ALIVE IN THEIR GARDEN

Alive in Their Garden

The True Story of the Mirabal Sisters and Their Fight for Freedom

Dedé Mirabal

Translated and Edited by Ana E. Martínez and Heather Hennes

Introduction by Julia Alvarez

A Translation of *Vivas en su jardín. La verdadera historia de las hermanas Mirabal y su lucha por la libertad*

UNIVERSITY OF FLORIDA PRESS

Gainesville

Publication of this work made possible by a Sustaining the Humanities through the American Rescue Plan grant from the National Endowment for the Humanities.

Preface copyright 2025 by Heather Hennes

Translation copyright 2025 by Ana E. Martínez and Heather Hennes

"Introduction: The Most Difficult Act of Heroism" copyright © 2012, 2024 by Julia Alvarez. First published in a slightly different form in *Vivas en su jardín: la verdadera historia de las hermanas Mirabal y su lucha por la libertad*. By permission of Stuart Bernstein Representation for Artists, New York, NY and protected by the Copyright Laws of the United States. All rights reserved. The printing, copying, redistribution, or retransmission of this Content without express permission is prohibited.

Originally published in Spanish as *Vivas en su jardín. La verdadera historia de las hermanas Mirabal y su lucha por la libertad*

All rights reserved

Published in the United States of America

30 29 28 27 26 25   6 5 4 3 2 1

Library of Congress Cataloging-in-Publication Data
Names: Mirabal, Dedé, author. | Martínez, Ana E., translator. | Hennes, Heather, translator. | Alvarez, Julia, writer of introduction.
Title: Alive in their garden : the true story of the Mirabal sisters and their fight for freedom / Dedé Mirabal ; translated and edited by Ana E. Martínez and Heather Hennes ; introduction by Julia Alvarez.
Other titles: Vivas en su jardín. English | True story of the Mirabal sisters and their fight for freedom
Description: Gainesville : University of Florida Press, 2025. | "Originally published in Spanish as Vivas en su jardín. La verdadera historia de las hermanas Mirabal y su lucha por la libertad." | Includes bibliographical references and index.
Identifiers: LCCN 2024025394 (print) | LCCN 2024025395 (ebook) | ISBN 9781683404880 (hardback) | ISBN 9781683405009 (paperback) | ISBN 9781683405214 (pdf) | ISBN 9781683405054 (ebook)
Subjects: LCSH: Mirabal, Patria, 1924–1960. | Mirabal, Minerva, 1926–1960. | Mirabal, María Teresa, 1936–1960. | Trujillo Molina, Rafael Leónidas, 1891–1961—Adversaries. | Women revolutionaries—Dominican Republic—Biography. | Assassination—Dominican Republic—History—20th century. | Political persecution—Dominican Republic—History—20th century. | Dominican Republic—History—1930–1961. | Dominican Republic—Biography. | BISAC: BIOGRAPHY & AUTOBIOGRAPHY / Women | HISTORY / Caribbean & West Indies / General
Classification: LCC F1938.5.M57 M5713 2025 (print) | LCC F1938.5.M57 (ebook) | DDC 972.93050922—dc23/eng/20241112
LC record available at https://lccn.loc.gov/2024025394
LC ebook record available at https://lccn.loc.gov/2024025395

University of Florida Press
2046 NE Waldo Road
Suite 2100
Gainesville, FL 32609
http://upress.ufl.edu

I dedicate this book to my people,
especially to our youth who
venerate the memory of my sisters.
To our friends who had the courage
to stand by our side
in the most critical and dangerous moments.
And to my family.
—Dedé Mirabal

CONTENTS

List of Figures   ix

Preface   xiii
Heather Hennes

Translators' Note   xxxiii
Ana E. Martínez and Heather Hennes

Alive in Their Garden: The True Story of the Mirabal Sisters and Their Fight for Freedom

    Introduction: The Most Difficult Act of Heroism   3
    Julia Alvarez

    Staying Alive   7

Part I. Memories of a Happy Time

  1. Our Family   21

  2. Our Childhood, Education, and Friends   33

  3. Temperament, Ideas, and Life Choices   45

Part II. A Time of Storms, Struggles, Tragedy, and Changes

  4. Fall from Grace   85

  5. Events That Impacted Our Family   94

  6. Fortunate Encounters, Liaisons, and Moving On   102

  7. The Early 1960s, the 14th of June Revolutionary Movement, Repression Continues to Grow   127

  8. The Tragedy   150

  9. The People Mourn   164

  10. Manolo, 1963   177

Part III. A Time of Recovery and Commitment

11. A Trial That Will Go Down in History   185

12. The Killers' Fate   213

13. Political Events Continue to Impact Us   223

Part IV. A Time to Preserve Memories

14. Raising the Children Brought Us Back to Life   237

15. The Value of Work   250

16. Love, Marriage, Divorce, and Stability   254

17. No More Room for Dictatorships   262

Chronology   271

The Plural Cause of Things   285
  Minou Tavárez Mirabal

When We Lost Everything, You Were There for Us   289
  Minou Tavárez Mirabal

Bibliography   291

Index   295

FIGURES

0.1. Mirabal Reyes Family Tree xi
0.2. Map of the Dominican Republic xii
0.3. Dedé and Julia Alvarez 2
1.1. Doña Chea (pregnant with Patria) and Don Enrique Mirabal 14
1.2. Dedé, Minerva, and Patria, between the ages of four and six 14
1.3. Patria at fifteen years old 15
1.4. A young Dedé with Minerva 15
1.5. Minerva representing the homeland 16
1.6. Patria surrounded by her garden 16
1.7. Minerva dressed as a rumba girl with guitar 17
1.8. Patria and Pedrito's wedding, 1941 17
1.9. María Teresa, Patria, Pedrito, and Minerva 18
1.10. María Teresa showing off her long hair 18
1.11. María Teresa with her parents in Ojo de Agua 19
1.12. María Teresa: "She was always a good little girl" 19
1.13. Marriage of Dedé and Jaimito Fernández, 1948 20
1.14. Minerva in 1946 20
1.15. Minerva sitting behind the steering wheel 20
2.1. Dedé and Jaime Enrique as a child 77
2.2. Minerva, expecting Minou, and Manolo in Montecristi, 1956 77
2.3. Birth of Minou Tavárez Mirabal, 1956 78
2.4. Minerva, Patria, Leandro, María Teresa, and Nelson in Montecristi 78
2.5. Manolo with Minerva at her graduation in 1957 79
2.6. María Teresa and Leandro's wedding, Manolo as best man 79

2.7. María Teresa and Leandro's wedding, 1958   80

2.8. María Teresa with her daughter Jacqueline, 1959 or 1960   80

2.9. Patria with Raúl as a baby, 1959   81

2.10. Patria, Dedé, and Minerva   81

2.11. Last photograph of Minerva   82

2.12. María Teresa   82

2.13. Dedé standing behind her sisters' caskets   83

2.14. Rufino de la Cruz Disla   83

2.15. Funeral mass in Salcedo   84

3.1. Pedro, Leandro, and Manolo in jail, 1961   183

3.2. Manolo during the assassins' trial in 1962   183

3.3. Manolo as leader of the 14th of June political party, 1963   184

4.1. Ana Antonia (Tonó) Rosario   233

4.2. Dedé surrounded by images of her sisters   233

4.3. Doña Chea with her granddaughter, Patria Román González   234

4.4. Jaime David, Dedé, and Juan Bosch   234

4.5. Dedé with her nine children   235

4.6. The Mirabal Sisters House Museum in Conuco   235

4.7. Dedé, the one who lived to tell the story   236

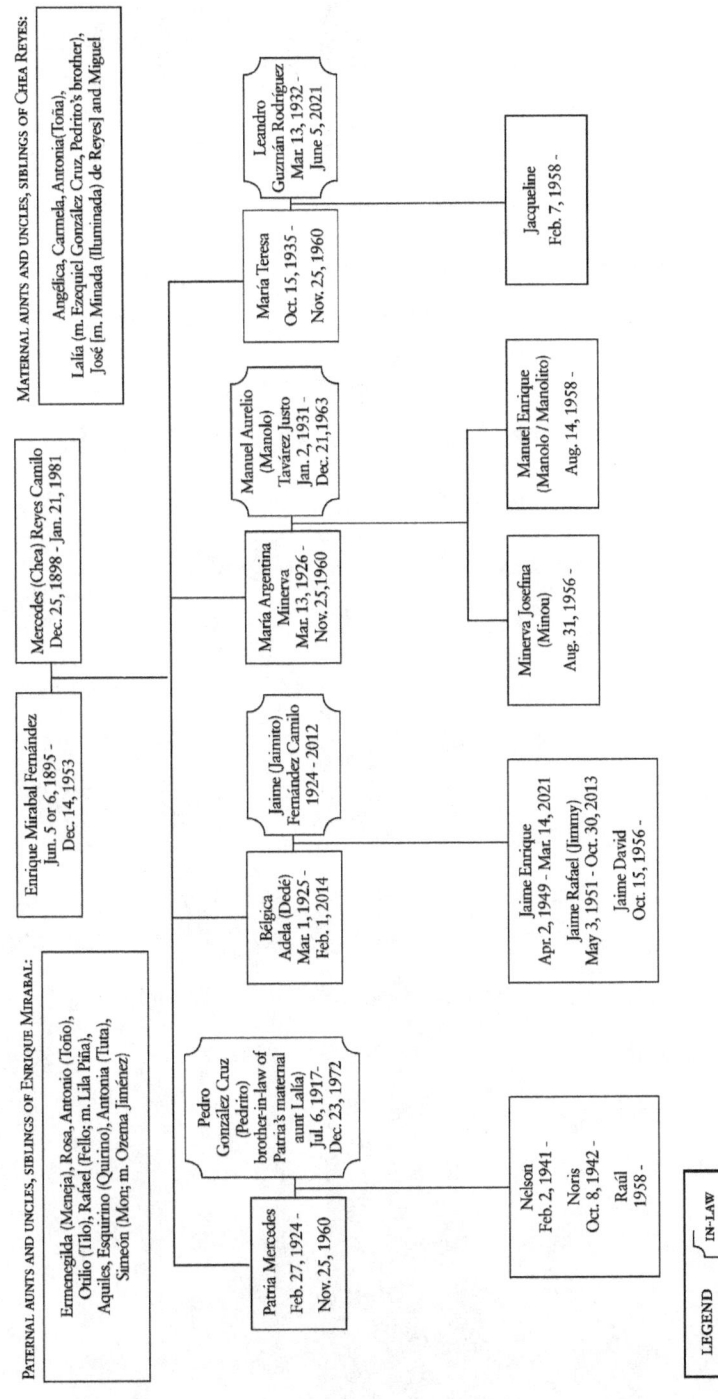

Figure 0.1. Mirabal Reyes Family Tree. Created with the help of Lisa Chicchi, Saint Joseph's University.

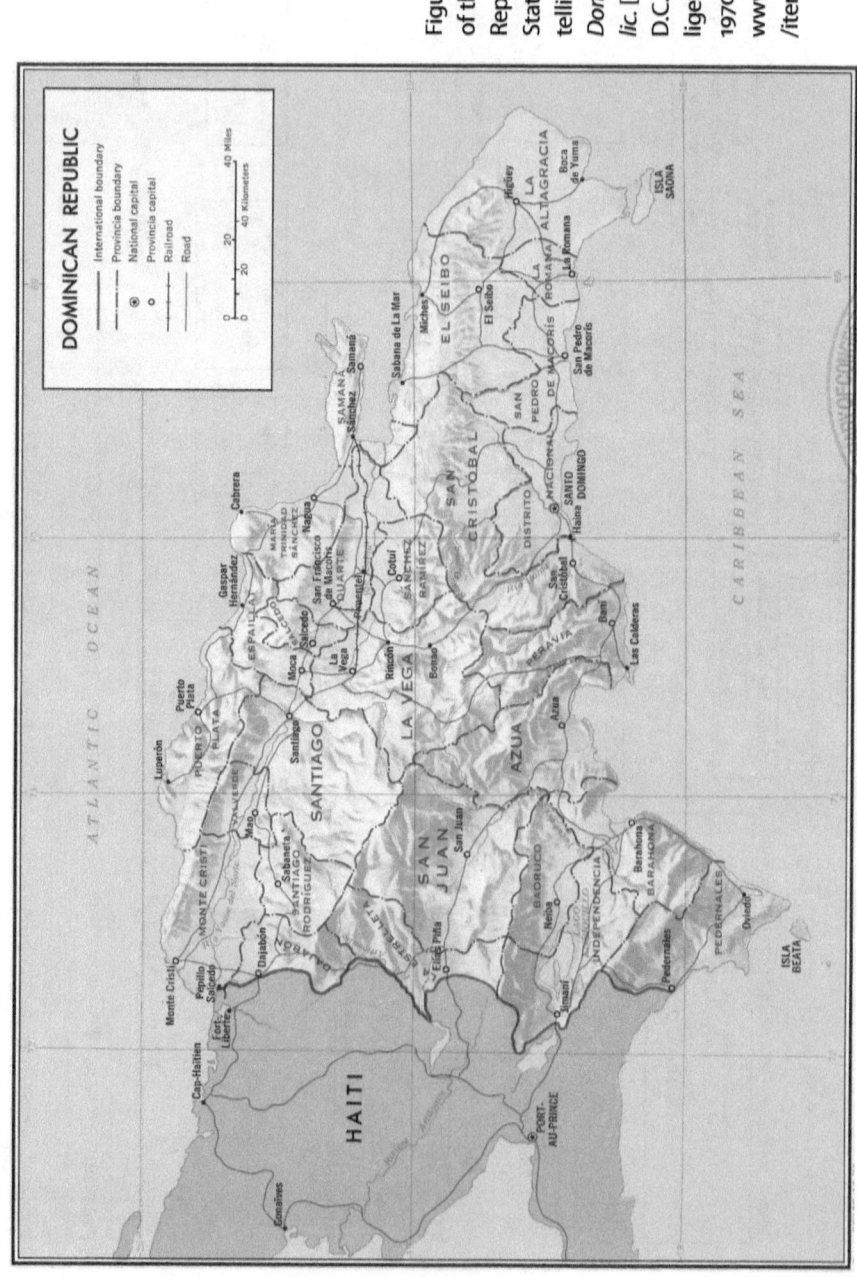

Figure 0.2. Map of the Dominican Republic. United States Central Intelligence Agency. *Dominican Republic*. [Washington, D.C.: Central Intelligence Agency, 1970] Map. https://www.loc.gov/item/2015861142/.

PREFACE

Heather Hennes

The story of the three Mirabal sisters—Patria, Minerva, and María Teresa, who in 1960 were brutally murdered by the dictatorial regime of Rafael Trujillo in the Dominican Republic—is becoming widely known throughout Latin America and, increasingly, in the United States and parts of Europe. The tragic death of these three young mothers known as "the Butterflies" shook the Dominican Republic in 1960 and since then has taken on mythical proportions, inspiring works of public art, literature, musical theater, documentary and feature films, a podcast, and other creative works.[1] We owe their growing presence in the public imaginary in large part to one woman's tenacious efforts to keep their memory alive: their sister, Dedé, the only one of the four Mirabal sisters who survived to tell their family's story and that of an entire generation of Dominicans. Their story is the central axis of Dedé's 2009 memoir, *Vivas en su jardín / Alive in Their Garden*, but as she conjures up memories from decades ago and reflects upon her own personal journey in the years following their loss, Dedé mirrors the experiences of many Dominican women who lived and struggled and pressed on through the three decades of the Trujillo dictatorship, the political turmoil following his assassination, and the subsequent Twelve Years of the repressive and bloody Joaquín Balaguer regime. In this way, *Alive in Their Garden* provides deep insights into the challenging past and the deep wounds that have helped shape contemporary Dominican society.

The Mirabal Reyes Family

Bélgica Adela (Dedé) Mirabal Reyes was the second of four daughters born to Enrique Mirabal Fernández (1895–1953) and Mercedes (Chea) Reyes Camilo (1898–1981). She was born on March 1, 1925, in the small rural community of Ojo de Agua in the mountainous Cibao region, in the center of the Dominican Republic. Her older sister, Aída Patria Mercedes, had been born only a year and two days before, on February 27, 1924. Her younger sister María Argentina Minerva was born a little more than a year after Dedé, on March 12, 1926. The three were very close, and as Dedé recalls in chapter 1 of her memoir, they spent their childhood playing together with children from nearby farms and the town of Salcedo. After Minerva, Doña Chea gave birth to a baby boy, Víctor Enrique, but he died shortly after his birth. When Dedé was ten years old, her family welcomed their youngest sibling, Antonia María Teresa, on October 15, 1935. Given their considerable age difference and Dedé's nurturing ways, she helped protect and take care of her baby sister, which would make María Teresa's death at the age of twenty-five all the more devastating for her.

The family lived on their farm in Ojo de Agua. They produced cacao, coffee, rice, and other agricultural products there and on some other parcels they owned. Don Enrique eventually became a successful merchant, and Dedé grew up helping him in the store, keeping inventory and other financial records. They relied heavily on her. In chapter 2 of this memoir, she describes how painful it was to stay behind temporarily to help in the store while Patria and Minerva went off to school. Still, her father's successful business allowed the family to send all four daughters to boarding school at the Immaculate Conception School in the nearby town of La Vega. His business also led Don Enrique to create a strong social network, and he became a respected member of the community. In addition, it both required and allowed the family to have several employees on their property and in their household. Dedé recalls several of these cherished individuals in her memoir, describing how their solidarity during the family's most trying times was their lifeline. In particular, she tells us about Ana Antonia Rosario (Tonó), whose parents were employed by the family. She grew up in the Mirabal Reyes household and who would eventually become a third mother to Dedé's children, nieces, and nephews after her sisters were killed.

Dedé's memoir presents a vivid image of her sisters, the childhood they shared, and the different paths their lives took. There is a happy nostalgia in her voice as she recalls tiny details and shares memorable anecdotes. These are the unique insights that her narrative contributes to the body of literature on the Butterflies. Much of what has been written about the Mirabal sisters mythifies and distorts their life stories. Their sister, Dedé, who knew them better than anyone, reveals them as flesh-and-blood human beings with unique quirks, gifts, flaws, and dreams. She also situates them within a tight web of social relationships, which helps us understand both the pervasive surveillance and repression in which they lived and the resistance movements that grew in response. In many ways, Dedé's narrative and reflections help the reader make sense of how her sisters engaged in the resistance, how they lived their final months, and how their loss impacted those they left behind. It also immerses the reader in the collective psyche of the time. How did Dominicans experience and navigate the intricate web of surveillance and the threat of violence that pervaded everyday life? How did they carry on after having lost loved ones to political violence? What lessons can we learn from their experience?

The Era of Trujillo

Dedé's memoir is the story of one family's journey through the repressive years of the Trujillo dictatorship and its aftermath. Known as the *Trujillato*, the thirty-one-year dictatorship of Rafael Leónidas Trujillo Molina (1891–1961) is often cited as one of the most brutal in Latin American history. But supporters to this day credit Trujillo for having modernized the Dominican Republic by building infrastructure, developing industry, fortifying public institutions and services, paying off the national debt, and fostering a strong sense of national identity.

At the turn of the twentieth century, Dominican politics were characterized by frequent and futile uprisings, revolutions, and armed conflicts between different groups under regional strongmen called *caudillos*. Dominicans—predominantly laborers and small-scale farmers—lacked the basic infrastructure, government services, and protections they needed, and the country had significant foreign debt. In 1904, President Theodore Roosevelt, in keeping with the Monroe Doctrine, agreed to Dominican president Carlos Felipe Morales Languasco's request for intervention. The U.S. began asserting authority over Dominican politics, finance, and public works and sent warships to Dominican shores.[2] In 1916, the U.S. deployed the Navy and Marines onto the island after General Desiderio Arias led a revolt against President Juan Isidro Jiménez, whose administration had been bolstered by the U.S. The U.S. cut off funds from the customs receivership (the country's largest source of revenue), established a military governorship, outlawed gun ownership, suspended freedoms of speech and the press, and took control of political processes, including the cancelation of elections and the suspension of the legislature.[3] The stated objective of the occupation government was to stabilize the Dominican economy and modernize the military, public institutions, and services, including education and healthcare. This new government required the centralization of power and increased surveillance of citizens in a country in which, historically, power had been highly localized and land use had been loosely regulated.

This first U.S. occupation lasted until the election of President Horacio Vásquez Lajara in 1924, but as we gather from Dedé's narrative about her parents' experiences, its impact on Dominican society, politics, social institutions, and identity were long lasting. Among other significant changes brought about by the U.S. occupation, there was increased access to education for Dominican girls, which played a significant role in the lives of all four Mirabal sisters. Women also entered the workforce, primarily in the fields of education and public assistance, and they participated in political life in new ways, particularly in pro-sovereignty campaigns.[4] In 1931, shortly after the end of the occupation, the Acción Feminista Dominicana formed as a civic organization that allowed women to engage in public life in new ways. Historian Elizabeth Manley explains that it "provided the foundation from which the Trujillo regime [would later involve] women in the politics of the dictatorship through the rhetoric of maternalism and appropriate modernity."[5] Traditional Dominican customs and values were highly patriarchal, and the first U.S. occupation introduced certain American ideals of secular modernity that disrupted customary patterns of domestic life and created tension with Dominicans' desire for sovereignty.[6]

Dedé's narrative reveals how many Dominican families suffered through the first U.S. occupation, with its suspension of civil rights, abuse of individuals, and destruction of property. In chapter 1, she tells how her mother's family had to flee their home when U.S. troops burned it down and how many people from Salcedo were killed in the campaign to wipe out resistance. The experience of the U.S. occupation was always in the background of Dominican collective memory, and it shaped many Dominicans' views, not only of the U.S. but also of Trujillo. He had joined the Dominican National Guard in 1918, been trained by U.S. Marines, risen to the rank of Chief of National Police and later Commander of the Armed Forces, and used his military command to allow the 1930 coup against President Vásquez, led by Rafael Estrella Ureña. That coup paved the way for the sham election that gave Trujillo the presidency in 1930, initiating what would be called the Era of Trujillo.

When Trujillo assumed the presidency in August 1930, the country was suffering from an economic crisis due largely to a dramatic drop in the price of sugar. This turmoil was exacerbated weeks later when Hurricane San Zenón decimated the capital, Santo Domingo. Trujillo seized the opportunity to present himself as the decisive patriarch who would rebuild the nation out of the literal and proverbial rubble and look toward the future. In what Lauren Derby calls "a seminal moment [. . .] in the foundational myth of the Era of Trujillo,"[7] the newly elected president saw to it that the reconstruction of Santo Domingo projected a new image of the Dominican Republic as, in his words, "clean, magnificent and modern."[8] The monumental government buildings and grand avenues in the new modern architectural style were the outward signs of a nation set on asserting its sovereignty, modernizing its economy, ending its foreign debt, and culturally aligning itself with white, Western culture. Trujillo and his supporters put his mark on much of the growth, renaming streets, parks, natural features, and public projects after members of the Trujillo family. In 1936, the Dominican National Congress changed the name of Santo Domingo, the oldest European settlement in the Americas, to Ciudad Trujillo (Trujillo City).

The modernization of Santo Domingo was one visible sign of the transformations taking place throughout the country under Trujillo's direction. New infrastructure would connect rural and urban areas, contributing to economic development and facilitating the centralization of power. The state was able to establish its control over rural areas, enacting land distribution and public assistance programs, but also increasing surveillance, regulation, and intervention.[9]

While the economy grew, the Trujillo family generated vast personal wealth, including property (equivalent to about 9 percent of Dominican territory), liquid assets, and control over about 60 percent of wage labor and 75 percent of Dominican industrial production. Much of this wealth was acquired unethically.[10] With political deftness, Trujillo leveraged his growing wealth through displays of generous gift-giving to individuals and institutions, serving as benefactor to organizations, schools, and the Catholic Church. While his oversight of reconstruction and economic development earned him the title Padre de la Patria Nueva (Father of the New Nation), his grand displays of patronage inspired another title: El Benefactor (the Benefactor). Trujillo's political economy of favors created a sense of indebtedness from those who received his favors and all but assured their compliance with his dictates.[11] Not surprisingly, one of his most commonly used monikers was El Jefe (the Boss). Trujillo's public image reflected deeply rooted notions of patriarchy and paternalism in which the Father of the New Nation would provide work, protection, and prosperity as long as the Dominican people complied.

Much of the protection and prosperity that Trujillo promised, particularly in the first decade of his rule, was framed as a necessary rejection of Haitian influence in order to make progress.[12] Although he himself was from a lower-middle-class family of Spanish, Cuban, and Haitian ancestry, Trujillo rejected his Haitian heritage, encouraged the country to embrace its Spanish heritage over its Afro-Caribbean roots, and he diligently whitened his meticulously groomed personal appearance, even wearing makeup to this end. Trujillo's vision of a white European cultural identity was aligned with the ideals of the urban elite and may have deepened resentment on the part of the mixed-race rural majority. However, Trujillo managed to promote this cultural identity while simultaneously gaining favor among the previously disenfranchised rural majority by presenting himself as a strong leader, promising new infrastructure, protection, services, and upward mobility in exchange for the people's support.[13]

It was in this socio-cultural climate that, in 1937, he ordered the mass killing of Haitians and Haitian-Dominicans in the Dajabón region, along the northern shores of the Massacre River that forms the Haitian-Dominican border. For generations the borderland had been a place where Dominicans and Haitians had intermixed, intermarried, and crossed the border to work. In an effort to control the border, Trujillo entered into a border agreement with Haitian president Sténio Vincent and would later justify the massacre as necessary to enforce that agreement. The massacre was not only an assertion of Dominican sovereignty, it was also an attempt to cleanse the borderland of Haitian culture and of blackness.[14] Known as the Haitian Massacre or the Parsley Massacre,[15] it demonstrated that the new Dominican state had control over all of its territory, even the remote countryside, which until that time had suffered from violent conflicts under regional caudillos. Only twelve years old at the time, Dedé observed the trauma caused by this massacre. In chapter 2, she recalls how "the deadly echoes of the Haitian massacre hit very close to home and shook us deeply." Her recollections bear witness to that terrifying time, as seen through the eyes of a child.

For his transformation of the Dominican state, institutions, economy, and landscape, Trujillo was celebrated in civic ceremonies, school performances, and works of public art. It became not only customary but obligatory to show one's support for Trujillo by hanging a photograph of the dictator in the family home, stating that, in that house, "God and Trujillo" ruled. Public speeches hailed him as the hand of divine providence,[16] and several *merengue* singers praised Trujillo in some of their songs, enjoying his endorsement of their genre as the true national dance of the Dominican Republic.[17] The Father of the New Nation was seen as having brought the Dominican Republic into a new era, and his presence was felt everywhere.

The establishment of state control, particularly over rural areas, allowed for the development of infrastructure and public assistance programs that improved the rural economy, making Trujillo popular in many of those communities.[18] But the consolidation of power and increased economic and even social control that made these developments possible laid the foundations for the repressive regime. Maintaining this control relied on an intricate web of intelligence, state entities, and armed forces. The regime appeared to be omnipresent, and there was a prevailing sense that Dominicans were always being watched.[19] Dedé's narrative brings to life this atmosphere of constant surveillance and fear of being denounced for not supporting El Jefe. She describes how her family, like many others, was watched, harassed, detained, and ultimately murdered by agents of the newly formed Servicio de Inteligencia Militar (Military Intelligence Service), commonly known by the acronym SIM. This agency, which Trujillo formed in the mid-1950s, patrolled the streets in Volkswagen Beetles, which Dominicans called *cepillos* (brushes) because they "swept" the patrolled areas clean of dissidents. Any time Dedé mentions a Volkswagen in her memoir, the reader can feel the chilling presence of the SIM.

The regime's intricate web of surveillance and censure included the press. The state-controlled newspaper *El Caribe* (*The Caribbean*) included a "*Foro público*" ("Public Forum"), a column where individuals were denounced for their actions or ideas in opposition to the regime. The deeply engrained clientelism, patronage, and fear for one's own safety led neighbors and family members to denounce one another to avoid harm themselves or to gain favors. Dedé shares the many ways in which her family suffered the consequences of these denunciations: financial ruin, social marginalization, loss of livelihood or employment, and ultimately imprisonment, torture, and murder. At the same time, she expresses gratitude toward those friends and family members who risked their own well-being to support her family during the most dangerous moments. Her narrative helps us appreciate how strained Dominican society was and how difficult it was to trust anyone, when simply associating with a person who had fallen out of favor with the regime could result in personal or familial ruin. Dedé's narrative brings this painful reality to life for the reader, challenging us to ask ourselves how we would have acted in such circumstances.

During his dictatorship, Trujillo also solidified his control through a deft leveraging of gender relations and an appeal to Dominican morality. This appeal to morality is evident in the slogan of the Partido Dominicano (Dominican Party), the only official political party under Trujillo: "*Rectitud. Libertad. Trabajo. Moralidad*" ("Honesty. Freedom. Work. Morality"). Led by Trujillo, the Father of the New Nation, the regime promised to provide work, protection, and peace for its people. But Trujillo required compliance in exchange.

Under Trujillo, women were given juridical equality, the right to vote starting in 1942, and greater legal protections against harassment, abandonment, and abuse.[20] As scholar Elizabeth Manley explains, rather than excluding women from civic engagement, the Trujillo regime encouraged women to participate in particular ways. The Partido Dominicano established a Sección Feminina (Women's Division) to support *trujillista* women who held public office, particularly governorships. Women became spokespersons for the regime abroad, did the work of the regime's social and educational programs, and promoted the regime through public discourse, ceremonies, and events. However, as Manley points out, even women who worked outside the home and held political office typically followed traditional gender norms within the household, and the regime employed a discourse of maternalism to encourage public engagement as an extension of women's traditional roles as mothers and caretakers.[21]

With the onset of the Cold War, there was a heightened sense that the regime's stability was necessary to ward off the threat of communism, which was spreading in the region. Women's work at home and in the public sphere was cast as a critical link in the country's defense against the encroaching ideology.[22] At the same time, however, a growing number of Dominican men and women in exile in places like Puerto Rico, Cuba, and New York began to manifest their opposition to the regime by organizing anti-Trujillo campaigns, holding public demonstrations, publishing articles, writing letters, and seeking the support of politicians and diplomats.[23]

In spite of Dominican women's increased participation in civic affairs, public life, and the workforce, they were still held to clearly binary gender norms, and their sexuality was still very much under paternal control. One particularly sinister aspect of Trujillo's regime compelled numerous families to offer their daughters to Trujillo for his sexual pleasure in exchange for protection, favors, or pardon. At the same time, designated members of his regime arranged sexual encounters for him with young women and even school girls. Many families tried to keep their daughters out of view, since denying such a request was considered an afront to the dictator. As the Boss, the Benefactor, and Father of the New Nation, Trujillo seemed to embody the epitome of masculinity within this highly patriarchal society. His physical appearance projected strength and order. Often described as a megalomaniac, he was notoriously vain and obsessively presented himself as physically robust and meticulously groomed. But his exhibition of masculine virility was also an assertion of political power. As Lauren Derby explains, Trujillo's sexual exploitation of women and girls, particularly the daughters of the white elite, was in part an act of vindication, a way of reaffirming his dominance over the social and political elite after having grown up poor, minimally educated, and of Haitian descent.[24]

Understanding the gender landscape that the Mirabal sisters had to navigate helps the reader appreciate the tension surrounding various moments that Dedé recalls. During one particular episode, in 1949, the Mirabal sisters' mother implored their father not to take them to a party in San Cristobal that was organized by the regime. The event has become legendary, as Minerva rejected Trujillo both politically and personally in his presence, prompting a series of retaliations against the Mirabal family that would lead to Don Enrique's imprisonment and death and the persecution of Minerva for eleven years. Understanding the paternalism projected by Trujillo also helps us better understand how women like Patria could actively conspire as part of underground movements while escaping incarceration, while hundreds of her male peers were imprisoned, tortured, and killed for the same or lesser acts. Appreciating these deeply ingrained gender dynamics also helps us understand why simply killing Minerva as a political adversary was not a simple "solution" for Trujillo, why the public was so shaken by the sisters' murder, and why, as Dedé tells us, Trujillo was haunted by his obsession with Minerva in the months after he ordered that murder. Finally, understanding these gender dynamics helps us appreciate Dedé's role in the family and the personal journey that she shares with us.

Resistance

In her memoir, Dedé tells about several resistance movements that took shape in the country and among Dominicans in exile. Her narrative helps us appreciate the perilous atmosphere in which these movements formed and how political activism affected the families and friends of those involved. It also shows that her sisters' activism did not emerge in a vacuum, but rather as part of a larger wave of resistance that was emerging in pockets throughout the country.

During the first decade and a half of the Trujillo regime, the only official political party was the Partido Dominicano. However, increased access to higher education, especially for women, and contact with professors who had escaped the fascist Franco regime in Spain increased pressure internally. At the same time, waves of antifascism swept across the hemisphere, increasing international pressure on Trujillo. In 1946, this pressure compelled Trujillo to temporarily permit opposition parties. Dominicans living in exile in Cuba founded the Partido Socialista Popular and the Partido Democrático Revolucionario Dominicano (PDRD). The PDRD had a branch called Juventud Democrática (Democratic Youth). Dedé recalls that her parents were afraid that Minerva, who in 1944 was studying at the Immaculate Conception School in La Vega, would become involved in the organization.[25] To prevent her political involvement, Enrique Mirabal ordered Minerva to return to Salcedo for a brief time between 1944 and 1945. Dedé also describes Minerva's close friendship with Pericles Franco, one of the leaders of Juventud Democrática and a known enemy of the state. (Minerva's future husband, Manolo Tavárez Justo, was also active in Juventud Democrática, though they did not know one another at the time.) Her retelling of those days helps the reader understand how Minerva grew into political activism alongside many Dominican youth of her generation. Her narrative also gives us a sense of how risky such activism was, especially in the early years of the Cold War, when Trujillo and his supporters—called *trujillistas*—labeled his critics as communists. Her narrative also gives us a sense for the growing unrest among the opposition, especially among young people, helping us understand the formation of cells of resistance in the 1950s, culminating in the establishment of the Movimiento Revolucionario 14 de Junio (14th of June Revolutionary Movement).

Contrary to the popular myth that Patria, Minerva, and María Teresa Mirabal were the first to speak out against the dictator, several resistance movements formed in the late 1940s and in the 1950s, including multiple groups of women opponents. The first two significant attempts to topple the dictator were the Cayo Confites Expedition in 1947 and the Luperón Expedition of 1949. Assisted in part by the U.S., the regime quashed both planned invasions. There were other failed attempts in the 1950s, as several opposition movements formed both internally and among the Dominican diaspora in exile, especially in New York, Venezuela, Puerto Rico, and Cuba.[26]

The Cuban Revolution under Fidel Castro was a significant impetus for cells of Dominican resistance, both on the island and abroad. With this event as the backdrop, Dedé tells how on January 6, 1959, just days following Castro's victory, Minerva, Manolo, María Teresa, and María Teresa's husband Leandro Guzmán were at a Three Kings Day luncheon with family and friends. Some in attendance were related to prominent trujillistas but were themselves opposed to the regime. As Dedé recalls, Minerva proposed that they form a movement to take down Trujillo. It was a decisive moment for what would eventually become the 14th of June Revolutionary Movement, commonly written as "1J4." Dedé explains that anti-Trujillo resistance was spreading among young people from diverse political backgrounds, including the sons and daughters of Trujillo supporters and agents of the regime.

In March 1959, three months after the Cuban Revolution and the aforementioned Kings Day luncheon, Dominicans in exile set on ousting Trujillo and implementing political, economic, and social reform in the Dominican Republic formed the Movimiento de Liberación Dominicana (MLD). Approximately 250 revolutionaries of the MLD trained in Cuba and planned to land in the Dominican Republic on June 14, 1959. They were intercepted by Dominican armed forces, captured, tortured, and executed. This expedition came to be known as the Expedition of Constanza, Maimón, and Estero Hondo for their intended landing points on the northern coast and in the Central Mountain Range, not far from where the Mirabal family lived.

The resistance movement that Minerva had proposed at the January 6, 1959, luncheon would grow and eventually adopt the name "Movimiento Revolucionario 14 de Junio" as a way to take up the torch passed on by the failed 1959 expedition. While several versions of the story have made their way into the myths surrounding the Mirabal sisters, Dedé provides testimony from members of the movement—called *catorcistas*—such as Fernando Cueto, who had first- or second-hand knowledge of the events surrounding the movement's naming. Cueto's testimony is one of the many instances in which other voices speak through Dedé's memoir. These other voices include testimonies by those who participated in the events, newspaper clippings, diary entries, and letters. These accounts complement, reaffirm, and build upon Dedé's own recollections. She was committed to telling this story as completely as she could because, as she states in her introduction "Staying Alive," this is not only her sisters' story, but the story of a generation of Dominicans who fought for freedom. The inclusion of multiple texts, testimonies, and voices is one of the many merits of her memoir.

Dedé briefly mentions two other resistance movements. One is the group of lower-middle-class youth in Santiago that formed the Unión de Grupos Revolucionarios Independientes (UGRI) under the leadership of twenty-year-old Wenceslao (Wen) Guillen Gómez. Members of this movement became known as Los Panfleteros de Santiago after dozens of them were arrested and tortured in January 1960 for having disseminated *panfletos* (pamphlets or flyers) that harshly criticized Trujillo. Twenty-seven of them were held in La 40 (La Cuarenta), the same clandestine torture center where Minerva, María Teresa, five other catorcista women, and hundreds of catorcista men would be incarcerated days later. The twenty-seven panfleteros were hung on January 29, 1960.

The other resistance cell that Dedé briefly mentions is Acción Clero Cultural (Clergy-Cultural Action), a group of seminarians, university students, and farmers who came together in July 1959 in Salcedo, Conuco, and Tenares under the leadership of Father Daniel Cruz Inoa from the Archdiocese of Santiago.[27] Among the collaborators in Acción Clero Cultural were the Mirabals' neighbors, friends, and family, including their first cousin on their mother's side, Antonio Ezequiel González Reyes. He was also Patria's nephew since he was her husband Pedro González's brother's son. Another of Pedro's nephews, Francisco Aníbel (Pachico) González, was also involved in Acción Clero Cultural, as was the family's close friend, Rafael (Fafa) Taveras, who in 2018 shared his recollections of these events in an interview on the Dominican daily program *El Día*.[28] Patria's family, including Pedro and their teenaged children Noris and Nelson, became involved, as did María Teresa. Meanwhile Minerva and Manolo were establishing contacts among *antitrujillistas* in Manolo's hometown of Montecristi, where they were living at the time. Patria and Pedro's property in Conuco was one of the places where the group assembled and stored small explosives.

The group began building a network of contacts that extended beyond the Cibao region into other parts of the country. It merged with other cells of resistance under the leadership of Minerva, Manolo, Leandro, Rafael (Pipe) Faxas Canto, and others, forming the largest network of antitrujillista resistance to that date. As Dedé points out, it was a diverse group, including Dominicans from various social and political circles, including many young people from important trujillista families. Leaders of that merged group met at Patria and Pedro's home in Conuco on January 9, 1960. They elected Manolo, Pipe Faxas Canto, and Leandro Guzmán as officers. Though not elected to a leadership role as a means of protection, several accounts, including that of Rafael Taveras, identify Minerva as a central figure in the organization's leadership.[29]

Tragedy

As Dedé details in her narrative, the SIM cracked down on the newly named movement within days, arresting, incarcerating, and torturing hundreds of catorcistas, including several members of her family. Her harrowing recollection of those days brings to life the anguish that families suffered across the nation as their loved ones were stolen away and their homes were ransacked. She reminds us that the "subversives" who were detained were integral members of families and communities and that their detention and torture was an attack on entire families. As Dedé grapples with these painful memories, she reveals to us the deep wounds that still afflict Dominican society.

The mass detentions and clear abuse of human rights drew international pressure and finally convinced the Catholic leadership in the Dominican Republic to speak out. On January 31, 1960, parish priests across the nation read what is known as *La Carta Pastoral* (The Pastoral Letter), which Dedé quotes in part. After decades of silence, the Church finally appealed to the Trujillo regime to avoid abusive excesses and to respect its citizens' basic human rights.[30] While international pressure mounted, including from the U.S., the detained catorcistas were tried and sentenced. Many were given excessive fines and prison terms. Most of the prisoners were sent to La Victoria National Penitentiary in Santo Domingo. Minerva, María Teresa, and five other women were among them, but increased international pressure, as well as pressure from within Dominican society, forced Trujillo to release them and commute the sentences of several other prisoners. Minerva and María Teresa were sent home under house arrest.

The arrests of the 1J4 revealed how extensive anti-Trujillo opposition had grown and how closely it had come to the regime itself. It was also clear that Minerva continued to be an important leader and formidable enemy. Even under house arrest, her leadership presented a real problem for Trujillo, whose public image as the nation's patriarch was predicated upon the idea that he would protect families, women, and children. His repressive tactics were already fueling international scrutiny and protests from Dominicans in exile, including groups of women.[31] In spite of the likely political repercussions, word circulated through the Cibao countryside that Trujillo was planning to have Minerva killed. Dedé recalls the warnings they received, giving us as readers a chilling sense of the danger they faced, but also an appreciation for the courage that it took for them to simply carry on with family life and visit their husbands in prison. On one level, Minerva seemed to think that Trujillo wouldn't dare have her killed. But small references in Dedé's narrative suggest that she probably did realize the risk she faced.

The popular narrative and many historians point to the Mirabals' assassination as the event that set into motion the conspiracy that would culminate in Trujillo's assassination six months later. That group of conspirators has become known as the Héroes del 30 de Mayo for the date on which they carried out the assassination, commonly called the *ajusticiamiento,* an execution for a capital crime. Antonio de la Maza, who had held positions within the regime, led a group of eleven men, many of whom also worked for the regime, to ambush Trujillo on the highway between the capital and the dictator's house in San Cristóbal on May 30, 1961. Almost all of the conspirators were hunted down by the SIM and executed. Each one had suffered at the hands of the regime, mainly by having lost a loved one. But the Mirabals' assassination was one of the proverbial straws that convinced them to take action. One of the only survivors, General Antonio Imbert Barrera explained in a 2018 interview that news of the sisters' so-called accident prompted him to ask himself, "Where the hell are the men in this country?"[32] María Teresa's widower, Leandro Guzmán, also affirmed that the Mirabals' murder led that group of men to say, "Enough! We can't take any more. That man is killing women too."[33] In short, while women abroad were calling Trujillo out for his attacks on Dominican families, the murder of these three young mothers was a pivotal moment because it was viewed as a blatant attack on Dominican families and morality.[34]

Survival, Fortitude, and Memory

As the surviving sister who picked up the family's broken pieces and carried on through the aftermath of this tragedy, Dedé helps us see beyond the gruesome details and the popular myths. The intimacy of her narrative reveals to us the painful day-to-day struggles through the months and years that followed the family's tragic loss. Dedé dedicates a significant part of her memoir to the events surrounding her sisters' murder on November 25, 1960, to the way it shook their family and community, to the trial of their assassins, and to the killers' ultimate impunity. She tells how her family continued to live under SIM surveillance in the months following the murder and how the SIM ransacked and destroyed their property and threatened the lives of Minerva and Manolo's children. Once again, what comes to the foreground in these pages is the solidarity of the friends and family who stood by them. This solidarity helped them survive, even when they suffered the devastating loss of Manolo, who had continued to lead the 14th of June Movement–turned-political party and was assassinated in 1963. But she also describes the various attempts to erase the Mirabal sisters' murder from collective memory. With this memoir, she corrects those erasures and insists that not only their sacrifice, but that of their generation, not be forgotten.

The backdrop for this phase in Dedé's life was the turbulent period following Trujillo's assassination, through the brief presidency of Juan Bosch, the coup that ousted him, the Dominican Civil War known as the April Revolution, and eventually the period known as Los Doce Años, the twelve-year authoritarian presidency of Joaquín Balaguer. A Dominican lawyer, intellectual, historian, and writer, Balaguer was a loyal trujillista functionary who was the puppet president from 1960 to 1962 and then assumed the presidency from 1966 to 1978 and again from 1986 to 1996.

It was during this turbulent political time, from June to November 1962, that the assassins of the Mirabal sisters and Rufino de la Cruz were tried and convicted. The trial was covered extensively by the press, and Dominicans followed the proceedings closely on radio and television.[35] Dedé recalls in painful detail the information that emerged during the trial and how it affected her personally. In November of that same year, during a moment of political aperture, the exiled antitrujillista writer, activist, historian, and educator Juan Emilio Bosch Gaviño (1909–2001) returned to the country and was elected to the presidency. However, President Bosch was ousted by a coup in September 1963 and was replaced by a military triumvirate. This coup is what compelled Manolo to lead a group of guerrilla fighters into the mountains at Las Manaclas with the aim of restoring Bosch to the presidency. Dedé recalls the devastating end to that mission.

As she dedicated herself to raising her children, nieces, and nephews, Dedé carried on amidst the political turmoil of the April Revolution in Santo Domingo (April 24 to September 3, 1965). The revolution was the attempt by civilian and military "constitutionalists" to restore Juan Bosch to the presidency to which he had been elected. The "loyalists" were aided by the U.S. and the Organization of American States. This began the second

U.S. occupation of the Dominican Republic (1965–1966) and led to the 1966 elections in which Joaquín Balaguer became president, beginning the period known as *Los Doce Años* (the Twelve Years).

Balaguer's regime during the Doce Años cloaked authoritarianism in a veil of democracy. He included more women in political positions, invested heavily in public works, promoted economic development, and distributed basic goods among the lower class. However, the majority of the new wealth remained among the upper-middle class and elite and favored foreign investors. Corruption and cronyism were rampant, and he maintained his hold on the political landscape through censorship and political persecution, including the incarceration and murder of dissidents.[36]

This is the political climate in which Dedé raised the children through adolescence and young adulthood. Understanding this helps us as readers appreciate the fear that lingered over the family home as she and Doña Chea tried to protect the children. This is especially evident in chapter 14, when we read about young Minou's maturing political awareness and her family's concern that she was following in her parents' footsteps, a legacy upon which Minou reflects in her book *Mañana te escribiré otra vez*.[37] Dedé's recollections also help us understand how and why the deep wounds of the Trujillato festered for so long before now, finally, being addressed.

These are the challenges—and the joys—that Dedé recalls in the final part of her memoir: "Time to Preserve Memories." This final section is an affirmation of life and a commitment to building a better future for the Dominican Republic. In many ways, it reflects the experiences of many Dominicans, and particularly women, during the turbulent years following Trujillo's assassination. Dedé points to the repression that continued under Balaguer and to the corruption and cronyism that took deeper roots in Dominican politics.

The repressive and bloody Balaguer regime is the backdrop for what would become Dedé's mission in the last decades of her life: creating and maintaining the Casa Museo Hermanas Mirabal in her mother's home in Conuco and sharing her knowledge about an entire generation of Dominicans with its many visitors, especially school children. Her work through the museum and, indeed, this memoir, aim to address the silences and erasures that have distorted Dominican historical narrative. As the memoir comes to a close, we are reminded that this is not the work of a historian detached from the events they relate, but rather the testimony of a woman who has reopened deep wounds in order to recall and retell the details of the past, in the hopes of steering the next generation away from a similar course. While the popular narrative surrounding the Mirabal sisters focuses on the heroism of Patria, Minerva, and María Teresa, the conclusion of this memoir leaves no doubt that what Julia Alvarez wrote about Doña Dedé Mirabal's narrative is resoundingly true: that it is a "brave," "moving," and "invaluable" act of heroism, "the hardest heroism that survives and forgives but does not forget. The heroism that teaches us how to be human again."[38]

Notes

1. See bibliography for a list of creative works.
2. Roorda, *Dictator*, 15, citing Bruce Calder, *The Impact of Intervention: The Dominican Republic during the U.S. Occupation of 1916–1924*. (Austin: University of Texas Press, 1984), 1–5 and note 15, 246.
3. Roorda, *Dictator*, 16.
4. Elizabeth Manley, *The Paradox of Paternalism: Women and the Politics of Authoritarianism in the Dominican Republic* (Gainesville: University Press of Florida, 2017), chap. 1.
5. Manley, *Paradox*, 23–24.
6. For more on this see Maja Horn, *Masculinity after Trujillo: The Politics of Gender in Dominican Literature* (Gainesville: University Press of Florida, 2014), 27–28.
7. Lauren Derby. *The Dictator's Seduction: Politics and the Popular Imagination in the Era of Trujillo*. (Durham: Duke University Press, 2009), 69.
8. Trujillo, quoted by Héctor Minaya in "Dictador llegó al colmo de cambiar el nombre de la capital por Ciudad Trujillo," *El Nacional* (Santo Domingo, Dominican Republic), May 26, 2016. https://elnacional.com.do/dictador-llego-al-colmo-de-cambiar-el-nombre-de-la-capital-por-ciudad-trujillo.
9. Richard Lee Turits. *Foundations of Despotism: Peasants, the Trujillo Regime, and Modernity in Dominican History*. (Stanford: Stanford University Press, 2003), 181–82.
10. Turits, *Foundations*, 5.
11. Derby, *Dictator's Seduction*, 259.
12. Turits, *Foundations*, 178.
13. Turits, *Foundations*, 178 and Derby, *Dictator's Seduction*, 92; 257–60.
14. Roorda, *Dictator*, 129.
15. It is said that troops distinguished between Dominicans and Haitians by their distinct ways of pronouncing the word *perejil* (parsley). See Turits, *Foundations*, 164–65.
16. One significant example was a speech by Joaquín Balaguer upon his induction into the Dominican Academy of History in 1954. He argued that the Dominican Republic owed its existence to two supernatural forces: the Divine Intervention that began with the 1492 arrival of Christopher Columbus and the emergence of Trujillo as national leader in 1930. See Joaquín Balaguer, "Dios y Trujillo. Una reinterpretación de la historia dominicana." in *Clío*, La Academia Dominicana de la Historia,

Año 23, no. 101 (Oct.–Dec. 1954), republished on Cielonaranja (2016), http://www.cielonaranja.com/balaguer-diostrujillo.htm.

17 Darío Tejeda explains how Trujillo entered into a mutually beneficial relationship with *merengue* singers who wrote songs celebrating the Father of the New Nation and legitimating his regime. In exchange, Trujillo promoted merengue as the new national music and dance, in spite of it having been historically looked down upon by the nation's elite society. See Darío Tejeda, "Las políticas musicales del poder en la Era de Trujillo en República Dominicana, 1930–1961," in *Raíces comunes e historias compartidas: México, Centroamérica y el Caribe*, edited by Alain Basail Rodríguez, Inés Castro Apreza, María Luisa de la Garza Chávez, Teresa Ramos Maza, and Mario Eduardo Valdez Gordillo, 329–44. CLACSO, 2018. https://doi.org/10.2307/j.ctvn5tzmv.19.

18 Turits, *Foundations*, 181–82.
19 For a more in-depth discussion, see Derby, *Dictator's Seduction*, 209–11.
20 Turits, *Foundations*, 221–22.
21 Manley, *Paradox*, 6.
22 Manly, *Paradox*, 62–63. For more see chapter 2.
23 For more on Dominican women's opposition movements abroad, see Manley, chapter 3.
24 Derby, *Dictator's Seduction*, 185–86.
25 For more on female participation in the Democratic Youth, see Manley, *Paradox*, 97–99.
26 For details see Manley, *Paradox*, 80–92.
27 For more information see Pedro Camilo, "La Acción Clero Cultural, una organización de la resistencia antitrujillista." *Historia dominicana*. Jan. 18, 2008. http://www.historiadominicana.blogspot.com/2008/01/la-accin-clero-cultural-una-organizacin.html.
28 Rafael Taveras, "Entrevista con Rafael (Fafa) Taveras, Comunicador." *El Día*, YouTube. Uploaded by *El Día RD*. Nov. 23, 2018. https://www.youtube.com/watch?v=4JgUzNtSMYg.
29 Taveras, "Entrevista," 13:31–14:06.
30 For the full text in translation, see "Text of Pastoral Letter Read to Dominican Republic Catholics," *New York Times*, Feb. 3, 1960. https://www.nytimes.com/1960/02/03/archives/text-of-pastoral-letter-read-to-dominican-republic-catholics.html. The translation we have provided in this volume is our own and differs significantly from the version published in the *New York Times*.
31 Manley, *Paradox*, 93.
32 Antonio Imbert Barrera, "Entrevista al General Antonio Imbert Barrera, uno de los ajusticadores de Trujillo." *El Día*, YouTube. Uploaded by *El Día RD*, May 31, 2018. 0:57–0:59.
33 Interview with Leandro Guzmán in Cecilia Domeyko, dir. *Code Name: Butterflies / Nombre secreto: Mariposas*, Dir., Writ. & Prod. Cecilia Domeyko. Accent Media (2008), 55:22–55:31. Original text: "¡Ya! No se puede más. Este hombre está matando a mujeres también." The translation is ours.

34 Manley, *Paradox*, 94.
35 For a discussion of the trial and its implications see Manley, *Paradox*, 133–35.
36 For more on women's political participation and maternalist discourse during Balaguer's Doce Años, see Manley, *Paradox*, chapter 5; characterization of the Doce Años, 162.
37 The book is a collection of Minerva and Manolo's personal correspondence framed by Minou's reflections and explanations. Minou Tavárez Mirabal, *Mañana te escribiré otra vez. Minerva y Manolo. Cartas* (Santo Domingo: Fundación Hermanas Mirabal, 2013). Translated into English as *The Letters of Minerva Mirabal and Manolo Tavárez: Love and Resistance in the Time of Trujillo*. Introduction and Translation by Heather Hennes (Gainesville: University of Florida Press, 2022).
38 Julia Alvarez, introduction to the present volume.

TRANSLATORS' NOTE

Ana E. Martínez and Heather Hennes

When Minou Tavárez Mirabal asked Nani if translating the book into English was a worthwhile project, she immediately thought of the more than two million Dominicans who now live in the United States, Europe, Latin America, and other parts of the world. That number represents roughly 20 percent of the Dominican population. So, what an opportunity this would be to honor Doña Dedé's commitment, following her sisters' assassination, to tell their story and, through that, the stories of thousands of Dominicans who also fought tirelessly to rid the Dominican Republic of the Rafael Trujillo dictatorship, one of the bloodiest the Americas has suffered. With this translation, we hope to convey Doña Dedé's tenacity, fortitude, and, most importantly, her will to live, heal, and contribute to Dominican collective memory as a building block of the democracy that Dominicans have merited and currently defend with all their might.

Vivas en su jardín

Doña Dedé's memoir was first published in 2009 as *Vivas en su jardín: Memorias* by Editorial Aguilar (Santo Domingo) and as *Vivas en su jardín. La verdadera historia de las hermanas Mirabal y su lucha por la libertad* by Penguin Random House, Vintage Español (New York). It begins with an introduction by Julia Alvarez, the acclaimed Dominican American writer whose 1994 novel *In the Time of the Butterflies* introduced the Mirabal sisters to a U.S. readership. That introduction was translated into Spanish by Minou Tavárez Mirabal, the daughter of Minerva Mirabal and Manolo Tavárez Justo. The introduction you will read in this volume is the original English-language version of Alvarez's text. The first edition of *Vivas en su jardín* also contains eighty-one photographs organized in two sets. We have retained forty of those photographs with their captions and have added a map of the Dominican Republic and a Mirabal Reyes family tree. The appendix of *Vivas en su jardín* contains a chronology prepared by economist, historian, and former Dominican ambassador to the United States, Bernardo Vega. We include it here in translation with one addition: Minou Tavárez Mirabal's first election to the legislature in 2002.

The present translation of *Alive in Their Garden* is based on the third edition, published in 2014 by Editora Búho in Santo Domingo. This 2014 edition contains two additional texts, both by Minou Tavárez Mirabal. One, titled "The Plural Cause of Things," is the reflection Minou presented at the April 27, 2009, book launch of *Vivas en su jardín*. The other is the farewell letter that she read at Dedé's interment in Salcedo, "When We Lost Everything, You Were There for Us." She concludes the letter with a statement that summarizes Dedé's determination to carry on and always remember: "It was you, Mamá, who, when we lacked everything as a nation, as a world, as a family, as sons and daughters, you were the one who was there filling the void with your committed and eternal presence, always telling the story—over and over again—a story you never tired of telling, so that your sisters would never become a part of the past. It was you, Mamá, it was you, who when we lost everything, you gave us your all."

Dedé's memoir took shape through a collaborative effort, as she explains in her introductory chapter "Staying Alive." It began with the encouragement of family and friends, in particular Dr. Juan Tomás Estévez, whom Dedé thanks in her preface. The narrative itself began as a series of oral testimonies that were recorded, transcribed, and organized by Ángela Hernández. Finally, Dedé's nine children, especially Minou, helped polish the narrative into its final form. We are honored that her family has trusted us to join this project by translating her story for the English-speaking public.

The Present Edition

One of our primary goals and challenges has been maintaining Doña Dedé's voice while providing any additional information readers might need in order to understand her memoir on multiple levels. Her narrative is peppered with references to people, events, places, and aspects of daily life that may be unclear to a readership unfamiliar with the cultural, political, and physical landscape of that time and place. While the original text includes a few explanatory footnotes, we have added several more. To distinguish between

Doña Dedé's notes and our own, we have labeled the former as "Author's notes." All other notes are ones that we have added. We have also eliminated three notes from the original text, as we were able to clarify the material in the body of the translation. Whenever the author cites excerpts from other texts, including poems, magazine articles, letters, and testimonies, we have provided bibliographic information to the best of our ability. At times we were unable to do this fully for lack of information in the original text.

One challenge of this translation has been providing the needed clarification while preserving Doña Dedé's voice and the intimacy of her narrative. She speaks to us directly from the painful memories in her heart, without flourishes or pretenses. With this in mind, we have left certain terms in Spanish because of their strong affective connotations and because some terms have no direct equivalent in English. Besides the widely recognizable *Mamá* and *Papá*, we have retained terms such as *comadre* and *compadre*, which parents use in reference to their children's godmother and godfather, respectively. We have also retained the titles of respect *don* and *doña*. These terms remind us of the close familial ties and friendships that sustained the Mirabals throughout their lives and that are a central theme of Dedé's memoir. For a similar reason, we have also retained words with strong connotations related to life under the regime. One such term is *calié*, a reference to the regime's spies and henchmen that conjures up chilling memories to this day. Other such terms include *trujillista* and *antitrujillista*, references to Trujillo supporters and opponents, respectively, and *catorcistas*, members of the 14th of June Revolutionary Movement. By retaining these words in Spanish, we hope to situate the reader in the Dominican Republic at the time and hear Doña Dedé's voice more clearly as she tells us her story.

Concluding Thoughts from Nani Martínez

During the translation process I frequently asked myself how was Doña Dedé capable of writing this story, of bringing up so much suffering and despair. They say it is better to leave the past where it belongs . . . in the past. And, on many occasions during the translation process, I had to put the book aside, let it be, and simply stop in order to take a deep breath of air, close my eyes, and try to listen and understand the words Doña Dede kept repeating for decades: "I was left behind to tell their story." Those words kept me going.

What an honor to share her words with an English-speaking audience who, otherwise, would never know the true story of las Hermanas Mirabal.

Alive in Their Garden

The True Story of the Mirabal Sisters and Their Fight for Freedom

Dedé Mirabal

Figure 0.3. Dedé and Julia Alvarez, who re-created the tragedy in her novel *In the Time of the Butterflies.* Courtesy of the Fundación Hermanas Mirabal.

Introduction

The Most Difficult Act of Heroism

JULIA ALVAREZ

"'Why didn't they kill you?' the children who visit the museum sometimes ask me."

So opens Dedé Mirabal's brave, moving, and invaluable testimony of her own and her sisters' lives and struggles during the Trujillo dictatorship. Brave, because just reading these pages is a gripping and terrifying reminder of that oppressive and not distant time in Dominican history. Moving, because the losses of those years, which can blur into facts and figures, become real and immediate when we experience them in detail through the testimony of a person who lived under that regime and lost three sisters and a dear brother-in-law to it. Invaluable, because those of us who have had the great privilege of hearing Dedé recount these stories firsthand have long felt that they must not be lost but should be written down. As those of you who are about to read this book will soon discover, we have here what amounts to a national treasure. Dedé in person is a natural and lively storyteller, and the magic of this testimony is that her voice has been captured in these pages!

I admit that when I first met Dedé Mirabal in the late 1980s, that child's question was the one in my head. "Why didn't they kill you?" But I was a thirty-something-year-old woman who knew better than to ask that indiscreet question. Instead, over the course of several years researching and writing *In the Time of the Butterflies,* a novel based on the lives of the Mirabal sisters, I discovered the answer for myself. It is the same answer Dedé gives to these ingenuous, curious children: "I stayed alive to tell you this story."

I first began to contemplate writing about the Mirabal sisters when a women's press in the United States asked me if I would contribute a short paragraph about a Dominican heroine for a series of postcards they were publishing about extraordinary women from around the world. The three Mirabal sisters instantly came to mind. What I did not know on setting out to research their lives was that a fourth sister had survived. Because ours is a country where everyone knows everyone else, and there is always a cousin married to the brother-in-law of someone you want to talk to, I was able to meet, interview, and befriend Dedé Mirabal.

What happened to me during our first meeting was that the story came alive in my imagination from hearing Dedé recount the lives and deaths of her sisters. Instead of a postcard, I now envisioned a whole book. At first, I debated whether it should be nonfiction, but as I listened to this expert storyteller, I knew I wanted to tell a story, not of facts focused on the dictatorship and the sisters' tragic ending, but a story of complex, vibrant personalities who kept faith with what was grand in the human spirit in spite of persecution and terror. Back in the late '80s and early '90s, there wasn't much written about them, and so I took refuge in historical fiction. As a German novelist once wrote, "Novels arise out of the shortcomings of history."

This memoir, along with the detailed and helpful chronology by Bernardo Vega, now provides a wealth of information and a complete account of the history. This is the book I wish I'd had on hand as I was writing *In the Time of the Butterflies*. But perhaps had this wonderful testimony existed, I would have felt no need to fictionalize a story already so well told by one of its protagonists. In addition, this book includes not just the lives of the Mirabal sisters, but also the lives and struggles of their husbands, most particularly that of Manolo Tavárez, Minerva's husband, whose charismatic and noble character represents an important balance to the bestiality of Trujillo. We must never forget that we are capable of being both types of human beings, and while we must denounce our inner Trujillos as well as the outer ones, we must also reach for the stars, the Manolos and the Mirabals inside each and every one of us. Furthermore, we must demand their standard of integrity, courage, and service from our public servants.

Over the years since the publication of my novel, I have become friends with Dedé Mirabal and her niece-daughters Minou Tavárez Mirabal and Jacquelín Guzmán Mirabal. We have been together at any number of events commemorating the Mirabal sisters. Among these commemorations has been the United Nations's gratifying proclamation of the day of their murder, November 25, as the International Day for the Elimination of Violence against Women. Around the world, from Denmark to Zimbabwe, from Ecuador to Jordan, women and men gather in their name and under their symbol, the butterfly, to affirm the ongoing struggle against gender-based violence, a struggle which we, who will always be in debt to the Mirabal sisters and to others who died during the dictatorship, must continue.

How far our little butterflies from a tiny half-island nation have flown!

At all these commemorations, and here in these pages, Dedé speaks of her sisters as flesh-and-blood women, thus underscoring that their heroism is possible for all of us. What she does not mention, and what perhaps we have taken for granted as we admire and acknowledge the grand sacrifice of her sisters and other fallen heroes, is her own heroism. It's easy to overlook the heroism of daily discipline, of dozens of seemingly insignificant choices that make all the difference in the world. This is the hardest heroism, one that survives and forgives but does not forget. "Revolution only secures the territory in which life can change," Rebecca Solnit observed in writing about the Zapatistas. "Change is a discipline lived every day."[1]

When the children ask us why they did not kill Dedé Mirabal, we must tell them it's so she could stay alive and model that daily discipline, so she could teach us how to be humane human beings again.

The thirty-one years of the Trujillo dictatorship were the darkest moments of our history. After his death, Trujillo lived on in many of his minions, perpetuating long years of corruption and "democratic dictatorship," disgraces that continue to plague our history. It is still the time for Butterflies to act as forces, locally and globally, threaten to pull us back into the morass of *Trujillismo* without Trujillo. Often, we encounter willful ignorance, which dooms us to repeat the past and set the blueprint for the future. But to offset that historical amnesia and present confusion, we have the inspiration and example of the remaining Mirabal sister. Patiently, quietly, persistently, with dignity and grace, Dedé has been showing us how to live, as her sisters showed us how to struggle and how to die. She is the unacknowledged mother of the new nation that we are still constructing, leading us with her stories and her strength, her vivacity, tenacity, and most importantly with her example. I don't think we fully understand to what

---

1 Rebecca Solnit. *Hope in the Dark: Untold Histories, Wild Possibilities* (New York: Nation Books, 2004). Translators' note.

extent Dedé Mirabal has been, and continues to be, our guiding spirit. Perhaps these pages will allow us to realize what she means to us as a nation and to feel gratitude at this last butterfly still alive,[2] not just in the gardens that surround the Museum of the Mirabal Sisters but alive in her own words in these pages.

Revised on March 8, 2024, International Women's Day

---

[2] Dedé Mirabal was alive when this book was originally published in 2009, but she passed away on February 1, 2014, at the age of eighty-eight. Translators' note.

Staying Alive

"Why didn't they kill you?" the children in all their innocence often ask me when visiting the Mirabal Sisters House Museum in Conuco, or my home in the town of Ojo de Agua. "I stayed alive to tell you their story," I respond. "Of course!" they agree with surprise.

Over the years, I've gotten used to telling my sisters' story to all the individuals and groups who have asked me, knowing that my testimony honors an entire, exceptional generation of women and men, and the Dominican people as a whole, who fought for freedom during the dreadful years of the Trujillo dictatorship.

There is an anecdote that I would like to share because I believe it is important. Early each morning, I go out and tend to my garden. Most days, the son of a woman who works with me follows me about. I pick up every little dry leaf. I clean here and there while he asks me different questions: "What about the Mirabals? Where are the Mirabals?" I stop and point to the butterflies: large and beautiful; yellow, orange, and brown; flying about the anthuriums, the impatiens, the roses, and the robust orchids because we grow everything organically. "Is that them?" he asks, wide-eyed. And I answer, "Yes, that's them. So, start picking up the leaves so that when they come, they'll see that everything is clean and tidy." Day after day, as he follows behind me, he cries out, "They're here! Look, the butterflies!" Other times, he looks at me and asks, "Will the Mirabals come today?"

Children and teenagers are often drawn to stories about the struggle against Trujillo and the tragic end of the Mirabal sisters. Maybe it is because they have studied the historical events in school, or because they have overheard adults mention them, albeit vaguely.

The Truth of the Matter

When you reach a certain age, you become more acutely aware of our inescapable reality as human beings, of that great journey that lies ahead for each of us. I am eighty-two years old, and there are so many things that I have witnessed personally, so many things that I have lived through and must tell . . .

People often ask me, "Dedé, why don't you write your memoirs?" I have given many interviews and been involved in several book projects. Still, all these bittersweet memories that I carry inside me have yet to be written.

Today I feel more at peace. A friend is encouraging me, my children are insisting, and I have a writer and a photographer acting as accomplices. The time has come to stop and reflect on my life from the day I was born to the present. My sole purpose is to share in detail my experience of the events that impacted my family and my country during much of the twentieth century.

I would like to give this testimony as clearly as possible.

What do I want the reader to discover in this memoir? The truth of the matter. The facts. Many pages have been written and much has been said about my family, but I have always thought the story to be distorted, whether for simple lack of information, because of special interests or convenience, or even because of imagination and myth.

Julia Alvarez's novel *In the Time of the Butterflies,* originally written in English, shared the story of my sisters with the world and the United States, where more than one million Dominicans and thousands of Latin Americans live. Many of these people experienced firsthand what a dictatorship is all about, which is partly why the book was so well received. Its translation into Spanish was an even greater success. But as the author herself has explained, the book is a novel, a work of fiction. One day Julia Alvarez confessed to me that, as a woman, she wrote the book mainly thinking of women, and that the participation of men would be the subject of another project and of other writers. I suppose this is why Julia left out even Minerva's husband Manolo Tavárez, who deserves this country's respect for his extraordinary leadership and who made the ultimate sacrifice for his beloved nation. Her novel does not convey his importance.

Those who have asked me about the facts behind certain situations, specifically regarding this or that detail or, for example, how my husband is portrayed in the novel, I always remind them that even though it is based on facts, the novel is a work of fiction.

The novel responds to the author's needs and style. They will at times exaggerate or downplay the events in order to capture the reader's interest. As historian Bernardo Vega has pointed out, *In the Time of the Butterflies* has the merit of piquing the reader's curiosity. It encourages the reader to search for the true facts behind the events. The adaptation of the historical events for the sake of the narrative makes sense, is understandable, and meets a specific purpose.

However, ignorance and perverse interests have distorted our recent history. Such is the case of Alicinio Peña Rivera,[3] one of my sisters' murderers. He conveniently altered the historical facts for his own personal gain, benefitting financially from the books he wrote. In his version of the events, everyone else is to blame, except himself. Not long ago, I was visited by an acquaintance of Ciriaco de la Rosa, another one of my sisters' murderers.[4] He told me that the men who killed the girls and Rufino were furious with Alicinio because he washed his hands of the murders and pegged it all on them. This should not surprise us because the majority of hardened murderers try to justify themselves and blame others.

My memoir will set the record straight for the reader; it will lead them toward the truth.

What motivates me, above all else, is that the younger generations learn our history. I want our young people to better understand the facts so they can discern between historical reality and imagination when they read fiction or other kinds of books containing anecdotes that aren't necessarily true, even though the intention of those narratives is not to downplay my sisters' sacrifice. A great many Dominicans couldn't have known what really happened during those years. For a long time, one would speak of the Mirabal sisters, and of many other cases, with certain discretion, with fear, because it was dangerous to do so. The repressive machinery of the regime did not disappear when Trujillo did.

In these pages, I insist on mentioning certain names and events that might seem insignificant or repetitive. I am committed to preserving the memory of many known or unknown individuals who played a fundamen-

---

3   Victor Alicinio Peña Rivera, regional head of the SIM in the north, was one of the intellectual authors of the plan to assassinate the Mirabal sisters. In his 1977 memoir *Trujillo: Historia oculta de un dictador / Trujillo: The Hidden History of a Dictator* (New York: Plus Ultra), he admits as much but claims he was not at the scene of the crime, an assertion that contradicts witnesses' testimonies. In 1962 he was tried and sentenced to twenty years of labor, only to be freed during the April Revolution in 1965. He went on to live in Puerto Rico and Boston.

4   Ciriaco de la Rosa was one of the five men who participated in the murder of the Mirabal sisters. In 1963, after the fall of the dictatorship, four of the men were given thirty-year sentences, while de la Rosa received only twenty years for the crime. All "escaped" from their jail cells during the chaos of the April Revolution in Santo Domingo in 1965. They later resurfaced in the United States. De la Rosa settled in Lawrence, Massachusetts, where he lived for three decades and later died in 2002 or 2003.

tal role at a particular moment in time and faced tremendous risks, individuals who sacrificed themselves along with so many young men and women of that glorious generation. They deserve to be remembered.

In order to tell my story as effectively as possible, I have organized it in four parts. The first three parts summarize three important stages of my life. The fourth tells of the work that I have undertaken over all these years to preserve the memory of my sacrificed sisters.

The first pages reminisce about a happy period in my life. They span from my most distant memories to the moment when our family definitively fell from grace from the Trujillo regime, a turn that would forever mark our destiny. It is during this period that our parents met, we were born, and my sisters and I grew up. It is a time when my family established its livelihood and its social and commercial relationships. I am referring to my father, Enrique Mirabal Fernández, and my mother, Mercedes Reyes Camilo, known as Doña[5] Chea, as well as the family's closest relatives and friends. During those years we received an education, our characters took shape, we chose different occupations, and we formed long-lasting personal bonds.

The second part of this memoir begins with the tragic party in San Cristóbal in 1949, when Minerva politically challenged Trujillo. It concludes with the death of her husband Manolo Tavárez Justo in 1963. It was during this time that the storm came upon us. These were years of struggle and tragedy, when we lost Patria, Minerva, María Teresa, and Manolo. We had already lost our father earlier, in 1953. In spite of it all, these were also years of loving our family and spouses, years when our children were born and friendships were put to the test. They were years that brought learning and awareness.

The third part recounts the most relevant events following my sisters' deaths, including the murder investigation and the trial of those responsible. In writing this section, I have drawn from documentation to help reconstruct the events. It is my intention to provide an account that is as faithful to historical fact as possible, for the benefit of all those men and women, especially our youth, who are interested in this period of our history. At the same time, this third section summarizes my life without my sisters: the personal challenges of having survived and of recovering from the tragedy.

The fourth and final part tells of how my mother and I have worked to keep our family together, to provide for and educate my sisters' children, as well as my own. It tells of my life into the present and the challenges I have

---

5 "Don" and "Doña" are forms of address used with a person's first name to show respect.

had to face, including the responsibility for keeping my sisters' memory alive. I also reflect on the responsibilities that we have toward our country today.

I cannot conclude this introduction without expressing my deep gratitude to Dr. Juan Tomás Estévez, who insisted on this project and took it upon himself to assure that my story be put down in ink on paper; to Angela Hernández, who dedicated long hours to recording, organizing, and transcribing my memories; to historian Bernardo Vega, who carefully prepared the chronology included in this book; and to my nine sons and daughters, especially to Minou Tavárez Mirabal, who gave form to this book, who pruned, cleaned, and watered these pages, in which—as in the garden surrounding the house museum—my butterflies will live forever.

I

Memories of a Happy Time

Figure 1.1. Doña Chea (pregnant with Patria) and Don Enrique Mirabal. They were married in 1923. "My father, although he was not rich, was well off financially. My mother owned a farm." Courtesy of the Fundación Hermanas Mirabal.

Figure 1.2. Dedé, Minerva, and Patria, between the ages of four and six. Courtesy of the Fundación Hermanas Mirabal.

Figure 1.3. "Today Patria Mercedes celebrates fifteen Februaries . . ." Courtesy of the Fundación Hermanas Mirabal.

Figure 1.4. A young Dedé (*right*) with Minerva. "When I look back now and remember what we were like, I think that I was probably the boldest and most flirtatious of the four . . ." Courtesy of the Fundación Hermanas Mirabal.

Right: Figure 1.5. Minerva representing the homeland with a dress that featured the national emblem. Courtesy of the Fundación Hermanas Mirabal.

Below: Figure 1.6. Patria surrounded by the flowers in her garden. "She was always in a good mood and was always up to date on fashion and decorating trends." Courtesy of the Fundación Hermanas Mirabal.

Left: Figure 1.7. "Minerva enjoyed everything: she embroidered, sewed, went on outings, danced if she had to dance, but her passion was reading." "For [a] party she dressed up as a rumba girl, wearing a white skirt with red polka dots . . ." Courtesy of the Fundación Hermanas Mirabal.

Below: Figure 1.8. Patria and Pedrito's wedding in 1941. María Teresa was the flower girl. "[Patria] was lucky to find a quiet and indulgent husband who always supported her . . ." Courtesy of the Fundación Hermanas Mirabal.

Above: Figure 1.9. María Teresa, Patria, Pedrito, and Minerva. Courtesy of the Fundación Hermanas Mirabal.

Right: Figure 1.10. María Teresa showing off her long hair, which was never cut and which she usually wore in one or two braids. Courtesy of the Fundación Hermanas Mirabal.

Above: Figure 1.11. María Teresa with her parents at their home in Ojo de Agua. Courtesy of the Fundación Hermanas Mirabal.

Left: Figure 1.12. María Teresa. "She was always a good little girl, extremely kind." Courtesy of the Fundación Hermanas Mirabal.

Above: Figure 1.13. Marriage of Dedé and Jaimito Fernández, 1948. "I knew him all my life. His mother, Doña Lesbia Camilo, and my mother were first cousins . . . I caught his eye at a very early age." Courtesy of the Fundación Hermanas Mirabal.

Right: Figure 1.14. Minerva in 1946. "The last few years of the 1940s were perhaps the happiest and the ones that Minerva enjoyed most." Courtesy of the Fundación Hermanas Mirabal.

Below: Figure 1.15. Minerva sitting behind the steering wheel with Violeta and Normita, 1946. Courtesy of the Fundación Hermanas Mirabal.

1

Our Family

Settling in Ojo de Agua

My father, Enrique Mirabal Fernández, was born in Don Pedro, in Santiago Province. His father was Simeón Mirabal Núñez and his mother was Adela Fernández. On my father's side we had nine uncles and aunts: Ermenegilda (Aunt Meneja); Rosa; Antonio (Uncle Toño); Otilio (Uncle Tilo); Rafael (Uncle Fello); Aquiles, who died as a child; Esquirino (Uncle Quirino); Antonia (Tuta); and Simeón (Uncle Mon).

A friend of grandfather Simeón and my father's godfather, a man named Clemente, had a small farm in Clavijo, which is the present-day site of the Salcedo cemetery. It was he who one day invited my grandfather to come work in this town that, at the time, was known as Juana Núñez. My grandparents arrived at the farm with almost all their children. This is where they grew up, except for Uncle Tilo, who stayed with his godfather. He later joined the family as a young adult.

From a very young age, my father and his brothers had the idea of going into business for themselves. Clavijo was situated about one kilometer from Salcedo, and they came into town every day to work in small hardware shops owned by Arabs. They went to school at night.

When they turned about sixteen or seventeen, Uncle Fello and my father moved to Ojo de Agua, a small village that was further away but still close to Salcedo. That must have been in 1916 or 1917 because my father said that by then the Americans were passing through the villages, which meant that the occupation had already begun.[6]

They started working for Mr. José Espaillat in what was apparently a two-story store since they said people would pass by on the street below. José Espaillat was originally from Tamboril. He was the father of Che Espaillat, who would later join my sisters in the struggle. He decided to move to the

---

6   Reference to the first occupation by the U.S. Marines from 1916 to 1924, aimed at protecting U.S. and European investments by imposing institutions and policies that would increase political and financial stability in the Dominican Republic.

United States and sold his business in Ojo de Agua to Uncle Fello and my father.

The rest of the family stayed behind in our home in Clavijo. Later on, little by little, they all began to migrate, except Aunt Meneja, the only one of my aunts who did not have children and who lived in that house until her death. We always visited her when we were little or accompanied her to Mass on Sundays, and she was the one who took us to celebrate our first communions. She was very loving toward us. By that time, my father was more financially stable, and he helped Aunt Meneja and Aunt Rosa.

My father and Uncle Fello were doing very well with the new business, which consisted of buying and selling cacao, coffee, beans, rice, corn, and other agricultural products. So they decided to buy about an acre of land and build a home there, which is the same house that we still maintain and where I currently live. It was a solid structure for the time, and little by little we continued to improve it. We changed the walls and built an outdoor porch. It was in that house that my father, who always distinguished himself as a man of progress, vision, and dynamism, opened his first grocery story. Later on, he took interest in the construction of the Ojo de Agua-Conuco road and bought more land.

We were very close with some of our aunts and uncles on both sides of the family, and we were familiar with the regions where they lived. They were part of our experience from the time we were born, as you will appreciate later in this story.

Uncle Fello married a woman named María Michel from the town of Moca. She died soon thereafter during her first pregnancy. Uncle Fello then took ill with hemoptysis, a kind of tuberculosis. His doctor, Dr. Pascasio Toribio, who had studied in France, recommended he move to a cold climate to recover, such as the mountain town of Jarabacoa. When he left, he and my father reached some sort of agreement. My father probably bought Uncle Fello's share of the house and the business. At the time, property was not worth much.

In Jarabacoa, Uncle Fello recovered and got remarried, this time to Lilia Piña, with whom he had two children.

During his entire life he remained very close to my father and to us. He came to visit, and during our childhood and youth, my sisters and I loved to spend our vacations at his home in Jarabacoa.

My Mother, Her Family, and the Wounds Left by the 1916 American Occupation

My mother, Mercedes—or "Chea," as everyone knew her—was born and raised in Ojo de Agua. Her father, Miguel Angel Reyes, had immigrated there from Canca la Piedra in Tamboril and fell in love with my grandmother, María de los Angeles Camilo (Mamá Chichí), whose family owned various cacao farms in the area. He married her, and they settled here. They had my mother, as well as Angelina, Carmela, Antonia (Toña), Lalía, José, and Miguel.

My mother remembered her father as a hardworking man, who took her and her brothers to the farm to help plant, even as small children. When he was young, perhaps only thirty-six, he died from the influenza epidemic, a kind of pneumonia that was ravaging the country at the time. I remember my mother's nostalgia, standing in front of the land that I still own, telling us, "Look at those plum trees. My father planted them to divide the properties."

It was here in this region that the U.S. Marines killed the sons of Mrs. Rita Campos, suspected of being accomplices to the *gavilleros*,[7] an accusation they were never able to prove. Juan Osorio's novel *Silvana, o una página de la intervención* is based on these events.[8] It tells the story of how one of these men died, uttering his final words, "Silvana, my Silvana." Back then, there were individuals who loved their country and defended it from the invaders. They were self-respecting, dignified men such as Linito Camilo and Perún de la Cruz, who went to the mountains to fight against the occupation.

Aunt Fefita was my grandmother's first cousin and someone very close to us. It was near her home that the Americans branded Cayo Báez on the chest with a branding iron. They tortured him to get him to identify the *gavilleros*, who were operating in the region, and confess to being one of them. They left him for dead on the roadside, but Aunt Fefita courageously picked him up and took him to her home. She didn't let him die. She nursed him back to health and later told us that he was an extremely skinny man, who did not have an ounce of fat in his body.

---

7   Derogatory name given to Dominican guerrilla fighters who opposed the 1916 U.S. occupation. Author's note.
8   Reference to the 1919 novel by Juan A. Osorio Gómez, of Salcedo in the Cibao region. It tells the painful story of a girl in the countryside whose father is pursued and killed by the Marines.

My father always mentioned that, during the invasion, the Americans killed several people in the vicinity of Salcedo because the area was a gavillero stronghold. Charles R. Buckalew commanded the U.S. Army troops in this region. Something happened within this context that gravely impacted my mother's family. The revolutionaries went to my grandmother to seek her help. Mamá Chichí told them, "I have nothing to give you. I'm a widow. The only thing I have is my family." But there was a mole in the group, a snitch, who Dominicans call caliés,[9] who went and told the Americans that my grandmother was helping the gavilleros. The next day the invaders came to the house and told my grandmother that they were going to burn her house down. That evening, she had to leave the house with her children to seek refuge with her brother, who lived nearby. When they returned the next day, everything was burned to the ground.

My mother was about eighteen years old, and her brother, my Uncle José, was almost ten when this happened. It marked my entire family, but most especially my uncle. That is why during his entire life he was a radical anti-American and a staunch Trujillo adversary. "The Americans left Trujillo in place. That's what they left us," he would say.

My grandmother bought my mother a Singer sewing machine so she could learn to sew and help support her family financially. I still have the little book that she used to learn how to sew. She probably received it as a gift from Josefa González de Garrido (Aunt Fefita), the daughter of Pedro González, a landowner who was so rich that it was rumored he planned to pave his driveway with gold coins. Aunt Fefita, my mother's sewing teacher, was a progressive woman for that time. She truly loved my mother and was always praising her natural intelligence and her many talents, noting that, despite not having the opportunity to attend school, she had learned to read, write, and even paint.

Mamá's much younger sister, Aunt Carmela, did go to school. She studied with a teacher from the town of San Francisco de Macorís, who was brought to Conuco by some of the many wealthy families that lived there. Since Conuco was very close to Ojo de Agua, Aunt Carmela was sent there to study. But my mother could not go because my maternal grandmother had gone mad due to what had happened during the occupation. Mamá had to stay behind and keep sewing to help pay for her siblings' education.

---

9 This term for a snitch or informant would take on an added dimension during the Trujillo regime (1930–1961), as the caliés also served as the regime's henchmen.

My mother sewed, embroidered, appreciated the beautiful things in life, and loved her gardens. She told us that after their house was burned down, they built a smaller one with a pyramid-like roof, and that back then it was known as a "Lima house." She and her sisters planted a beautiful garden there, with many blooming carnation bushes. "Those flowers were the only decoration at our humble home," she recalled.

She used to tell us how she learned to sign her name on the charcoal stove. She wrote it in the ashes. It always astonished me that both she and Mamá Chichí had such beautiful penmanship despite having never gone to school.

As a reaction to the American occupation, my mother preferred German-made products because, as she put it, they were of good quality. "Look at that vase. I bought it right around the time I was married, and look how it's holding up," she would comment. She believed the Germans made top-quality products. When she talked about Singer sewing machines, for example, she would point out how wonderful they were. She always named her dogs "Nazi," and even though she didn't have a clear idea who Hitler or the Nazis were, she admired the Germans. Until the end of her days, she liked to point out, "My God! Everything the Germans make is good!"

Another important event that she always talked about when I was young was Hurricane San Zenón, which in 1930 destroyed the city of Santo Domingo but hardly impacted our region. The majority of homes in the area were not built of wood and nails, but rather of palm tree boards. The rain would come in through the cracks. I remember there was a butcher who, as he chopped meat, would sing of the tragedy that had swept through the capital:

Santo Domingo, how beautiful you were
With your boulevard-lined neighborhoods.

He would hang the pieces of meat on a stick made of palm tree wood. He used to give us the sticks while singing about the tragic event. At the time, there was an abundance of everything, but because there was no refrigeration, the meat—especially beef—was cut into small strips and left out to dry. The meat was first seasoned with salt and bitter orange juice. I can still see the portico of our house full of those meat strips, drying in the sun.

My Parents' Marriage

My father met and fell in love with my mother at Aunt Fefita's house, where my mother would go to learn to sew and embroider. When they married on March 17, 1923, my father was doing well financially, although I wouldn't say he was rich. My mother owned a farm, though she had not yet inherited it.

They were married by Father Rodríguez, the parish priest in Salcedo, who would later father several children. I think I once heard that my parents were driven to their wedding ceremony in a car, which would not have been common at the time. They had to ride on horseback from my mother's home at Los Limoncillos in Ojo de Agua to the place where the cars were waiting because the road did not reach the house. There was only one road, and it was of very black dirt. The horses' hoofs would stick in the mud, creating large puddles that made travelling very difficult. So much water accumulated that the region came to be called Ojo de Agua.[10] Slightly further away was a river passing through a ravine called La Quebrada Prieta.

The home was furnished with original Maria Theresa–style furniture and bronze beds that were purchased from a Mr. Peralta, who sold imported furniture. These same furnishings are currently on exhibit at our house museum.

My parents had very different personalities and characters. They had a good marriage, but they also had their share of crises, almost always related to one of my father's amorous adventures. He was a model husband until he reached a certain age, but after that, he began having extramarital affairs.

Perhaps his behavior began to change after he contracted hemoptysis (he must have been thirty-five or thirty-six years old), an illness for which the family doctor, Dr. Toribio, prescribed several medications. Antibiotics were not widely used at the time.

I can still see my mother serving him coffee in bed, with a few drops of a medicinal oil that she was convinced would keep his bronchial tubes clean. What was strange is that Papá, who had always been so healthy and who'd never caught so much as a cold, came down so quickly with an illness that made him spit up blood.

My mother, who was very jealous and always sought a logical explanation for everything, explained that during his illness, my father took too many vitamins and calcium and that, because of that, he began to fall in love and father children outside of his marriage. He became such an ardent

---

10   Literally "Eye of Water," or natural spring.

lover that he had a daughter (Iris) and a son (Ezequiel) with another woman and later on four daughters with yet another (Margarita, Ana, Zunilda, and Adalgisa). We knew that jealousy was eating my mother up inside, and it deeply saddened us to see her suffer in silence. But we never heard them argue.

My father liked to have a drink before dinner, but he wasn't the kind of man who went out to get drunk. He poured himself into his work. But sometimes he would mount his pretty black mule with the pretext of checking on the farm. Because he was a young, good-looking man, so white that you could literally count his veins, and with money in his pockets, he did what he wanted. But he always slept at home. My mother would be seething with rage but never said anything to him, at least not in front of us. They never exchanged insults. Mamá always kept her spirits up and kept busy with the store and the house.

During those days it was not common for couples to go out and have fun. My mother did not like to go out, but my father did. He would go to Uncle Fello's home in Jarabacoa to spend a week there. "To get a little rest," he would say.

At the time Ojo de Agua was considered part of Moca, a nearby town. Since my father was a friendly person who enjoyed all kinds of social relationships, we frequently had the local authorities come to lunch at the house. My poor mother was the one who had to cook for all those people. It's not that my father was a politician—he really didn't like politics—but he maintained good commercial relationships and was friends with lots of people. Included among his good friends were almost all the important leaders of Salcedo, such as Mr. Víctor Rodríguez, Mr. Jaime Fernández, Mr. Porfirio Montes de Oca, and attorney Juan Rojas. The same thing happened in Moca, where he was friends with Mr. Carlos Mena, originally from Puerto Plata, and the Bordas family, cacao buyers also from Puerto Plata. Their son, Diego Bordas, eventually went into exile.

At one point my father was appointed as the government official in charge of rural statistics. No one consulted him prior to this assignment, and there was no salary. He was responsible for surveying agricultural products and people. I was the one who sometimes had to fill out those lengthy forms. I often dragged my feet until we received word that they were due.

Another business my father had was a rice factory. Since there was a special tax on rice crops, we had to declare to the Internal Revenue Service how many quintals[11] of clean rice we had gotten from the bushels of unmilled rice that came in from the paddies. We recorded this information in a book that we called "the inspection registry." When it came to coffee, one had to fill out a special form for export and another for internal consumption. Only the coffee used for export was washed, pulped, and hulled. I remember the inspectors would arrive on huge Harley-Davidsons, which made me very nervous because I was afraid of making a mistake. If we did make a mistake, we had to pay hefty fines.

The word that best describes my mother is "austere." She was also meticulous and always concerned about cleanliness. One of her favorite phrases, which she would later repeat to her grandchildren, was: "God loves poverty, not filth." That's what she taught us: to love cleanliness and maintain beautiful surroundings in impeccable condition, with flowers in every corner of the house, with a lush garden and a well-set table. She believed that even though the food on the table may not be the best, if the table was beautifully set with a pretty tablecloth, napkins, and pretty plates, the food would taste better. Even at breakfast, and even though we were a large family, she arranged the plates with small pieces of red and white cheese placed around the scrambled eggs. Because of his work schedule, Papá would eat breakfast a little later. He always found a well-set table when he got home, sometimes accompanied by a friend who would join him for breakfast or lunch.

Mamá was the one who taught us the basics of sewing. She said that no one should walk around with torn clothing and that a woman's dignity was reflected in the way she took care of herself. Who dared get up in the morning and not make their beds? She would not allow it. And she insisted on always giving us advice. When it came to finding a spouse, she would tell us that girls shouldn't wait too long to get married or they'll end up with the first warm-blooded creature that comes along.

Mamá was the one who taught us respect in the home. She was very strict with us about all sorts of things. She was protective of us. She never let us sleep over at someone else's house or go on school trips. She was the disciplinarian. Sometimes she made us kneel as punishment, but then my father would come, tell us to stand up, and give us a kiss.

"Trusting people can be dangerous," she used to say. On one particular occasion I suffered terribly when I asked for her permission to go on an outing to see a nearby hill called Cerro de la Cruz, where the Americans had placed a commemorative plaque. No matter how much I pleaded with

---

11 Approximately one hundred kilograms.

her, she said no, arguing that boys would be on the excursion; she was so terribly overprotective. "The hands of a man are poison! If a man places his hand on you, you will give in," she would tell us. I was the one who suffered the worst of Mamá's overzealous protection because Patria married young and Minerva was devoted to her reading and her commitment to freedom.

In 1944, there was a huge celebration in the town of Moca to commemorate the Republic's centennial. I was so excited about attending that I had Mrs. Gelín, a famous dressmaker in the region, make me a beautiful dress for the occasion. Papá was going to accompany me but did not feel well, and even though I cried incessantly, Mamá would not let me go to the party with anyone else. She gave me all sorts of excuses. Later, to console me, she kept saying in a sweet voice, "Look, Dedé, look at all the pretty chickens we have here. Look at the hens." But I could only cry and think of my dress and the party. I snapped back at her, "Those darn hens! I don't care about the darn hens!"

Mamá was more concerned about our education than Papá. She wanted to send us to the best school available. She continuously inquired about schools until she heard from her cousin Arturo Burgos about the Immaculate Conception School in the town of La Vega, where he had sent his own daughters.

Sometimes her reactions were truly original. She fiercely rejected games of chance and gambling but once purchased a raffle ticket from a local priest to benefit a parish in Salcedo. Then, bam! Her number was called. The priest brought her the radio she had won, but she firmly rejected it and told him, "That's the Devil tempting me to keep on playing so that I keep on gambling away everything I have. I don't want the radio. No, that's temptation."

She was always busy, bustling about, working hard, sewing, helping out in the store, handling the farm workers, and taking care of the garden. Tonó,[12] who was like another daughter to her, a sister to us, and a mother to our children, would always say of my mother, "Doña Chea is what you would call a first-class lady."

She never liked parties. Work was everything to her. She wasn't interested in enjoying herself. But we did manage to convince her to go on the occasional outing, like the time when Patria took her to the capital

---

12 Ana Antonia Rosario, who grew up in the Mirabal household and helped care for the Mirabal children. After Patria, Minerva, and María Teresa were murdered, she also helped care for their children.

and to the town of Higüey to spend a few days. I don't remember her being excited about those trips.

She had a peculiar kind of peasant wisdom, which revealed itself in the many popular expressions she would often repeat or that she herself made up. She was always wary and could sniff out dishonesty in others. At the store, for example, she could identify a thief from afar, and on several occasions, she caught them red-handed with stolen merchandise.

Mamá was very supportive and nurturing toward others. Everyone always came to her for advice. They respected and cared for her, and she was always ready to step up and help people when they faced difficulties. My ex-husband's maternal grandmother was also my mother's aunt by marriage. She would say, "If you're with Chea, you are not alone. When you are close to her, you feel that someone is standing by you."

Business Ventures and Working with Papá

Upon moving to Ojo de Agua, Papá opened a small store in a room in the house where I currently live. The store did well right from the start, and within a few years he owned several warehouses. The locals began to comment that Enrique Mirabal was a "money magnet."

Back then it was not common practice to export goods directly, so Papá would sell his products to local stores, such as La Curacao, Casa Munné, and La Importadora (known later as Indubán), which had branches in Moca. I was always fascinated by the non-stop activity at the store, the number of people who came from all over the region, the mule trains, the merchants who came to buy or sell goods, and the enormous sacks of sugar that weighed about 320 pounds each, which a worker would have to carry on his back. Life was hard then.

My job was to help Papá with invoicing at the store. Our warehouse was stocked with rice, sugar, bolts of cotton fabric and denim, and military uniforms as well. We even had a small pharmacy. Papá was a good, reliable, and very trustworthy client. He purchased merchandise in Santiago at the Parisian Bazar, the Tavárez warehouses, and La Opera. He even managed to purchase life insurance, which was rare back then. He purchased it from Augusto Vega, from the Canadian Confederation. That is why we received two thousand dollars from the insurance company when he died. There was a safe in our office, and it was filled with cash since back then it was not yet common to deposit money in banks. Everything was paid in cash. When Papá went to Santiago, he would take rolls of cash to make his payments, but he was never robbed because such attacks were practically unheard of in those days.

I had a small office in the store where I kept the books and handled the wholesale side of the business, something I truly enjoyed. There were no complications. The business was doing so well that we didn't even have to take inventory. We purchased everything with cash. We paid everyone. Papá gave people advances, and they paid him back. It was that simple.

Even though we had two employees, Mamá was always there with me. She handled retail sales because we also had a small retail store. We sold fabric by the yard. I remember that when stores began to sell Japanese fabric, which faded in the sun, people preferred to buy American-made fabric because it kept its color.

We purchased our first vehicle when pickup trucks arrived in the country in the 1940s.

My father would wake me up early in the morning. "Come on, Dedé! The clients are here!" The truth is even though I answered, "I'm getting up," I always managed to sleep a little more. He would then come in and give me a kiss on the head. He was so good and understanding with us, so supportive and affectionate. As I said, the safe was always full, and though I didn't receive a salary, I could take whatever I needed. When we went shopping in Santiago, we simply took cash from the box and purchased what we wanted at a store called El Gallo. I never wasted money, though. I was very much like my mother: austere, so much so that today my children accuse me of being stingy.

There was abundance and trust. My father took risks, was ambitious, and had vision. We got along really well, even though he sometimes put me in very difficult situations. "She's the one that knows," he would say when the inspectors visited us on those huge motorcycles. It made me nervous, and I didn't know what to do. They came to see him, but through a small window he would say, "Tell them I'm not here." "He's not here," I would say, but immediately he would start yelling, "Tell them that I just arrived!" I would start crying, wanting to kill him. "Papá, they can hear you!" I would scold him. But he'd be completely at ease. "Let them hear!" he'd respond.

Papá left us some farms, but unlike Mamá, he didn't like to work the land. He preferred business: buying, selling, and making life easier for many people. He loaned money that people would pay back with the harvest, interest free. The agreement was that they would sell the harvest to him. "Enrique is such a good man," they would say, and many appreciated the support he had given them.

This was a very prosperous region. It was a common sight to see four or five trucks in front of a warehouse unloading plantains from the nearby hills, including from the Gaspar Hernández region. It was easier to reach us than to travel to Puerto Plata. They would cross paths with the mule trains that were coming to bring or purchase merchandise.

At one time, one hundred kilos of coffee sold for two pesos. Papá purchased a large amount and later sold it at a very good price. When, in 1937, the price of cacao went up, he again did very well. He had a knack for business. He purchased kerosene gas and nails because he predicted that their prices would go up, and sure enough, the prices jumped, and he earned very good returns.

He used to say that anyone could work, but very few knew how to manage a business: "Management is the key to success."

2

Our Childhood, Education, and Friends

Births

We were born in the following order: Aída Patria Mercedes, February 27, 1924; me, Bélgica Adela, March 1, 1925; María Argentina Minerva, March 12, 1926; and Antonia María Teresa, October 15, 1935. We were all born by natural childbirth.

As you can see, three of our birthdays were very close to one another, between February 27 and March 12. Patria was only one year older than me, and I was exactly one year older than Minerva, while there was close to a decade between María Teresa and the rest of us.

Patria was given her name, which means "homeland," because she was born on February 27, Dominican Independence Day, while the Americans were still in the country. They left in July of that year. I was named Bélgica Adela after my paternal grandmother, whose name was Adela, but Argentina Minerva and I were given the names of countries, mine being Belgium. María Teresa owes her name to the calendar of saints. She was born on St. Theresa's Day.

After Minerva, Mamá gave birth to a baby boy who died immediately after childbirth. He came into this world with a hole in his spinal column. It must have been spina bifida. Although they never requested a birth certificate, they did give him a name: Víctor Enrique. Papá's hopes of having a boy were crushed when he died. Years later, when María Teresa was born, he was still hoping for a boy.

I was told that the day Mamá went into labor was the same day that Uncle Tilo, my godfather, came to live with us. Papá sent him to get the midwife on a mule that Uncle Tilo said gave him all kinds of trouble. When he arrived with the midwife, I was already born and in the hands of Isabel Durán (Mamá Chabela), my mother's aunt by marriage, who also lived with us. Uncle Tilo used to complain that my father made him take the midwife back that same day and refused to pay for her services.

I remember the day María Teresa was born. Patria, Minerva, and I were older and hoping for a boy, the boy my father always dreamed of. "Another girl!" said the midwife. But still, it was such a joy to see María Teresa, so chubby and with those precious little legs.

Uncle Tilo was one of the family members who most impacted us during our childhood. Extremely intelligent and educated by a Spanish priest, he was the first person to talk to us about the Bible, which at the time was not commonly read. We were fascinated by the stories he told us, especially the one about the Good Thief and the Bad Thief.

His skills and memory were amazing. He would grab a fist full of beans and throw them on top of a table, immediately declaring, "There are X number of beans there. Count them!" He always gave the exact number. I have never seen another person who could do that, nor did we understand how it was possible that he always came up with the right number of beans. He worked in the store, and in his spare time, he made small talk with everyone who was sitting around. He also arm-wrestled.

He constantly joked with us. "Uncle Tilo, give us a cookie," we used to beg, but he would give us bread. We would throw a fit!

He told us that he was jailed in 1922 during the construction of the Duarte highway, on which he was forced to work. He said the reason there are so many mango trees along the highway is because the workers would eat mangos and throw the pits nearby. Even when he got married later on in life, he didn't move away from our family. He lived next door to my mother's house until his death.

Uncle Tilo, Uncle Fello, Uncle José, and Aunt Meneja always pampered us. They loved us very much, and we were like daughters to them.

Childhood, Games, and School

We had a truly happy childhood. When we were very little, Patria, Minerva, and I had three doll houses that Mamá had a local carpenter make for us. He used leftover wood from the boxes in which gas cans were delivered to our store. Uncle Tilo would come and play with us. He would take a doll and we would say to him, "Take this one, but don't mess up the house." We would dance around in a circle with other girls, and sing:

El alelí del matutí
tú sabes que yo no duermo
nada más pensando en ti.[13]

And also:

Las cortinas del palacio
son de terciopelo azul.
Entre cortes y cortinas
ha llegado un andaluz.[14]

We also used to play hopscotch by drawing the squares on the floor or go swimming at the river and in the Pichardos' pond, especially when our girlfriends from Salcedo visited. Doña Lucila Ariza, Minerva's godmother, was raising a couple of girls who would visit us often. At the river where we would swim, there were big rocks and we would rub against them because they allegedly helped exfoliate our skin.

In the evenings we enjoyed listening to Irenita, the cook, tell folktales about Juan Bobo and Pedro Animal and Bible stories, especially the one where Herod sent Salome the head of John the Baptist. We became enthralled by these stories, especially Minerva, who was extremely bright and paid close attention. The tales of witches and bloodsuckers also captured our imaginations. The bloodsuckers were creatures that had one foot here and the other in the capital, while the witches were women who could fly.

We had next-door neighbors named Mateo and Estebanía, who lived on land that today is part of the garden. My father gave them another plot that he owned in exchange for that one. They had no children, but Mateo's brother Polo and his mother, old lady Jacoba, lived with them. People around here used to say that Estebanía was a witch. She always had one ear covered with cotton, and people would say that her ear had been marked while she was flying around. Mateo, who had an ulcer on one leg, grew very irritated when people referred to the ulcer as "Mateo's spur," whispering that he had also been marked because he walked like a bloodsucker.

In spite of those fascinating stories, which were perfect for our childhood imaginations but which made us fear them somewhat, we got along

---

13 Morning pansies / you know I can't sleep / just thinking of you.
14 The curtains of the palace / are made of blue velvet. / Between the court and the curtains / the Andalusian appeared.

very well with them. We would sit open-mouthed, listening to all those stories that came from who knows where. For example, they would say—and even my mother said she heard the sound on several occasions—that an "evil apparition" with a loud laugh was roaming around, accompanied by barking dogs and surrounded by a swarm of fireflies. (In the countryside people believe that fireflies are the spirits of the dead.) When "the thing" passed by the house, the small dogs began to bark one after another.

Even Uncle Tilo, whose girlfriend lived a kilometer away, used to say that one evening when he was coming home late from visiting her (back then, ten o'clock was considered late), he heard small dogs barking. He was so terrified that he couldn't make it all the way to the warehouse where he had a room and instead hid in the passage dividing the warehouse from the house. That's where he heard the vision panting and the small dogs barking nearby, followed by the neighbors' dogs barking as well. The next day, a man we used to call Uncle Dimas asked my mother, "Comadre Chea, did you hear that last night?" "Yes," said Mamá, "we heard it."

Uncle José baptized the vision *Caco e'nima*, Big-Headed Spirit, and this character became the protagonist of many tales told during our evening story time.

My father sent the cacao to the town of Salcedo. He would stack two sacks on top of a horse and would place us in the middle. Nino Mojito, Aunt Meneja's husband, would be waiting for us at the grocery store to take us back home. We would sometimes spend a weekend or Holy Week there. It was a beautiful time. I remember that, back in those days, a man from Moca began selling ice cream. I have never since tasted such delicious raspberry ice cream. Perhaps it was because children have privileged taste buds. My mouth still waters when I remember the street vendor announcing, "Ice Cream! Ice Cream!"

In my mind, our childhood years were full of happiness. We played. We ran. We visited Uncle José and his wife, Aunt Minada, who every Good Friday would take us to the procession on buses the locals called *Palé*. Back then those buses began traveling between Santiago and San Francisco de Macorís. They charged a couple of pennies per ride.

We had everything. At Christmastime my father would travel to Santiago to buy dolls and other gifts that the Three Kings would leave us on January 6. We innocently believed in this tradition for a long time, until one year we discovered the dolls, hidden away. Then we stopped leaving grass for the Three Kings' camels and water for Baby Jesus.

Ana Almánzar, my mother's godchild and a very good friend of mine, would visit me every day so we could play. Later on, in the 1940s, she worked at my father's store until she went to live in the United States. The daughters of David Camilo, my mother's first cousin, also came over to play with us. We went to the same school. We had a lot of friends, and we played all kinds of games and did lots of fun activities.

Patria would scold Minerva because she would sit on the floor and get dirty. Minerva loved to roller skate, and once, at the school in La Vega, she fell and got three stitches in the chin.

In school we began playing volleyball. I was a better player than Minerva. We put together a team with nearby friends and played inter-collegiate tournaments with girls from Macorís and Conuco. When the store closed at five o'clock, I would hop on a bicycle that my father had given me and ride two kilometers to play with a group of friends. We played on various courts. That's where I fell in love with Jaimito, who would later become my husband. He also played volleyball back then.

I hold beautiful, unforgettable memories of my childhood girlfriends: Aunt Fefita's daughter, Flor Garrido, who currently lives in Miami, and her sister Clara. We were very close. There was also Alia Cruz; Ana Almánzar who, as I said previously, practically lived with us; and our cousins Tata and Dulce Pantaleón, the daughters of Aunt Carmela, who frequently visited and spent time with us.

Life back then was not like it is now. Everything was so different, so simple. Personal relationships were so strong. For example, Aunt Fefa was the one who took us to the Three Kings Day parties at the club in Salcedo because my mother did not like parties. Aunt Fefa would come and say, "Comadre Chea, let the girls go. I'll take them." We didn't go every year, but the times we did go were truly some of the happiest moments I remember from our early childhood.

Aunt Fefa was a fine lady and was very advanced for her time. I remember that when Patria turned fifteen, she wrote her a poem. I only remember these verses:

Hoy cumple Patria Mercedes
quince febreros cabales
y le ofrecen sus amigas
flores, música y cantares.[15]

---

[15] Today Patria Mercedes / is fifteen years old / and her girlfriends offer her / flowers, music, and songs.

When we were older my father took Patria, Minerva, and me to Santiago, where we boarded an airplane and flew to the capital. He wanted us to have that experience.

On another occasion we traveled to the coast to see the sea for the first time and to go swimming at the beach. Patria was already married, so we weren't small children. We had so much fun! I was in awe! The sea looked like a giant plantation of broad beans.

Another delightful trip was the one to Long Beach in Puerto Plata. We went by bus. Patria had already been there, and she wanted Minerva and me to go. That trip is one of the most beautiful memories that I cherish to this day.

Mamá, Our Health, and Education

Although we were never seriously ill nor hospitalized, Mamá worried about María Teresa's health and about a patch of skin on Patria's foot, which I think was simply a scar left by a slight scratch. The truth is Mamá was almost obsessive when it came to her family's health. She was mortified because María Teresa had some sort of asthma. She was always overprotecting her, giving her homemade remedies because she worried that María Teresa might have inherited Papá's hemoptysis, even though my sister was born before he took ill. She would prepare her all kinds of concoctions with sesame oil and who knows what other ingredients, such as onions in juice from an herb called *apazote* and milk with garlic. Minerva would warn my sister, "Don't just drink everything she gives you," and scold Mamá, "You are poisoning her!" If María Teresa coughed, she had to stay in her room for fear that she might catch a cold or who knows what. And then came Mamá with all her potions and homemade remedies.

Once there was an outbreak of an illness called uncinariasis, or something like that. They often treated it with a laxative known as the "Three Strikes." You had to travel to La Vega three times in eight-day intervals. On the first visit, they ran all the tests, and if you tested positive for parasites, you had to return two more times. We were all tested, and the only one who didn't test positive for parasites was María Teresa. How could she possibly have parasites with all the potions Mamá used to give her?

We learned to read and write in Ojo de Agua. We learned our first letters at a little wooden school that back then went up to the third grade. It is still open today. Our main teacher was Nicolás Camilo, from whom I learned almost everything I know. As a matter of fact, I learned more from him than at the Immaculate Conception School. A follower of Eugenio María de Hostos,[16] he even taught us how to graft plants. On Arbor Day we planted small trees, especially mahogany trees, and we had a vegetable garden. He was truly a wise teacher in the full sense of the word. He taught us a lot, about everything. Another teacher, Lidia Acevedo, taught us how to embroider and the basics of home economics.

We went to school mornings and afternoons, and for us it was like taking a nice stroll. The school was nearby, some two hundred meters from our home. We not only learned all kinds of things, but we also got to play with the other girls.

I have vivid memories of us as little girls running after Mr. Camilo's mule as he traveled back to Salcedo on Fridays. We used to walk the two-and-a-quarter kilometers to the highway, where Uncle José and Aunt Minada lived in my mother's old house. We spent weekends with them and late on Sunday afternoons, Patria, Minerva, and I would walk back home, scared to death. Patria, the most easily spooked, would suggest, "I'll walk in the middle, and you two walk next to me, one on each side." Minerva and I would respond, "Oh yeah, right! You stay in the middle so we can protect you!" People used to say that a dead man would appear in a coconut grove along the path, and that another would appear in a huge fig tree that once stood where the sports complex was later built, next to my home. Childish nonsense! But today they are happy memories.

Mamá was the one who saw to it that we studied, learned discipline, and built sound friendships. Once we finished the first three years of elementary school, she convinced Papá to register us at the Immaculate Conception School in La Vega. Patria and I were registered in fifth grade, and Minerva, who knew much more than we did, in fourth. But before the end of the first month, she was moved up to fifth grade. So, we were all in the same grade pretty much from the start.

We didn't all start school at the same time because Papá had decided that my sisters would start in September and that I would stay home until January to help him run the store. I can see myself as if in an old, black-and-white movie the day Mamá, Papá, and I went to take Patria and Minerva

---

16 This Puerto Rican educator, philosopher, sociologist, and writer who settled in the Dominican Republic is known for his innovative pedagogy. He advocated for laic education rooted in science, logic, and reason and maintained that such education should be available to female students as well. He is also known for having fought for Puerto Rican independence from Spain and the United States, and for the unity of the Antilles.

to school. I remember feeling heartbroken, fighting off the tears as we said goodbye.

In the beginning, we traveled mainly by train. The La Vega Station was on Gregorio Rivas Avenue, close to the school. Later on, we would go in cars that would come from Moca. Papá himself made the arrangements with the drivers. He was convinced that you had to be wary of drivers and military officers. Papá was careful with his money because he said it was well earned, but he believed that paying forty-five pesos for the three of us to attend school was not expensive at all.

The day when I was finally sent to study in La Vega, I remember traveling from my house to the train station in Salcedo on a mule with a nice gait. A little boy went with me, riding on the mule's hind quarters. He then brought the mule back home.

I arrived at the Immaculate Conception School for the first time one late afternoon, but since Patria and Minerva had already been there for a couple of months, I felt safe. Dinner was usually rice and black beans with fried eggs. The beans seemed so dark to me because we were used to red beans. Sometimes we had a piece of cheese and chocolate. They never served us plantains or bread.

The daily routine was to get up, go to church to pray or attend Mass, have breakfast, and then go to class. At noon we went to the dining room. Then we had recess while the nuns ate. When they finished, they came back and we all prayed again. We prayed all the time. In the afternoons we went back to our studies. Some went to art class. Others learned typing, while the rest of us went to study in a place called The Court, where there was a Sacred Heart of Jesus. Two older students were charged with supervising us while we studied. They were María Luisa Osterkri and Pucha Rodríguez, the sister of José Horacio Rodríguez, who would later be one of the leaders of the June 14, 1959, expedition[17] to overthrow Trujillo. We were organized in different groups: "the little ones," "the middle ones," and the "older ones." We belonged to the first group.

We would arrive at school in September and not return home until December. We also had vacation during Holy Week, before Easter, but only

---

17   Reference to the failed attempt by exiled revolutionaries of the Dominican Revolutionary Movement to land in the Dominican Republic and topple the Trujillo regime. After having trained in Cuba, the 198 freedom fighters planned to land on the northern coast at Maimón and Estero Hondo and in the Central Mountain Range on June 14, 1959. They were discovered, overcome, and killed. The survivors were interrogated, tortured, and then executed.

two or three days. Some of our unforgettable friends at school were María Krant, Gladys García, and Leyda García. There was also a small group of girls from Salcedo, like us, including Jaimito's sisters. Another student there was Pura de la Maza. Her brother, Antonio de la Maza,[18] was instrumental in the plot to assassinate Trujillo in 1961.

I also remember Olga and Deysi Rojas, members of an aristocratic family in Moca. Much later we heard the news that once Olga Rojas finished school, Trujillo fell in love with her. She became his lover, and he built her a mansion in Santiago. After the regime's demise, the Villa Olga neighborhood was built on its grounds.

Sundays were visiting days for parents and families. In the entrance hall I met Mr. Juancito Rodríguez, sitting there very straight, red-faced, and dressed in a white suit. I was rather impressed with this man, who was rumored to be one of the richest men in the country. He had been a general and senator but later on was forced into exile and dedicated his entire fortune and life to fighting against Trujillo. "That's Pucha Rodríguez's father," they would say.

On Sundays the nuns took us for walks through the city of La Vega, which we really enjoyed. They would organize us in lines. The boys were always hanging around, even though we were little girls.

During Carnival we would agonize because we wanted to see the "devils" in their colorful costumes. Rather than take us to the town square where they gathered, the nuns would take us down Rivas Avenue, where the outskirts of the city met the countryside.

At the time, La Vega was a sort of cultural center. Back then, and even today, it is known as the Olympic City because of the many outstanding athletes born in the area. It had an active intellectual life, and many young writers and artists would meet there. But the school kept us far away from all those activities.

The Franciscan nuns in charge of the Immaculate Conception School were very strict, very demanding, and had very clear no-nonsense policies. The vast majority of the nuns came from Spain, although there were a

---

18 Antonio de la Maza (1912–1961) had a lumber business and was a long-time critic of Trujillo until, in an attempt to reign him in, Trujillo offered him a position as an army cadet. He eventually became second lieutenant. After witnessing the regime's abuses, including the assassination of his brother Octavio, Antonio de la Maza led a group of eleven Dominicans in a plot to assassinate Trujillo on May 30, 1961. Agents of the Military Intelligence Service killed de la Maza five days later. Today, the group of men who killed Trujillo are remembered as Los Héroes del 30 de Mayo.

couple of Dominican nuns, such as Sister Remedios from Puerto Plata, Sister Altagracia from Bonao, and the piano teacher, Sister Africa, who played really well and had a very pretty face and a limp.

Aside from the teachers, Victoriana Pérez and Marcia Cordero, I also fondly remember Sister Inés who, though she was never my teacher because I was very young, did teach Minerva later on. And I could never forget Sister Eloisa, whose real name was Laurita Geraldino before she became a nun and who opposed Trujillo until the very end. Years later, during the final months of the dictatorship and during the events that involved Monsignor Francisco Panal Ramírez,[19] the nuns sent her to Puerto Rico to protect her.

We had an area where we could skate, a painting studio, a reading room, and a volleyball court. Among the students, the majority of whom came from the country's most important families, were Cesarina Rubio, from La Romana; the Casanova girls, from San Pedro de Macorís; Elsa Aristy, from Higüey; Gisela and Zaida Aybar, from El Seibo; Colombina Marrero, from Villa Rivas; Violeta Martínez, from San Francisco de Macorís; Emma Rodríguez, from La Vega; and Aniana Vargas, from Bonao.

When Patria finished the eighth grade, my father took her out of school so she could help in the store. That's when she met Pedrito González, who fell in love with her, and they got married almost immediately.

Since I was the oldest living at home, and I was strong and healthy, they also pulled me out of school to work in the family business. Just like Patria, I was only able to complete the eighth grade. We were only at the Immaculate Conception School for four years, but the education was of such high quality that what we learned there, including simple accounting techniques, was enough to help us run the business.

I wanted to protest when they forced me to interrupt my studies to help in Papá's store, but I respected the decision because back then you obeyed your father. I had always dreamed of being a pharmacist, but I don't think I ever told Papá so as not to upset him. Besides, I really learned a lot by working with him. The truth is, deep down, I enjoyed that lifestyle. It was somewhat dynamic: full of visitors and unforgettable characters.

Perhaps it was because I always compared myself to Minerva's impressive intellect and personality, but ever since I was a little girl, I always considered myself to be of average intelligence. Because I was strong and always prepared to work, my parents had it in their minds that I was the one who should work. And even though I would sometimes go to them and com-

---

19   The bishop of La Vega who, on March 4, 1961, delivered a sermon in Trujillo's presence that was considered an afront to him and his regime.

plain that I was the "Cinderella" in the family, I gladly accepted my responsibilities.

After María Teresa was born we hired a maid, whom Mamá ordered me to supervise. If the woman came to wash the floors, I had to make sure it got done. If she had to fetch water or sweep the patio, it was my responsibility to help.

Still, I wouldn't say I felt frustrated. I dedicated myself to the business and only much later, when the Radio Santa María education programs came along, I registered to study for my high school diploma. By then my vocation had changed, and I wanted to study law.

Memories of Bodó and Fefa

The Haitian Massacre took place when we were teenagers.[20] One of our domestic employees back then was a woman named Fefa. She was such a character that even today people ask me about her.

In 1937, the deadly echoes of the Haitian massacre hit very close to home and shook us deeply. It so happened that a Haitian named Bodó Atidó lived in Ojo de Agua. He was married to a Dominican woman whom people called Pajayola. He ran a little store near the banks of the Cenoví River and would buy his goods at my father's store. I remember it well because he would bring us small bananas and mangoes. He was very friendly, and when he smiled, you could see his beautiful set of brilliant white teeth. One day, people began to say, "They took Bodó!" He disappeared forever, but his family remained here.

Something similar occurred to all the Haitians in Salcedo who, in most cases, worked in the tanneries and fields. Jaimito's father tanned leather, and several Haitians worked for him. People said that one day they rounded up all the Haitians in the province of Moca and stabbed them all to death. Niningo Santos had to hide Bautista, a Haitian who worked in his home, for a long time so they wouldn't find him.

Fefa was our cook and worked and lived in our home for several years with her son, whom we affectionately called Negro.[21] Fefa believed in spir-

---

20 In 1937, the Trujillo regime began carrying out mass killings of Haitians and Haitian-Dominicans, primarily in the Dajabón region, along the northern part of the Massacre River that marks the border with Haiti.
21 In English, the word "negro" means "black," almost always used contemptuously, but in the Dominican Republic, it is often used as a term of endearment and as a nickname.

its, and she liked to tell us about her mystic experiences. Mamá would get upset and scold us because one of her half-sisters on her father's side, Aunt Chela, also read the bottom of coffee cups. "What you're doing is breaking my cups," she used to tell us, as we dried the cups in the fire so Fefa or Aunt Chela could read them to us. "A sweetheart, a package from afar, a journey, a sad man who will turn his back on you, a gift, a parcel, a man who left, another who will arrive . . ." They always said the same things, but their stories were entertaining.

Somewhere around 1940 the situation began to change where we lived. A number of fights and conflicts broke out among folks in the area. The people requested that a police precinct be set up, and Papá lent one of his warehouses so they could set it up there. We gave food to the recruits assigned to the precinct, and that's how Fefa met Corporal Marte, whom she later married.

Soon after, she stopped working for us. I'm not sure how it came about, but she became a very popular healer, so much so that people would come from all over the country, including the United States, to consult with her and ask her for remedies to cure all kinds of illnesses. It had nothing to do with witchcraft. She would simply prescribe remedies. Her cure for eczema became famous. After the girls were killed, she began saying that they would come to her and help her cure people. Then she became even more popular and received people from all over who would camp outside her home while her husband controlled the flow of visitors.

3

Temperament, Ideas, and Life Choices

"What was María Teresa like?" people ask me. I try to imagine her, but I end up crying when I realize that, for some inexplicable reason, many details of her personality or her appearance have been erased from my memory. I've come to the conclusion that this mental vacuum is a defense mechanism against the pain and helplessness I've experienced from my inability to prevent our little sister's death. She was my baby, and the adored "baby" of the entire family, killed just when she was beginning to blossom.

On the other hand, I remember Patria and Minerva more vividly. Sometimes I think I see Patria on the patio, wearing her form-fitting gray slacks and a red blouse with straps tied in a bow. That was how she was dressed the last time I was with her.

I remember much more about Minerva, perhaps because her personality and ideas had a decisive influence on all our lives and destinies. I have those images and experiences "all jumbled up in my mind" as Minerva would say, but I will try to organize them so readers of this memoir might clearly envision the events and influences that shaped our individual personalities.

Aída Patria Mercedes: The Supportive One

How can I define Patria? Not long ago, her photograph was printed in the crossword puzzle published by the newspaper *Listín Diario*. The following week I read the description they had written of her: "*Mujer prínclita.*" I wasn't familiar with the term *prínclita*, so I looked it up in the dictionary: "exceptional person." That was Patria, an exceptional woman.

She was always Mamá's favorite. We used to be jealous of their relationship. She had a soft spot for Patria, and she justified it by arguing that Patria had a birthmark that indicated a liver problem. She was always so concerned about the birthmark that she even took Patria to a French doctor who had recently arrived in Santiago.

Pedro González (Pedrito) was from Conuco, a rural community near Ojo de Agua. His brother, Ezequiel González, was married to Aunt Lalía, Mamá's younger sister. Pedro saw Patria at Aunt Lalía's house and fell in love with her.

I still have two affectionate letters that Patria sent Pedrito. They reveal my sister's youth and innocence:

Ojo de Agua, June 18, 1940

Mr. Pedro González
Conuco, D.R.

Dear Pedrito,

I am writing this note to say hello and to ask how your cold is. I assume you're feeling better because I haven't heard anything from you. Let me know if you received the letter that I asked Ezequiel to give you.

I thought that you were going to come by today, so I didn't write. If you're feeling better, stop by in the afternoon.

A wasp stung me yesterday, and it hurt a little last night, but I didn't scream or cry when it stung me.

Please stop by. I'd really like to see you so we can have nice, long conversations. Come with lots of stories and dreams. My regards to Mamita and Sofía, and to the others as well. Papá says that the price of cacao rose yesterday afternoon, ten cents more than the price he told you. He also asks that you give Mon Camilo 25 sacks.

Everyone here sends their regards.
Please come, make sure you stop by.
Sending a kiss.

Yours,
Patria

Ojo de Agua, August 16, 1940

My dearest Pedrito,

I'm writing to say hello to you and to everyone else, and to ask how you are. I'm so happy that you are well, as am I.

Pedrito, we are thinking of going to the concert this evening in the town square, so come prepared, or go into town so that we can meet there. Please do go, and have lots of stories for me.

Regards to everyone. And to you: hugs and kisses from the one who thinks of you always and loves you very much.

Until this evening,
Patria

They had a short romance, approximately one year. Although Patria was only sixteen years old when she married, Pedrito was financially stable. I remember he had an iron pickup truck, a sort of jeep—I think it was German—and a fine horse with a very rhythmic gait. The marriage took place in 1941, in this very house in Ojo de Agua. María Teresa was their flower girl. She was six years old at the time.

A terrible tragedy had struck Pedrito's family. His father was attacked while using the latrine, but he managed to walk back to the house, screaming "They've killed me! They've killed me!" Pedrito was the only son who was still single, so maybe that's why he added, "If I die, build a home for Pedrito!" That's where the couple went to live: in the house that was built at the request of Pedrito's dying father.

Patria abandoned her studies when she was very young, and she took on all the household responsibilities. Nelson was born less than a year later, in early 1942. After she was married, Patria began learning how to draw with crayons and pencil. Miriam Burgos, a friend of ours who had studied art, taught her. Her drawings were almost all inspired by flowers and are on exhibit at the house museum. Unfortunately, we lost the only oil painting she made.

She would refer to the domestic employees who helped her in the garden and in the house as "my secretaries." She was exceptional in how she treated people with decency and respect.

I remember how much she was admired by others, like Dr. Abel Fernández, father of the well-known magistrate Aura Celeste and one of the collaborators of the 14th of June Movement in San Francisco de Macorís. He tried to find words to express how much he admired her, but all he could say was, "Patria! Patria!"

Many years after Patria's death, the beggars would stop by the ruins of her house in San José de Conuco, which the regime had completely destroyed. They would kneel down and thank the Lord for that woman who gave everything with so much love. Tonó, who knew her as well as I did, remembers that Patria was so loved that all the poor folks around here wanted her to be the maid of honor at their weddings.

Recently, while visiting the ruins of what was once her home, I struck up a conversation with the neighbors. We talked about the death of Leví González, Pedrito's first cousin, who died in an accident, and how Patria picked up the mangled body, bathed it, and prepared it for burial. She did the same with a neighbor who had complications during childbirth. Patria drove her to the doctor, but she died. Patria brought her back, prepared her body, and buried her. That's how Patria was, and that's how she is remembered by those close to her.

She would leave her kids to go and pick up my son, hug him, take care of him, and shower him with love. She was a very special sister to me. I always knew I could count on her. I felt as if her home were my own. I knew her well, and I admired her humanity, how organized she was, how kind, supportive, and nurturing toward all those around her.

She took me to parties, social events, and every Saturday in December to the Christmas parties organized by the young people in the area. She managed to convince our overprotective mother to let me go to parties because, of the four sisters, I was the one who enjoyed them the most. When Mamá would say "no," I would start to cry. Then along came Patria in her car, and she took me to the dance, or wherever, so I could enjoy myself.

They say that the first thing we forget about our deceased loved ones is their voice. However, one of the things I remember most vividly about Patria is her warm voice.

She was always in a good mood and was up to date on fashion and home decor. She was super advanced and refined, and had excellent taste. You should have seen the gardens she designed and kept! In Santiago, she used to buy *American Home* magazines and would order items from the Sears catalog through a man named Peter Prasmoski. We all went with her to Santiago to place those orders. Papá was so proud of his daughter. Every time we had visitors, he would take them to her home because even if she only served coffee, she would serve it with grace and good taste. If she prepared lemonade, she would add a few green drops, garnish it with small leaves, or add some other special detail, and then serve it.

Her profession? She was an expert when it came to coming and going. She loved to take trips. She organized them and enjoyed them. She always had her overnight bag ready "just in case the opportunity arose." On Sundays she would drop by with that overnight bag, in which she kept little rollers, face powder, a dress, a small pair of scissors, and a copy of Psalm 23, which she used to recite. I always think of her every time I hear it: "The Lord is my shepherd. I shall not want..."

She dreamed of traveling, even more than Minerva, and she especially wanted to go to Havana. And how she loved Christmas! In October the El Gallo store would begin displaying its Christmas merchandise. "Christmas is coming!" she would announce, and thus began her trips to Santiago to buy Christmas ornaments or other decorations. Papá would sometimes go with us, and he enjoyed taking us out to eat at restaurants like the Yaque or Antillas.

She was lucky to find a quiet and indulgent husband who always supported her because, when it comes to couples, the woman makes the man, and the man makes the woman. They complement one another. A good partner not only complements a person, they help them grow as an individual. Pedrito did not like to dance, but he took Patria to parties because she enjoyed them.

Patria was always conscious of her appearance and was always nicely made up. "I always think people are looking at me," she used to say. That's why she always stood tall and wore makeup. Even when she went to bed, she would primp. She wore luxurious pajamas, and since I was so different from her in this regard, she would scold me, "Dedé, you don't sleep in torn pajamas, do you? Oh no! That won't do!"

María Argentina Minerva: A Spirited Young Woman

People are usually most interested in learning about Minerva. They often ask about her exceptional personality or if it's true that she was such a brave and bold woman. My response is that, aside from having a strong character, she was very friendly, kind, straightforward, and a bit absent-minded, perhaps the most absent-minded of the four of us. She was very well rounded, always talking about books, politics, and paintings. She also had a true passion for gardening and animals. She was a very attractive woman: tall, slim, well-built, with plumpish legs and long, slender hands. With her cadenced walk and piercing and intelligent gaze, she never went unnoticed. I'd say she was a stunning Dominican woman, with very beautiful black hair and eyes.

Minerva remained at the Immaculate Conception School until she finished high school. But Papá, who was aware of his daughter's ideas and was afraid of them, took her out of school in the middle of the 1944–1945 school year when the Democratic Youth was founded.

She refused to be confined for long. She wanted to travel to the capital or to La Vega. I remember packing a small overnight bag and asking merchants from La Vega to deliver it to her behind my parents' backs so she could spend her Christmas vacation in La Vega and would not have to travel to the countryside.

We got along really well, though we sometimes fought, like most siblings do. There was one fight in particular I'd rather not recall. Minerva always took very good care of her hands, and she loved having long nails. I had short, stumpy nails because I was always working in the garden. One day she proudly showed me her nails and said, "Dedé, look how pretty my nails are." With a "wham!" I broke one and started to run. She ran after me, and when she caught up to me, she tore me to shreds. My goodness! What a temper that girl had! That's how she was. Mamá would make us kneel before the Sacred Heart of Jesus when we misbehaved, even though they were just childish skirmishes. She would hit us with a small strap. As soon as I'd see the strap, I'd begin to cry. But Minerva could be struck four times and not make a peep. That's how she was.

She loved reading and reciting poetry and was wonderful at it. She read the poems of Pablo Neruda, José Asunción Silva, Gustavo Adolfo Bécquer, Fabio Fiallo, Amado Nervo[22] . . . I can still hear her, standing somewhere in the house or the garden, reciting "For Ever," one of the most popular poems by the Dominican writer and politician Fabio Fiallo: "Cuando esta frágil copa de mi vida . . ."[23] I heard it so many times that I know the poem by heart, just like this one, although I can't remember the name of the poet:

Fue la alondra más hermosa
que naciere en la campiña
rubias alas, piel de rosa

---

22 In other words, Minerva was reading some of the most influential Spanish-language poetry of the late nineteenth and early twentieth centuries, including referential figures of Spanish Romanticism (Gustavo Adolfo Bécquer, 1836–1870) and Latin American Modernism (José Asunción Silva, Colombia, 1865–1896, and Amado Nervo, Mexico, 1870–1919). The celebrated Chilean poet, diplomat, and communist politician Pablo Neruda who, in 1971, received the Nobel Prize in Literature, is known for his deftness at a variety of poetic forms and styles, as well as themes ranging from the erotic to the historical and political. Fabio Fiallo (1866–1942) was a Dominican writer, poet, diplomat, and politician. Though his most well-known literary works are his modernist poetry and short stories, he is also known for his fervent opposition to the American occupation of the Dominican Republic from 1916 to 1924.

23 "When this fragile cup of my life . . ." Our translation. No citation is provided in the original text.

y el andar como de niña voluptuosa
[. . .]²⁴

In this house, in this very garden, I can still see her with her head held high, gazing into infinity with a lost stare, reciting these poems and so many others, like the verses of Gustavo Adolfo Bécquer. She never tired of reciting them.

Recently, I saw the play *Yo soy Minerva*,²⁵ written by Mu Kien Sang Ben and masterfully interpreted by the Dominican singer and actress Edilí at the National Theatre. Afterward, when I was at home, I would swear that I saw her. Yes! I sat down to have breakfast, and I saw her! I saw her standing there! Her presence was so real that all I could do was cry. I felt so sad that I called my cousin. She was shocked when I told her screaming, "I'm seeing Minerva! I can see her. I saw her. I'm sure that I saw her! So beautiful and in love with Manolo. She was waiting for him."

Minerva's love for poetry began when she was a small child. When she was a little girl, Professor Camilo would make her recite "A Prayer for Us All" by Andrés Bello.²⁶ The poem is long, with some thirty verses, and begins like this:

Go and pray, my daughter. It is time
awareness and deep thought
[. . .]²⁷

In the evenings, after closing the store, we would have dinner, bathe, and sit on the front porch. Papá would sit with us, while Mamá was usually inside doing chores. As it rose above the trees, the large moon would cast a

---

24 "It was the most beautiful lark / born in the countryside / blonde wings, skin like a rose / and the sashay of a voluptuous girl." Our translation. No citation is provided in the original text.

25 *¡Yo soy Minerva! Confesiones más allá de la vida y la muerte / I Am Minera! Confessions from beyond life and death* is a monologue written by the Dominican historian Mu-Kein Sang in 2003 to be adapted to theater. The narrator is Minerva's spirit, and she addresses the monologue to Dedé. The first part focuses on Minerva's life, and the second imagines her response to the conditions and events in the Dominican Republic following her death in 1960.

26 Venezuelan intellectual, educator, poet, philologist, diplomat, and legislator whose writings are seminal works of the Spanish American intellectual tradition, particularly of the Independence and Early Republican periods of the early nineteenth century.

27 Our translation.

giant shadow in the night. Minerva would then begin to recite a poem by José Asunción Silva:

> A night,
> a night quite full of murmurs, of perfumes,
> and the music of wings
> [...][28]

These moments are so vivid in my memory that I still feel as if I am reliving them all over again.

Back then there was no television. Perhaps that's why Minerva read so much and why we always got together to make plans, to talk, and to enjoy her poetry recitals. We used to gather on the porch or in the dining room. I have the impression that it was colder back then than it is now. There was no electricity in that part of the country, but we had a generator that supplied us with energy twenty-four hours a day. It made Papá very nervous to think that we might have visitors and no electricity. Even before then, we had a gas refrigerator.

Tonó got along really well with Minerva and was always fussing over her. She helped her with the flowers, took care of the rabbits, and cleaned the fish pond that Minerva herself had designed in the backyard. She loved animals. Minerva had dandruff, and I remember her asking Tonó to scratch her head with a comb as she read, sitting in bed. I would tell her, "Minerva, go to bed already," and she would answer me by saying that sleeping a lot was a waste of time.

Minerva enjoyed everything: she embroidered, sewed, went on outings, and danced if people were dancing. But her passion was reading. She made sure to get the best books available in Santiago or the capital. She frequented the bookstore owned by Alfonso Moreno Martínez, a staunch antitrujillista—an opponent of Trujillo—in San Francisco de Macorís. She bought tons of books, and her friends Violeta Martínez and Pericles Franco would lend her theirs. Franco, a known antitrujillista, would send Minerva letters and books by way of Minerva's seamstress, Doña Pepé Bodden, who lived in Salcedo.

Back in the 1940s and 1950s Minerva, used to tell me what she thought

---

28 "Una noche, / una noche toda llena de murmullos, de perfumes / Y de músicas de alas [...]," José Asunción Silva, "Nocturne," in *The Penguin Book of Latin American Verse*, ed. and trans. Enrique Caracciolo Trejo (Harmondsworth, England: Penguin, 1971), 173.

about books like *Man, the Unknown* by Alexis Carrel, *Anna Karenina* by Leo Tolstoy, and *Les Misérables* by Victor Hugo. She also read books by Eugenio María de Hostos, Goethe, Horatio, Anatole France, Shakespeare, Émile Zola, Thomas Mann, Sigmund Freud, Homer, Cervantes, Federico García Lorca, Esquilo, José Enrique Rodó, and Alexander Dumas, just to mention a few of the authors she told us about.

She spent nights reading until Papá would tell her to "turn out the light!" "Okay, all right," she would answer. Papá would fall asleep. Later, he would wake up and say, "Minerva, I told you to turn off the lights, now!" She was still awake at one or two o'clock in the morning. She suffered from insomnia, and she would get up very early in the morning, wrap herself in a blanket, and go to the kitchen to drink coffee and continue reading.

What didn't she read? If they sent a book of government statistics to the house, she would read it. She read everything. The Bible, everything. However, she never read Karl Marx, Lenin, or Engels.[29] She never had access to them. I don't think anyone in this country did. Sometimes she would be so engrossed in thought that Patria and I would whisper to one another that she looked like a famous intellectual who had once passed through these parts. She would complain, "I know you're making fun of me," and would return to her reading. All that reading was probably what shaped her ideas about democracy and patriotism.

She influenced us quite a bit. I, for one, read some of the books she recommended, such as the biography *Mary Queen of Scots* by Stefan Zweig. She made me read that book and others, even though I was not a very good reader. But it was easy to enjoy those books. "Come, come and read what Mahatma Gandhi said: 'People who do not love their liberty must accept their destiny...'" She would read a small passage like this and then leave.

I still have a vivid impression of Lin Yutang's *A Leaf in the Storm,* a novel that Manolo lent us and that has always reminded me of Minerva. When I read a copy of Aimé Césaire's *The Tragedy of King Christophe,* which she had given me, I wanted to travel to Haiti to learn more about their reality.

By listening to Minerva constantly quoting authors or reciting poems, they became forever fixed in my memory. This was the case with Manuel del Cabral's poem "Letter to My Father,"[30] which she would often recite to

---

29 By making this statement, Dedé distances her sister from accusations of being a revolutionary socialist or Marxist.
30 Renowned Dominican poet, writer, and diplomat (1907–1999).

Papá when responding to him as we sat around the table. A few of the verses went more or less like this:

> What more do you want from me? What better things?
> My Father, what you gave me in flesh I give back to you in flowers.
> Understand that I cannot remain silent about these things.[31]

She identified with these verses because they expressed her ideas about not abandoning her books and her vocation of studying law in order to take on the heavy burden of a business. She insisted on becoming an attorney.

Mamá criticized her vocation. She was concerned that, because of the environment in which we lived, such knowledge would only lead to spinsterhood. My mother was being realistic. Perhaps things have changed for women today, but back then, that was our reality. "Women can't know too much because men don't like women who are too smart. Oh, no! You've read all those books! . . . Just pretend you never read them. Men don't marry women who know too much," Mamá would tell her repeatedly.

Minerva's love for poetry spilled over to the entire family. Once, around 1940, my father suffered a stroke that left him in a coma for almost a month. He would get desperately thirsty and would ask for water, delirious. The San Francisco de Macorís aqueduct was under construction at the time. As Minerva and I were taking care of him, he would say, "If only they would finish the aqueduct. Water! Water!" He made no sense when he talked to us, and I thought he was reacting to the treatment. Because I was the strongest one, I had to take his temperature through the rectum, something Patria or Minerva wouldn't dare to do. When he recovered and we told him what had happened, he told us that the only thing he remembered from that month was Minerva reciting her favorite poems.

Minerva became interested in politics on her own and at a very young age. I would say that her interest was somewhat spontaneous, were it not for the influence of Uncle José, Mamá's brother. He was only ten years old when the Americans burned down his mother's house. Uncle José had developed a visceral hatred for Trujillo because he said that the Americans had left him in power. He constantly referred to the United States as "The Master" and to Trujillo—the tyrant—as "the Master's Pawn." In fact, I think the only

---

31 "¿Qué más quieres de mí? ¿Qué otras cosas mejores? / Padre mío, lo que me diste en carne te lo devuelvo en flores. / Estas cosas, comprende, ya no puedo callarte." Manuel del Cabral, verses from "Carta a mi padre." No source is cited. The rough translation is ours and does not capture the rhyme or rhythm of the original.

topics he ever talked about were "The Master," the dictatorship, and how the Americans supported it.

When the United States invaded our country for the second time, in 1965, Uncle José must have been about sixty-five years old. He was still so thirsty for vengeance that he asked one of his grandsons to take him to the capital, where the war against the invaders was taking place. He wanted to take up arms and kill some Marines, unless they killed him first.

His obsession was so great that he never accepted a ride in my car because it was a Volkswagen Beetle, the same model used by Trujillo's Military Intelligence Service (SIM).[32] He preferred to walk rather than get in the car because "that was the car that the caliés used," he'd say, referring to the regime's "snitches." "Uncle, get in the car," I would tell him. And he would answer, "God forbid! Never!" That was the first car I bought after the April Revolution of 1965, when I learned to drive and began working as a saleswoman for an insurance company.

Many people in Ojo de Agua were against the Trujillo regime, from the peasants who had never been to school to businessmen and all sorts of people.

Mamá used to say that Minerva could sniff out those who opposed Trujillo "with that nose of hers," that she could pick them out anywhere. Her friends in San Francisco de Macorís were Alfonso Moreno Martínez, Jacintico Lora, Don Paco Martínez, Violeta Martínez, Brunilda Soñé, and an entire legion of women who opposed Trujillo. Minerva sought them out. She was involved in that. She had *always* been involved in that.

When she first arrived at the Immaculate Conception School, she was assigned to sleep near a little girl who was always very sad, which intrigued Minerva. The girl told Minerva that she had seen her father vomit blood and then die, murdered. Trujillo often gave scholarships to the daughters of some of the opponents he had killed. This story lit a spark of hatred and rebellion in Minerva while she was still a child. Back then, in 1946, they announced a rally in La Vega in which Chito Henríquez and two brothers, Félix Servio and Juan Ducoudray, were supposed to participate. I remember that Minerva wanted to go. The following year, when a group of militants attempted what is known as the Cayo Confites Expedition,[33] Minerva tried to figure out how to contact them.

---

32 Dominicans referred to these cars as "cepillos" (brushes), as they swept through the country rounding up suspected antitrujillistas.
33 In the summer of 1947, approximately 1,200 militants, mainly Dominican exiles,

From the time she was a little girl, Minerva had a certain sensibility that she further refined through her readings. A writer has something to say from a very early age. A painter begins to draw . . . People develop these qualities little by little in response to the situations they face in life. I think that was the case with my sister, and that's how her ideas matured.

A gentleman by the name of Gustavo Ramos, who lived in the region, tells the story that Minerva once passed by on horseback while he was painting the front of his house. She was intrigued by what he was doing. When he told her that El Jefe was going to pass through the area and that, like everyone else, he was obligated to tidy up the front of his home or he would be fined, Minerva told him, "But Don Tavo, don't be such a chickenshit." This anecdote surprises me a bit because Minerva was very measured in her ways and was not the type of person to use that kind of language. But then again, she could have said something like that given how close we were with the Ramos family. "I long for this country to be free. That's what I'm fighting for," she often said.

She was also blessed with other qualities. She bought small fish, birds . . . She would get very upset when we told her that she was a spendthrift, throwing away money like that. I have often told the story of a gray heron that she attentively raised in our garden. Jaimito, who at the time was my boyfriend, had rescued the beautiful large bird from Samaná, where it would have been killed. He gave it to her. One day the heron escaped. Papá declared, "What an ungrateful bird! After eating your fish and the pound of meat you bought for it every day, it decides to run away." Very calmly, Minerva responded, "Even birds love freedom." I guess what she meant to say was, "That's what I love, freedom," as if comparing herself to the heron.

Jaimito used to tell her, "You like fancy things" because she loved to buy high-end products. We would make the trip to Santo Domingo in her car to buy magazines such as *Vanity, Vogue, Para Ti, Atlántida,* and the Cuban magazine *Carteles,* which she especially enjoyed.

In the capital we would go shopping at the Immaculada Nursery, which was owned by Mario Bobea. It was in the area called Alma Rosa, which at the time was not part of the city. There, we would buy imported flowers and exotic plants. Our garden was one of the first in the country to have bougainvillea bushes in all colors.

---

organized in Cuba and plotted to invade the Dominican Republic, connect with the anti-Trujillo underground, and topple the dictatorship. They were arrested before leaving Cuba.

It was Minerva who laid the stone path at our home in Ojo de Agua. It remains intact to this day. She placed the stone slabs with her own hands. Maduro, a hardworking little boy from the neighborhood, helped her. Just like Tonó, he was always following Minerva around, helping her. She carried the slabs, rid the rose bushes of crickets, and weeded the garden. During World War II cement was very expensive and hard to come by. At one of my father's farms, there were some stone slabs, which he began to use in place of cement to create areas for drying cacao. Minerva took several of the slabs to build a stone path around hundreds of rose bushes that she had ordered from a nursery in California. They arrived by ship at the port in Puerto Plata. Getting those rosebushes from the port ended up being such a difficult task and took such a long time that some of the bushes perished. Dr. Pericles Franco would become nostalgic as he recalled that rose garden and Minerva's efforts to create it.

As she lay the stone path, Minerva argued with Maduro to do things the way she wanted them done. He would place the slabs, and she would remove them. Mamá felt bad seeing her work like this and would tell her, "*Mi hija,* leave those stones alone. Those lovely hands of yours aren't meant for that." And I would tell Minerva that she should have been an architect. She used wooden squares to build a trellis for the bougainvillea vines, which climbed up over them beautifully. In the new home that Mamá built in Conuco in the 1950s, she began to gather stones with the idea of building a Spanish patio. But she never had the chance to build it. Today, in the museum that was once our home, those stones now adorn her tomb.

From the moment she began to study at the Immaculate Conception School, she took an interest in painting. Today, the paintings exhibited at the house museum are from that time.

Back in those days, the Salcedo Casino was in a small wooden structure on a plot of land across from the home of my mother-in-law, Doña Lesbia. Anyway, in 1945 there was a pageant to elect Miss Casino, and the winner was Lesbiolita Fernández, Jaimito's sister. Young people from the neighboring provinces came to the after-party, which was held at the club. Among them was an officer whose last name was Lluberes. When he asked Minerva to dance, she told him that she was talking with some friends and that she didn't feel like dancing, which sent him raging out of control. Toward the end of the party, Minerva got up to dance with a friend named Cucho. The officer, who apparently was still interested in her, and who may have been aware of her political ideas, ordered the party to stop. Even though everyone begged him to be reasonable, pointing out that the orchestra had traveled a long way to be there, he refused to let the party continue. They even introduced him to Miss Casino so he could dance with her and calm down, but he was still very upset.

Years later, when Minerva was arrested and transferred to Trujillo's offices as a detainee, accompanied by mother and father, she ran into this same officer. By then he was a colonel. He just looked at her and smiled, without comment.

When Jaimito and I were married, we moved to San Francisco de Macorís. So, the only ones still living at our home in Ojo de Agua were Mamá, Papá, María Teresa, and Minerva, who had to help Papá at the store for a few months. But Papá adored her and knew that this was not what she wanted, so he tried to please her with other things.

That's when he bought her a gray Ford, in 1948. We had always had pickup trucks for the store, but she was the first in the family to have her own car. Papá thought that by giving her the car he would make up for not allowing her to go to college. As I mentioned before, Papá had forced her to interrupt her studies during high school because he was afraid of her anti-Trujillo ideas. My father thought that with a car, Minerva would be happy because she would be able to visit her friends, travel to the capital, have some independence, and that she would stop pressuring him so much with the whole idea of studying at the university. What he feared the most was that being in that environment would strengthen the opposition to Trujillo that had been growing in her since she was a little girl.

So, Minerva learned to drive. I'm not entirely certain, but she likely learned from José, "El Búcaro," one of the drivers employed by our family. Around here it was not at all common for a father to buy a car for his daughter, and much less common for a woman to drive. Back then, very few women studied at the university, and rarely did girls from the countryside pursue higher education. However, I do recall that Mamá's first cousin, David Camilo, sent his daughter to study pharmacy. He was one of the first men in the region to have this new attitude regarding women's roles in society.

The last few years of the 1940s were perhaps the happiest ones for Minerva, the years that she enjoyed the most. She was invited to parties, spent time with friends, traveled, and read . . . Once, she went to a carnival party at Santiago's Recreation Center dressed up as María Montez,[34] wearing

---

[34] Dominican actress of the 1940s known for her fanciful costumes and for playing the seductress in Hollywood-produced adventure films.

all kinds of necklaces. For another party she dressed up as a rumba girl, wearing a white skirt with red polka dots.

During those years she spent a great deal of time with her friend Thelma Benedicto, who would often make the trip from Santiago to Salcedo to visit her maternal aunt. Concerned because Thelma was so thin, Minerva invited her to spend a few days in Ojo de Agua. Thelma stayed about a month or two with our family. They would go to the river to swim and would drive around in Minerva's car. The photographs we took during that visit are probably the nicest ones we have of my sister since they show how happy we were back then.

Our home was filled with friends, with young people, with boys who may or may not have been romantically interested in her, but who would stop by to visit her: Arturo and Bartolo Antuña, Carlos Sully Bonnelly, Rafael Llenas, and Poppy Bermúdez, who would visit her when he was back home on vacation from his studies in the United States. They would sit on our porch in Ojo de Agua and talk with Minerva for hours. It was also a time spent with girlfriends: Adalgisa Nicolás, Adalia Cordero, Gilda Pichardo, Cecilia Cortiñas, and the Pou sisters.

However, her dearest friend from childhood was Emma Rodríguez from La Vega. Emma would visit our home and spend weeks, even months, during summer vacation. Minerva enjoyed spending time at Emma's house as well because there she could have long conversations with Emma's grandfather, Don Rafael Rodríguez, a staunch critic of Trujillo and a relative of Juancito Rodríguez.

When Minerva finished high school and came back to Ojo de Agua, Emma left to study pharmacy at the university and married Rubén Suro, a poet from the La Vega group known as Los Nuevos. Perhaps part of the reason they became estranged was because Emma had already graduated and was married by the time Minerva finally started college.

Two of my sister's best friends were cousins who shared the same name: Violeta Martínez. The Violeta from San Francisco de Macorís went to school with Minerva at Immaculate Conception. Her parents, Don Paco Martínez and Doña Amalia de Martínez, were Spaniards who opposed the dictatorship of Francisco Franco, and Minerva would spend hours talking with them. It so happens that Minerva met the other Violeta, who was from the town of Moca, at the home of the first Violeta. They developed a strong friendship since they shared political and literary interests. At a time when discussing politics was strictly forbidden, these young women were keenly focused on the political struggle.

One of the most talked-about aspects of Minerva's life was her relationship with Pericles Franco Ornes, whom she met in 1947. I am going to tell this story because people have always said that they had a romantic relationship, but that is not true. Manolo was her only boyfriend.

Pericles Franco was a very attractive young man: tall, handsome, well educated, a brilliant speaker who could charm you with his words. He had studied medicine in Chile, where he met important intellectuals and writers, such as Pablo Neruda, who wrote the prologue to his book condemning Trujillo.[35] But most importantly, he knew a different reality, one with more freedom, unlike the oppression and terror we were experiencing here. Upon returning to the Dominican Republic, he became a key leader of the Democratic Youth movement and helped found the Socialist Party along with Chito Henríquez and the Ducoudray brothers, among others. So, when he started coming to our house to visit Minerva, he had already been imprisoned and was marked as one of the most important leaders of the opposition to Trujillo. Simply being in contact with him put one in serious danger.

Someone had told him about this beautiful and progressive young woman, and he arranged to meet her. He and Minerva were attracted to one another, they identified with one another, and they liked one another. But apparently, they never openly talked about their feelings. As a matter of fact, she hid many of their encounters from us. Unbelievable! We definitely would have scolded her had she told us! We learned about them many years later after Minerva's death because Pericles told Minerva's daughter, Minou, the story of that love that never came to be, and he showed her some of the photographs they had taken together during a visit to the capital. What I did know at the time was that he had written her the most beautiful letters, like something out of a novel.

In late 1949, Pericles was once again released from prison and went into exile. Before leaving, he unsuccessfully tried to contact Minerva, using extreme caution to avoid putting her at risk. Later on, while in exile, he tried sending her a letter through a friend of his parents, asking Minerva to seek asylum in the Colombian Embassy and marry him. When the messenger came to deliver the letter, Minerva—who had already been in prison and did not know the woman—refused to accept the letter, thinking that it was a trap. My sister never knew the content of that letter. Neither did we.

Before meeting Minerva, Pericles had been engaged to Gilda Pérez, a

---

35   Pericles Franco, *La tragedia dominicana. Análisis de la tiranía de Trujillo* (Santiago de Chile: Federación de Estudiantes de Chile, 1946).

young woman from an anti-Trujillo family in Santiago who had also been forced into exile. Being an upright man, he told Minerva of his engagement. Perhaps this is why their relationship was never more than platonic. I don't know the details, but apparently Pericles spent some time in Central America, then in Mexico, and finally the United States. Anyway, when he arrived in the United States, he discovered that Gilda had married an American. That was when he wrote that letter to Minerva. He had not acted on his desires while still in the Dominican Republic out of respect for his engagement to Gilda. Years later, Gilda Pérez divorced the American and married Pericles. I think Minerva had already met Manolo by then.

Two months before his death, already ill, Pericles came to visit me. He came with Gilda and Consuelo Despradel, a TV and radio commentator. He had kept all those memories a secret, but he wanted to reminisce and share them with me. He wanted to return to the places where he had such fond memories. Walking with me through my garden, he sadly noted that the rose bushes that Minerva had planted were no longer there.

During his visit, Pericles spoke of his utopias, of when he was a communist, and of the time when he believed that he could change the world with his ideas. At the end of his visit, he confessed that knowing Minerva had been a sublime experience. He gave me a copy of Johann Wolfgang Goethe's eighteenth-century novel *Werther* and told me, "This book that Minerva once gave me sums up what she and I felt for one another. I want you to keep it in the museum." This particular copy bore the seal of Alfonso Moreno Martínez's bookstore in San Francisco de Macorís. On the first page was the following dedication in my sister's handwriting: "To Pericles: a keepsake. It speaks of my sincere affection. Your friend, Minerva. September 1949." In *Werther*, Goethe tells the love story of a young man who returns from exile, I believe, and falls hopelessly in love with a young girl who cannot return his feelings because she is already engaged to marry someone else.

We agreed to meet again after I returned from a trip that I had already planned. Upon my return we agreed to visit the following Saturday, but he died two or three days before then. I was left with the pain of not being able to meet with Pericles Franco one last time.

Probably the most intimate and spiritual of my sister's friendships at the time was with Tobías Emilio Cabral, whom she fondly called "Larry" in honor of the main character of William Somerset Maugham's novel *The Razor's Edge*. By the end of the 1940s, Larry, too, had to emigrate to the United States. The letters they wrote to one another, with their code words and references to personal events, reveal their deep level of trust and friendship. Minerva's sensitive, revolutionary spirit, always full of dreams, comes through clearly in these letters. It was from these letters that we learned that she kept a diary, which she destroyed out of caution and for fear of being misunderstood.

It's not possible to understand all of the subtext in Minerva's letters. But in one particular letter, which I now share in this memoir, the date suggests that she is referring to what happened with Pericles Franco, whom she calls "Hafiz," probably a reference to the famous Persian poet.[36]

> Larry,
>
> It is for you that I write this letter, which is the story of my life. I don't pay much heed to the gusts of wind that, from time to time, rattle my life with hurricane strength. But the friendship that unites me with you, that tenderness that seems to surround me with a sweet sadness in both joys and sorrows, is the reason why I write to you today with hope, a hope that is always ephemeral, swept away by the wind. Again, I write with the hope that my words reach you. I carry in my heart that afternoon when we last said goodbye to one another. (Do you remember?)
>
> Remember how you thought that you would see me again soon? But it has been three long years—centuries—that have brought us spiritually closer or, to be more precise, have brought me closer to you. Now it is only with you that I can entrust my mysterious inner space.
>
> In this immense spiritual solitude that surrounds me, your memory is always with me. Feeling my spirit in imminent need, I search for you, and you come and speak to me.
>
> Let's return to that afternoon. Remember when you told me you wanted to read my diary? I destroyed it. It was too indiscreet, a true reflection of the conventionalism that keeps me from adapting to my surroundings, and I feared that it would fall in the hands of someone that would not have the level of understanding that you have. But

---

36 Iranian poet Khwāja Shams-ud-Dīn Muḥammad Ḥāfeẓ (1320–1389), better known as Hafiz. In the book *Mañana te escribiré otra vez. Minerva y Manolo. Cartas*, Minerva's daughter Minou Tavárez Mirabal explains that in the late 1940s, Pericles Franco gave Minerva a copy of Hafiz's *Divan*, a collection of seven hundred short poems known as "ghazals," or short odes consisting of couplets. (Tavárez Mirabal, 223). The poems are revolutionary, capricious compositions that reject poetic conventions, allowing greater freedom for feelings and imagination. Author's note, modified by translators.

today, I want to leave on this page not the evening conversations that brought my spirit so close to yours, but rather those situations that have turned me into what I am today and so that tomorrow, when "I tire of my tiredness" and my spirit reaches out to find you and accompany you as you have accompanied me in my solitude, I will then become a reflection. I dedicate to you the portrait in which I appear with my dog. Keep it. It is a companion to the one I once gave you and that you later gave Hafiz. It hurt me a little that you gave it away, but what happened later led me to reflect on your words to make up for the selfishness that I harbor within me. Your soul, if indeed I did see it, appeared so sublime that the tears that I normally repress flowed freely from my eyes. But this brings me back to the purpose of my letter: You thought that I loved him! No, that was not true, and I once told you so. As always, I needed the company, the understanding, because solitude is my tragedy. His letters were so beautiful, but there was more than friendship. It was not my fault that he was attracted to a mirage, and that he idealized me. Had I reminded myself of my intolerance when it comes to infidelity, I never would have made that mistake. He had his fiancée.

And I myself once told you that he adored her. How would it be possible then for me to think of him as anything other than a friend? I don't care that everyone believed that, but it hurt me that you were "one of them." But don't interpret this as me reproaching you. It is only natural.

I remember that he sent me part of a diary and poems with the following message: "Minerva, these ghazals are very much like you, and I want to be like Hafiz, and the truth is that something brings us together in this beautiful book." With my normal insistence on calling things by their names and leaving them crystal clear, I answered him that we were undoubtedly united by a love of beautiful things, a love of the Oriental poet's beautiful language. His response... well, his response was what fed all the accusations that befell me.

Now that I see destiny before me, I want to navigate this deviation carefully. (Do you see?) He wears modern clothes and is known as a playboy, and you know him as well as I do. But in spite of everything that's happened I am terribly fond of him. I thank God that aside from my sorrow, I have never felt bitterness nor resentment. I forget my enemies entirely, even their names. How can I blame him? Destiny was sending him to me, and he endured all kinds of difficulties.

I couldn't object, and if I did, I would do anything to go back to that dance floor, the place where it all started.

But that fatalism is not an excuse for my errors, for I have committed so many that I don't quite understand how I haven't lost all confidence in myself. I recognize my many faults. My outbursts will certainly not lead to happiness. But I hear Nervo's verses echoing inside me:

> If I extracted sweetness or bitterness from things,
> it was because I infused bitterness and sweetness into them.[37]

Minerva

Antonia María Teresa: Intelligent and Kind

Minerva, María Teresa, and I lived together for seven years after Patria married. But Minerva spent a good deal of her time in school, which meant that María Teresa was my source of entertainment. She was like a daughter to me because when she was born, in 1935, we already knew how to embroider and knit.

As soon as Patria got married, María Teresa—who was still a small child—became my mother's world. After that, I was the one who spent most of the time with her. I remember that once, in 1942, I was left in charge of the house and the store because Patria was about to give birth to Nelson. My mother went to spend a few days with her, but apparently they got the dates wrong. I complained, "So Mamá is not coming. I'm here by myself taking care of María Teresa. I'm tired. Mamá had better come soon."

My little sister was also the shortest, and the one who most resembled my mother. She was very attractive and had a body that one might call sculpted. She had two physical characteristics that attracted everyone's attention: legs that were so shapely that they looked as if they had been sculpted by hand, and extremely long black hair that she never cut. She always wore it in braids. In the oldest photograph I have of her, her hair is in three small braided buns.

The students and children who visit the museum sometimes ask me how I would characterize each of my sisters. The first of María Teresa's quali-

---

37 Amado Nervo. "En paz" / "At Peace," originally published in *Elevación* (Madrid: Editorial América, 1916). This translation is one of a few that are published on multiple websites without crediting a translator.

ties that I highlight is her incredible kindness. She was always so kind, so wholesome. She was one of those people who always thought the best of others, to the point that some people took advantage of her kindness. One of her best friends—who is still alive—told me that in school she had to stick up for her because the other students pulled her braids and picked on her, and, rather than defend herself, María Teresa would just burst out crying. She cried very easily ... and hard, so hard that her tears effortlessly flowed from her wide-opened eyes.

Tonó says that when they brought her to live with us to keep María Teresa company, she was impressed when she saw my sister sitting out in the arbor telling stories to the workers. They were completely engrossed in her tales. María Teresa was not only an excellent storyteller, but she also had a prodigious memory.

We used to point out how curious she was because she inquired about everything. She would ask Uncle Tilo about our ancestors, where our great grandparents came from, the trips that great grandfather made through the woods, his journey from the moment he landed in Puerto Plata until he reached Don Pedro, in Licey ... She inquired about everything, absolutely everything, and she managed to remember the smallest details. She knew everyone by name and knew where everyone came from, how they were related to one another, and could even recall anecdotes or specific details about people she barely knew.

She was very intelligent and read a lot, which Minerva encouraged. It was also Minerva who got her interested in political issues. When Minerva was forced to drop out of school and return home, María Teresa, who at the time was only eleven years old and went to the local country school, became Minerva's student in a way, always following her around, asking about everything. The two of them spent a lot of time together. "She's always following me around," Minerva would sometimes complain. I remember clearly how one day Minerva was sitting on the porch talking with friends. María Teresa was sitting nearby, carefully listening to the conversation, until Minerva spotted her and scolded her. María Teresa ran crying to Papá, complaining that Minerva had scolded her in front of company. He intervened, asking Minerva, "My dear, why are you mistreating María Teresa like this?" Minerva's response was that the political matters that she and her friends were discussing on the porch were not for María Teresa's ears.

It seems fitting to share with you how María Teresa's husband, Leandro

Guzmán, describes her in his memoir, *1J4: De espigas y de fuegos*.[38] He describes the impression she made on him the day they met, when she was twelve years old and he was fifteen. They met in the summer of 1947 when some friends invited them over to a farm near Patria and Pedrito's house:

> One's first true love brings a delight and exhilaration that is once in a lifetime. This is probably why I find myself swept up in a dizzying whirlwind of emotion when I think of her, of scenes filled with her long hair. She and her braid, racing down the dirt road on her bicycle, jumping over the bumps and ditches . . . I fell in love, and she fell in love with me. She was so beautiful, with her deep eyes. It was difficult to win her hand, with her possessive family where practically no one liked me.
>
> She enjoyed cooking. I particularly liked her stews. I would ask her, "María Teresa, what's in turkey stew?" She would then explain the recipe, "That's what they taught me. It's a stewed turkey with lots of peppers and no tomato sauce, so that the meat takes on the color of the pan."
>
> She visited me frequently in San Francisco de Macorís where she made friends, as she often did wherever she went. One such friend was Jean Awad Canaán, who later on would be the central figure in a series of tragic events that inspired rumors of foul play. People said that Trujillo's daughter, Angelita Trujillo, fell in love with him when she met him, despite knowing that Jean was married and that his young wife, Pilar Báez, was pregnant. In short, he was sent to a military post on the border as punishment, and there he died "in an accident." It was widely rumored that Angelita had him killed because she couldn't have him. The even greater tragedy was that Jean's wife died during childbirth. It was rumored that they let her die.[39]
>
> Milagros Ortega, Minerva Mues, Milagros Piña, and Tina Rizek were some of María Teresa's friends from school. I remember their names because our friendship continued over the years.

---

38 Leandro Guzmán, *1J4: De espigas y de fuegos. Aportes para la memoria necesaria: testimonios de un militante* (Editora de Colores, 1998). Unofficial translation: *The 14th of June Movement: Of Spikes and Fire. A Militant's Testimony to Expand Our Collective Memory*.

39 The couple's daughter, Pilar Awad Báez, tells her parents' story in the book *La verdad de la sangre* (Santo Domingo: Editora Búho, 2013), which she co-wrote with author Eva Álvarez.

Me, Bélgica Adela

When I look back and try to remember what we were like, I see that I was probably the most flirtatious and pretentious of the four of us. I loved to spend time with friends, meet new people, go to parties, and make more friends. However, in Salcedo we had very few opportunities to have fun, and convincing Mamá to let us go to a party or on a special outing took a lot of effort, Papá's intervention, and the intervention of other family members. Perhaps that's why I recall that one of the happiest times in my life was the month I spent at Uncle Mon's house during the 1944 centennial celebrations.

Simeón (Mon) Mirabal was a prosperous businessman from La Vega who had received a much better education than his brothers and sisters, including Papá. I felt free in his home. Uncle Mon took me to all the parties and outings. He'd say, "Enjoy yourself, my dear." And when my father would send for me, telling me to return home, my uncle would respond that I couldn't go back just yet because they were still fixing my teeth.

I had never gone to so many parties in my life. We would get up very early and go to the La Vega Casino or the Angelita Country Club with a group of girlfriends that lived near my uncle's home: Mireya and Carmen Estela Jiménez, Anselma Alonso, Gladys Calventi, and Aura Fernández. I remember meeting lots of interesting young men, but I never dated any of them. Back then, you couldn't become someone's girlfriend just like that. That did not go over well and was even forbidden. At one of those parties, I met a young man who really caught my attention. He had alluring eyes that never stopped watching me during the dance. I met him a few times after that, and he visited me, but it never came to more than a few fleeting glances because he had dated one of my friends.

Every year the Salcedo Club celebrated its anniversary with a dance. Many young people from nearby San Francisco de Macorís and Moca would attend. Mamá accompanied us to one of the dances, where Lope Balaguer[40] and the San José Orchestra were performing. We were still dancing at six o'clock in the morning! As one song was ending, I continued dancing to the next one so I wouldn't have to go back to the table and be told that we had to leave.

---

40 The nephew of Joaquín Balaguer, not officially linked to the regime.

I liked to put up a fuss, but it wouldn't be fair to say there weren't pastimes to enjoy at home. I loved thoroughbred horses. Papá bought me a couple, one beautiful horse in particular. He was large and mellow. I loved to ride him because when I was on top of a good horse, I felt like I owned the world.

On Saturdays, my friends Patria Camilo, María Teresa Toribio, María Cristina Suazo, Mercedes Michel, and I would get together to ride between Salcedo and Tenares, which back then was just a village. We rode around the village, through the town square, and went around again. The ride from Salcedo to Tenares took us about two hours. People would come out of their homes to see these young ladies on their horses. There were very few cars back then. We were accompanied by Jaimito Fernández—who was not yet my boyfriend—Blanco Camilo, and other young men. Efraín Camilo, who according to friends was in love with me, had two beautiful horses: a black-and-white one and a pure thoroughbred. Sometimes he would lend me one, and he would ride the other. We wore fashionable gaucho-style pant-skirts that Aunt Fefita had made for us.

Sometime later, during the most repressive years of the dictatorship, I enjoyed riding past the caliés' homes on a beautiful horse that Jaimito had given me. I would gallop past their homes in Salcedo as if to tell them, "You will not defeat us!"

Even though I only had one boyfriend, whom I eventually married, there were lots of young men who wanted to court me. Apparently back then I was the popular one, the one who was "in style." Young men from nearby towns came to see me, but Mamá was extremely overprotective and would not let them visit me.

One of these young admirers serenaded me and even rented Salcedo's only movie theater to show a special movie in my honor. He had seen the movie, which was based on a song that went, "If at your window a dove appears / treat it tenderly, for it is I . . ." He sent me a card in which he told me that he had rented the movie theater especially for me so I could see the film. But Mamá refused to give me permission, although Papá tried to persuade her. He felt terrible about my refusal, which he saw as ungracious. He said that it would be rude for me to not attend the showing.

My sisters and I all married our first boyfriends. In those days, romantic relationships were under tight restrictions. If you went anywhere with your boyfriend, you had to be accompanied by a chaperone, and the most you could get away with, if you were lucky, was to steal a kiss or a hug here and there . . . and sometimes not even that because mamás were always nearby, watching.

Over the years I've come to think that I should have had at least one other boyfriend. I even joke with my children about this, asking them their opinions about this old custom of marrying your first boyfriend.

Jaimito Fernández and I knew each other all our lives. His mother, Doña Lesbia Camilo, and Mamá were first cousins. His sisters were some of my best friends. He set his eyes on me at a very early age.

During Holy Week, we used to come home from school for the Easter holiday. On Good Friday we went to the procession. On Holy Saturday we went to Mass dressed in our best dresses and then would walk to the Salcedo town square for a stroll and to hear the concert by the municipal band. On one such occasion, Jaimito saw me and later told me, "Dedé, when I saw you with those beautiful, plump legs, I said: 'That's the one I like,' and I decided then that one day you would become my wife." Jaimito said that I was the prettiest of all. Perhaps it was that I was so full of life, and that attracted young men, and even some dirty old men too!

He was the only boy in a family of five sisters, who doted on him constantly. After we were married, I asked his Mamá, "Is Jaimito so pigheaded because you never spanked him?" She laughed and said, "One day I smacked him with a rag." "Well then! That's why he's so spoiled and conceited," I replied.

When Jaimito began to fall in love with me he serenaded me. They brought a piano and the popular poet and troubadour Héctor J. Díaz[41] dedicated the song to me: "For Dedé Mirabal, the most beautiful song, made woman . . ." Then he sang, "In one kiss, a lifetime . . ." I remember that the low tone of his voice sounded like Rafael Solano, one of our finest musicians and composers.

On May 15, 1946, St. Isidore's Day, Jaimito's father, Don Jaime Fernández, came to my house to ask for my hand in marriage. He did so after meeting all sorts of requirements and with great formality, accompanied by Don Juan Rojas, Don Víctor Rodríguez, and Don Porfirio Montes de Oca. My father celebrated with a toast. They sat down to talk. Don Víctor is a funny man and said more or less, "Well, we are here to ask for Dedé's hand in marriage. She and Jaimito are in love, and we have to bring them up to speed."

---

41   Popular poet, radio host, and troubadour from Azua de Compostela, celebrated for his smooth, deep voice. He died in New York City in 1950, at age forty.

Papá accepted. Mamá said nothing because from the very beginning she didn't think Jaimito was right for me. She thought he was too much of a Don Juan, and, besides, before we dated, he was seeing a cousin of mine.

Mamá was so adamant that she would tell me I'd stolen him from my cousin, even though it was not true. Or she would say, "Don't get involved with him. He's fooled some fifty thousand girls." During our two-year courtship we never went out by ourselves, and when he came to visit, Mamá would sit by my side. However, before the wedding, she told me, "Come to the kitchen a couple of days to learn how to cook." And, of course, she taught me to cook. We had a lot of help at the house, so I also learned by preparing them rice, beans, and meat.

The truth is I fell in love with Jaimito, a violent and handsome man. I was madly in love with him, and I think he loved me too. In an interview he gave to Angela Hernández, he tells his version of how we fell in love and got married:

> When I was in love with Dedé, I would cross over the hills and through cacao fields—sort of hidden—to reach her house. Doña Chea loved my Mamá very much. They were first cousins, and she would let her daughters come visit at our house. If they went to a party, it was with my sisters. I had a brief romance with Tata, Dede's first cousin. She was so beautiful that even today as an old lady she is still beautiful. That's why Doña Chea didn't want me for her daughter. I was so arrogant. I fell in love with this girl, I fell in love with that girl, and I usually fell in love with my cousins because they were the only girls I thought were pretty. We were all related around here, in one way or another. When Dedé began to fall for me, I was still seeing Tata, but Doña Chea didn't know that. But was I even thinking about that? Dedé was still very young, and I couldn't think of getting married, but I knew very well that when I did go after Dedé I'd better be settled and financially stable if I wanted to marry her because Dedé was the one who handled the finances for the rice mill, the coffee accounts, the cacao accounts, and the books for the entire business, including the grocery store, the pharmacy . . . everything. If I wanted to win her hand, I had to be serious about it.
>
> Besides, Dedé had all sorts of suitors! I had a cousin of marrying age who was in love with her, but I didn't want to lose her to someone else or let any of those other guys beat me to her. So, I would go to Dedé's house and take up her time. We talked about volleyball, went

horseback riding... When we went riding, I would slip in a couple of words here and there because back then it was difficult to go out with a girl. Doña Chea did not allow her daughters to go to parties, unless Don Enrique took them. I would come from Salcedo to see Dedé play volleyball, but my cousin was also there watching her. He was an "old bachelor" who was starting to lose his hair, so that encouraged me. I'll never forget that. A small kiss, a little something... Dear God! But anyway, that's how she eventually said yes. I was like one of those dogs that when they fall in love, they migrate toward their mate. But since Doña Chea was so difficult, I would keep my distance.

Once Dedé and I were in a relationship, I stopped thinking about other women. In fact, I spent too much time thinking about Dedé. I was desperate to get married, but I didn't have the means. My parents were comfortable but poor. My father worked hard, and so did my mother, but they didn't own a farm where I could make a living. I thought I'd open a small grocery store, so that's what I did. They helped me, and I opened the store in Salcedo. I had already worked for Munné and Company, but a hired hand is a hired hand. You can't get far on that salary, and I was very ambitious.

We were married here in Ojo de Agua, on May 27, 1948. We planned a huge celebration with lots of guests, followed by a honeymoon in Sosúa. My sisters were so happy. Patria was the maid of honor. Minerva was a bridesmaid. Patria's children, Nelson and Noris, were my flower girl and ring bearer. My wedding dress was made by the talented designer Pepé Bodden.

As luck would have it, around five in the afternoon, after I had put on my wedding dress, it began to rain. But it wasn't just any downpour. No. The skies opened up, and it poured. All the rivers overflowed. The two bridges that went from Tenares to Salcedo, crossing over the Jayabo and the Juana Núñez Rivers, were completely destroyed, and no one could cross for several days. It rained so much that day that, for a while, folks around here would say, "It rained more today than when Dedé and Jaimito got married."

When we saw that the rains could lead to flooding, we decided to leave earlier for Salcedo, where the wedding ceremony was to take place. We left in several cars in the middle of the downpour, but when we got to the river, we saw that it was impossible to cross. Everything was flooded. We had no other choice but to turn around and go back to the house. As we approached the house, I told everyone that I wasn't married yet so that they wouldn't start congratulating us. A group of friends waited until the waters receded a bit and placed wooden planks over the river. They went to pick up Father Javier and bring him back across the river so he could marry us.

All of Jaimito's friends stayed at the house until the whisky ran out. To return to Salcedo they had to go by way of San Francisco de Macorís and La Vega. Jaimito's relatives had to stay overnight in Ojo de Agua. That's what my wedding day was like. We also had to cancel our honeymoon in Sosúa. To make matters worse, when we finally got to our house in Macorís, there was not one drop of water. All that rain . . . and we didn't even have water to drink! Unbelievable!

It was around that time that ice cream pops became popular. Jaimito's mother set up an ice cream shop in Salcedo, and he opened a similar one in Macorís which he baptized Helados Casino. Things were going more or less well until he just up and closed it. He tended to be fickle when it came to these kinds of endeavors. He would begin a business, grow tired of it, and then start a different one.

That's where my sons were born, in Macorís: Jaime Enrique on April 3, 1949, and Jaime Rafael (Jimmy) on May 3, 1951. Jaime David was born in Salcedo a few years later on October 15, 1956. The first of my sons, Jaime Enrique, was born on a Sunday evening at around nine o'clock after a long labor that ended with the doctor using forceps because the baby was so big and chubby. He was beautiful. Jimmy was also born on a Sunday, but early in the afternoon. Jaimito's family had spent the day at our house, and when I began to feel the contractions, my obstetrician was unavailable. He was on a call at a farm. My husband went to look for him on a huge motorcycle that he owned back then, but because he couldn't find him, he called on Dr. Adolfo Ortega. One good contraction, and it was over! That's how my second son was born. Eleven pounds. He was huge, just like people say about May babies: they're big and strong. But even though it was a quick delivery, I couldn't get out of bed for nine days.

One of my comadres, Jaimito's cousin's wife, gave birth before me, but the little girl was very small. Because she produced so much milk, her breasts would swell and she would send word to "send Jimmy over" so she could nurse him. After he nursed from those breasts, which gave so much milk, he didn't want mine. Unlike Jaime Enrique, Jimmy was not a pretty baby when he was born. Mamá used to wonder, "Who does this child take after?" Lucky thing he grew out of it.

Because Jaime Enrique was the first grandchild for Jaimito's parents, they would come to our house, pick him up, and take him to stay with them for several days. He meant the world to Jaimito's sisters, especially Clara. Jimmy would stay with me, and I would take him to the shoe store I had back then. I remember him squatting down to catch a glimpse of some children who used to play on the other side of the street. One of the girls, Rosita, used to hit the little ones. That bothered Jimmy, and he would tell me, "Mamá, Osita ang'y! Osita ang'y!" Today, I still say to him jokingly, "Jimmy, Osita ang'y!" Years later, when Jaimito and I spent a great deal of time working on a farm that we'd bought, Jimmy would routinely stay behind in Conuco with Mamá. Jaime Enrique would stay in Salcedo with Jaimito's parents and sisters.

From the time I was very young, my family would call me "Aunt Rosa," after an aunt who was known for being obliging and tolerant. Later on, it really took hold when they saw how I put up with my husband's complicated, explosive temperament. I'd put up with his temper tantrums, staying calm and carrying on. A train could run me over, and I wouldn't even flinch.

Things happened between Jaimito and me. Back then he was like a dictator in our house. Fortunately, now that our lives have taken different paths, now that he is happy, and I am happy, we have become good friends. He comes to eat at my house, and he visits me. We talk about our children, and even though he is always complaining, I don't harbor any bad feelings toward him at this stage of my life.

That marriage lasted thirty-four years, and I would say that the first eighteen were normal. But then problems arose that we couldn't fix. I made the decision to get a divorce when I finally convinced myself that the relationship could not be saved. Now that I look back, I'm glad things turned out the way they did, for his sake and for mine.

II

A Time of Storms, Struggles, Tragedy, and Changes

Figure 2.1. Dedé and her oldest son, Jaime Enrique. "He was born on a Sunday . . . he was so big and chubby, so beautiful." Courtesy of the Fundación Hermanas Mirabal.

Figure 2.2. Minerva (expecting Minou) and Manolo at their home in Montecristi. "Without looking, they found one another, and each complemented the other with their ideas." Courtesy of the Fundación Hermanas Mirabal.

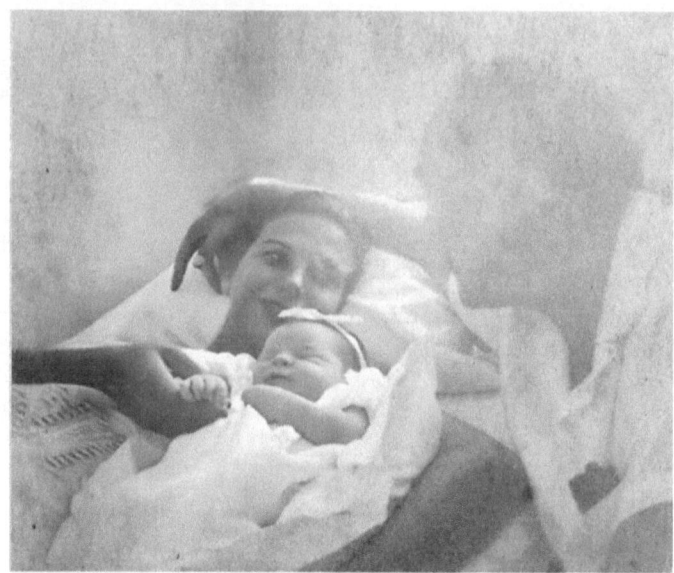

Figure 2.3. Birth of Minou Tavárez Mirabal, 1956. Courtesy of the Fundación Hermanas Mirabal.

Figure 2.4. In the town of Montecristi: Minerva, Patria, Leandro, María Teresa, and Nelson. Courtesy of the Fundación Hermanas Mirabal.

Left: Figure 2.5. Manolo was Minerva's sponsor at her graduation in 1957. At the time she was pregnant with Manolito. Courtesy of the Fundación Hermanas Mirabal.

Below: Figure 2.6. Leandro and María Teresa's wedding, 1958. Manolo was the best man. Courtesy of the Fundación Hermanas Mirabal.

Above: Figure 2.7. Leandro and María Teresa's wedding reception, 1958. Courtesy of the Fundación Hermanas Mirabal.

Right: Figure 2.8. María Teresa with her daughter Jacqueline, 1959–60. Courtesy of the Fundación Hermanas Mirabal.

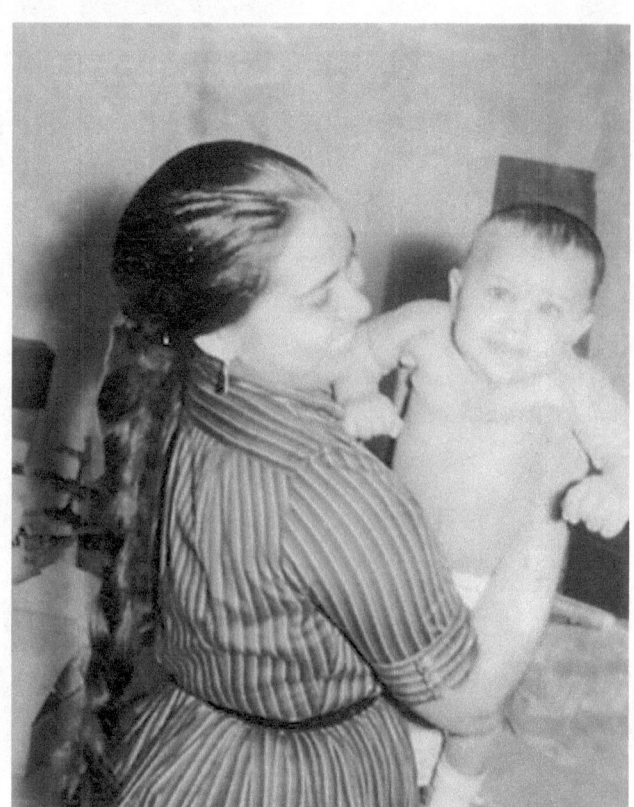

Figure 2.9. Patria with Raúl, who was born in 1959. Courtesy of the Fundación Hermanas Mirabal.

Figure 2.10. Patria, Dedé (who is sometimes mistaken for María Teresa in this photograph), and Minerva. Courtesy of the Fundación Hermanas Mirabal.

Right: Figure 2.11. Last photograph of Minerva. She had the photograph taken for her identification card. She lost her first ID when she was arrested in 1960. Courtesy of the Fundación Hermanas Mirabal.

Below: Figure 2.12. María Teresa. Courtesy of the Fundación Hermanas Mirabal.

Above: Figure 2.13. Dedé standing behind her sisters' caskets at Doña Chea's home in Conuco. "The greatest pain, however, came the following day, when I left the house. I thought my soul had abandoned my body, and I felt faint." Courtesy of the Fundación Hermanas Mirabal.

Left: Figure 2.14. Rufino de la Cruz Disla. "We have never forgotten his sacrifice and endless courage." Courtesy of the Fundación Hermanas Mirabal.

Figure 2.15. Funeral mass at the San Juan Evangelista Church in Salcedo. Courtesy of the Fundación Hermanas Mirabal.

4

Fall from Grace

October 13, 1949: The Party in San Cristóbal

To better understand why the events at the famous ball in San Cristóbal were so significant, I need to clarify certain details and events that took place. Back then, Trujillo frequently held balls in various cities. He held one of these balls in honor of the "very prestigious" members of society in Moca and Salcedo, which were municipalities in Espaillat Province.

Minerva and Trujillo had met during the inauguration ceremony for Santiago's City Hall, which took place before the ball in San Cristóbal. She was later invited to a ball at the Hotel Montaña, where she had to dance with one of the Trujillos. I can't remember if it was with the dictator himself or with his son Ramfis.

One day, Miguel Rodríguez Reyes came to see me in San Francisco de Macorís. He was the general who was killed when troops were sent to break up the Liborista movement in Palma Sola in 1962.[42] It turns out that he was my mother's cousin and my maternal grandmother's godchild. Despite the fact that we had never been in contact with him, he came to visit me that day and asked me who my husband was. I immediately suspected that there was a hidden motive for the visit, and that this man, who was a staunch supporter of Trujillo, had come to find out something specific. As it turned out, my Uncle José's sister-in-law, María was married to Miguel Rodríguez Reyes's brother, who was a sergeant. María told her husband that Minerva was against Trujillo and that she "listened to foreign news programs" on the radio. When Uncle José found out, he was furious and forbade María from ever stepping foot in our house.

---

42 This is commonly known as the Palma Sola Massacre. The Liborista movement was the religious following of the popular healer and messianic figure Olivorio Mateo, known as Papá Liborio. General Rodríguez Reyes is said to have been trying to minimize the bloodshed by speaking with the Liborista leaders when he was brutally stabbed and beaten.

This is why I believe that the San Cristóbal ball was plotted from the start. Attendance was mandatory since events like this were a way to promote public support for the regime. So even though my mother objected, my father said that we must go.

We left for the ball. When we reached the capital, we went to the home of Arturo Burgos, my mother's cousin. He and his wife Doña Fifa ran a small hotel in the historic Casa del Cordón in the colonial quarter. There we ran into people from Salcedo who were also invited to the ball, and we were given more information about where the ball was to be held.

At the time, the town of San Cristóbal was as clean and shiny as a silver teacup. We finally got to the hotel that was being inaugurated by Trujillo, who had lately taken to building hotels throughout the country, such as the Hotel Montaña and the Hotel Nueva Suiza. We asked where the event was taking place and were told that it was at the Hacienda Borinquen. Upon arriving, we were surprised to see Don Enrique Arzeno, president of Trujillo's Dominican Party in Moca and a good friend of ours. He told us that they had been waiting for us at Trujillo's beach house in Najayo, just west of San Cristóbal.

Jaimito went to park the car, while Papá, Minerva, Patria, Pedrito, and I went in. The place was completely full. It took Jaimito a while to return. When he finally appeared, he explained that he had taken so long because he made sure to get a parking spot near the entrance so we wouldn't have a problem when we left. As soon as we entered the party we saw Manuel de Moya Alonzo, famous for his role as an official matchmaker for Trujillo. Both he and Isabel Mayer[43] had the shameful reputation of recruiting women for the dictator. "Good evening! Good evening!" said de Moya, looking directly at Minerva. He had seen her a few times before: once in La Vega and, on a separate occasion, when my sister represented the Homeland dressed as the National Emblem at an event organized by the dictator's brother, Petán Trujillo, in the town of Bonao.

We were finally seated at a table that, according to Jaimito, was apparently reserved for us. There were several people we knew from Moca and Salcedo. All of a sudden, we heard a commotion. Several guests stood up. I turned my head, and there was Trujillo. That was the only time in my life that I saw him. He had entered through a different door. He remained standing and

---

43 Prominent pro-Trujillo politician who was the first woman senator in the Dominican Republic and also served as governor of Montecristi and Santiago. Coincidentally, she was the first wife of Manuel Francisco Tavárez Ramos, Minerva's future father-in-law.

did not sit down. The orchestra began to play two very popular merengues: "Ay Tana, la maricutana" and "El jarro pichao." In the meantime, Trujillo decorated several military officers, promoted others, and, as always, gave his customary public performance. I remember that even though he was dressed in military uniform, he was not wearing his famous bicorne hat. The orchestra was playing, but he remained standing. I still remember the image of a woman standing close to him, wearing an extravagant stole made of marabou feathers.

A short while later Manuel de Moya approached our table asking to dance with one of us. Patria said she didn't dance, and Minerva refused. But the man insisted until Minerva had no other choice but to accept or risk offending him. As they were dancing in the middle of the dance floor, de Moya passed her to Trujillo, and they danced to a couple of songs. They only danced to maybe one or two sets, but to us it seemed like an eternity. When the orchestra finished one piece, Trujillo would just stand there, as would Minerva, just like the other couples on the dance floor. We were worried that Minerva might take a sip from a drink that Trujillo had offered her. We had heard rumors about such drinks being spiked with a drug that would make women fall into his arms. Watching nervously from our table, we kept our eyes fixed on the glass and prayed that Minerva would not drink from it.

At one point, Minerva said to Trujillo, "I would like to return to the table." Trujillo then passed her on to Negro Trujillo, and he to Manuel de Moya. We all breathed a sigh of relief when she sat down and said, "I didn't drink anything." After that incident we stayed a while longer. I got up to dance several times. All of a sudden it started to rain, and because we were dancing in the band shell, out in the open, everyone went inside. Patria had a headache, and she asked Pedrito for a painkiller. We were all very upset, as you can imagine. Minerva had danced with Trujillo. She told us that Trujillo had asked her if she had a boyfriend, to which she responded no. He also asked, "Are you not interested in my politics, or is it that you don't agree with them?" Minerva answered, "No, I don't like them." Trujillo continued, "And what if I send my followers to convince you?" Her response was, "And what if I convince them?" Finally, Papá decided to take advantage of the chaos provoked by the downpour and said, "Let's get out of here."

Our car was very close to the main entrance. We headed back to the capital, where we filled up with gas and continued on to Salcedo. When Trujillo asked where Minerva was, everyone went looking for her: the governor, the senator, the officials from Moca. All were concerned about the situation we had created by leaving early. After a while they had to inform Trujillo that Minerva and her family had left. They called La Cumbre, a highway checkpoint, to have us detained, but we had already passed through. They say that when they informed Trujillo that we had left, he threw a fit, created a scandal, and berated Antonio de la Maza, who was governor of Moca, and Senator Juan Bautista Rojas, an eminent and prestigious attorney from Salcedo.

In the meantime, we were all relieved to have gotten out of there. Jaimito kept the pedal to the floor, while Patria talked with him nonstop to keep him awake.

Granted, we had heard that it was prohibited to leave a party before Trujillo, but we forgot all about that as we headed home. So we never imagined the consequences our behavior would bring in the coming days. I remember that Doña Paulita and her husband, Dr. Renán González, left the party with us, but they were not reprimanded. Nothing happened to them. We were the only ones they persecuted.

What was later said, that Minerva had slapped Trujillo and left him standing in the middle of the dance floor, simply never happened. But I do think she delivered a verbal slam. Minerva's words and attitude were enough; she didn't need her hands to "slap" him in the face.

As they danced, she was hostile toward this man accustomed to having people kneel before him. Trujillo perceived her disgust and saw her for who she was: a beautiful twenty-two-year-old woman, well educated, competent . . . and an enemy of his government. Here he was, the all-powerful, a man whom everyone feared and who no one dared contradict because he had his opponents killed . . . and then here comes Minerva, a young, courageous woman who dared tell him that she could convince those he sent to convince her.

Did Trujillo know that we were going to the ball? Of course he did! The clearest testimony came from Doña América, the wife of Juan Bautista Rojas and a very passionate and extroverted woman. After Trujillo berated Don Juan, she said she had told her husband not to invite Minerva to the ball. He replied that he had no choice and that he was obligated to make sure she attended.

Repression Against the Family Begins

We arrived home from the ball in the early morning hours, unaware of the problems ahead. On Sunday morning, a man sent by Senator Rojas arrived at the house to tell Papá that he should immediately send a telegram to

Trujillo to apologize for having left the ball before he did. Papá said he did so, but on Monday they came and picked him up for questioning. On Tuesday afternoon military officers from La Vega came to pick up Minerva. My mother objected, "My daughter cannot go by herself. I'm going with her." When they reached the capital with the military officers, they were taken to the Hotel República on 30 de Marzo Street. The owners, Tulio Zorrilla and Antigua Peralta, were friends of ours from Salcedo. Mamá asked the officers to let them use the bathroom. In the lobby they learned that Papá was also being detained and was there under house arrest. So was Juan Rojas. Papá told them that Don Juan was up all night, typing, which led him to believe that the situation was quite serious. They still did not know that Juan Rojas had been berated the night of the ball.

Immediately after, they took Minerva and Mamá to the Ozama Fortress[44] but were sent back to the hotel because it was so late. They were ordered to return the following day. Very early the following morning, different military officers arrived, but they only took Minerva, and they transported her in a paddy wagon. This was one of the most painful and frightening moments for Mamá because she didn't know what they would do to her daughter. "I couldn't even eat, just thinking that they were hurting her," she told us later. She knew Minerva too well and knew that she would not give in to pressure.

When Minerva arrived at the fortress, she discovered that there was an entire group of young men and women being detained there who, according to the intelligence services, were somehow connected to her: Jacinto Lora, who later disappeared without anyone ever finding out what happened to him; Francisco Ornes; Violeta Martínez; Rubén Suro. Many of Minerva's friends and acquaintances were being "investigated." I'm not sure if Pericles Franco was still in jail at the time or if he had already gone into exile. Minerva was almost always interviewed by then Colonel Fausto Caamaño. They would pick her up at the hotel in the morning, put her in the paddy wagon, and bring her back at night.

There was a gentleman by the name of Don Chilín Camilo, who lived in San Francisco de Macorís and was related to my grandmother. They used to say that years ago, he had been named brigadier but, because of health problems, he relinquished the position to Trujillo. Apparently, Trujillo was grateful to him because this boosted his career. That's why we turned to Uncle Chilín, as my mother used to call him, when my father was arrested and

---

44 Spanish colonial fortress dating to 1502. During the Trujillo regime, many political prisoners were tortured and imprisoned there.

we didn't know where else to turn. Even if people wanted to help us, they didn't dare. We asked him to write to Trujillo, telling him that Don Enrique Mirabal was not a troublemaker, but a very hardworking man.

On Saturday, they took Minerva and my parents to the National Palace to meet with Trujillo. He asked Mamá, "Are you related to Don Chilín?" She answered yes. That's when Trujillo told them that their relative had informed him that Don Enrique was a hardworking man, and that he was not involved in politics. Then, as if he owned Minerva, he asked, "What do you want me to do with your daughter?" My mother was very aware that Minerva was a revolutionary and that she faced serious danger. She replied, "I'm responsible for her and I'll take her home with me." "Very well, take her with you," Trujillo conceded.

For a brief period of time everything was quiet. Trujillo's caliés had not yet begun to surveil our house. Minerva and Trujillo never met again. The tyrant did not visit Salcedo for many years. However, my sister remained under a kind of house arrest and under permanent surveillance. Papá describes her situation in a letter that he sent to Antonio de la Maza in January 1950. I obtained the letter not too long ago thanks to Luciano García, the son of Tamara Díaz, Minerva's friend from Montecristi.

The letter was written on Papá's stationery, which reads, "Enrique Mirabal, Merchant-Landowner." It refers to the time when de la Maza and Manuel de Moya Alonzo questioned my father about Minerva's activities "following the incident." It also makes reference to a certain anonymous letter that was circulating regarding our family.

When I read the letter, I couldn't stop thinking of how paradoxical life can be: the same governor who had interrogated my father and my sister in 1950 would later be part of the group of courageous men who, outraged by the assassination of my sisters, among other things, decided to assassinate the tyrant in 1961. The letter said:

Mr. Antonio de la Maza
Provincial Governor, Moca, D.R.

Distinguished Governor,

I write to you in reference to the conversation we had yesterday. I returned home worried that my responses may have left you with doubts, or rather led you to think that I was misleading you, Mr. de Moya and, by extension, the President of the Republic.

When I arrived, I asked my wife if she and Minerva had ever gone to the movies during a trip to see the doctor. My wife was surprised by the question. Minerva then explained to me that in the conversation she had with you and the President of the Dominican Party, she simply mentioned that she had wanted to see an art exhibit once when she was going to the movies. She explained that since it had happened so long ago, she didn't think it necessary to mention that it had been in February of the previous year. I hope you understand why I hesitated to answer your question; at the moment I did not understand exactly what you were asking, nor was it clear to me to which time period you were referring. I could only assure you that if the event had taken place after the incident, then Minerva would have been accompanied by her mother. Kindly pass this information on to Mr. de Moya.

Since you mentioned that Minerva had attended events for entertainment, I wish to remind you that the wedding she attended was that of a close relative and that it was a very private event.

You also referred to the fact that I have a store, which is frequented by other vendors. You took issue with the fact that I did not inform you of these visits. I did not mention them because dealing with such middlemen is a normal part of doing businesses, and to this day I have never seen anything suspicious, and therefore I didn't consider it necessary to report them to you. But I will do as you say. I am explaining all of this because I noticed that you were uncomfortable, and even upset with me. Once again, I assure you that the Honorable President of the Republic has my full and loyal support and friendship. Therefore, I do not want my good faith to be called into question and to lead to accusations. I was honored by the President who, in an act of kindness that I will never forget, entrusted my daughter to me unconditionally, trusting in my sincere friendship and proven loyalty. I cannot allow the slightest shadow of doubt to betray this trust, and I accept full responsibility for my daughter's actions. Any actions taken against my daughter would harm me directly. This is why I believe that the letter that I showed you from Moca, full of slander and accusations, was sent not to malign her, but to malign me. I brought the letter to you because you are the head of the region, which means that I have treated you with the consideration and respect due to an authority of this province. In so doing, I informed you of something that would likely be of interest to you and that might be to your detriment.

I have nothing further to add but do send my regards, as always.

Your servant and friend,
Enrique Mirabal

In most Dominican households it was customary to hang a portrait of Trujillo in a visible spot in the house. But not in our home. I also don't remember my father registering with the Dominican Party. During elections, Uncle Tilo would pick up the national identity cards and take them to the town of Tenares so they could be officially stamped. That's how we voted.

In 1951 my father was arrested once again. This time the excuse was that he had refused to give money to Porfirio Dantes Castillo and Lico Canto for an album that would be dedicated to Trujillo. Papá told them that, just days before, he had donated five hundred pesos for that very purpose. They still locked him up. We immediately started trying to get access to see him and get him released. We spoke to Governor Brea of Macorís, and we also visited Tomás Rodríguez Núñez, a very important person and a friend of Jaimito's father. No one knew where my father was. He disappeared. No one told us anything.

The next day they came to the house and arrested Minerva and Mamá. They said they were under investigation. Because there were no jails for women, they took them to the Hotel Presidente on 30 de Marzo Street, across from Independence Park. The hotel was owned by Don Javier Abraham, a good friend of my father and Uncle Fello. I remember being struck by the fact that even in the middle of all this terror and tension, Mamá took interest in a couple of trees she hadn't seen before, and she picked up a few seeds to plant back home. People around here call those trees foreign oaks. They have purple leaves. We still have some of those trees in the garden at our home in Ojo de Agua.

Without first notifying Mamá and Minerva, they took Papá to Ozama Fortress. Mamá began to send him clothes and food, but we were unable to find out anything more regarding his circumstances. Lupita de Albert and her American husband, who were friends of the family and were also related to the dictator's brother, Virgilio Trujillo, visited Minerva and begged her to write letters asking about our father and expressing her remorse over what had happened. But with her usual attitude and composure, Minerva told them, "I'm not going to write those letters." I imagine that Trujillo was informed of her response.

While my father was in jail, he suffered another stroke. It was more severe than the first one. Julito Brache, the District Attorney in Moca and a friend of Minerva's, who in the future would have our home searched repeatedly, let us know that our father was alive. He told us that Papá had been taken to a small hospital where they used to treat the guards stationed at Ozama Fortress. That's where Julito saw him. Later on, Papá told us that they even asked him who his doctor was, and he responded that it was Dr. Bernardo Pichardo, who back then was a prestigious cardiologist.

Virgilio Trujillo had visited the region several times to attend cock fights. Cockfighters tend to become good friends, and even though my father did not have roosters, he sometimes went to the cockfighting rings to bet on the fights. He and the dictator's older brother became friends. Virgilio visited Minerva to propose a meeting between her and Trujillo at the Hotel Jaragua so she could speak with him. He was surprised by her response: "Look, Don Virgilio, I'd rather throw myself from this third floor than do that." Later on, Minerva told us that Virgilio looked at her with contempt, as if to say, "Do you think my brother is in love with you?" She didn't care and was not frightened by his reaction. She simply was not going to meet with Trujillo.

Several days later, a car with my father and a military officer arrived at the Hotel Presidente, where Minerva was being held. They picked her up and brought them both to the Hotel San Cristóbal, the government-operated hotel in the town that bears the same name. In other words, they were bringing them to a pack of wolves. They were left there as prisoners. Very early the next morning Patria, Jaimito, Pedrito, and I went to the hotel in San Cristóbal. We had lunch with them. That made Papá very happy. But in the afternoon, we were ordered to return home.

In less than twenty-four hours, they were freed from that small cell and transferred to the prison that was the Dominican Republic in 1951.

As soon as he got home, Papá demanded to know why we had not sent him food or clothing. Every single day, without fail, Mamá had sent him clean clothes and a canteen with food, right from the hotel. They never gave them to him.

5

Events That Impacted Our Family

Uncle Fello's Son: Another Mysterious Death

Uncle Fello had two sons. The oldest, Fellito, was close to my age and a very handsome young man. He joined the Navy at a very early age.

In 1947, Fellito met Dwi at a party. She was one of the young girls that Trujillo became infatuated with. She was the daughter of an Austrian couple that had come to the country to work in the San Cristóbal armory. "One day I was riding my horse through the streets when Trujillo saw me and fell in love with me," she would later reveal. Trujillo used her sexually and later on donated land to the family where today stands the La Vega sports complex.

Completely unaware of her background, Fellito became interested in her. They were immediately rushed into marriage. Behind their backs we criticized him for marrying a damnificada, which is how people referred to the women who had fallen victim to this type of abuse by the dictator. She became pregnant, but because my cousin was not really in love with her, they separated as soon as she gave birth. I imagine that she complained to Trujillo, and she probably told him that Fellito had mistreated her. The truth is we never really knew what happened.

One day Fellito was having lunch at the Sans Souci naval base with his colleagues. When he finished, he got up from the table and went to his room. A little while later they announced he was dead. But how? How did he die? A young, healthy, athletic man . . . His colleagues said they had all eaten together and that Fellito was fine. They took the body to the mountain town of Jarabacoa, and his burial included an honor guard. However, they did not allow Uncle Fello to open the coffin to see him. They'd killed him. His own colleagues said so. From then on, Uncle Fello lived and eventually went to his grave with that terrible pain, convinced that his son had been murdered. Just a few weeks later, Fellito and Dwi's son, Gustavo Mirabal, was born.

My Business Ventures and Minerva Goes off to the University

In the meantime, I continued living in San Francisco de Macorís. In 1951, the year when Jimmy was born, I opened a shoe store where I sold imported shoes. I closed the store when my father died in 1953. I bought my merchandise at a store in Santiago called Los Muchachos and resold them at my store. I sold other merchandise at the store, which was a common practice back then.

I personally tended to my clients, and I also did manicures. I took care of my children, got them ready for school, and tended to the needs of my husband, who was a special case to be reckoned with when it came to demanding personal attention. I was able to do so much because I always got up at the crack of dawn.

After the arrests, Papá decided to relax his stance on Minerva attending the university. She'd finally convinced him. He no longer wanted to get in the way of her wishes to study. He made his decision precisely when the dictator was away on a long trip to Spain.

Minerva registered at the university in 1952 and completed her first year of studies. At first, she lived in a dorm managed by the Carmelite nuns, next to the university. She was so happy! But her happiness only lasted until September 1953, when she was denied the right to register. Rafael David Henríquez, a clerk at the university, gave her the news. The university had approximately one thousand students registered. My sister tried to find out if they had denied registration to students who were against the Trujillo regime. No, she was the only one. That's when she realized that Trujillo had never forgiven her. When he returned from Spain and found out that Minerva had registered at the University of Santo Domingo, Trujillo took drastic measures. She took this interruption in her career really hard because of how much she wanted to study and graduate.

By then, Papá's health had deteriorated significantly. In September 1953, when Salcedo became a province, there was a special event in honor of Trujillo at the club in Salcedo. Some suggested to Minerva that she deliver special remarks during the event in the hope that she would then be allowed to register for classes again. She had Chachita Brito, a dear professor at the local school and an enemy of Trujillo, write the short remarks. She toned down all praises to Trujillo. Minerva felt that she couldn't write even a single word of those remarks. Papá never found out about this because we wanted to spare him any more suffering on his death bed.

Minerva felt humiliated, but she gave in because she wanted to continue with her studies. I suppose this episode is what inspired the reference to a supposed contract signed by Minerva in the movie based on Julia Alvarez's novel. In this contract, my sister promises to stop participating in anti-Trujillo activities. This is a fabrication. Such a contract never existed.

Soon after, she was allowed to register once again at the university. She rented a room from Chelito Conde, a resourceful woman who, already married and with two adolescent sons (Narciso and Tony Isa Conde), began to study architecture. Later on, María Teresa also stayed there. Minerva found out that Rodríguez Reyes, the military officer I mentioned before, lived nearby and had said that Minerva "was a communist." She decided to move. For a short time, she rented a room from one of Vincho Castillo's relatives and then went to live with Hortensia Marcial, a fellow student, and Father Marcial Silva's sister.

Papá's Death and María Teresa's Diary

In late 1953, Papá returned from the capital, where he had been hospitalized at a local clinic. One day he said he had a toothache. María Teresa took him to San Francisco de Macorís to have the tooth pulled, and they stopped by my house to visit. I found him to be really slow and distracted. That's when I found out they had given him insulin in the capital. We were never able to determine why he had been treated with insulin if he was not a diabetic. That Friday afternoon he returned to Ojo de Agua with María Teresa and Jimmy. The next day, on Saturday, I went to see him. He was very ill, depressed, and sad. Tonó told me that he had stayed in bed, listening in silence as María Teresa read to him for a long while. When he said he wanted a priest to listen to his confession, Mamá sent for Patria and Pedrito. We brought the priest, and he received the sacrament of confession.

I remember that on Sunday we were all at the house with relatives who had come from La Vega and Jarabacoa to visit Papá. Uncle Fello was there and so were Patria, Pedrito, and their children. It was our custom to spend Sundays at the house after going to church. They were preparing a Dominican stew for lunch that no one ever touched. The last thing Papá told me was that he wanted to pee. I was in the process of helping him when he suffered the brain hemorrhage. Jaimito had left for the capital mid-morning to pick up Minerva, but when they arrived in the afternoon, Papá was already in a coma.

María Teresa's diary ended up in my hands, thanks to Picky Lora,[45] who found it and sent it to me in 1997. It contains only a few entries over the span of a few weeks. She began to write on December 28, 1953, and ended her entries on February 11, 1954. In her diary María Teresa details the emotional state of our home after Papá's death. She describes the sadness and tensions that existed due to certain problems that the family had to face, her relationships with friends, her relationship with and admiration for Minerva, as well as her own feelings and health during this period. At the time, she was the only one who lived with our mother. The diary also reveals her goals as a student and her concerns regarding the family assets.

I'll comment on some of the entries to help clarify what they mean. At the time, my sister was getting ready to go to college. Back then, you had the choice of earning a high school degree in three specific areas: mathematics, social studies, and science. María Teresa graduated high school under the science program in Santiago. During the summer she completed the social studies curriculum in Salcedo through the open studies program. She also traveled to Macorís to complete the high school program in mathematics because she had already decided that she was going to study engineering, and she needed to complete that requirement. That's why on several occasions she mentions that she is studying or that she had to study.

Monday, December 28, 1953
Today I've been in bed all day with a cold. Chachita[46] stopped by and we talked a lot, I also read some philosophy from a booklet.

Tuesday, Dec. 29
Chachita is still here. I got up because the Guzmans stopped by and also Tommy R.;[47] we talked about regionalisms. An unforgettable day.

---

45 Picky Lora was the only woman among the 150 guerrilla fighters who, in 1963, attempted to return President Juan Bosch to power after he was overthrown.
46 Chachita was very close to our family. Very intelligent. She was the first principal of the Salcedo School. I remember she used to say: "You can say anything you want, what matters is how you say it." Chachita Brito, Efigenia Rodríguez, and Ms. Gómez were the three women who embodied teacher excellence in Salcedo. Author's note.
47 Antonio Guzmán was our attorney. He handled our affairs after Papá's death. Tommy Román was a friend of Minerva's from Santiago. Author's note.

Wednesday, Dec. 30

Chachita left, and I've gone back to bed because of a high fever. News of Papá's death was published in the newspaper *El Caribe*.

Thursday, Dec. 31

Years ago, this was a happy day for all of us, but due to our father's death, we are devastated.

Friday, January 1, 1954

All our sisters visited to wish us the best in the coming year, which I hope will not be as sad as the one that just passed.

Saturday, Jan. 2

Today I began to cut a pattern for a dress but, as always, I put it aside without finishing it.

Monday, Jan. 4

Yesterday, Sunday, my dear nuns stopped by. So many memories of my happy childhood came to mind. Nené[48] and Dilia also visited.

Tuesday, Jan. 5

The only thing we've done is talk, Minerva and I visited Mireya, and in the afternoon Chachita, Fe, and the Guzmans stopped by.

Wednesday, Jan. 6

This has been a hectic day. The nephews were thrilled with their new toys.[49] Aunt Minada visited, and Mela slept over.

Thursday, Jan. 7

I've received many letters from my friends, expressing their condolences over the death of my father. I'm so grateful to all of them!

Friday, Jan. 8

I'm so sad because Minerva will be leaving soon. I'm going to be so lonely! Rosario told me she was coming on Sunday.

Saturday, Jan. 9

I did very little yesterday, but today Rosario and Crimilda stopped by and we talked a lot. I have decided that I am going to study engineering.

---

48 Nené Rojas, from Moca. Author's note.
49 Three Kings Day, when Dominican children receive gifts.

Monday, Jan. 11

Minerva has already left. I still can't believe it. Today we received more letters, some that were very moving. I've felt nervous today.

Tuesday, Jan. 12

I still feel nervous. I don't understand what is going on with me. Patria bought me a blouse and stopped by to help deal with our situation.

Wednesday, Jan. 13

Today was a terrible day that I will never forget. When I write, the tears begin to flow. We've gone through so much.

Thursday, Jan. 14

Today is Papá's one-month anniversary. Went to Mass and also to the cemetery. Mamá is so sad. We're dealing with a terrible conflict.

Friday, Jan. 15

I feel very depressed, and sometimes I just want to disappear so I don't have to deal with so much injustice.

Saturday, Jan. 16

I just received a letter from Minerva. She knows almost nothing, but, what's worse, she wants to know it all.

Monday, Jan. 18

Today I've been organizing things around the house; a lot of old documents, some that hold great spiritual value for us.

Tuesday, Jan. 19

Today has been really hectic because of all the legal documents we have to deal with. A certain person was insulted by something I said, and I'm glad.

Wednesday, Jan. 20

A lot of people have stopped by these last few days to express their condolences for our great loss and everything we are going through.

Thursday, Jan. 21

Uncle Fello and Uncle Mon visited today. As always, they think that things will take care of themselves, but the problems are getting really complicated.

Friday, Jan. 22

I'm studying to see how much I can learn. I have excellent goals. God will help me stay focused on them.

Saturday, Jan. 23

I visited Macorís yesterday, where I talked with Marilí who asked me to come over and study with her. I saw Violeta, Nelly, etc.

Monday, Jan. 25

I found out someone said something about me, I didn't like it much because it was just not true. Yesterday, I read in the Gospel: "Never pay back evil with more evil," and since it seemed to be speaking to me, I will put it into practice.

Tuesday, Jan. 26

The girls came to spend the day, as did Mr. Guzmán. Today I remembered someone whom I had almost forgotten.

Wednesday, Jan. 27

We received a letter from Minerva and the package from Sears. She says that a young man she knows keeps asking about me. I'm dying to know who it is.

Thursday, Jan. 28

I've studied a lot today, and I really want to visit Minerva because I imagine she has a lot to tell me.

Friday, Jan. 29

Since I've been studying, I'm really excited with my studies, and I think if I keep this up, I'll do well in this profession.

Saturday, Jan. 30

I received a letter from Minerva that truly moved me. My dear sister really knows how to express herself! If only I could write like she does.

Monday, February 1, 1954

I just returned from Santiago, where I went shopping, and then I visited Conuco. Everything went well, but today I feel sadder than ever. Nelson turned 12.

Tuesday, Feb. 2

Today I have a sore throat, but I did some sewing. I cut a dress from a pattern that I think will turn out quite nice.

Wednesday, Feb. 3

I've spent the entire day in bed feeling terrible and with a fever. Uncle José came today and we talked a lot. He brought a lot of fresh news.

Thursday, Feb. 4

Patria and P. stopped by this morning to pick me up and take me to the doctor. We spent the day in Macorís at Dedé's; talked to Minerva on the telephone.

Friday, Feb. 5

Today I have very little to say. Doña Lupe and Mr. Albert visited yesterday. We brought . . . (I feel something is missing here) over, who updated me on my old school friends.

Saturday, Feb. 6

Minerva came yesterday and stayed until today. She told me a lot of things that truly pleased me. This afternoon we took her to Macorís.

Monday, Feb. 8

I was in Salcedo today. I visited with Alcides[50] and we talked a lot. Later I stopped by Chachita's. It was an enjoyable afternoon.

Tuesday, Feb. 9

I've spent the day working on the inventory of our properties and did not have time for anything else, not even to study.

Wednesday, Feb. 10

Doña Lupe and Mr. Albert stopped by and we chatted for a long while. They spent the day here. I was able to study some this evening, but there are so many things going on that I hardly have the time.

Thursday, Feb. 11

I've spent the entire day painting and fixing up the house because I think on Sunday Minerva is coming over with someone. I waited for Alcides, who promised he would stop by.

---

50 Alcides Camilo was the son of Nicolás Camilo, a very good friend of Minerva and María Teresa. Author's note.

6

Fortunate Encounters, Liaisons, and Moving On

Minerva and Manolo in Love

During those years, many young men who were interested in Minerva came by our home. But the truth is she never expressed a particular interest in any of them until Manolo appeared. "She's just not interested. She only cares about politics," Mamá would say.

If I remember correctly, Minerva and Manolo met in La Poza, Jarabacoa, either during Easter week or in the summer of 1953, just before she was about to begin her second year at the university. Jarabacoa had become a popular vacation destination, and many wealthy families built vacation homes there. La Poza turned into the most popular meeting place for young people. María del Rosario Rodríguez de Goico, the mother of Dominican singer Charytín Goico, introduced them at a bonfire that the Díez twins organized at their home. Manolo was dating a girl from the capital, Ana Matilde Cuesta, the daughter of Dr. Pelayo Cuesta, who was a famous attorney back then.

That's why I believe nothing happened between them during that first encounter, even though they were smitten with one another from the very beginning. Manolo's sister Angela, who was also vacationing at Ana Matilde's home, remembers that even though she and Ana did not attend the bonfire, she heard the rumors over the next few days about the impression that Minerva had made on Manolo and how they spent the entire night talking to one another. According to Angela, the family began making fun of Manolo because two or three days after meeting Minerva, he went to visit her at Uncle Fello's home. Apparently, he was so enthralled with staring at her that when an avocado fell on his head, almost killing him, he didn't even flinch.

In the capital Manolo lived near Minerva, at the home of his cousin Isabel Tavárez, the widow of Dr. Enrique Lithgow Ceara, who was also assassinated by Trujillo. I still remember the impression Isabelita made on me the day I met her, not only because she was very beautiful and attractive, but because I had never seen a woman wear shorts before. The thing is they were practically neighbors; they lived near one another close to the university, but they had never run into one another. When Manolo saw her again, he was already madly in love with her. But it wasn't until the end of 1953 or in January 1954 when they formally began to date. At least the first letters between them were written between February and March 1954.

I believe that María Teresa's diary entry dated February 11 refers to Manolo's first visit to our home. Minerva made Mamá buy new furniture before his visit. She gave the house a make-over in a whirlwind of preparations. Manolo ate at the house and made quite the impression on all of us. He impressed everyone; he was so handsome and well educated; he spoke carefully and was so well mannered. Mamá, in particular, was not only impressed, but she felt quite at ease after meeting him.

I vividly remember Minerva that day. I can see her dressed in her mourning clothes because Papá had died recently. She was standing on the porch, with makeup on, in love, happy, waiting for her prince.

After Manolo's visit to Mamá's home, he wrote her a very nice letter, in which he comments on his shyness and his intentions.

Mrs. Mercedes R. Vda. Mirabal[51]
Salcedo

Dear Doña Chea, whom I remember fondly,

It is with true pleasure and respect that I write to you. I would have liked to have done it sooner, but my shyness prevented me from doing so. It was stronger than the sincerity of my wishes! But yesterday, after reading one of Minerva's letters, I made up my mind to write to you, motivated by the deep respect and affection that you inspire in me.

I would like to take this opportunity to express the admiration that you have inspired in me because of your personal qualities and for the exemplary family that you and your husband—may he rest in peace—have raised.

I am very proud to have had the honor of meeting you and of visiting with you at your home. I will always remember the moments

---

51 Vda. is an abbreviation of the Spanish word *viuda* (widow), referring to the fact that she is the widow of Mr. Mirabal.

we shared. Once more, Doña Chea, I reiterate my deepest gratitude for the attention that you and the girls bestowed upon me, and I assure you that one of my greatest wishes, and that of my family, is to someday have the infinite pleasure of having you all here, visiting us, further strengthening the bonds between us. I have already expressed my feelings to Minerva, to whom I am bound by the most noble and beautiful feelings.

Perhaps this is not the most appropriate way for me to express these sentiments, but I feel obliged to do so. Besides, it is a bit easier this way. I am sure you will understand.

I have been very happy since yesterday, and from a distance I share in your joy at being once again reunited with the girls. Minerva wrote to me, telling me in her letter that she was leaving yesterday to visit you, and even though she did not mention whether or not María Teresa would be staying, I assume that she too will be by your side. Please give my warmest regards to her and to everyone else.

Doña Chea, allow me to express to you my most sincere and respectful regards. I also send you my family's best regards, as they are aware that I am writing to you.

Respectfully yours,
Manolo Tavárez

On one occasion Manolo came all the way from Montecristi to serenade Minerva. He actually brought a piano with him in the bed of a truck. He had a lovely voice, but the piano arrived all out of tune because the trip was long and the roads were in very bad shape. Minerva was madly in love. So many young men had fallen in love with her, but this was the first time she felt love's flame.

Not long ago I reread several notes that Emma Tavárez Justo, one of Manolo's sisters, published in the magazine *¡Ahora!* on December 9, 1974. I reproduce them here because I think they express, much better than I ever could, the happy days my sister lived during their courtship:

I took a quick glance and tried to capture the mysterious image in the photograph that Manolo had been contemplating for the longest time. Seated in a rocking chair, he was listening to soft music, intensely admiring the face that he found so beautiful. Intrigued and curious, I walked past him several times and, over his shoulder, I spied the smiling silhouette of the woman in the photograph. I assumed from her dress that she was a school girl. Inside, I was dying to know who Manolo had fallen in love with this time. I couldn't stand it anymore, and so standing beside him I said, "She's so pretty! Who is she?" "Her name is Minerva," he told me.

Later in the article Emma Tavárez describes the impression Minerva made on her when they first met, as well as the pleasant gatherings that took place between the two families. She also details her visit to Ojo de Agua, along with her twin sister Edda, revealing Minerva's happy and youthful spirit and the fact that she was very much in love and full of hopes and dreams:

> I met her at our home in Montecristi one sunny morning. She was accompanied by her sisters Dedé, Patria, and María Teresa, along with the husbands of the first two: Jaimito Fernández and Pedrito González. They were still in mourning over the death of Don Enrique, their father. Minerva said to us: "So these are the two little twins that Manolo has told me so much about." We were all seated at the table and I just fluttered around Minerva, Manolo's new girlfriend, and her sisters.
>
> She wanted to take my twin sister Edda and I back home with her on vacation. We arrived in Salcedo in the evening. Mamá Chea greeted us sweetly and lovingly. The next day, I was impressed by the exuberant vegetation of Ojo de Agua, the place in the country where they had their home. It was cool and very green, with a tremendous variety of plants that came in all sizes and colors. I compared the lush landscape with my hometown, which was rough, dry, and dusty.
>
> We would get up very early, when the evening dew still covered the early hours of dawn, and go to the kitchen, which was a bit removed from the main house. Standing close to a welcoming, warm oven, I couldn't understand how Minerva could calmly stand there and sip from her steaming cup of coffee without burning her mouth.
>
> I would sometimes watch Minerva in the mornings as she kneeled down next to the flower beds, planting and replanting with her hands embossed by veins that stood out like webs on her skin. Fun and chatty, she would tell us the names of her favorite plants.
>
> Sometimes we sneaked over to the warehouse next door, where she kept a bunch of *La Familia* magazines, and we would laugh at the outdated fashions that at the time seemed so extravagant to us.

In the afternoons she would sometimes recite long poems in a pleasantly modulating voice. I remember the feeling she expressed while reciting the poem of St. Francis of Assisi. She would leaf through her books with us, pulling them from the bookcase mounted on her bedroom wall. At the foot of the bookcase there was a small bed where I would sit and read excerpts from some of her books. We enjoyed poems by Juan Antonio Alix.[52] With great enthusiasm she showed me the albums where she kept her paintings, some of which she had painted at the Immaculate Conception School [. . .].

On other occasions María Teresa, with a spoon and a large gourd bowl in her hands, would ask me to help her beat the batter for the cakes she periodically baked.

One Sunday we went to eat at Patria and Pedrito's house in Conuco. It was like an oasis, surrounded by huge trees and a beautiful garden. Patria, very sweet and with soft, quiet gestures, was the perfect housewife down to the smallest detail of her home and family. With talents in music and painting, she turned the place into a small, personal paradise, which she shared with her children Nelson and Noris. Raulito had not been born yet [. . .].

Sometimes we went to Salcedo, where her other sister Dedé lived with her husband Jaimito and their children Jaime Enrique, Jaime Rafael, and Jaime David. With extraordinary skill and speed, Dedé would use the sewing machine to embroider beautiful monograms on sheets and pillowcases. One afternoon, Minerva took us to the home of a woman who read teacups and cards. Her name was Fefa, and she was very well known in Ojo de Agua. We were thrilled because it was something new, and she told each one of us our future. Later on, Minerva commented with a smile that the lady had predicted that she would soon marry.

On Sundays Minerva would take us to church in Salcedo in the family's old Buick. After breakfast we went for a drive to the nearby towns of Tenares and San Francisco de Macorís. In Tenares she introduced us to Dr. Concepción, an old and very dear friend of hers and her family.

Once María Teresa confided in me that she was in love with a young man from San Francisco de Macorís, but that her family did

---

52 Popular Dominican poet (1833–1918).

not yet approve of the relationship. One morning, during a visit to San Francisco, she and I went for a stroll to the town square. She pointed out a young man who was waiting for her on one of the benches. It was Leandro.

Communion of Ideals

Minerva and Manolo shared the same ideals. Without looking, they found one another. They bonded. Even before she met Manolo, she had a good number of anti-Trujillo contacts who, years later, would collaborate with the 14th of June Movement.

Manolo had grown up in a very different environment than Minerva. He went to high school in the capital. He was handsome, young, and very charismatic. He played the guitar and sang well. He harbored anti-Trujillo ideas before he met Minerva and had even been a member of the Democratic Youth. But I don't think he developed his political ideas at a very young age, as had Minerva, nor had he manifested them to the same extent that my sister had. She held fast to her anti-Trujillo ideas. I remember once when, right in front of our mother, she was openly critical of the dictator in a conversation with a government employee whose last name was Portes. My mother became alarmed and asked, "Have you gone crazy?" Mamá also said that Nené Rojas, a gentleman from Moca who worked in La Curacao and who was connected to Dr. Alfonseca, was always observing Minerva: "Look at her, look at her; those two are together just to 'bash' the government."

Many people have asked me, "Did Manolo influence Minerva, or did she influence Manolo?" My answer is always the same. Without looking, they found one another, and each one complemented the other with their ideals.

There's an anecdote that illustrates how Manolo's attitude against tyranny was just as audacious as Minerva's. Manuel de Jesús Estrada Medina, who in his youth had been a protégé of Isabel Mayer, became senator at the same time that my son Jaime David was also elected to the Senate. One day he came up to him and said: "Jaime, I want to tell you a story. Once, during the Trujillo Era we were all spending the day on the banks of a river when I handed Manolo two checks for the work he had done either as a substitute for a justice of the peace or as a supervisor. Manolo shred them to pieces, threw them into the water, and said to me: 'Listen Rooster'—that's what Manolo and I called one another—'I don't want them. They're covered in blood.'"

One had to live during that time to understand the magnitude of his actions. They lived in an environment of fear, where the great majority of people—even if they were unhappy with the regime—would remain silent in order to avoid falling out of favor with the regime or finding themselves in danger. They thought of their families, their jobs, or simply staying alive. No one wants to die. It's one thing to cry out "Let them kill me!" and another to be aware that yes, they could very well kill you.

My mother, very pleased, would say, "Minerva has found a man that will keep her under control." She was constantly concerned about Minerva's ideas and her strong character. "*Mi hija*, they are going to kill you. If you look for trouble, you will find it. They are going to throw you off a cliff. They are going to kill you," she would continuously repeat. And how right she was!

She knew that Minerva was doing her thing, participating in politics. That's why when she met Manolo, my mother thought he would rein her in, that "he would get her to control her political statements and ideas." Mamá completely ignored the fact that he was doing the same thing. She only saw him as a young man who was deeply in love with her daughter. During this time, they encouraged and supported one another in their conspiracies. In Manolo, Minerva had found encouragement, complete support: a true comrade in life and in political struggle.

Minerva insisted that Manolo become a notary public.[53] He dodged the idea without revealing the reason why: he didn't meet the legal age requirement. He had not told Minerva his true age because he was younger than she was. When Minerva found out, she stood her ground: "I am not getting married," she said and ended the courtship. But, because she was so much in love, she let herself be convinced, and finally, they were married on November 20, 1955.

Minerva had already celebrated her twenty-ninth birthday, and at the time, she was almost considered a "spinster." Her marriage lasted exactly five years and five days, until death parted them.

The church ceremony and the reception at our home in Ojo de Agua were simple and took place under torrential downpours, just like my wedding, and Patria's too. Minerva was not interested in parties, and she organized things in a rush. The beautiful cream-colored dress she bought from Virginia Dalmau is on exhibit at the house museum.

---

53   In the Dominican Republic, one must have extensive legal training to be a notary public since they draft legal documents and advise clients, unlike in the United States.

As guests, I remember Francisco Gómez, Alfredo Parra Beato, an attorney from San Juan de la Maguana and a friend of Manolo's, Rafael Acosta, and a few other guests. The photographer was late, and when he finally arrived, Minerva had already taken off her wedding dress. Mamá was desperate: "She's not into this. She's into that other thing, her politics." The truth is Minerva showed very little interest in certain details of the wedding, things that are usually very important to brides.

I can't exactly recall the date, but just a few days after the wedding a commentary appeared in the feared *Foro Público*—a malicious column published by the daily *El Caribe*, used by Trujillo to attack or instill fear in those who opposed his regime. The column stated that Dr. Manuel Tavárez Justo had recently married a "red communist," Minerva Mirabal Reyes. That was not the first time the cowardly column referred to my sister, publishing her first and last names. A few months before, in June of that same year, the column accused the clerk of the Law School for allegedly letting himself be corrupted by her and for binding her books using materials belonging to the university. It said, "It would be wise to put an end to the corrupt tactics of Mr. Horacio Geraldino, the head of the university's book binding department, who uses university-owned materials to do work for law student Minerva Mirabal, for whom he has bound some 20 books [. . .]."[54] They sacked that poor man because of that lie.

They went to live in Manolo's hometown, Montecristi, where their enthusiasm for political activism intensified.

Minerva traveled by airplane between Manzanillo and the capital to continue her studies. She spent weeks at the home of Isabelita Tavárez, where Manolo had once lived.

There is no better window into Minerva's heart at the time than the letters she wrote to Manolo between 1954 and 1955. Minou shared excerpts from these letters[55] in a keynote speech she delivered about her mother. It was summarized in the morning daily *Listín Diario* on November 22, 1987. Through her own intelligent eyes, and the eyes of a daughter, Minou

---

54 "Foro público," *El Caribe* (Santo Domingo, Dominican Republic), Jun. 25, 1955. Author's note.
55 Minou published her parents' intimate correspondence in the book *Mañana te escribiré otra vez. Minerva y Manolo. Cartas.* Santo Domingo: Editorial Santillana, 2014. The English translation is: *The Letters of Minerva Mirabal and Manolo Tavárez: Love and Resistance in the Time of Trujillo.* Translated by Heather Hennes. University of Florida Press, 2022. The latter is the source of the excerpts included here, some with slight revisions.

revealed the political qualities—but most of all the human qualities—of a complex, perceptive, and determined Minerva.

Minou observed, "During that period, when the predominant values were the traditional masculine values of violence, repression, and brute force, when the dictatorship was nothing more than a big hyperbole for '*machismo*,' it was in that masculine world that Minerva emerged to demonstrate to what extent the feminine presence was a form of dissidence."

I believe that in that speech, Minou revealed for the first time the soul of Minerva the dreamer, who, at the same time, was bestowed with tremendous common sense.

"As a woman"—says Minou—"she faced the same concerns faced by all women, but managed to shake them off." In one of her letters, dated October 20, 1955, she responds to Manolo's insistence that they get married and live with his parents until they could have their own home. She tells him:

> I ask that we set up our house before I finish my studies. Otherwise, I might feel inhibited. It doesn't matter if it's not the yellow house across from the courthouse. So what if it's a modest little house? I'll make it beautiful for you with my own two hands. It will be our home, and together we will watch the gardenias and jasmine grow, the ones I have planted to adorn it, and I will place their flowers on your desk every day. My love, you'll see that we won't need riches to make us happy. I prefer spiritual tranquility and love a thousand times over.[56]

In a letter dated February 5, 1955, we discover the enthusiastic, passionate, and tender expression of a love that knows it is mutual. Minerva writes to her boyfriend:

> Today my heart calls you by a thousand different names, one affectionate synonym piling on top of another.[57]

In a letter dated March 8, 1955:

> I love you so much. I depend on you for everything; you are my crutch, my old shoe, my love. It's terrible to feel so weak to the bone and to not have your beloved shoulder nearby.

---

56 Tavárez Mirabal, *Letters*, 199.
57 Revision of the translation in Tavárez Mirabal, *Letters*, 97.

On July 18, 1955:

It seems like a century has passed since you left. I reach out my hand to touch you, and it tightens in a fist against my chest. I hear your voice and feel deep inside the tenderness with which you called me "beautiful" yesterday.[58]

On September 14, 1955:

Don't call me a charlatan . . . you know that I adore you, that I laugh about our situation, and that I make comments to you about "providing," etc. because laughter and happiness are sisters. Look Manolo, without realizing, I've stopped writing this letter to think, and the conclusion is that you can rest assured: that's your Minerva for you, the one who pokes fun at sentimental things, perhaps to hide her own sentimentality. When I'm not like that, it's because something is wrong.[59]

From a letter dated October 20, 1955:

[. . . W]hen I'm with you I think only about that beautiful moment and the infinite Heaven of our love. But when I'm alone, I think about the broom, the ironing board, the basket of dirty laundry, and in all those mundane things that one must keep in mind at a wedding.[60]

Other letters that Minerva wrote to Manolo and that Minou presented reveal her thought process, such as the letter written on December 14, 1954, when she tells him:

It's possible that there is a discrepancy between the ideal and reality, and I can't help being an incurable idealist. When I try to conform to reality, I resemble one of those rivers whose murky waters hide its bed from view.[61]

Her letters reveal Minerva's ideals on love and relationships, such as the letter dated September 12, 1954:

You know that I've deprived myself of many things—things that come very naturally for any girl—only because of my character. Although

---

58 Slight revision of the translation in Tavárez Mirabal, *Letters*, 148.
59 Revision of the translation in Tavárez Mirabal, *Letters*, 179.
60 Revision of the translation in Tavárez Mirabal, *Letters*, 199.
61 Tavárez Mirabal, *Letters*, 179.

I've made every effort to tame it, it's always extremist at its core; it gives of itself completely and it demands everything. That's why I'm rather guarded about entrusting my friendship and affection. I don't want to assume more than what others feel *spontaneously* toward me. This is why, until now, I have repressed my attraction toward you: because I was afraid that you wouldn't return the intimacy and affection that I have desired for so long. Could you possibly satisfy my soul, my longings?[62]

In another letter, dated September 23, 1955, she writes:

I am convinced that two people who love one another are better off when each one maintains a certain amount of independence.[63]

Getting back to Minou's analysis of her mother's personality, I quote:

But, nevertheless, Minerva is clear about her intellectual and spiritual goals. She demands the best from herself and strives for her own ideals of perfection. But she also influences Manolo. When she confronts what she believes are character weaknesses, it is terrible. These moments of self-awareness, of a person who meditates and longs for perfection, are frequent. In particular, it is interesting to note the frequency with which Minerva describes herself with adjectives such as "selfish" or "strong-headed" or she begs forgiveness for this "girlfriend of yours, so super-intolerant, over-sensitive, and overly boisterous."[64]

Minou accurately interprets this as nothing more than Minerva's search for truth and authenticity. And Minerva also encourages Manolo. In letters from March 1955, she writes:

My love, I am happy that you are studying and have goals. At least our common ambition links us, in addition to our great love.[65]

And:

Your father told me that its best to go with the flow. I hope that you become a current that's at least convincing if not overwhelming . . . [66]

---

62 Tavárez Mirabal, *Letters*, 62.
63 Tavárez Mirabal, *Letters*, 181.
64 Minou Tavárez Mirabal, speech delivered in November 1987. No further information available.
65 Revision of translation in Tavárez Mirabal, *Letters*, 112.
66 Revision of translation in Tavárez Mirabal, *Letters*, 104.

A letter dated November 13, 1954, shows how much Minerva valued their careers. She tells Manolo:

> Remember, too, that I'd prefer that you defend your thesis. In other words, put this ahead of me, ahead of everything. Later, if you want, you can put me in that place.[67]

I remember Minerva's joy, her happiness, when she arrived in Montecristi. She was thrilled with the ocean, which was a true novelty for her. Manolo, Angela, Angela's husband Jaime Ricardo Socías, and Minerva, would frequently go fishing and listen to the underground radio programs of exiled Dominicans living in Cuba, Puerto Rico, or Venezuela.

Tamara Díaz, a young woman from Santiago married to Dr. Carlos García, Manolo's cousin, was the person with whom Minerva bonded the most when she moved to this new town.

In a letter that I still keep, Tamara tells me how happy Minerva was and how deeply in love. She describes her arrival in Montecristi with her husband and how she immediately began to plant a beautiful garden for her house.

Montecristi is one of the Dominican Republic's oldest towns. It experienced a significant economic boom in the late nineteenth century. Many wealthy families built beautiful homes there, some brought over from France piece by piece and assembled there. When the economy fell, those same homes were abandoned by their owners. One of these was the home of Doña Emilia Jiménez, practically sold for pennies by one of her grandsons.

Minerva bought ceramic tiles from the home of Doña Emilia, sold in the streets by young peddlers, to use in her garden. Even today there are people in Montecristi who remember the impact and the curiosity that surrounded her garden in a city that, by its nature, is arid and had no gardening tradition.

Regarding her friend and neighbor Tamara, there is an incident that led to some confusion. The book on the Mirabal sisters written by Chino Ferreras states that Minerva was suffering from tuberculosis. The truth is that although Minerva dearly loved her friend Tamara, she did not trust her enough to tell her the real reason for her frequent trips because Tamara had relatives who were high-ranking military officers. In order to hide her political activities from Tamara, Minerva told her that she was traveling to see Dr. Concepción for treatment for "a lung problem." Emma Tavárez writes about this period in the article that I previously quoted:

---

67 Revision of translation in Tavárez Mirabal, *Letters*, 72.

After her wedding trip, Manolo and Minerva temporarily lived in a room above my father's office, annexed to our home in Montecristi. Minerva, seated on her bed in the loft and already well along in her pregnancy with her first child, Minou, asked me to read aloud several chapters from her law books, which at the time seemed to me quite dense and unintelligible. She would soon take the final exams of her last year in law school.

With the birth of Minou (her name was in honor of Minou Drouet, a precocious, young French poet), Manolo and Minerva centered their dreams on that small child [. . .]

Later on, the birth of their second child, Manolito, balanced out the love they had initially concentrated on their cherished Minou. The birth of the much-awaited male heir filled both homes with sheer happiness.

After he was born, the loft became too small for them. Manolo and Minerva moved a few blocks away. Their new home was an expression of their characters and particular tastes. In their living room they had rattan furniture and area rugs made from agave plants. They also adorned their home with decorative pieces in unusual shapes and colors, books, paintings done by Minerva, and ornamental plants. Their backyard garden, which Minerva carefully tended, gave the home a special charm [. . .]

Minou's first birthday was coming up, and Minerva was very busy organizing the birthday celebration. She was excited, running around, helping my mother and sisters prepare the cake, making small baskets, bunnies, and party hats. That August afternoon, Minou ran all around the house amidst the jubilant whistle-blowing and the antics of her little friends. Manolo and Minerva really enjoyed seeing their first-born so happy.

One time, when Patria and María Teresa were visiting them, we went to spend the afternoon at Parolí in the foothills of Montecristi's El Morro, a seaside cliff. I remember climbing up some really high hills and then rolling down the slippery slopes. Minerva said that she was not staying behind, and holding on to one another, we managed to reach the top of the hill.[68]

---

68   Emma Tavárez Justo, in the magazine ¡Ahora!, no. 578, December 9, 1974. Author's note.

Of course, not everything was rosy between Minerva and Manolo. Perhaps this is the moment to mention a small situation they experienced during their marriage. Minerva had already given birth to Minou and was pregnant again. She made all kinds of sacrifices to travel to the capital to finish her studies. That's when it happened, something she never expected or imagined. During the weeks that she spent in Conuco to give birth, Manolo had a small affair with a young woman who worked at the courthouse in Montecristi, where he was working as an attorney.

When Minerva found out, she was furious. She and my mother were very jealous individuals, even though they disguised it. Minerva wrote to Manolo, chided him, and told him that she was getting a divorce. She was terribly upset. I tried to calm her down: "Minerva, you're pregnant. Sometimes this is how men behave." She did not accept nor tolerate this behavior. As she saw it, both members in a relationship are obliged to be faithful, not only the women, and she trusted that her husband would never look at another woman. That was what she thought a marriage should be.

Stubborn and obstinate, her behavior during this time led to complications, and she suffered a hemorrhage during the delivery. She had to stay in Conuco a few more days to recover.

For Manolo, his marriage to Minerva was never in question. But she was very hurt, like any other woman would be. She felt betrayed. Even though she was deeply hurt, with time I saw that the crisis had been resolved.

Interestingly enough, in a letter written by Minerva to Manolo before they were married, she said to him, "I dreamed that you had fallen in love with someone else and that we had broken up . . . When I told my mother yesterday that I was determined to break up with you, she had to remind me that it was just a dream."

Minerva would say to me, "You have no personality. You're just like Aunt Rosa! The reason you've ended up such a sucker is because you're such a good person." She never said that to me in front of anyone else, nor in a bad way, but when we were alone, she scolded me: "You tolerate too much." When I was dating Jaimito I wanted to visit Santiago to see Eva Garza, a popular singer back then. But Jaimito was not interested in going because he had already seen her. Minerva was so ticked off! She was much more upset than I was: "In other words, just because he went and saw her, he doesn't want you to go? He's so selfish!"

Once, I gave Minou a piglet that Uncle Tilo had been raising for her. He was really cute, but as soon as he fattened up, Mamá sold it for some sixty pesos. On one of Minerva's trips to Santiago, Mamá gave her the money she had received when she sold the piglet. "Take it so you can buy something for Minou." When she returned, we asked her what she had bought her. "I bought her books," she calmly answered. Mamá complained, but Minerva argued that there's no better legacy than a book. Mamá tried to defend her point of view to no avail and criticized Minerva's "addiction" to poetry books, novels, essays, and art. She explained that she was only trying to protect Minou's interests, as she was still very little.

I believe that during this period Minerva had already adopted the pseudonym "Butterfly." That's how her comrades referred to her. Since she was one of the best known and the most persecuted, no one wanted to say "Minerva is coming to a meeting" because it was dangerous. That's why they preferred calling her "Butterfly."

That pseudonym inspired our national poet, Pedro Mir, to name the long poem he wrote in honor of my sisters "Amén de Mariposas." Years later, Julia Alvarez would also use the name in the title of her novel *In the Time of the Butterflies*.

Falling out of grace means that everything you do is bad. We had very few friends left. Little by little most turned their backs on us. Those who used to come to the store to buy their goods also stayed away. That is why, beginning with my father's first arrest in 1950, the store began a downward spiral. They treated us as if we were lepers, so we had to close.

However, there were those who were the exception when it came to the way they treated us. Dr. Angel Concepción, for example, never stopped visiting us. Opposition to Trujillo was beginning to grow. I remember the priest from Tenares, Ercilio Moya, a very brave antitrujillista who was left partially paralyzed when he was a child and who walked with a limp. He was one of the friends that were never scared away.

No matter what, we still had friends, and our relatives never abandoned us. My father-in-law Jaime Fernández, a government official, remained close. Mr. Juan Rojas, a very honest and good-looking man, remained a good friend of the family even when he was a senator. Many blamed him for inviting us to the famous ball in San Cristóbal.

A Period of Very Hard Work

I became pregnant shortly after we moved from San Francisco de Macorís to Salcedo in 1956. I couldn't believe it, much less tell anyone. I'll never forget the day I ran into Clara, my sister-in-law, who was also pregnant. She was eating the meat of a coconut and I had a terrible craving to eat from that particular one. Sadly, no one offered it to me. During my pregnancy I craved coconut all the time, but none satisfied my craving. Jaime David was born with a birthmark that, if it's true what they say about cravings, came from my insatiable desire to eat coconut.

One Sunday afternoon I began to feel ill. Jaimito took me to Macorís and I was in labor until 9:00 the next morning. Jaime David was a big and beautiful baby, but I was heartbroken and couldn't stop crying when he was born because I was hoping for a baby girl that I was going to name Jacqueline.

I remember Jimmy watching me when I was sewing baby clothes, and I would ask him: "Who is this for?" and my son would answer: "For Quelín," that is, Jacqueline. I embroidered little garments and told Jaime Enrique and Jimmy that they were for their little sister Jacqueline.

I asked María Teresa to be his godmother and sometime later, when she had her little girl, she told me: "Dedé, since you're not going to have any more children, you are going to be my daughter's godmother and I am going to name her Jacqueline." Life is so strange! How could my sister have imagined that I would be the one who would end up raising her daughter Jacqueline?

I had my three sons by then. Jaimito and I were still very close. We were not in the best financial situation, but we were full of energy and drive to move forward with hard work. To help me write my memoir, I asked him to write his account of those days as he experienced them:

> Things had gone very, very badly on my rice plantation; I had sold my cows one by one, and I was left with only twelve and one bull, whose name was Gusará, and every time things began to get tight financially, I would tell him: 'You're in trouble, Gusará' because if the situation got any worse, I would have to sell him. I lost almost everything I had. Then Dedé and I took refuge at a small farm that we had bought in El Indio, just past El Abanico, some twenty-seven kilometers from Nagua. It was a pretty farm, with a small thatch-roof house with dirt floors. Once we covered the floor with sand, it looked very pretty.
>
> In order to purchase the property in El Indio, I sold a small farm that Don Enrique had bought for Dedé with her savings. The lot was

approximately ninety-eight *tareas*,[69] but the terrain was very rugged. I took advantage that the price of cacao was high and said, 'I'm selling it!' And I sold it for five thousand pesos.

That was truly incredible, and with that money we bought six hundred and fifty tareas in El Indio. It brings back bad memories of the comment someone made in front of Doña Chea: "He's already beginning to sell Dedé's properties." But I got lucky. There were some small hills on the property that I fixed up nicely and where I planted several palm trees. I worked the land with oxen my father had lent me, and I planted peanuts, corn, grass . . .

We were going through really bad times. We began working in El Indio in 1957. We took Jaime David with us. He was about one year old. We left Jaime Enrique with my mother and father so he could go to school in Salcedo. Jimmy stayed with Doña Chea, who enrolled him in a school in Tenares. They were happy to stay because Doña Chea spoiled Jimmy. For my mother and father, Jaime Enrique was the love of their life because he was my son, the oldest in our family, and Dedé's, who my father and mother loved even more than their own daughters. Two of my friends owned buses called La Altagracita and La Richi that traveled daily between Salcedo and Nagua. They had been manufactured in Salcedo, where they used to make the best buses. We used to milk the cows and send twenty-five bottles of milk to Nagua. All the money that came in went to pay off our debts, especially in the grocery store; that debt tortured us because we were strangers in that community.

Little by little, I managed to fix up the small farm beautifully. I cut down a bunch of guava trees and planted plantains. "Don't plant plantains, they don't grow here!" and I would say: "Let me plant them, will you let me plant them?" "Go ahead, the land is yours," they would answer, and I would say: "Well, then!" I planted some twenty tareas of plantains. Dedé was thrilled every time people would come up to the farm on horseback. The conversation would go like this:

"Do you sell plantains here?"

"Yes."

"How much for a load?" (A load consisted of two hundred plantains).

---

[69] Land measurement equivalent to 628.86 square meters.

"Three pesos."

When we sold a load of plantains, Dedé would shout: "Oh! The spirits! It's the spirits!"[70] Sometimes they would come and buy a bottle of milk or half a bottle, worth about five cents. We would buy three cents worth of sugar at the grocery store since we hadn't drunk our coffee for lack of sugar.

Dedé didn't want Doña Chea to find out that her daughter was going through such difficult times. We didn't want anyone feeling sorry for us. We spent almost two years like that. We visited Salcedo every fifteen days, more or less.

Dedé embroiders beautifully. In El Indio she embroidered sets of bedlinens with her small sewing machine and found a client that paid her three pesos for a set of embroidered sheets. Dedé would finish two or three sets per day. She spent the day embroidering. This was excellent income for us.

We were also lucky to have a lot of chickens that laid eggs, and we had milk and other supplies. We never lacked food.

After Doña Chea moved to Conuco, they closed her house in Ojo de Agua. I was dying to get out of El Indio. Financially I was much better off, and we were bored on the farm. So we decided to move to the house in Ojo de Agua, even though Pedrito, Patria's husband, did not want us to move in. I came in second or third place after Pedrito because for Doña Chea, everything had to be done according to what Pedrito said. That's the way it was. I don't know what Pedrito's problem with me was, but he was always getting in the way of things.

In spite of the difficult economic situation Jaimito describes, I was very happy in El Indio. That's where I think Jaime David, who was little back then, learned to love the land and animals. I enjoyed listening to him name the cows and the bulls, stumbling through his first words.

I have always worked, and even though I enjoyed embroidering the sheet sets, which helped me bring in extra income, I wanted to return to Salcedo because I wanted to be with my three sons.

In 1954, Mamá suggested that we build a house in Conuco and we immediately began the construction process. She made her decision based on the fact that Conuco was easily reached. The main highway passed by the

---

70 A common expression in the countryside when something unexpected or inexplicable happens.

front of the lot, and it was close to Uncle Tilo. Her sisters Aunt Carmela, Aunt Lalía, and Aunt Toña also lived nearby, and she felt much safer there.

I can still see Minerva and me on moving day in 1956, seated on the porch: she was pregnant with Minou, and I was expecting Jaime David. They were born only a month and a half apart. The large garden that surrounds the home in Conuco was created by Mamá and Minerva, who was an avid gardener.

Minerva not only designed the garden in Conuco, but practically the entire house. It was all her idea. I remember she once had a huge fight with the workers because they placed a column backward. Because she was such a perfectionist, and she liked things done correctly, she ordered they tear down the column. But Mamá intervened and said, "Impossible!"

In 1959, I moved with my family to our home in Ojo de Agua. Although the house had deteriorated because it had been closed for three years, the move brought me closer to my mother. The houses were approximately three kilometers apart.

María Teresa Goes to the University and Marries Leandro

María Teresa completed high school at the Sacred Heart School in Santiago. Mamá had transferred her from the Immaculate Conception School in La Vega because her asthma had gotten so much worse. In 1954, she registered at the university and moved in with Minerva.

Politically, we were considered enemies of the regime. There is nothing worse than to feel that you are being spied on, persecuted. You get to the point psychologically that when you spot a little bird, you think it is a serpent. I do not wish that fear, that anguish, on my worst enemy.

We were specifically singled out. We confirmed this when María Teresa participated in the Miss University beauty pageant. On June 1, 1956, the following article appeared in *El Caribe*:

> The slim and attractive candidate loves her profession and enjoys the poetry of Rubén Darío, Fabio Fiallo, and Franklin Mieses Burgos. She has a light-brown complexion and says she enjoys decorating. María Teresa likes the paintings of José Fulop and Leonardo da Vinci, and she enjoys theatre. Her favorite works include Shakespeare's *Hamlet* and *La vida es sueño*, by Calderón de la Barca, which she saw here in a production presented by the Compañía Lope de Vega. María Teresa says that she would like to travel abroad and that once she completes

her studies, she hopes to take special courses in the United States. She loves her home region of the Cibao.

But Magda Mejía Ricart was chosen to be Miss University. We were informed that María Teresa had been disqualified because she was against Trujillo. This sort of nonsense shows what this period was like.

That feeling of being constantly watched led us all to do the most absurd things. I remember that once, in 1954, they organized a teachers' parade along George Washington Avenue, one of the many parades organized to honor Trujillo. Patria and I decided to accept the invitation in order to keep up appearances. But when we got to the capital, Minerva said, "Forget about it. Don't go to the parade. Let's go to Casa Virginia so I can buy some clothes. Who's going to know that you didn't go to the parade?" We readily accepted and went to Casa Virginia. It's a good thing we listened to Minerva because there was a huge rain storm and the parade turned out to be a total disaster.

For the parade, the teachers had spent one or two paychecks to have special uniforms made of silk-wool cloth, which was very popular back then. The only problem was that when it got wet, it shrunk. Their enormous bonnets flopped under the rain. The poor women's dresses shrunk up to midthigh. We got out of that one and laughed about it afterward.

María Teresa's world in the capital—her friends and activities—were those of any young woman full of life and dreams. In the letters she sent to her boyfriend Leandro Guzmán between 1955 and 1956, she told him all about her outings and the games she played with her friends at the university and at the dorm. "Residencia Universitaria, Avenida Independencia 201, Ciudad Trujillo" was the return address on her envelopes. In her letters she explained to Leandro how she enjoyed going to the movies, her studies, her love, her plans, and her meetings with friends.

February 21, 1955

Yesterday afternoon I went to a meeting sponsored by a committee that is organizing a tribute to Angelita [Trujillo],[71] and I was selected to play an Indian girl in a special comedy. They are going to wear special skin-colored garments under the costumes, but I don't want to participate because we are still in mourning.

Regarding my studies, yesterday I began to study hard [. . .]. On Saturday afternoon I went to visit Maruja, but she wasn't there so

---

71 The dictator's daughter.

I went to run some errands, and on Sunday morning I went to the movies, which I regretted because the movie was so bad; in the afternoon I went to the parade and marched with C.E., and later I stayed on at the Fair with Perla and Manolín and we had dinner at El Vesuvio. Later on we went to the Spanish Pavilion, which by the way is very lovely and had many beautiful items on sale. At this very moment we are engaged in a conversation.

March 3, 1955

[. . .] Manolo and Minerva picked me up so I could go and have lunch with them. On our way we were talking about a certain girl and Minerva was telling Manolo who the person was and I said: "But Leandro knows her!" You understand, right? I said your name instead of his. Minerva laughed and said: "Of course, it's because you talk [to Leandro] every day!" And I explained that I was talking about you when they came to pick me up [. . .]

Yesterday [. . .] afternoon I went shopping with Angela, Manolo's sister, and this morning I went to the university to practice levelling.

February 29, 1956

This morning I went out with Minerva Mues to help her run some errands . . . Later on I went to see some things that I plan to buy with the money you are going to send. I'm so excited about this because you can't imagine how much a young woman enjoys setting up her future home.

March 21, 1956

Yesterday morning Minerva came to pick me up to go out with her . . . to buy things for the baby. I was so jealous! I bought some beautiful sheets for the baby. Right now I'm singing. If you could only hear me! But the girls say I am doing much better.

March 7, 1956

I planned to go home on Saturday, but on Friday I have to go take some measurements even though it is a holiday. The boys want to finish everything before Easter Week, and I was planning on telling you that perhaps it's better if you come next weekend. Monday is St. Joseph's Day, and it will be a three-day weekend. As I said, we have a pretty good and inexpensive itinerary all set up. I'll give you a brief summary: Saturday afternoon to the movies, Sunday, to the Fair (we'll bring sandwiches, etc.), and on Monday morning to a matinee and in the afternoon to the zoo. I think it's great, don't you?

April 7, 1956

I wanted to let you know that Josefina is no longer going to Puerto Rico because Father Quevedo, where she was going to stay, told her that it is better that she go in July and now I'm thinking about getting my documents ready so I can go with her and with Rosita. The money that I had given her I now plan to use to purchase some things for our future home. I was dying to begin preparations, but I was waiting for you to give me a little push because I couldn't do it on my own. Now I plan to get ready to go shopping and later to the movies with Luly and Linda.

April 8, 1956

Yesterday I went to the movies with Linda and Luly to see *All That Heaven Allows* with Rock Hudson and Janet Whitman,[72] which I truly enjoyed.

(No date)

I'm glad you enjoyed last weekend, as long as you always think of me, I don't mind if you have fun.

April 23, 1956

I had a very nice time at home even though my time there was so short, because on Saturday I spent the entire day at Dedé's and I got home at night, and the next day we left very early to visit Pedrito's farm in Güiza. We spent the day there and returned at seven that night. I picked up all my things and slept over at Dedé's and returned in the morning. I don't think Mamá liked the idea that I flew back to the capital.[73]

May 3, 1956

I've wanted to write to you since yesterday, but I decided to leave it for today because that way I had more things to tell you. The first thing is that I miss you terribly. Yesterday, after I saw that the airplane

---

72 María Teresa's error. The leading actress was Jane Wyman.
73 This aircraft traveled between the capital city and certain towns, such as Montecristi. Minerva frequently took the flight to which María Teresa refers in this letter. Author's note.

was well on its way, I went to El Conde Street with Linda to buy the material for your shirt. I found a similar one for sale at González Ramos, except that rather than the material being white it is pale blue, which I really didn't like that much. I finally ended up liking the one with fine blue stripes, which is the one I'm sending to you.

I was walking around as if I were from another world (a true Mirabal, no doubt). I didn't even understand what people were saying to me because I was thinking of the wonderful moments we had shared the day before.

[...]

... last night we celebrated Perla's birthday with a cocktail and lots of other stuff, and I made the girls believe that I was drunk and told them that I was a cat and I started walking around on all fours. They laughed so hard that the nuns woke up and, what a riot. The nuns couldn't stop laughing either.

May 4, 1956

This morning I went shopping with Minerva, who is leaving tomorrow to spend a week in Montecristi.

[...]

Don't forget to pray the rosary every day. It's only 15 minutes and it has many benefits.

May 5, 1956

Yesterday afternoon I went to the Olympia movie theater and saw *High Society* with Grace Kelly, very nice, and in the afternoon, I went with Perla and Manolín to see *Aida*, which I also enjoyed. This morning I went to study with Martha.

Leandro graduated as a civil engineer in 1954, and he immediately began to work as a municipal official in San Francisco de Macorís, his hometown. He was later transferred to Santiago as head of the Public Works Office in the Cibao region. Later on, he decided to emigrate to the United States to obtain a degree in Mine Engineering. When telling about this period in his book *1J4: De espigas y de fuegos*, Leandro recalls that once all the necessary documents were ready and he managed to put some money together (four thousand dollars), he talked to María Teresa about his plans. She insisted on going with him, and he told her that since the money he had was not enough to cover the trip for both, they could use some of the savings he had from his inheritance. Once they agreed, Leandro said:

We began to think, talk, and to come up with ideas of what we were going to do while we waited for the passport to be issued. Then one day we received a resounding and arrogant response: we could not travel to the United States because the Mirabal Reyes family was openly anti-Trujillo, especially because of her sister Minerva's actions and situation.

María Teresa and Leandro were married in a civil ceremony on February 14, 1958, and had a simple church wedding two and a half months later, on May 3. Family and a few friends were in attendance. They moved to Santiago.

Manolo and Leandro had met in 1949 at a meeting of the Dominican Democratic Youth and were friends. This was a main reason why the two couples—Manolo and Minerva and Leandro and María Teresa—developed such a strong bond, not only because of familial ties, but also because of their political activism.

The End of the Fifties

Trujillo never stopped monitoring Minerva, following her steps to the point that when she graduated from law school in 1957, even though she had excellent grades, the Law School of the University of Santo Domingo denied her all her academic recognitions. She was also denied the right to practice law. Today, the university's Law School is named Minerva Mirabal in her honor, and three decades later, in an act of justice, the Faculty Council decided to issue the law degree that she truly deserved for her outstanding grades: Doctor of Law, Summa Cum Laude.

From a very young age Mamá was known within the family for having premonitions. Papá always said so: "Chea can see things before they happen. When she has a sense about something." Irenita, our housemaid, would also say, "That woman screamed in her mother's womb," meaning that when my mother predicted something, you could bet it was going to happen. That's why it was not surprising that she was so frightened by the events that were happening around her. She talked about some French nationals that owned a farm in Rincón, in La Vega Province, who were murdered. The same happened to a gentleman whose last name was Pimentel who also lived around there. They said that Virgilio Trujillo had orchestrated the murders.

The French nationals used to visit the Hotel Jaragua in the capital to play at the casino. One night their bodies were discovered alongside a cliff, near the town of Rincón. Mamá reminded my sister about the incident: "Minerva, be careful. They are going to throw you off a cliff with the sugar trucks. They will do to you what they did to the French couple and to Donato Bencosme." He was the son of Cipriano Bencosme, from Moca. Donato was an archenemy of Trujillo. After killing Cipriano, Trujillo named Donato governor of Moca. What a farce! Later on, they arrested him when he was returning from Puerto Plata. They picked him up at the highway checkpoint in La Cumbre, killed him, and threw him off a cliff. It was the same cliff from which, years later, they would hurl the jeep containing the girls' bodies and that of Rufino de la Cruz, the friend who drove them that day.

7

The Early 1960s, the 14th of June Revolutionary Movement, Repression Continues to Grow

The most repressive years of the Trujillo dictatorship were from 1959 to 1961. During those two years the resistance movement intensified and became much more diverse, with the participation of the Catholic Church and an important sector of the country's youth. The group called Clergy-Cultural Action was founded in the town of Tenares, in the country's central region, headed by Father Daniel Cruz Inoa from the Archdiocese of Santiago; the 14th of June Revolutionary Movement was conceived; and in Santiago, a group of young individuals founded the underground movement known as Los Panfleteros. The group of university students used fecal matter to write on city walls: "Trujillo is a Piece of Shit." In the meantime, antitrujillistas in exile intensified their efforts in several countries.

Those years were full of terror and carnage, treason, betrayals, and overall destruction. But it was also a time when an entire generation of young people was more heroic than ever. My sisters were part of that youth movement that sacrificed itself so Dominicans could overthrow the dictatorship that had oppressed them for so many years.

Los Panfleteros suffered the most at the hands of the dictatorship, and most of its members were exterminated. The 14th of June Movement, which grew surprisingly fast, was severely attacked by the repressive forces and was nearly destroyed. More than four hundred of its members were arrested and tortured.

The history of this period is long and complex. We know a lot about it, and much has been written. But a lot has yet to be revealed. I will summarize some of the events that closely touched our family, shattering life as we knew it.

There are coincidences that can change history. That's what happened on January 6, 1959, in the home of Josefina Ricart and Guido (Yuyo) D'Alessandro, Manolo's nephew. The encounter began as a social event to celebrate the new year. Among the guests were Minerva, Manolo, Leandro, and Juan Bancalari, Yuyo's Italian business partner or employee at the Distribuidora Olivetti, a company owned by the D'Alessandro family. The triumph of the Cuban Revolution had taken place only a few days earlier.

Some of the guests have related that it was Minerva who said: "Why can't we form a similar movement in our country, if so many people here have been mistreated and are opposed to Trujillo? Why can they do it in other countries, but we can't? Let's make a commitment so that when we leave here, each one of us can start making contacts to build a movement."

Josefina Ricart, who was also Ramfis Trujillo's sister-in-law, and who was very much aware of the serious consequences suffered by all who conspired against the regime, became frightened and warned them "not to play with fire" because this proposal could turn out to be very dangerous. That event was the embryo of what later became the 14th of June Revolutionary Movement. The idea, according to witnesses, came from Minerva.

The landing and annihilation of the 1959 expeditionaries deeply upset Minerva and Manolo, as well as all the young people who aspired to freedom. In the article I quoted previously, Emma describes the environment that prevailed at Minerva and Manolo's home in Montecristi:

> Those days in 1959 were full of rage and powerlessness. News spread quickly that a group of anti-Trujillo expeditionaries had landed in Estero Hondo [on the north coast], Constanza [in the central mountain range], and Maimón [in the central region]. Near the town of Estero Hondo, the townspeople could hear the far-away sounds of explosions.
>
> At the dining room table in the home of my sister Angela and her husband Jaime Ricardo, Manolo and Minerva located on a map some of the geographic locations closest to where the June expeditionaries had landed. They were trying to organize ways to contact them.
>
> Minerva was making plans in the privacy of her bedroom. I remember watching her standing before the mirror dressed as a man, wearing Manolo's shirt and khakis. She cut her hair with a pair of scissors and tried to look as manly as possible by shadowing in a moustache with an eyebrow pencil. With a worried look, she turned around and asked me, "Do you think they'll recognize me?" She was aware of the possibility that the government troops might use her to reach the combatants, and this is how she was going to slip past them.

We were overcome when we heard the official radio station announce the names of the dead expeditionaries, aghast at the announcer's cynicism when he said that the troops were making the expeditionaries' brains "fly like butterflies." A few days later all our hopes collapsed.[74]

Founding of the 14th of June Movement

On January 9, 1960—one year and a few days after the meeting in Yuyo's house—the first meeting of what would be called the 14th of June Revolutionary Movement took place at Patria and Pedrito's house. People from various regions of the country attended the meeting. They came from San Pedro de Macorís, San Juan de la Maguana, San Francisco, Moca, Montecristi, Santiago . . . Aside from Manolo and Leandro, participants also included Julio Escoto, Efraín Dotel, Carlos (Cayeyo) Grisanty, Rafael (Pipe) Faxas, Abelito Fernández, Luis Gómez, and Niño Alvarez. Dulce Tejada and Minerva were the only women who participated in the meeting. They decided to hold the meeting in Conuco rather than in Ojo de Agua because the former was a much more secluded location.

That night, some stayed over at Patria's and slept in her daughter Noris's bedroom. Others traveled to Macorís and Santiago. The rest stayed at my mother's house. Being a very distrustful woman—especially when dealing with men—she locked their bedroom door from the outside. Later we would laugh about the things that occurred to my mother because, in the middle of the night, the men had to knock on the door to be let out to relieve themselves since she had locked them in!

People were becoming increasingly aware of the need to confront Trujillo. How could we keep putting up with the dictatorship? People like Patria, like me, like Juan Peña, a local farmer who suffered tremendously at the hands of the dictatorship, began to see the need to fight to end this insufferable situation.

The 14th of June Movement received its official name on January 10, 1960, in Mao, in the northwest region, during the second and decisive meeting that took place at the farm of Charlie Bogaert. In the year since its inception in 1959, the clandestine movement had branched out throughout the

---

74 Emma Tavárez Justo, as written in ¡*Ahora!* magazine, no. 578, December 9, 1974. Author's note. Title and page numbers not provided.

country, and all kinds of people had joined it, including family members of solid Trujillo supporters.

Only two women—Minerva and Dulce Tejada—participated in the January 10 meeting, which was the first formal meeting with an actual agenda and with the goal of establishing a central executive committee to lead the movement.

At that meeting they drafted the movement's statutes and objectives, as well as the National Liberation Movement program. Manolo was elected president, Pipe Faxas secretary general, and Leandro treasurer.

The original copies of the detailed minutes, drafted by María Teresa, are on exhibit at the Casa Museo Hermanas Mirabal. Some of the tenets and goals of the program were to remove the dictator, celebrate free elections every four years, carry out agrarian reform, and have a Constituent Assembly approve a new constitution. They also decided to gather weapons to combat the dictatorship.

Fernando Cueto shared that when Germán Silverio returned from Mao after having represented Puerto Plata at the meeting, Fernando and Juan Carlos Morales went to see him to find out more about what they had discussed. Fernando had sent a proposal suggesting that the movement be named General Luperón. The following is a detailed account of his conversation with Germán Silverio following the January 10 meeting in Mao:

> Germán Silverio told us that "that woman"—there was a baseball team here known as "Those Men"—had rejected my motion and proposed the name 14th of June. I said, well, that's fine. The impression we got of Minerva was that she was an extremely determined woman, much more determined than anyone else in regards to certain things that I don't even dare mention. We told Manolo that we needed weapons, because on one occasion Guancho Escaño and Melecia Victoria, who had tried to organize an attack on a specific target, were almost apprehended by some henchmen that suddenly appeared. They were able to save themselves because Guancho hugged Melecia and started kissing her in order to go unnoticed. They told me, "We're alive because of pure luck. We won't be able to do anything if we don't have weapons. You tell Manolo that we can't go on like this." So I sent a message to Manolo, through Germán: "Tell him that if there are no weapons, there is no sabotage. That they have to at least give us some revolvers because we aren't going to just let them kill us." Germán received an answer from Minerva, who told him that there were guns

out in the street and that we should go and find them. The sabotage consisted of burning sugarcane fields and throwing staples along the highway. We burned the Social Security building.

Our family was unfamiliar with this particular aspect of Minerva's personality. According to Fernando Cueto, she was like that, always achieving what she set her mind to. I still tremble when I think that my sister, after getting out of jail in August 1960, traveled to Montecristi to pick up some of her belongings and return to Salcedo. During that long trajectory she daringly traveled with a revolver hidden between her legs. She had stashed the weapon in Montecristi, and it was never detected during the raids.

Very little has been said regarding one particular aspect of her personality: that she inspired trust and security in others. For example, when she went to speak with Miguel Lama in Santiago to try to bring him into the movement, he knew that she was not setting him up and that he would not be reported. If it interested him, he would agree to be part of the movement; if he were to refuse, he would not feel threatened. Minerva contacted and managed to convince people. San Francisco de Macorís was one of the towns where she focused her efforts and had tremendous influence on friends and acquaintances. That's where Dulce Tejada, Abelito Fernández, and a group of truly valuable and respected citizens lived. She succeeded in recruiting them.

Now, almost half a century later and with the experience brought by the passing years, I can appreciate how advanced Minerva was for her generation. She impressed everyone with her remarkable ability and vision. For example, she was already talking about women's emancipation when it was not yet on anyone's agenda. Who at that time was thinking about these issues? Minerva was adamant that women had to study, to better themselves, and to earn their proper place in society. Women couldn't just limit themselves to having babies and taking care of the household.

She had won Pedrito over to her cause, so much so that, in addition to participating in the movement, he offered his home to hold meetings and stash away guns. The same with Patria. Minerva was very effective when it came to winning people over. However, my husband Jaimito would say, "Look, Manolo, when the guns get here, you let me know. As long as there are no guns, don't count on me. Where do you think we're going without guns?" The truth is the weapons never arrived.

"The guns" were stashed away in a warehouse owned by Pedrito, which was located near Patria's home. And what were these weapons? Firecrackers, shell casings, and small packets of gunpowder to make homemade bombs. That was all.

Leandro had taught at the La Salle School in Santo Domingo, making it very easy for him to contact and recruit former students from rich families. He won them over, brought them in, and organized them. In the movement, you became involved and participated through word of mouth. For security reasons, all information was handled personally by each member. Inspired by the Dominican independence movement *La Trinitaria*,[75] Manolo and Minerva recommended that the organization be structured in cells consisting of only three members. There were a lot of young people involved in the movement. Patria and Pedrito's oldest son, Nelson, who at the time had not reached his eighteenth birthday, was one of them.

Fafa Taveras,[76] a young man at the time, started working with a group of young men from the Church, primarily former seminarians. Father Disla, who lived nearby, was one of the leaders of this particular group.

The first person arrested was Marcos Pérez Collado, recruited while working in Manzanillo. He made a comment in front of a young man, I believe a relative of his, who snitched on him. He was later arrested. Cayeyo Grisanti was also arrested immediately after that.

During the last days of January, due to the problems and harassment against their household, Patria decided to move to our mother's home and asked me to go to her house to pick up some things. I went with Jaime David, who was about four years old then, but who remembers this episode really well because we went to pick up Raúl and Noris's toys.

Trujillo's henchmen raided and occupied Pedrito and Patria's home, as well as a farm in Güiza that my mother owned but that was in their names. The henchmen auctioned off their furniture and other belongings and distributed the cattle among themselves. Alicinio Peña Rivera, head of the Military Intelligence Service in Santiago, took over the house and set up a Military Intelligence Service office there, headed by the calié Silvio García.

Manolo was arrested on January 13 in Montecristi, three days after the meeting in Mao. Caonabo Almonte, also known as Quillona, was a nephew of Isabel Mayer, the well-known Trujillo supporter and Manolo's father's

---

75 La Trinitaria, founded in 1838, was the movement that spearheaded the independence of the Dominican Republic.
76 Rafael Francisco Taveras Rosario (Fafa Taveras) (b. 1938 in Salcedo) was a friend of the Mirabals. He would later become an important leader in the 1965 Revolution. To date, he is the only member of the 14th of June Movement who is still alive, and is an active member of the current ruling Partido Revolucionario Moderno (PRM) party.

first wife. Quillona had sent for Manolo with the excuse that he wanted to see him. In response to his request, Manolo went to the police station in his light green Buick, and Quillona arrested him right then and there.

Minerva sent her maid Francisca all the way from Montecristi to Salcedo to tell us not to call her and that we had to cut off all contact. She and Manolo had planned to escape to Haiti in the event that they were discovered. They had saved some dollars just in case, which Minerva sent to us with Francisca. There began a series of arrests. Leandro was jailed on January 19. That same day they arrested Sina Cabral and Rubén Díaz Moreno.

Patria, who was very much involved, went to the home of some relatives to pick up Nelson, who had fled from the student dorm at the Colegio Calasanz[77] in Santo Domingo. Nelson lived at the dorm because he was studying engineering at the university. While the arrests continued, Pedro hid at my mother's house. They arrested Renato González, Pedro Ramón, and Francisco Aníbal González, whose families were related to Pedro and who lived near him and Patria.

After they arrested Leandro on January 19, María Teresa, who a few months before had moved to the capital, also returned to Mamá's new home in Conuco. On the evening of the 20th, they came to arrest her. Mamá insisted on accompanying her, but when they reached the fortress in Salcedo, the military officer on duty received orders by radio to return them to their home due to Mamá's presence.

On the morning of the 21st, when I went to find out what had happened, María Teresa was the one who told me everything. I spent the day with her and Patria. After I returned to my home that afternoon, the military officers came back to arrest María Teresa once again. Mamá wrapped her in a blanket because she was running a fever. What did they do then? They left the car outside. They presented themselves, and when Mamá told them, "I'm going with her," this time they were prepared. They walked back to the car, using a flashlight to guide their way to the road. The car was parked to the right. They ordered María Teresa to get into the car, while the other military officer ordered Mamá "to turn around and get in on the other side." No sooner did she take a few steps, the car sped off, taking María Teresa with

---

77 The complete name of the institution was Colegio Mayor Universitario San José de Calasanz. At the time it provided housing for university students. It was situated on what is now the site of the Autonomous University of Santo Domingo (UASD) Law School that, in the mid-1980s, was named in honor of Minerva Mirabal. Author's note.

them. It still pains me to remember how Mamá suffered, how desperate she was even days after that.

That very evening, we moved quickly to determine their whereabouts. We hired a car and a driver so we could leave for the capital at the crack of dawn the very next day.

Jaimito stayed behind with Nelson and Pedrito, who were hiding in the cacao farm behind the house in Conuco. Mamá and I futilely knocked on various doors, asking for help. Virgilio Trujillo was not in. We called on Mario Abreu Penzo, secretary of the interior and police and owner of various farms in San Francisco de Macorís. We knew him, even though he was not a close friend. He said that when it came to those kinds of problems, no one could get involved, and that he could do nothing. No one wanted to intervene to help us. Finally, we were received by Romeo (Pipí) Trujillo, the dictator's brother, who told us, "Doña Chea, don't worry. This is a mistake. The problem is not with María Teresa, but with Minerva."

When we returned to Salcedo, Mamá left in the car for Conuco, and I stayed behind trying to contact Montecristi by telephone to find out about Minerva. There was only one public telephone in town. I finally reached Jaime Ricardo Socías, Manolo's brother-in-law, who also belonged to the movement. When I asked him about Minerva, all I heard was, "They arrested her just now."

When I arrived at my in-laws' house, Jaimito was waiting for me: "Dedé, run! You can't imagine what just happened at your house! The caliés barged into Doña Chea's home like wild animals looking for Pedrito. They started firing their weapons into the air. The kids are terrified. Patria is screaming. It's total chaos." To this day I tremble when I remember those moments. We left for my mother's house, and Patria said to Jaimito, "Compadre, let's go to my house to see what's going on." They left for Patria's, while I stayed with Mamá and my sisters' children. A while later I saw a couple of military officers approaching the house, and I thought they were coming to kill us. "Antonia, they're coming back! Throw the saints to the floor!" I screamed.

It's astounding that in those horrible moments, I, who have never been superstitious, remembered an old tradition we have in the countryside, which is to throw the statues of saints to the floor hoping they will perform miracles. Somehow, I mustered up the courage and opened the door. I immediately saw two officers, a member of the military, and a police officer, the latter a friend of ours whom we knew from Ojo de Agua when he was only a recruit. "Dedé, it's me, Murat González. We came looking for Pedrito." I told him that my brother-in-law had just turned himself in, which is exactly what he had done.

When Pedro found out about the atrocities the caliés had committed, he was determined to avoid further harm and suffering to the family. So he jumped a barbed wire fence, reached the highway, where he stopped a car, and asked the driver to take him to Salcedo. He turned himself in to the governor, Basilio Camilo, who took him to the fortress. After wreaking havoc at my mother's house, the caliés went to Patria's house, where they broke into cabinets, broke down doors, and destroyed everything until they found the "weapons" stored in a nearby warehouse.

January 22, 1960, was a day from hell. Mamá was praying on her knees. We didn't sleep that night thinking they had killed the girls. "Where can we go? What should we do? Who do we turn to?" we desperately asked ourselves. We had no options, and there wasn't much we could do. Everyone was in total anguish. We were truly beside ourselves. Her daughters, my sisters, were in jail.

Some friends stopped by to tell us things they had heard or to simply console us. Juan Bautista Santos, an engineer married to one of Jaimito's sisters and who was related to an important government official, came to tell us everything he had found out. He also belonged to the 14th of June Movement. One day he came to tell us that they had stripped one of the female prisoners naked. I can't bear the memory of how deeply anguished we felt, thinking that he might be referring to María Teresa. It's not that we weren't concerned about Minerva; it's that we knew how strong and courageous she was.

Luis Pantaleón, the mayor of Ojo de Agua, had also been taken away and submitted to a "series of investigations." Upon his return, he sent us a message telling us that Américo Dante Minervino, the head of La Cuarenta torture center and prison, had given the order to arrest Nelson. Jaimito and I ran to my mother's house to tell her, but when we arrived, we found all the children crying because the SIM had already picked him up. To this day I can still hear Jimmy screaming, "They took Nelson, Mamá! They took Nelson!" My son Jimmy, who was still a child, was forever impacted by these terrible events. To this day he is overcome by sadness and tears when he recalls them.

Sometimes I ask myself how we found the strength of spirit to carry out our daily activities. For example, one day we sent Tonó to María Teresa's home to pick up some of her belongings and take them to my mother's house. Tonó told us that as soon as they got there, a man who claimed to be a friend of Leandro's showed up and offered to help. At one particular moment he even shed some tears for Leandro, supposedly out of affection. He spent the day with her, helping her pack whatever belongings had been left after the raid and load them onto a truck that would take them to Salcedo.

We later found out that the man who had helped and accompanied her during the entire day was one of the Military Intelligence Service's most despicable caliés. Tonó's family became extremely concerned because the snitch already knew who she was. She, however, never expressed fear and was always there for us, first taking care of the children and later Mamá, until her death in 1981.

Throughout this memoir I've mentioned our Tonó (Antonia Rosario) and another person who was extremely important to our family: Pedro Díaz. Tonó was the daughter of a neighboring family who joined our household when she was nine or ten years old to keep María Teresa company. At the time, María Teresa had not yet turned six, but we were already off to boarding school. She became a part of the family, and with time, she practically became the head of our household.

I don't know why, but my father would say to Tonó: "Ana! Ana! My glasses!" And the poor thing would go off running looking for his eyeglasses, which he would leave all over the house. As part of our family, she was with us through the difficult times we endured. With her kindness and solidarity, she became a sister to us, a daughter for Mamá, and another mother for our children.

Pedro, on the other hand, was the son of Milita, a woman who worked in our kitchen, and Jazmín, her husband, who worked on the coffee farm, removing the pulp from the beans. I remember how we would laugh when María Teresa would stand next to Jazmín and say: "Min, pregnant; Min, pregnant," believing that Jazmín was pregnant because of his huge belly.

You could count the bones in Pedro's rib cage because he suffered from rickets. He was born here and grew up with us. You could say that Mamá cured and raised him. They used to call him Pedro-Chea. Pedro and Tonó accompanied us during the happy times and were there during all the difficulties we faced. They suffered insults and abuses from the military officers and caliés. When Pedro got married, Mamá gave him a house as a wedding present, and even though he moved off our property and had his own family, he always worked for her.

I was not a firsthand witness to Minerva's situation in Montecristi, but

Emma recalls that after Manolo was arrested, his parents wanted Minerva and Minou to go and stay with them. She refused, explaining that she would feel as if she had abandoned their home and Manolo. Given the situation, Emma and her brother Eduardo went to sleep with Minerva that night. Emma remembers:

> Those hours seemed endless. Late at night, we heard footsteps in our backyard that seemed threatening, and later we heard them going up the steps to the back porch. We knew when they were lying down on the porch because we could hear their bodies brushing against the wooden boards. Minerva finally agreed to move to our house.
>
> Very early on January 21, 1960, we noticed various unknown men standing at the corner of the park, across the street from our house. We knew they belonged to the SIM. At noon, I heard the door of a car that had stopped in front of our house. Frightened, I looked through the blinds and saw a Volkswagen that had just parked in front of the house. An officer and two armed military guards started to walk toward our front door. Moments later they knocked on our door.
>
> [. . .]
>
> I opened the door. The officer, a brawny man with light skin and light eyes, asked me if Mrs. Mirabal de Tavárez lived in the house. I answered yes. "We want to see her," he told me. "She's having lunch right now. I'll go and let her know," I responded. I asked him to wait in the living room, but he refused.
>
> With my heart in my mouth, I ran up the stairs to the second-floor room. Minerva, accompanied by my sister Angela, was still eating. "The Secret Police are looking for you," I said, anxious. By the way she reacted I knew then that she was waiting for them. She quickly changed and threw some chocolates into her bag. My parents and brothers were astounded.
>
> The anguish and nervousness in the air made Minou, who was still a toddler, begin to cry. When Minerva was preparing to walk down the stairs, Minou clung to her skirt. She asked her mother to take her along. Minerva picked her up and told her that she couldn't take her because she was going on a trip to the capital to see her father, but that if she didn't cry, she would bring her toys. I took the child in my arms and accompanied Minerva to the door.[78]

---

78 Emma Tavárez Justo, ¡*Ahora!* magazine, no. 578, December 9, 1974. Author's note. Title and page number not provided.

Our concern after Minerva's arrest was to bring Minou back to Salcedo because she had stayed behind in Montecristi with Doña Fefita and Don Manuel. We asked Luis Noboa for help. He was an executive of the Bermúdez Company and was married to Jaimito's sister. He was always very supportive of our family. Noboa sent his wife Olga to bring Minou to us. To cover up his intentions, he hired as a driver one of the meanest caliés in Santiago. Olga brought Minou back to us. Manolito was already with us because Minerva always left him with us.

By that time, they had already arrested Minerva, Manolo, María Teresa, Leandro, Pedrito, Nelson, and all the young men in Conuco. They also arrested several of Patria and Pedrito's neighbors: Pedro Ramón, Renato, Antonio Ezequiel and Francisco Aníbal González, Juan Peña, Candito and Otilio Portorreal... The national hunt for young dissidents was on. In Santiago they arrested Miguel Lama; in Macorís, Abelito Fernández, Dulce Tejada, and her husband Niño Alvarez... Each day we waited in terror to hear the list of the others who had been arrested.

The 14th of June Movement had managed to quickly engage a good number of the country's youth.

A specific tactic that Manolo used in jail and that others who were being tortured also used, was to mention those who had already been arrested or the sons of the country's most prominent and richest families, in a desperate attempt to stop the killings: Pipe Faxas Canto, Rafael Francisco Bonnelly, Moncho Imbert Rainieri... Many of society's pampered rich kids, as well as the sons of some of Trujillo's officials who also belonged to the movement, were eventually arrested. These included the sons of the Cáceres, Vega Boyrie, Troncoso, and Baquero families. When they reached Rafael Francisco Bonnelly, son of Rafael Bonnelly, the persecution slowed down.

Dr. Manuel Tejada Florentino had warned his henchmen: "Do not put me in the electric chair, because my heart won't be able to stand it." He died from the torture. He was sure he would die because of his heart problems. Curiously, Candito Portorreal, a very fragile and thin man from around here, was also placed on the electric chair and survived, as did many who were tortured on that macabre apparatus. One of the things they said was that the 14th of June Movement wanted Tejada Florentino to head the government once Trujillo was overthrown. It saddens me to remember his wife back then. Until the very end, she hoped that her husband would be found alive and that perhaps he was being held on Beata Island, in the country's southwest corner.

In the beginning Manolo, Leandro, and Pedrito were being held at La Cuarenta, along with the other members of the movement, but before the "trial" started and their sentences were issued, they took them to La Victoria penitentiary.

Minerva, María Teresa, and Other Jailed Women

Seven women were being held at La Cuarenta. Aside from Minerva and María Teresa, the following women were also detained: Fe Violeta Ortega (a dentist from Salcedo), Tomasina (Sina) Cabral (also from Salcedo), Dulce Tejada (from San Francisco de Macorís), Miriam Morales (from Puerto Plata), and Dr. Asela Morel (from the capital).

Sina Cabral was the first of the women to be arrested. She was an engineer and worked in the Ministry of Public Works. They took off her clothes in front of her comrades, who were also naked and handcuffed. They would later tell us that, impressed by Sina's dignity and integrity during those terrible moments, they all crunched together to form a human wall to shield her from view. This occurred the same day Dr. Tejada Florentino was killed in the electric chair.

A week passed. In Salcedo, no one slept. Only the children remained innocent, playing and running in the garden without realizing what was really going on. Not even the older ones could understand the seriousness of the situation we were going through.

On February 6, some military officers arrived at my mother's home and told us to go and get the girls. In that moment of tremendous confusion, Pedro, the young man who lived with our family, ran and brought me a mule: "Hurry up, Doña Dedé, they're arresting Doña Chea and taking her away." I didn't know what to do. I quickly put on a pair of pants and hopped on the mule, a very spritely animal. I stopped at a friend's house and asked him to run to the farm to tell Jaimito that they were arresting Mamá and taking her away.

I galloped on. Rather than take the highway, I took a shortcut until I ran into some sheets set out to dry on nets. The mule became frightened, jumped, and threw me right in the middle of the net, which was surrounded by bushes full of sharp thorns. In the Cibao region these bushes were used as farm fences. I screamed and screamed. A woman appeared and helped me stand up and get back on the mule. Riding as fast as I could, crying, I reached Mamá's front door. My cousin Dulce and her husband, Esperanza, who were always there supporting us, were leaving the house and managed to tell me, "No, they aren't taking Doña Chea away. But you need to go to the capital to pick up the girls." I could've killed myself en route to the house. *If they arrest Mamá,* I was thinking as I rode, *they are going to have to kill me too.* I cried some more and relaxed a little bit.

As soon as Jaimito arrived I asked him to get us a car to go and pick up the girls. Dulce, Esperanza, Tonó, Uncle Tilo, and Melania were at the house. Jaimito returned immediately with the car and the driver, Joaquín Baló, known for speeding on the highway. Patria decided she should stay with the children at the house. Mamá and I were ready to go. As we passed through Salcedo, the siren went off, announcing that it was midday. They still had not finished the highway to the capital. We had to go through Arroyo Vuelta and then through a place on the mountain, near the highway checkpoint La Cumbre, known as La U. Mamá was praying and praying in the car, nonstop. The driver was going full speed. I felt as if my heart was going to explode in my chest. At the entrance to the capital, across from the Leche Rica processing plant, we met up with Pepillo, another driver from Salcedo, who was returning in his yellow vehicle. He turned on his lights so we would stop. I asked him what time it was, and he answered, "One thirty-five." This meant it only took us one hour and thirty-five minutes to reach the capital. That was a record then, and still is today. However, I thought we were never going to get there, that the trip was taking forever.

We had to wait until three in the afternoon to pick up the girls, which is when they told us to pick them up. We waited in the home of my sister-in-law Rosario Fernández, who graciously made some soup for my mother that eventually neither of us tasted. I don't think we were capable of swallowing anything at the time, even water.

At two thirty in the afternoon, we reached SIM headquarters, which was situated just north of the National Palace. Waiting there were Manuel Tejada, Manuel Ortega, and other parents and family members of the seven detained women. They had informed each of the families. No one spoke. Soon the calié Faustino Pérez arrived. He threw a small bag down in front of us and said, "Look at the weapons they had." Those of us who were there looked at one another, as if to ask, "And these were the weapons?" Even the bag was useless because it had holes in it. And like I've said, the contents of the bag were a joke.

The wait was endless. Close to five o'clock Faustino returned and told us they had decided not to release them. What a horrible feeling, having to return to Salcedo without the girls! Oh my God! What a tragedy! What terrible suffering! What were we going to do?

I returned to my house to sleep with Jacqueline and Jaime David. Even though she was in jail, María Teresa could rest assured knowing we were with the children.

The next day, February 7, Jacqueline's first birthday, a local man named Otilio Portorreal[79] came to the house and said: "Dedé, run! I saw the girls on the highway accompanied by military officers."

When I reached my mother's house everyone was overjoyed! María Teresa was all bubbly, as usual; Minerva, very quiet. Both were exhausted, very sad. We sat on the porch to talk, and all of a sudden María Teresa asked, "Dedé, what's that on your legs? What are all those dark spots?" Days before, when I fell over the net, I had ripped my pants and a bush full of thorns had pricked me. But how could I notice under the circumstances? The fall occurred two days earlier. I had gone to the capital the day before, slept, got up, ran many errands, and I never noticed the thorns. María Teresa sat on the floor to pull out all the thorns with her tiny hands. It was then and there that I noticed how painful they were.

I don't quite remember the date, but it was probably the following weekend in the town church when the Augustinian fathers dared celebrate a Mass to give thanks for the girls' release. Many people attended the service. Later, there was a Way of the Cross procession between the town of Tenares and Salcedo. A large number of people participated in that too. By then, the now famous Catholic Church Pastoral Letter against the Trujillo regime had been read during masses on January 25, 1960. I feel it is important to quote certain passages of the Pastoral statement issued by the Church:

> [. . .] Each human being, even before birth, is guaranteed a series of superior and inherent rights that surpass those of any State. They are intangible rights, and not even the sum of all human powers can impede the freedom to exercise them, or diminish or restrict their field of action.
>
> [Citing Pope Pius XII . . .] "But this freedom can only flourish where rights and the law prevail and properly guarantee a respect for dignity, both for individuals and for the collective people. [. . .] In the meantime, millions of human beings continue to live under oppres-

---

79 Likely the father of Otilio Antonio Portorreal, who was one of the catorcistas arrested in January of that year.

sion and tyranny. They have no guarantees, no home, no private property, no freedom nor honor; and the last ray of tranquility—the last spark of passion—dies in their hearts."

[. . .] In order to eradicate from our dear homeland the evils that we are lamenting, and in order to obtain all kinds of spiritual and material gifts to which all men have an inalienable right, we fervently pray to the Holy Virgin of La Altagracia so that she may continue to be our hope and the bond that unites all Dominicans during this time of sorrow and uncertainty.

With all our heart we ask that all, both the clergy and the faithful, plead to God during these religious celebrations in honor of the Holy Virgin of La Altagracia so that in her infinite kindness she concede abundant gifts and consolation to those that are especially facing serious danger or grave difficulties, bereaved by life's tribulations. With these common prayers we implore our merciful God that mutual understanding and peace be restored, and that the sacred rights of human coexistence which contribute greatly to the good of all society, be recognized and that they be legitimately and happily exercised.

[. . .] Before concluding the present letter, we are compelled yet pleased to communicate to you that, in paternal response to your appeal—which we make our own—and out of duty to our pastoral ministry, we have directed an official letter to the country's highest authority so that, through a plan of mutual understanding, all excesses be avoided, for undoubtedly they will only harm those who commit them; that all the tears that have been shed be wiped away; that many wounds be healed; and that peace return to so many homes.

Convinced that this intervention will yield positive results, we have promised special prayers to God so that none of the authorities' family members ever experience during their lifetime the suffering that currently afflicts the hearts of so many Dominican fathers, so many children, so many mothers and so many wives.[80]

After this expression of solidarity with our family, there was not one Augustine priest left in the country. All were deported back to Spain. During

---

80   Our translation. To read the full Pastoral Letter, in a rendering different from our own, see "Text of Pastoral Letter Read to Dominican Republic Catholics," *New York Times*, Feb. 3, 1960. https://www.nytimes.com/1960/02/03/archives/text-of-pastoral-letter-read-to-dominican-republic-catholics.html.

this time period three seminarians were killed: one from the town of Moca, one from the north coast village of Sosúa, and the other from the eastern city of La Romana. Many Dominican priests did not dare manifest their opposition to the dictatorship, fearing that they or their families would be killed. The exceptions were Bishops Francisco Panal and Tomás O'Reilly. The latter was attacked by a group of caliés disguised as churchgoers.

Days after the girls were released, we were curious to find out what had happened to them and asked them questions, always trying not to overwhelm them. María Teresa told us that when they reached the town of Bonao, at a specific checkpoint where everyone had to stop and identify themselves, she, from the back seat of the car where she was being held prisoner, saw a couple of our relatives. "You can't imagine what I felt when I saw Uncle Mon's car returning from the capital, accompanied by my cousin Augusto. The last thing they imagined was that I was in that vehicle under arrest."

They took them to the courthouse in Santo Domingo. "We arrived under total darkness. I hid in a corner. After a while, I felt a small bulge in a corner." That "bulge" was Miriam Morales. María Teresa and she didn't speak a single word to one another. The next day in the morning they transferred both of them to La Cuarenta. Minerva was already there, along with Asela Morel, Dulce Tejada, and Sina Cabral. The last to arrive, two or three days later, was Dr. Fe Ortega. Apparently, no one had mentioned her name before then, since they imprisoned those who were named during the interrogations.

Sina Cabral was the only one who was tortured. The others were not physically abused. They interrogated and tormented them, but they also took them to see others being cruelly tortured, which for them was a form of psychological torture. They were forced to watch the men, comrades of the movement, naked, handcuffed, beaten, and abused. Seeing their husbands in this state, suffering such pain, was the most horrible, the most difficult torment they endured.

Not too long ago, Fausto Rodríguez Mesa, one of the organizers of the 14th of June Movement in the border town of San Juan de la Maguana, told Minou that the only time he saw Minerva was in the torture chamber. He said he would never forget that moment. He was naked, along with the rest of the men, waiting for his turn. They had just brought in the women to witness how their comrades were being tortured, when he heard one of the caliés tell Minerva not to be so arrogant because maybe one day one of them might want to marry her. Minerva's response came like a bullet that shook them all: "Don't worry. That is never going to happen because we don't like military men and much less if they are killers like all of you."

My sisters recalled with gratitude a man by the name of Salina Mota, the prison secretary, who would slip them chocolate bars under the doors. "No matter where you go there's always a good soul around," said Minerva, lost in thought. This man, Salina Mota, came to Salcedo to visit us soon after Trujillo was killed.

After arresting Minerva in Montecristi, they stopped in Santiago. Alicinio Peña Rivera began interrogating her, but soon he was sorry he did. No one knows what happened because he finally said: "No, no, take her. I'm not the one who should be interrogating her." Minerva's presence and attitude was such that she inspired respect.

During her stay at La Cuarenta, Minerva was taken at one in the morning to the "coliseum," the place where prisoners were interrogated and tortured. They stood her up in front of all those criminals who, upon seeing her, reacted like birds descending upon scattered seeds. Johnny Abbes,[81] the torturer, seemed to soften up, like all men standing before a beautiful young woman. He was all sweet and flirtatious. With him were Josecito and Virgilito García Trujillo, and José René Román Fernández. They were the leaders of Trujillo's assassination team. Minerva told us that from the first time she was interrogated she decided to use the strategy of not answering their questions, but rather responding with another question: "And why are you asking me that?" She was trying to find out what they were after or what their goal was, or to neutralize them in order to gain some time. Internally she would tell herself: "I'm much smarter than they are."

The men who were doing the interrogation insulted her: "You're nothing more than a conceited woman." "You're so manly that you don't even cry." And she defiantly answered: "Because I tell you the truth?" One time, when they saw that she would not buckle, they asked her, "Don't you know who we are?" "Haven't you seen us in the newspapers?" they insisted. When she said she didn't know who they were, they introduced themselves. She had only identified Johnny Abbes. Minerva told us that when they told her their names, she thought, "Oh, Virgin of La Altagracia! How foolish of me to provoke these hyenas! They're going to kill me!" She tried to control herself so they wouldn't notice her fear. But when she told us the story, she laughed when she remembered how upset they became when she said she didn't recognize them.

---

81 Head of the SIM, considered to be the cruelest henchman of the Trujillo dictatorship.

At eleven or twelve at night they would begin interrogating and torturing the prisoners of the 14th of June Movement. They would bring in the tough guys, the sons of high military and government officials or friends of Trujillo's son Ramfis, so they could watch as they were being tortured, as if it was a spectacle.

"I saw my friend Sully Bonnelly, all red, as he was given electric shocks," said María Teresa, while at the same time asking, "How could an old man, who probably has young sons, torture those young men? Didn't it occur to him that these young men could be his own children?" The old man she was referring to was José René Román Fernández.

Manolo was beaten much more than the other prisoners because when they interrogated the men as to who had recruited them to join the movement, in order not to implicate anyone else, they said "Manolo Tavárez." Someone who was in jail with him told me how impacted he was the first time he saw Manolo after he was tortured: "I figured that the man I was looking at was Manolo. He was very tall, about 6 feet 2 inches tall, so he couldn't be anyone else. But the beatings had turned him into a monster. His entire body was purple, they had pulled out his fingernails, and his arms were full of cigarette burns where they had put out their cigarettes. They had done everything to him."

In that physical condition, Manolo and many other members of the 14th of June Movement were brought to the courthouse. They were presented before a judge in a sham trial orchestrated by Trujillo to keep up appearances before the international community.

By then the international situation had gotten complicated for the dictator. The Organization of American States called a meeting of foreign ministers to learn more about the assassination attempt organized by Trujillo against Venezuelan president Rómulo Betancourt. Days later they issued the San José Declaration, condemning the regime. The United States had not yet closed its embassy here, but it was beginning to pull the rug out from under the tyrant. The deportation and murder of so many priests following the reading of the Pastoral Letter had seriously impacted the dictatorship.

In this context, Trujillo set up the mock trial. Many people attended, especially family members and individuals who Minerva and others had taken upon themselves to invite, in a provocative gesture that must have aggravated the dictator.

Right in the middle of the "trial," Minerva stood up and referred to a clause indicating a procedural violation. Victor Garrido, the chief prosecutor, ordered her to sit down. When the session ended, Minerva once again stood up and began singing the national anthem. There were a lot of people there because of the large number of defendants. All those present joined her in singing the anthem. Total chaos broke out because the henchmen found themselves in the midst of a protest that they were not prepared for and that they could not suppress.

According to the eyewitness accounts I received, my sister had not only convened all those present, but she had also carefully orchestrated the protest, explaining that it was important to raise the prisoners' spirits.

As a precaution, that night she didn't sleep in the home of the widow Isabelita Lithgow as she usually did. She checked into a hotel in La Opera building, in the Colonial Section. She spent the night there without anyone bothering her.

Arrested Once Again

My mother's household had begun adapting to the girls' presence and that of their children. We became very close, supporting them and keeping up on all that was happening around us.

On May 18 several SIM officers returned to once again arrest Minerva and María Teresa. Viterbo Alvarez (aka "Pechito") was with them, a calié working in Salcedo but who was originally from San Cristóbal. Later on, when the girls' assassins were on trial, he was sentenced as an accessory to murder and for "association with criminals."

María Teresa had bronchitis and was running a really high fever. Mamá told the SIM officials: "My daughter is sick. If you want, come in." They didn't want to come in. They only took Minerva with them. A little later the Volkswagen came back to pick up María Teresa. Mamá begged them not to take her because she was very sick. Officer Murat González, the same individual who had arrested Pedrito, told Mamá: "Doña Chea, I decided to come myself, so please trust me. Nothing is going to happen to her." Finally, Mamá had to resign herself and covered María Teresa with a towel. They took her to San Francisco de Macorís, where they had already detained Sina and Minerva. From there they were transferred to La Victoria.

This time they were placed in cells with common criminals. They would not let us talk to them, and they did not allow us to see them until their "trial" date. They sent us a little note through a family member of one of the prisoners, telling us to stop at a curve located just before arriving at the jail, from where we would be able to see their cell. Patria and I told the men that we were dizzy and asked them to stop the car. That's when we saw María

Teresa waving a towel through the iron bars. It was the towel that Mamá had wrapped around her the day she was arrested. When we saw the towel from afar, at least we knew they were alive.

The three were judged and sentenced to five years of hard labor "for threatening the security of the State." On appeal, the sentence was reduced to three years of hard labor. Manolo, Leandro, and other members of the group were sentenced to thirty years in jail and fined six hundred thousand pesos.

Patria and I visited La Victoria every week during May, June, and July. In the beginning, Minerva, María Teresa, and Sina were all together. But since Minerva was considered to be the most important of the three, they took her and placed her in a cell with prostitutes and lesbians. Minerva would later tell us, "The things I saw there!" One night, after several days, they pulled her out to interrogate her. They asked her how she felt being locked up in that cell. Minerva responded, "I feel fine because I have sixty-five assistants that do everything for me." The next day, they returned her to the jail cell with María Teresa and Sina. Their original plan was to humiliate her, but the "punishment" didn't turn out quite the way they had planned.

Minerva later told us how happy she was that the strategy she used to get out of that cell had worked because she had suffered terribly in there.

Minerva, who was very creative in many areas, asked us to bring her plaster while she was in prison. At first, they didn't allow it because they didn't know what she would use it for. But once she received some, she used it to sculpt from memory the head of her daughter Minou, which today is on exhibit at the house museum. If you place the sculpture next to Minou's photo, you can see the tremendous resemblance. She had her little girl fixed in her mind. She also used Sina as a model for another sculpture, but she was not able to finish either one.

On occasion, Patria, Tonó, and at one point I brought Minou, Manolito, and Jacqueline to the prison so they could see them. I'll never forget how María Teresa wept when she saw her little girl, who was just a baby at the time.

Even where you least expect it, there are compassionate people. In the jail there was a sergeant who, in spite of the dangers he faced, really treated my sisters well, so much so that when they were ready to be released, they didn't know what to give him, and so María Teresa gave him a radio they had. Unfortunately, there are also birds of ill omen everywhere. Such was the case with Colonel Frías, who, on one occasion, and in reference to Minerva, cruelly told Pedrito and Nelson, "That one is going to die with her shoes on." The man's wife, who was Pedrito's cousin, repeated the same words to Mamá.

This time they remained in jail until August. They released them when the scandal erupted that Trujillo had orchestrated an assassination attempt against the Venezuelan president Rómulo Betancourt. The scandal prompted a delegation of the Organization of American States to visit the country on a fact-finding mission. It was problematic for Trujillo to have those women in jail in that context. But there is proof that their release from prison was part of a plan that turned out to be worse than their prison sentence, as Manolo would later declare: "On August 9, 1960, the girls were irregularly released, and in that moment, the plot to assassinate the Mirabal sisters began."[82]

I remember that when they left prison and went under house arrest at our mother's house, Minerva spent all her time building a Spanish courtyard. During those months I saw her work tirelessly in the garden. She never lost heart, and she refused to allow anything to trample her spirit and her relationship with nature. I can still hear her reciting "Parasite plant, like the ivy, that climbs over the heart and consumes it . . ." while she worked on the Spanish garden. The majority of the sculptures exhibited at the house museum were made during this time period.

During the months that Minerva and María Teresa were in jail, rumors would fly around that they had been killed. Mamá became obsessed with an urgency to baptize the children. She asked Tonó to be Manolito's godmother. The children didn't even have birth certificates because, as Mamá would say, "Minerva is not thinking about that, but rather the other thing: politics." Tonó, Doña Fefita, and Dr. Concepción became the children's godparents.

Once Minerva was out of prison, Tonó said to her, "Minerva, I had to baptize the boy because no one would dare." To which my sister answered, "No matter, because you're the one who's going to raise them if I die." Tonó was crazy about Minerva's children, especially with Manolito who, of all the grandchildren, was the one who spent the most time with her and Mamá.

The pressure we experienced during those days was unbearable. Sometimes my son Jaime Enrique would stay in the park when he left Salcedo's public school, talking with friends about cars because ever since he was a little boy, he was passionate about them. But one day Ms. María Josefa Gó-

---

82 Statements made by Manolo Tavárez Justo before Judge Ambiorix Díaz Estrella during the trial against the assassins of the Mirabal sisters, December 1, 1961. Author's note.

mez, a teacher of teachers, told me that a captain by the last name Alegría, told her, "If you don't get that boy out of here, I'm going to kick him out myself with a beating." Since the school was across the street from the fortress, this official would frequently see the boy enter and leave. Ms. Gómez asked my husband to come in, and she told him, "Look, Jaimito, I don't want Jaime Enrique at this school because if they hurt him, they are going to have to kill me first." We had to enroll him in the Santo Cerro School in La Vega.

In July 1960, the government published a thick volume titled *Crimes Committed against the National and International Security of the Dominican State*,[83] which contained statements from the leaders, members, and supporters of the 14th of June Movement. The majority of the photographs published in the text showed men who looked like cadavers. Minerva's photograph, however, didn't look bad at all.

Earlier that year, in January 1960, a volume titled *Plot Discovered*[84] had been published in the name of Rafael Valera Benítez. He was in jail for his participation in the movement. The volume describes the beginnings and the evolution of the 14th of June Movement against the Trujillo dictatorship. It was discovered by the SIM.

I never read the first book, but I always felt that I should because Minerva, who had read it, was appalled and shocked by the statements they attributed to some of the prisoners. I remember her saying, "Oh my God! What is this? If these statements are true, they are disgusting, praising Trujillo, and blaming themselves for having fought the dictatorship. What are we going to do with them?" It also mentioned how some of the prisoners, especially Manolo and Luis Gomez, but also others, demonstrated immense courage and resistance in spite of the torture they suffered.

---

83   Luis Henríquez Castillo, *Crímenes contra la seguridad interior y exterior del Estado dominicano* (Ciudad Trujillo/Santo Domingo: Editorial La Nación, 1960). Author's note.
84   Rafael Valera Benítez, *Complot develado* (Ciudad Trujillo/Santo Domingo: Editorial Handicap, 1960).

8

The Tragedy

Before they transferred Leandro and Manolo to the jail in Salcedo, we received news that on August 20, Tomasina (Sina) Cabral had sought asylum in the Argentinian Embassy. I was the one who told Minerva, and I will never forget the impact the news had on her. Sina's decision led us to think that they had transferred the men to Salcedo for fear that Minerva and María Teresa would also seek asylum when they traveled to the capital.

We realized what was actually going on, thanks to a comment made by the head of the SIM in the Cibao region when he went to see the prisoners. This is what Manolo declared before the investigating judge, Díaz Estrella, in December 1961:

> while imprisoned in Salcedo's military jail, on November 5, 1960, Alicinio Peña Rivera, first lieutenant of the National Army and head of the Military Intelligence Service of the Northern Department, told me and the engineer José Ramón Leandro Guzmán that the Intelligence Service had received information that the Mirabal sisters continued conspiring against the Government and that if they received any further complaint regarding these activities, we and they would be assassinated.

Their meals were prepared at my mother's house each day. Pedro, the faithful young man who was just like a member of our family, delivered them.

Pedrito was left behind in La Victoria because he was not considered a leader of the movement and because of a comment made by Américo Dante Minervino Matías, a very cruel man who was later named head of La Cuarenta prison. His father had married a woman from Tenares who was related to Pedrito, meaning that Minervino was her stepson. When he saw Pedrito in the prison, he said: "He's a poor man, a farmer. The others were the ones that put him up to this."

Minerva and María Teresa remained under house arrest. They only had permission to leave the house to visit their husbands in jail, but before doing so, they had to stop and report to the SIM office in Salcedo. The office was located in a house that my mother owned, across from the Governor's Office. We were prohibited from visiting my brothers-in-law. Only my sisters could visit their husbands.

At the end of October, Trujillo decided to go on tour, visiting towns throughout the country. He visited Salcedo on November 1. They said when he visited one of the various homes in the town he asked, "How are things in Salcedo?" A military officer, or a well-known lackey—no one knows for sure—said, "Those women continue to cause problems." The next day, in Villa Tapia, Trujillo stated, "I only have two political problems to resolve: the Catholic Church and the Mirabal family." That comment spread like wildfire in the region, and of course, it reached our ears. Earlier, on May 15 in Santiago, Trujillo said that the place where the Jehovah's Witnesses and the communists had spread their deepest roots was in the town of Conuco, Salcedo. He again mentioned the Mirabal family. The story made the headlines the next day in the newspaper *El Caribe*.

A week later, on November 8, my son Jaime Enrique was riding his bicycle to school, and near the fortress he saw that Manolo and Leandro were seated in the back seat of a Volkswagen. The boy returned to my mother's house and told María Teresa—Aunt Teté, as the nephews and nieces used to call her—what he had just seen. Immediately she and Minerva headed over to the fortress to find out what was happening. They were told that their husbands were being transferred to a jail in Puerto Plata, on the north coast.

That same afternoon they rented a car and headed to Puerto Plata, accompanied by Doña Fefita, Manolo's mother, who had been spending a few days with us. Doña Fefita remembered that she had a very close friend in Puerto Plata, Rafael (Chujo) Pimentel, whom she would ask to send the men's daily meals. Just imagine. Nobody wanted to get involved in this situation. Don Chujo, on the contrary, showed us what a loyal friend he was. The girls finally reached his house, and he immediately said yes, that he would send Leandro and Manolo their daily meals. And he did.

That occurred on a Wednesday. When my sisters arrived at the fortress, they were not allowed to see them, but instead were told, "Your visits will be on Fridays. But since today is Wednesday and Friday is just a few days away, come back on Friday next week." On Friday, November 18, they traveled again to Puerto Plata in a rented car, driven by Joaquin Baló. They were accompanied by Nena de Guzmán—Leandro's mother—Doña Fefita, and Jacqueline, María Teresa's baby. They visited the prisoners. Nothing out of the ordinary occurred during that trip. I was waiting for them at my mother's house when they returned. As soon as María Teresa saw me, she said: "Dedé, you see? We've returned safe and sound." Even though they knew of the dangers that surrounded them and what could actually happen to their husbands, they never wavered when it came to their duties, nor did they ever think of seeking asylum.

During those days Minerva and I argued terribly. I, as the big sister, would tell her, "Minerva! Minerva! Don't be so stubborn! Don't go to Puerto Plata!" This fell on deaf ears. She would look at me with her big dark eyes and extend her long, thin hands, like the hands of a pianist, and respond, "But Dedé . . .," and she would keep on pressing the pedal of the sewing machine where she was sewing children's clothing to sell so she wouldn't be a burden to our mother. Many of Minerva's friends had small children, and they would buy clothes from her. At the house Patria also sewed, while María Teresa cut the patterns. They had all learned to sew at Aunt Minada's school. At that time, a certain style of Italian shirts were very popular. María Teresa bought one, took it apart, made a pattern from it, and began to sew handmade shirts.

I would ride my horse every day to visit my mother and my sisters, passing by the house in Salcedo that they had confiscated from Mamá. It was occupied by caliés. When I passed by, I felt a sort of pleasure, a satisfaction. It was as if by galloping past the house on my beautiful horse I was letting them know that we were not defeated. What's more, I was lucky, because one day the horse slipped in a roadside gutter, right in the middle of town, and I was injured from the fall. But what matters is that I didn't fall in front of them.

On November 20 or 21, Disnalda María paid us a visit, bringing the news that Juancito Rodríguez had died in Venezuela. We were seated under a tree in the backyard. Minerva sprang to her feet, distressed and grieving. Holding back her tears, she said, "How sad for this country. That man gave up everything for freedom, his entire fortune, and he even lost his son on June 14." Who could have told my sister, who was talking about this man with such admiration and respect, that two of her grandchildren, Camila and Manuel Aurelio, would also be the grandchildren of Juancito Rodríguez's son, José Horacio Rodríguez, the commander of the June 1959 expedition? In other words, they would be Juancito's great grandchildren![85]

---

85   José Horacio Rodríquez commanded the failed expedition of Maimón, Constanza, and Estero Hondo, which trained in Cuba in 1959 and set out to land in the Dominican Republic on June 14 of that year. Their mission was to topple

Manolo and Leandro's transfer to Puerto Plata concerned us more and more because the rumors kept spreading, and they were truly terrifying. Jaimito said that he "expected something like that would happen." Referring to those days, he explained:

> Someone sent me a message, I don't know who it was, but it was a friend of the person whose name I could not reveal ... A friend of mine from Macorís, Negrito Castellanos, who had been our neighbor, came and told me, "I'm in the Intelligence Service. I've come looking for you, and I'm glad you're out here so that I don't have to go in." We met on the highway. I don't remember if it was close to Doña Chea's home or near Salcedo. I asked him, "What's going on?" And he continued, "A friend of yours—and please don't ask me who because I'm not going to tell you because this is very serious—they transferred so and so to Puerto Plata ... If you or your wife want to see them one day, don't go on the days when the wives visit. You take your car, and you and your wife go on your own. Don't go with the sisters, because something really bad is going to happen ... they're going to kill Leandro and Manolo. That's what will probably happen: they are going to kill them. And if you go with Minerva, you know how Minerva is, he wants me to tell you that he knows how she is ... very outspoken ... and she can get you tangled up in this, so it's better that you not go, and when (the wives) go, they should go with the mothers," (Minerva with Leandro's mother and María Teresa with Manolo's mother), but they shouldn't go together.
>
> I relayed the message to my comadre Patria, who was at Doña Chea's, and she asked, "And who told you this?" "They just told me," I answered, and she insisted, "But tell me who told you." I told her that I couldn't say, that I had sworn that I would not say anything because I was putting my life at risk as well as the life of the person who told me, and the life of the person that had told him as well. She apparently dismissed what I said. She just said to me, "You're just afraid."
>
> I told Dedé, "You are not going over there; you are not going to Puerto Plata." If I didn't love her, I would have let her go. But since I

---

the Trujillo dictatorship. Dominican intelligence learned of the mission and the expeditionaries were captured, tortured, and killed, including José Horacio Rodríguez. However, his son, Doroteo Rodríguez, would later marry and have two children with Minou Tavárez Mirabal, Minerva Mirabal's daughter. So, those two children, Camila and Manuel Aurelio Tavárez Mirabal, are Juancito Rodríguez's great-grandchildren and Minerva Mirabal's grandchildren.

did love her, I wasn't going to let her go. I didn't want to lose her. This was no game; it was much too serious, and I took it seriously. I would tell Manolo, "You don't mess with Trujillo." I know because I too participated in the anti-Trujillo movement, but not like a game, like Pedrito, who spoke openly against Trujillo . . . I knew how things were because I grew up in a small town . . . Minerva and I fought continuously. I cared deeply for her, and she cared a lot for me. She was very strong-headed, very intelligent, she liked good literature, we talked about a lot of things because I was also somewhat of a reader. She was naïve, even though she had seen so much and in spite of being so very intelligent. She didn't believe that there were bad people . . .

Maybe that's why she never thought they would actually kill her. As for the message I was sent, I suspect it may have come from Arturo Rodríguez Espaillat, "The Gillette" or "The Razor"—as he was known—who at the time was the head of the Intelligence Service. His uncle was Dr. Víctor Rodriguez, my father's compadre. Don Víctor and my father were both from La Vega (there were many families from both Salcedo and La Vega: the Mirabals, the Rodríguezes, the Braches . . .)

The following week, on Thursday, November 24, Patria went to see her husband Pedrito, who was imprisoned at La Victoria. Her idea was to sleep in the capital because she had no one with whom to return to Salcedo. But during the visit at La Victoria, she ran into Memelo, a driver from Salcedo who had brought Celeste Fernández, the sister of Dr. José Fernández Caminero, to the capital. He was returning with her that day to Macorís. Patria asked if he could bring her back because, that way, she wouldn't have to sleep in the capital. They left for Salcedo at around two or three in the afternoon.

Patria arrived at my mother's house. The next day she announced, "Mamá, I'm going to Puerto Plata to see the boys." Mamá, with tears in her eyes, begged her: "Patria, don't go. Patria, your children!" Tonó, who was at the house when the girls left for Puerto Plata, heard my mother tell Minerva to return early. Tonó would later recall:

> Doña Chea would not stop repeating, "They transferred the husbands to Puerto Plata to kill the girls." Not long ago they had thrown Donato Bencosme off a cliff and said it was an accident. That's why she incessantly warned the girls: "The same thing that happened to Donato will happen to you."

We were all convinced that they had transferred the prisoners to Puerto Plata to kill the girls. A friend sent them a message with me: "Dedé, tell Minerva that the voice of the people is the voice of God. They are making them go there to kill them." Another woman, who was close friends with a high military officer, sent Juan Fernández Mirabal to tell us, "Tell the girls not to go. There's been an order to kill them." But Minerva would answer, "Do you think that Trujillo is going to kill everyone traveling with me? He's not going to kill all those people." That was what she thought because she was thinking politically. Much later we found out that Trujillo had ordered that if there were more than five people in the car, they should abort the mission. On the day of the massacre, there were only four in the car.

Perhaps Minerva thought that with all the international pressure against the tyrant, he was not going to risk carrying out crimes involving a lot of people, where innocent bystanders would also be killed for simply being at the wrong place at the wrong time. The most horrendous case of this type was the assassination of Porfirio (Prin) Ramírez, a businessman from San Juan de la Maguana. His brother was General Miguel Angel Ramírez Alcántara, one of the leaders of the 1947 expedition. Trujillo suspected that Prin was helping his brother prepare for a new expedition, so he sent Federico Fiallo to kill him. That day Prin had given a ride to nine people, and all were beaten to death and later thrown off a cliff in the outskirts of San Juan, making it appear to be an accident.

Juan Bosch wrote an article about that horrendous crime, titled "The *El Número* Crime," published in the Cuban magazine *Bohemia*. I don't know how we got hold of it, but I remember reading it.

That Friday, Joaquín Baló could not drive the girls to Puerto Plata, so they went looking for another vehicle and driver to take them. On the 24th in the afternoon, René Bournigal, a friend and neighbor from Conuco, offered to lend them his jeep and said he would talk to his driver to see if he would agree to take them. The vehicle was one of those Toyotas that was used to travel through the mountains. They spoke to Rufino de la Cruz, René's driver, and he accepted.

They had arranged for Aunt Melania (Uncle Tilo's wife) or Aunt Lalía to accompany the girls to Puerto Plata. But that changed when Patria decided she would go.

I can't help feeling angry whenever I think that Patria didn't have to go. To this day I haven't been able to accept it because she shouldn't have gone, she *could* not go. She didn't even have permission to visit them. When they discussed the issue, and I guess to calm my mother, she said, "They won't notice anything in Puerto Plata." And Minerva said, "Patria, the scenery you see when you go up the mountain . . . Just absolutely beautiful!" Now, looking back through time, and knowing Patria's personality, always fulfilling her role as the big sister, I believe she decided to go to protect them. I know she was aware of the danger, even though she didn't show it. She had paid close attention to everything that was said, including the warning that Jaimito had told her. But she went, convinced that with her presence she would protect her younger sisters.

On the afternoon of November 24, I talked for a long while with Minerva and María Teresa, but I returned to my home in Ojo de Agua before Patria arrived from the capital. Of these last moments I shared with Minerva and María Teresa I hold on to certain memories that often pass through my mind like scenes from a movie: Minerva sewing three blouses with the colors of the Dominican flag, to wear when the dictator was overthrown. One was for Sina, another for María Teresa, and the third one for her. The unfinished blouses were left on top of the sewing machine. I recall seeing María Teresa walk to the kitchen, with her slow, feminine stride, so much like Mamá.

In spite of everything they had lived through that year, my sisters were always in good spirits. Tonó tells how one day María Teresa was sewing, and all of a sudden, she turned around and said, "Tonó, we almost overthrew him, right?" She meant that the movement had made the regime tremble.

On the 25th, the girls left Conuco and stopped at the calié office in Salcedo to inform them of their trip to Puerto Plata, as had been previously arranged. In Santiago, they stopped at a store called El Gallo to purchase various items. During their trip they did not stop to visit relatives so as not to create problems for them. We were treated as if we had some kind of contagious disease. I say this to highlight how Don Chujo treated us; he was so courageous and supportive. He offered us his home when no one else dared. They arrived at his home in Puerto Plata and waited there until the scheduled visiting hours. They left his house at two o'clock and went to the fortress.

The visit was supposed to be until five o'clock, but at four, Ciriaco de la Rosa went in and told them that the visit was over. Minerva, as always, protested, "The visit is until five o'clock." In spite of their protests, they were forced to leave. That day Miriam Morales got to see them, but, apparently, they didn't see her, or they didn't respond to her greetings in order to protect her. They passed by Don Chujo's home, said goodbye, and began their journey back to Salcedo.

Just outside Puerto Plata they noticed a car following them. It was not a Volkswagen like the caliés used to drive. We know this from the testimony of witnesses who were riding in a truck from the Caja Dominicana de Seguros Sociales, who just happened to be passing by at the time. During the following months those witnesses suffered anxiety attacks and paranoia. They believed they were being watched everywhere they went. I was never able to talk with them personally, even though they came to visit my mother after the regime was overthrown. I was not in Salcedo at the time.

Don Chujo's wife had given Patria a dessert to take back with them. It was wrapped in a linen napkin that I later recovered from her purse, completely soaked in blood. I kept it. I have also kept Patria's rosary, sent to me by Professor Onésimo Jiménez through a student at Santiago's Sacred Heart School. Both the bloody napkin and the rosary are on exhibit at the *Casa-Museo*.

It was Friday night. Jaime David, who was four years old at the time, had an eye infection. Jaimito had gone out with Nelson in our pickup truck to run some errands, and they took longer than usual to return. I grew tired of waiting for them to take me to my mother's house, so I laid down with Jaime David. They finally arrived at around nine in the evening, and Jaimito said he thought it was too late to go out. I hardly slept that night, concerned, wondering if the girls had arrived safely. Mamá and Tonó were up all night, waiting. This is how Tonó tells her story:

> At nine Doña Chea and I were in the living room, waiting. Then we heard some footsteps, and I said: "Doña Chea, the girls' jeep broke down, and they left it in the gas station, but they are coming." But that didn't happen! We didn't hear the steps anymore. Every once in a while, Doña Chea would begin to cry, and say, "They already killed my daughters. This is the end. Who knows where they threw them." Doña Chea didn't sleep. I laid down next to the small crib where Raulito, Patria's son, was sleeping. I was barely starting to fall asleep when, all of a sudden, I felt someone grab my hand and say, "My son, my son! Take care of my son!" I knew it was Patria because I was with her son and also because Minerva had already asked me to take care of Manolito. Months before, when she had returned from jail, she said to me: "You baptized Manolo. I'm glad because you are the one that is going to raise him." I was half asleep when I heard Patria's voice, and it was so real that I saw the three of them all wet, thrown over a cliff, just like that, one on top of the other. That image has

stayed in my mind forever. I jumped out of bed to tell the three girls that were taking care of the other children—Malú, who was taking care of Raulito; Margarita, in charge of Jacqueline; and Hilda, who was taking care of Minerva's children, "They're dead," I said, "I felt them. Get up!" We all got up and began to pick up everything around us. We began to arrange things around the house, and Doña Chea was in her bedroom, praying and praying. At dawn, we woke up Pedro and told him to take a mule, ride to Dedé's house, and tell her that the girls had not arrived. By the time Dedé, Jaimito, and Nelson reached Doña Chea's house, a local man had already arrived carrying a small piece of paper that said that the girls had been involved in an accident and that they were at the Cabral y Báez Hospital in Santiago.

Early in the morning Pedro arrived at my house on the mule. I had spent the entire night dozing on and off, but at that moment, I jumped up and screamed, "Pedro! What's happened?" "The girls haven't arrived yet," he said to me. All doubts dissipated, and I began to scream what I would repeat nonstop during the next few days, everywhere I went: "He killed them!" "Nelson, get up, they killed the girls," I said. Nelson jumped out of bed. Jaimito did the same. We hurriedly dressed and left for my mother's house. Before we got there, we ran into Rufino's wife on the highway, desperate, crying. I screamed, "Look at Delia! He killed her husband too!"

By the time we arrived at the house, rural police officers were already there, reporting on the accident and giving us instructions. They said that before going to Santiago we had to stop by the police precinct in Salcedo. At that moment I thought of Patria and hoped that perhaps she wasn't dead. Maybe that hope was what gave me the strength to continue making the necessary arrangements and give so many orders. I said, "Nelson, get in. Mamá, you come here with me." I asked Tonó to get some clothes ready and to put them in the back. We all left in the pickup truck.

In my desperation I became hyperactive, as if by giving out orders I could deny what my instincts were telling me. When we arrived at the police precinct in Salcedo, all doubts dissipated. Jaimito got out of the pickup truck and told me to wait there for him, but I couldn't sit still. When I reached him, he had a telegram in his hands and told me, "Dedé, please, don't read it." I grabbed it from his hand and read it out loud: "Patria Mirabal, María Teresa Mirabal, Rufino de la Cruz, and another unidentified woman died in the accident." Minerva. They hadn't dared to write the name Minerva Mirabal.

I ran out of the precinct, and I told my mother that they had killed her daughters and that she should go with Nelson. "Murderer!" I screamed as I ran through the streets to my in-laws' house about a block away. I remember stopping a pickup truck that was coming in the opposite direction, and I begged the unknown passengers to take my mother back to her house.

Jaimito finally caught up with me, and we left for Santiago right away. But first we stopped at his sister Olga Fernández de Noboa's house. I asked her to give me sheets and towels. I realized that the clothes I had asked Tonó to prepare when I still had some hope that at least Patria had survived would be of no use now. Luis Noboa, Olga's husband, accompanied me to make all the necessary arrangements. At the hospital we ran into Dr. Víctor (Vitico) Camilo, Jaimito's cousin, and Toñito Canto, also a doctor and a member of the 14th of June Movement who had previously been jailed by the regime. Both helped us, especially Vitico, who went with Noboa to purchase the coffins. Meanwhile, I stayed there, talking nonstop, desperate, screaming at anyone who dared listen to me: "They killed them! They're murderers!" Mamá Lesbia, Jaimito's mother, arrived right after us. So did Esperanza Saba, my cousin Dulce Pantaleón's husband, and Vicente González, Pedrito's brother.

I simply cannot forget the incredible amount of paperwork we had to fill out for the hospital to release the bodies. But we finally succeeded. We loaded three of the bodies in the ambulance, and I took María Teresa with me in my pickup truck. As if we hadn't already received enough devastating blows, when we were near Moca, I believe, we drove past several trucks full of oak logs from Patria and Pedrito's farm, which Trujillo had confiscated.

I brought Rufino's body to Delia, who was crying inconsolably. Mamá offered to take him, along with the girls, to our pantheon in Salcedo, but his family decided to bury him in Tenares.

We reached my mother's house at around eleven in the morning. "Salcedo, here are your daughters! They have died for the freedom of your people!" I screamed when I got out of the pickup truck. A lot of people were already waiting for us. Everyone knows how supportive country folk are. María Teresa's friends from Macorís were there: the Duarte, Rizek, and Mues girls; there were people from Santiago who worked with Noboa at the Bermúdez company, as well as some others. Uncle José was in despair, more than anyone else, and I just held on to him.

I insisted on changing the girls' clothing. However, when we tried to bring the caskets into the bedroom, they wouldn't fit. I decided to do it in Tonó's bedroom, which was in the back of the house and which had a very wide door, but my cousin Antonio Mirabal brought me to my senses: "Dedé, they are already dead. Why change them?" And I repeated after him, "You're right. Why change them if they are already dead?" I placed each one's portrait on her casket. The other uncontrollable impulse that overcame me was to cut María Teresa's braid. I was so desperate that I tried over and over again to cut it, but I couldn't. Perhaps I did it because I had heard that hair doesn't deteriorate, and I wanted to keep something alive from her.[86]

We kept vigil with the bodies at the house until four o'clock. We then left for church. I kept María Teresa's body with me, and the other two were transported in the ambulance. Up until the very end, I felt that María Teresa was my daughter. "I'm always protecting you," I would continuously tell her and myself.

At the entrance to Salcedo, we all got out of our vehicles and walked the rest of the way to the church. The place was packed. The entire family was there. Father Juan Antonio Flores officiated the Mass. He was a parish priest back then but is now Bishop Emeritus of Santiago. I remember Mayor Pablo Yermenos was there with his wife Alida, who placed a veil over my head.

We took them on foot to the cemetery, but before burying the first casket, I said, "We are going to open the casket to see who is who." When I opened it, I cried: "Oh, Minerva! You were always the determined one, always the first!" We then buried Patria and the last one was María Teresa. There were no eulogies. Who had the strength to say anything at such an agonizing moment?

Father Flores almost had to physically remove me from the cemetery because I couldn't stop screaming, "Murderers! You killed them!" Of all the crying faces there I can't forget the face of a young boy whom I didn't know. With a troubled look, he kept gesturing to me, as if trying make sure that nothing would happen to me too. "Be quiet! Don't talk so much!" he seemed to be saying. The priest embraced me and said, "Christ, on your cross, grant me patience! Say that, say it like that."

I don't want to remember the trip back home. My mother was in her bedroom, seated, and I told her, as if sleepwalking, "Mamá, they are buried." She then said to me something completely unexpected: "Dedé, I have forgiven my daughters' killers so that my daughters may also be forgiven!"

Mamá refused to go to the church or to the cemetery. And from then

---

86   Dedé did manage to cut the braid, which is now on display at the house museum.

on, she refused to visit their graves: "I never go to the cemetery, because I expect them to return. I prefer to wait until you take me there the day I die."

Manolo's sister Angela and I stayed up talking until dawn. Consoling one another, I suppose.

The greatest pain, however, came the following day when I left the house. I thought my soul had abandoned my body, and I felt faint. Facing reality, facing what could never be undone, knowing that they were already buried, I felt as if the life had been sucked right out of me. I felt empty, as if I were in a vacuum. What a tragedy! I am not a writer, so I don't know what words I could possibly use to express such despair.

I saw a boy on a bus that I used to take frequently with Jaime David when he was little and we would travel to our farm in El Indio. I screamed at him, "Oh God! Bolívar! They've taken my soul from me!" More than forty years have passed, and I cannot think of those moments without reliving everything all over again.

I would enter the house and notice that my mother didn't know what to do with herself either. I can't imagine how you can live with such terrible pain. I didn't even remember that I had left Jaime David home sick. Luckily, Jaimito had taken him over to his Aunt Naná so she could take care of him until I returned. Two or three days later I went to pick him up, but before doing so we stopped by the home of Jaimito's unmarried aunts. When they saw the state I was in, they scolded him, "But Jaimito, how can you let her leave the house looking like that?" During those terrible endless days, lost in time, I didn't sleep or eat. I could only pray.

During the next nine days I didn't utter a word. I would sit at home in a rocking chair, without the strength to move. To top it all off, the psychological torture continued. Moncito, one of our employees, would come to me again and again and say, "Ma'am, they're here, they're here!" referring to the Volkswagens that would continuously go by the house to spy on us. They turned around when they reached the front of the house. Those were terribly cruel times. However, every time I heard one of the cars, I thought about something that would calm me down a bit: if they come and kill me, it will be very clear that the girls' death was no accident.

Jaimito stayed by my side at all times. He protected me and gave me his full support. He also took it upon himself to distract and support Nelson, who was terribly shaken by it all.

We all prayed for my sisters' souls for nine days, a ritual that is known in the Catholic Church as a novena. On the last day of the novena, something happened that clearly reflected the dictatorship's cruelty. There were a lot of people visiting our home in Conuco. Uncle Fello was there. Suddenly, Alicinio Peña Rivera arrived carrying a letter for my mother to sign. He was accompanied by the governor of Salcedo, Dr. Jesús María Camilo, who we called Uncle Chu because he was my mother's cousin and Jaimito's uncle. The document stated that the death of Minerva, Patria, and María Teresa was the result of an accident, and that the rumors spread by the anti-Trujillo exiles abroad were false. The exiles were blaming the government for their murders. Uncle Chu came in. Alicinio remained standing in the backyard.

I screamed and carried on with all my strength, completely opposed to Mamá signing the letter. However, Uncle Fello, who was a very prudent man, took me and locked me in María Teresa's bedroom. He went to my mother's bedroom and told her, "Comadre, the only one you have left alive is Dedé. What does it matter if you sign that document, if everyone already knows that it was no accident?" My mother agreed to sign it. I was screaming in the bedroom, furious, telling her not to sign it.

On December 6, the morning daily *El Caribe* published two international wire stories from AP and UPI specifically referring to the letter. The first story said that "a press release from the Dominican Revolutionary Party issued on December 2 to the news agency in New York reported that Mrs. Mercedes Reyes, widow of Mr. Enrique Mirabal, declared that she was currently in perfect health." The press release also stated:

> The widow declared that, in regards to the untruthful stories circulating abroad, "it is my duty to declare that I am in perfect health, at my country residence in Conuco, Salcedo, and those who are rudely speculating about the grief that currently overwhelms me due to the death of my three daughters Minerva, Patria, and María Teresa, which occurred in an automobile accident on the highway to Puerto Plata, can come and verify this for themselves."

The UPI wire story said the same, supposedly quoting my mother who allegedly stated, "I repudiate, for the abovementioned reasons, the attitude adopted by sensationalist groups abroad with regards to the death of my daughters and my husband, and to the lies being spread that I was assassinated."

Tonó, who was always close to my mother, revealed that she would not keep quiet and that she cried and cried, but said that she had to stay alive for the sake of her grandchildren so she could help raise them. "After Trujillo died, a lot of people visited Doña Chea. She talked to them about her daughters. She never believed they were dead. Sometimes she said that she felt them around her, that she felt they were looking at her. She called to them by their names. Every night she dedicated her prayers to them as if they had gone on a trip, as if they were expected to return at any moment. All of us there would pray alongside her."

It hurts to think that my mother was one of those people who come into this world to suffer. There are people like that, who seem to be pursued by tragedy, by suffering. But she never complained. She never said, "Why me?" "Why my daughters?" She suffered with tremendous dignity and was resigned to the comfort she found in her faith.

Trujillo, a murderer with the instinct of a hyena, sized Minerva up and saw her unbreakable will to fight. She was a woman who dared defy him politically and who did not hide her ideals. On many occasions I have thought that if my sister had gone alone with the driver, he would have killed just the two of them. Minerva was his problem, his obsession.

This was so much the case that around that time, Trujillo's chauffeur Zacarías commented to Trujillo's sister Japonesa that El Jefe clearly was not well because on several occasions Trujillo had said to him, "Look at that woman! Look at her over there. It's Minerva," but that when Zacarías looked, there was no one there.

For a sick, criminal, and authoritarian mind like his, accustomed to having women throw themselves at him, it must have been inconceivable to encounter a woman like Minerva. She not only rejected him but also dared to challenge him politically, and she led and organized the most important opposition movement that his regime had faced in thirty years. Trujillo pardoned no one who dared confront him. No one. And he was certainly not going to forgive a woman of such courage and audacity.

Joaquín Balaguer, who was always Trujillo's minion, was the president when the girls were killed. He had replaced Negro Trujillo, the dictator's brother, who was removed from office due to the pressures imposed by the OAS after the tyrant's assassination attempt against Venezuelan president Rómulo Betancourt. In his memoir and in a poem, Balaguer tried to wash my sisters' blood from his conscience, but I am convinced that he was very much aware of Trujillo's order to kill them. How could the president of the republic not know of the order, even though he was a "puppet" president the day the crime was committed? And if he wanted us to believe that he knew nothing of the plot, why didn't he resign, denounce the crime, or do something?

9

The People Mourn

The Uncertainties and Tragedies Continue

During the months that followed, beginning just a few weeks after the murders, there were several demonstrations throughout the country repudiating the crime. The majority were spontaneous, although some were organized. A kind of tribute called "The Way of the Cross of the Mirabal Sisters" also emerged. People began to slip notes under doors. "A kiss for the Mirabal Sisters" they called them. People began a telephone chain to express their support for my sisters, and many wrote poems in their honor. If anyone was caught participating in these acts, they were jailed. That is what happened to Caridad Cordero, an intellectual from Santiago, owner of the Atlántida bookstore. The same with Fifa Estrella, the sister of Salvador Estrella Sadhalá, one of the men who physically participated in the assassination plot that ambushed and killed Trujillo.

The cruelty toward our family was so intense that it did not stop with the assassination of the girls and Rufino. After the massacre, and as a way of deepening our pain, Trujillo came to visit one of Patria's neighbors who lived across the street from what was once her home. Although Patria's house had been ransacked, the people of Salcedo were ordered to go to the neighbor's house to pay homage to the dictator.

"Trujillo is coming to Salcedo," they announced. "Where will they take him for lunch?" No one could believe it when they announced that the luncheon would be held at the home of Isolina, Pedrito's cousin and neighbor and Patria's comadre. She was extremely upset but could do nothing about it. "Fill the house with people. Everyone must go and demonstrate that Trujillo has no enemies, that everyone supports him, and that no one thinks he ordered the killings of three defenseless sisters." Of course, lots of people went; all the officials, all the lackeys, the entire region was there to honor him. They prepared a tremendous buffet out in the backyard, with roasted pork and lots to drink.

And what brought about this inconceivable production? It was said that a Brazilian psychiatrist was brought in to treat Trujillo and that he had recommended that he be taken to the sisters' hometown so he could see that everyone loved him and thereby rid himself of his obsession with Minerva. I have already told how Trujillo's chauffeur Zacarías had made comments about this obsession to Japonesa Trujillo and the dictator's other sisters. So that is why they took him there, to a house where all those in attendance could see the ruins of my older sister's home, destroyed by Trujillo's snitches and lackeys. That was on March 6, 1961, some three months after the girls and Rufino were killed. Manolo, Leandro, and many of the young men from the area were still in prison or had simply disappeared. I asked myself, "How dare he mock us like this?" I remember that we even put locks on the door because people told us, "Trujillo is going to come here and will enter the house."

It must have been terrible for Isolina and her family to be forced into such a painful and humiliating experience, to have to open up their home to Trujillo. They were very close to us, like relatives. As a matter of fact, the day before the girls left for Puerto Plata, Isolina visited Patria at my mother's home. She said goodbye and reminded them to leave early. She was one of the last few people to see them alive.

Another painful blow we received at the time was Aunt Lalía's death. She was Mamá's sister and Patria's sister-in-law because she was married to Ezequiel González, Pedrito's brother. When we were little, we were her favorites. We ate tons of sweet cherries at Aunt Lalía's home! She only had one son, late in life, Antonio Ezequiel, who was imprisoned along with Nelson for participating in the 14th of June Movement. She was very close to Mamá, so when Mamá moved to Conuco, she built her house nearby. During that period, she would visit frequently to look after Raulito.

On November 25, Aunt Lalía was also going to go with Minerva and María Teresa to Puerto Plata. But she had heart problems, and the day before the trip she went to my mother's house and told her that she wasn't feeling well. After the tragedy, she became obsessed: "I should have gone, and not Patria. I should have been the one who died because my heart is already sick. What's there to live for?"

One day she returned from the doctor's office, ate with my mother, and played for a little while with Raulito. When she got home, she committed suicide. When they told me the news, I felt so helpless. This was yet another, very painful blow. We couldn't tell Mamá of the suicide. We decided to tell her that Aunt Lalía died of a heart attack, and that is what she believed until the very end.

On the day of Aunt Lalía's last prayer vigil, Tonó and I were walking from Ojo de Agua to Conuco under the hot sun. When a car would drive by, we would hide our faces so the people in the vehicle wouldn't be obligated to greet us or offer us a ride. If they gave us a ride, they would put themselves at risk. If they did not give us a ride, they would feel bad. We saw Pablo Yermenos's jeep come toward us. He was the mayor of Salcedo, and he was accompanied by the head of the SIM. They were making the final arrangements for Trujillo's visit, which would be the following day. I hid my face, but Pablo saw me, turned around, and offered to take us. I asked him to drop us off at an intersection near our destination.

"The Mirabal Sisters' Husbands Are Alive"

The tragedy occurred on a Friday. The following Monday, Ciriaco de la Rosa and some other men took Manolo and Leandro by car to the capital, to La Cuarenta. Pedrito was also taken from La Victoria to La Cuarenta. Leandro told us that every day he would climb on Manolo's shoulders and peer through a small crack in the wall, trying to see what was happening in the adjacent cell.

A year later, Manolo recalled those moments before the judge who was investigating the crime:

> On November 28, 1960, at 10:30 at night, my comrade, the engineer Leandro Guzmán Rodríguez and I were transferred to the Dominican Military Intelligence Service prison, known as La Cuarenta. On December 4 of that same year, they took my brother-in-law, Mr. Pedro Antonio González Cruz, to cell number six of the aforementioned prison, where the engineer Guzmán Rodríguez and I had been taken.
>
> The day before, on December 3, at four in the afternoon, they brought an agent from the Military Intelligence Service into our cell. His last name was Núñez.
>
> On December 4, at noon, a National Police captain, Miguel del Villar Alvarez, came to our cell accompanied by other agents stationed at the jail and told us, speaking directly to me, "Doctor Tavárez, you know that in this country, political prisoners are forbidden from receiving newspapers in prison, but there is something in this paper— he showed me a copy of *El Caribe,* dated November 27—that may be

of interest to you." And in a very cynical, mocking, and cruel way he threw the newspaper inside the cell with a grotesque laugh. He closed the door and left.

That's when we learned that our wives had died. After about half an hour, Captain Del Villar returned, accompanied by the same agents, and with the same mocking attitude he asked us, "So, now you know." He let out a laugh and said, "That's what this great government does to wretched individuals who, like you, attempt to overthrow it. And that's nothing. Terrible things are going to happen here because we are going to continue with the killings and perhaps the next victims will be all of you." Once he said this, he left and slammed the door behind him. The next day, Núñez, the calié, was removed from our cell.[87]

In his book *1J4: De espigas y de fuego*,[88] Leandro reveals that as long as the spy remained planted in their cell, he and Manolo would only look at each other without uttering a single word. "Those were by far the longest, most agonizing hours of my life, being constantly on alert."[89] When they removed the spy from the cell, the two prisoners finally managed to express their anguish. They speculated that perhaps the newspaper was fake. Trujillo was capable of ordering the newspaper to print false information in order to destroy their morale. In his book, Leandro explains:

> We continued to believe that a crime of such magnitude was simply not possible, that the tyrant could not have reached such levels of infamy, that it would be horrific, a direct afront to public opinion, something that Trujillo would not risk.
>
> [. . .]
>
> As more and more prisoners arrived at La Cuarenta, our desperation continued to grow. We asked them all if they knew anything about the Mirabal sisters. Most of them knew nothing. But one of them, Hugo Rivas, who had fought many times against Trujillo and who was a member of the Movement, assured us that he had seen them at La Victoria. Our spirits were lifted. We wanted to hold on

---

87 Statement made before Investigative Judge Ambiorix Díaz Estrella on December 1, 1961. Author's note.
88 Leandro Guzmán, *1J4: De espigas y de fuegos. Aportes para la memoria necesaria. Testimonios de un militante* (Santo Domingo: Editora de Colores, 1998).
89 Guzmán, *1J4: De espigas y fuegos*, 162.

dearly to that possibility. We convinced one another that that edition of *El Caribe* was fake.[90]

They were desperate, but they continued to feed their hopes and interpret the information they received in favor of that hope. Leandro says that when they were transferred to La Victoria months later, they were put in a cell that's walls were covered with the writing of those who had been there before. One of the writings took their breath away: "Trujillo is dead, but his regime of terror is still amongst us. Through these cells passed three innocent women, who were viciously brutalized. May 31, 1961." It wasn't until their release in July of that year that they would know for certain that their wives had been victims of that tragic crime and that Trujillo had been assassinated.

As for us, we thought for sure that Leandro and Manolo had been killed, but people came to us and told us the opposite. Ana Matilde Cuesta, who had been Manolo's girlfriend, and a military official we knew sent us messages: "They are alive." I doubted it: "Mamá, do not get your hopes up. They are dead." After my sisters' deaths, we learned of new killings almost daily.

Later on, Leandro and Manolo told us that in La Cuarenta, when prisoners arrived who had been tortured nearly to death, they would hear when the guards threw them into the adjacent cells. They would wait a while until the men calmed down and stopped crying before they started to shout: "The husbands of the Mirabal sisters are here," with the hope that someone would listen to them and eventually pass on the information. And, sure enough, from time to time we would receive these messages without knowing where they came from. A man named Héctor Osorio, who had been in jail, was one of the individuals who came to tell us that they were alive. "Liar!" I kept screaming, while Mamá said to me, "You're such a skeptic, Dedé."

When Leandro was released from jail, he told me that he saw them kill Domingo Russo and Eugenio Perdomo, and how their bodies were thrown in the back of a pickup truck. The latter was the father of Virgilio Perdomo Pérez, who died fighting the Balaguer regime in 1972, along with student leader Amaury Germán Aristy. Russo and Perdomito were falsely accused of having placed a bomb in the entrance of the St. Thomas of Aquinas Seminary. Trujillo's caliés had placed the bomb themselves. They say that the devil's sheets are long and narrow. One way or the other, a piece of him

---

90 Guzmán, *1J4: De espigas y fuegos*, 163.

will be exposed. There is always a witness, and in this particular case, there was more than one.

After six months of the same routine, of peering through a crack in the wall, one day they heard when someone who had just been tortured was thrown into the adjacent cell. He told them his name: Pirolo de la Maza. He was one of the De la Maza brothers,[91] an engineer who had worked with Leandro. Leandro pointed out, "Manolo, something's happened. I've noticed strange movements that are very different from the daily routine." Indeed, Trujillo had been assassinated, but Leandro and Manolo did not know it yet.

In late June 1961, an Organization of American States mission visited the country, and one of its first decisions was to visit and interview the political prisoners that remained in La Victoria. As soon as the delegation arrived at the prison, they demanded that the prison director bring them the husbands of the Mirabal sisters.

Thanks to the investigations and pressure from the OAS mission, the government began releasing important prisoners. On July 2, Leandro Guzmán, Pedro González, Miguel Lama, and Juan Rodríguez, Jr., were released. I remember that Esperanza, my neighbor and cousin, came to tell me, "They released Pedrito." I cried so hard that I thought I had used up all my tears. Leandro arrived later. They all returned, but not my sisters. They were dead. Those were very difficult days for my mother and me. Nelson and Noris could not stop crying either.

When I saw Leandro again, I relived all the pain. It was like poking at an open wound that would never heal. He himself wrote of the moment he arrived at my mother's house in Conuco. And he did it much better than I ever could:

> It was ten thirty at night when Patria, Minerva, and María Teresa's mother hugged us. The world came crumbling down on top of me. I cried, and cried, along with those who surrounded me and those who kept arriving, all trying to support me and ease my pain. But it was like adding sorrow on top of sorrow.
>
> Everything that was, and wasn't, passed through my head. I knew

---

91 Antonio, Ernesto, and Mario de la Maza Vásquez were conspirators in the plot to assassinate Trujillo, which Antonio orchestrated. A few years earlier, their brother Octavio (Tavito) had been framed for murder and was himself murdered by the regime. They were all executed by the regime and are now remembered as Héroes del 30 de Mayo.

then what loneliness is. I lost myself emotionally in knowing, and yet not knowing, if all this had been worth so much risk and sacrifice.

The past hit me with full force. Thirteen years before, precisely when she was thirteen years old, I met María Teresa, and together we began to build our happiness through the way we would look at one another, through tiny flowers left along the way, through secret messages. How would I ever survive this anguish?[92]

Manolo was released on July 26, along with Ramón (Moncho) Imbert, the Imbert brothers, and José (Che) Espaillat. Trujillo had already been assassinated, and Balaguer was the president, but Trujillo's son Ramfis, was in power.[93] They were truly difficult times. With a criminal fury, Ramfis dedicated himself to personally torturing all those who had participated in the assassination of Trujillo and many of their relatives. The most horrible crimes were committed during those months.

Manolo's nephew, Yuyo D'Alessandro, also happened to be Ramfis's brother-in-law since he was married to Ramfis's sister-in-law, Josefina Ricart. She was the sister of Ramfis's wife, Octavia (Tantana). Yuyo was one of the very few members of the 14th of June Movement who managed to escape prison and torture. He was of Italian ancestry and was taken in and hidden by an Italian couple. He managed to leave the country on board a ship, disguised as a priest. The crew had gone out to do some shopping. When they returned, Yuyo slipped in with them. The situation was so difficult that his family published a paid advertisement in the newspaper stating: "Yuyo is missing. We need to know his whereabouts."

In Yuyo's opinion, Ramfis was even more of a murderer than Trujillo. Although Trujillo would send people to kill, his son killed his opponents

---

92 Guzmán, *1J4: De espigas y fuegos*, 178–79.
93 Rafael Leónidas Trujillo Martínez (1929–1969)—known as Ramfis—was notorious for being an impetuous playboy with no interest in assuming the responsibilities in the regime. Though unprepared, he was named head of the Armed Forces. In the late 1950s, Ramfis's reckless behavior led the elder Trujillo to send him to Belgium. When the dictator was assassinated, Ramfis returned to the Dominican Republic, set on seeking vengeance. On the night of November 18, 1961, aided by other members of the regime and in a twisted plot that resulted in the deaths of three innocent prisoners, he personally killed six of the ten Héroes del 30 de Mayo extrajudicially before sailing off into exile on his father's yacht. Balaguer was left in control of the country. For more information, see Alejandro Paulino Ramos, "18 de noviembre de 1961: el día en que Ramfis Trujillo asesinó a los Héroes del 30 de mayo," *Historia de la República Dominicana*. 10 Nov. 2022. historiarepublicadominicana.com.do/18-de-noviembre-de-1961-el-dia-en-que-ramfis-trujillo-asesino-a-los-heroes-del-30-de-mayo.

with his own two hands. Such was the case with Luis Manuel (Tunti) Cáceres, Salvador Estrella Sadhalá, Modesto Díaz, Pedro Livio Cedeño, Roberto Pastoriza, and Huáscar Tejeda, all of whom were involved in Trujillo's assassination.

Once out of jail, Manolo came right over to our house. I remember him sitting down to talk with my mother. He tried to talk, but could not. He just cried. Then he went behind the house, sat Minou on his lap, and cried, cried, cried, hugging her. By that time, he had become a true national leader.[94] The people turned out en masse to follow him.

That day happened to coincide with a large rally sponsored by the Dominican Revolutionary Party (PRD) in San Francisco de Macorís. In the afternoon, when the massive crowd learned that Manolo had been released and that he was here, at our house, they marched right over. The crowd surrounded the entire property. The house and the backyard were packed with people screaming, "Manolo! Manolo!" They wanted to see him. And Manolo, overwhelmed with so much pain, could not stop crying. He had returned to the house for the first time without his Minerva.

When I saw all those people, I became very concerned. Manolo was a quiet man, and he spoke slowly, just like Minou. She inherited that from her father. "Manolo, come out, come out!" they insisted, until I finally made him step out. I remember seeing him walking, slowly, while the people around him clapped, honoring him. He did not speak. He could not. He was so overwhelmed with sadness and despair that the people cried along with him. What an unforgettable moment. Everyone cried in silence alongside their leader!

On that very same day, many were massacred. That same crowd headed to Santiago. The people had finally taken to the streets. There, they killed Erasmo Bermúdez Espaillat and Fausto Jiménez Guzmán. It seems that they confused Erasmo with the journalist Brinio Rafael Díaz. Pedro García Monclús and Marino Guzmán Abreu were viciously killed in the town of Moca. On the esplanade of the Juan Pablo Duarte Bridge, in the capital, they machine-gunned protesters, killing Dr. Víctor Rafael Estrella Liz and Manuel Martínez Cabrera. In Puerto Plata, where the 14th of June Move-

---

94   Following Trujillo's assassination, a variety of political parties emerged to challenge Joaquín Balaguer and the Partido Dominicano leading up to the November 1962 presidential election. Manolo led the 14th of June Revolutionary Movement through its evolution into a political party called the Agrupación Política 14 de Junio. Juan Bosch won the 1962 election, but when he was ousted by a coup in September 1963 and replaced by a military triumvirate, Manolo led an armed resistance to restore Bosch to the presidency.

ment had always been strong, repression was fierce. They killed Dr. Alejo Martínez, who was from San Pedro de Macorís but was the head of the Movement in Sosúa, and Dr. Pedro Clisante, among many others.

During those days that Manolo stayed at the house, he would sit for hours in an easy chair on the small back porch. With Minou on his lap, he let out all his pain and sorrow. He didn't want anyone to see him crying, so he hid back there, in the back of the house, to answer all of his little girl's questions. She was five years old at the time and was a very curious child. Minou remembers that he would tell her about Minerva and about his time in jail, while she softly caressed the marks left by his torturers when they put out their cigarettes on his arms.[95]

That's when people began to reproduce photographs of my sisters and sell them. Everyone wanted the photographs. Manolo did not like this commercialization. But who could control it? The people were in pain, and this was a way for them to express their feelings.

In late July and early August 1961, Manolo found himself in the capital, overseeing the mobilization of the political party that had formed out of the 14th of June Movement: the Agrupación Política 14 de Junio. From the capital, Manolo wrote an affectionate letter to my mother in which he expressed his feelings and mentioned his political activities, which were consuming all his time:

August 6, 1961

> My dearest Mamá Chea,
>
> I thought that by now we would be there, with all of you, whom we miss so very much. But work is all-consuming, and, in spite of our personal wishes, we are bound by obligation to meet our responsibilities. But we will be there, dear Mamá Chea. I am trying to resolve some urgent matters before I can leave. I need to see all of you again, share with you my spiritual solace and enjoy with my children the small pleasures that life holds for me.
>
> The three of us are in good health. We are taking good care of one another. I always remember your advice, and I try to conduct myself accordingly. Our endeavors are coming along fine. The people's sup-

---

[95] Minou details her recollection of this moment in *Mañana te escribiré otra vez. Minerva y Manolo. Cartas*, p. 270. In the English translation *The Letters of Minerva Mirabal and Manolo Tavárez: Love and Resistance in the Time of Trujillo*, this passage is on pages 259–260.

port for the 14th of June continues to multiply on a daily basis, and at a surprising pace. Our sacrifice has not gone unnoticed, and we are beginning to reap the fruits of the struggle. This is the only thing that heartens me in this noble struggle. Kisses to my beloved children, and for all of you my deep affection.

Your son,
Manolo

Manolo rented an apartment in the capital and asked that we let him take Minou with him: "I want to enjoy my daughter, and Manolito is too little." The boy had been living with my mother since the time he was a baby, and so he stayed with us. In Santo Domingo, Manolo enrolled Minou at the Santa Teresita School, headed by Minetta Roque, a teacher who cared for her very much.

Don Manuel and Doña Fefita, Manolo's parents, had also moved to the capital. Carmen Tavárez Mayer, Manolo's older half-sister on his father's side, had moved them in with her. Carmen was the daughter of Don Manuel and his first wife, Isabel Mayer, who was a high-ranking member of the regime and the country's first woman governor. Carmen enjoyed a very solid economic position because she was married to Guido D'Alessandro, an Italian engineer who lived in the country and had received important government contracts, including for the construction of the National Palace. Carmen Tavárez Mayer and Guido D'Alessandro were not only the parents of Yuyo, but also of Aldo, their twenty-year-old son who was killed by Trujillo on November 19, 1960.

Pedrito no longer had a home. They had destroyed it. He and Leandro stayed at my mother's house for a while.

The End of the Trujillo Era

On November 18, 1961, the Trujillo family was forced to leave the country. We felt liberated, as if we were breathing for the first time. We joined in the celebration and chanted what became a very popular Christmas song: "¡Navidad, Navidad, Navidad con libertad!" We would board buses and trucks. We went to political meetings and screamed along with the people, "¡Navidad, Navidad, Navidad con libertad!"

Balaguer sought asylum in the diplomatic mission of the Papal Nuncio on December 31. But even there he must have heard the people chanting in the streets, screaming, "Balaguer, paper puppet!"

Soon after, the Council of State was introduced. It was headed by Rafael Bonnelly, who would govern until the national elections were held in December 1962. In my opinion, Bonnelly organized an honest electoral process in which his party, the Civic Union, the party of the "well-off," lost. The winning candidate, Juan Bosch, had a simple message and was a known mediator. People listened to him and understood his messages, not only through his radio programs, but also in the last debate he held with Father Láutico García. The new president was sworn in on February 27, 1963. He only lasted until September because the army that Trujillo had built was still intact. The Americans also played an important role in his overthrow.

A few days after Trujillo was killed, Alicinio Peña Rivera destroyed Patria's home and burned it to the ground. During the trial, which was televised nationally, he declared that he had used the wood from Patria's home to build his own home in Santiago, on Estrella Sadhalá Avenue. Enraged, a group of citizens headed to his house and destroyed it.

Not too long ago I went to visit Pedro Ramón Rodríguez Echavarría to thank him because he was the one who arrested Alicinio Peña Rivera and stopped him from leaving the country with Ramfis, as they had planned. Rodríguez Echavarría told me, "I was the one that led the counter-coup. That's where I found Alicinio. It was like this: either he killed me, or I killed him. I took his machine gun and arrested him." By then, Manolo had already investigated the crime and knew who was directly responsible for murdering the girls and Rufino.

When Manolo was released from jail, he and Jaimito reclaimed the farm that Alicinio had taken from us, the farm in Güiza, as well as another one of our farms in the same region. As for Pedrito, he returned to the land where his house had once stood. Today, the property where Patria and Pedrito's home once stood, and where their children were born, belongs to them. I have tried to rebuild Patria's gardens, the gardens that she so loved.

In the mornings I like to go to Conuco to visit what was once Patria's home, to water the plants that survived and the new ones I have planted. I see the water tank, the columns, the fish pond, and everything else that survived the looting by the caliés. Patria built a small dam to retain the water from a small river nearby. With rocks and sand, she built a small swimming pool. My sons Jimmy and Jaime Enrique remember how they used to love to swim in "Nina Patria's" little river. "Nina Patria" was always ready to go out exploring. She was like a turbine that energized us all. We had so much fun together! Most of the rivers around here have dried up, but not the one that runs near Patria's home. Sometimes, not knowing if I am talking to her or to myself, I tell her that perhaps it is true that nature tends to be very grateful.

Seeing those ruins pains me deeply. I remember how Patria took care of her home and her garden. I've planted orange blossoms, just like my sister had planted before, with the hope that they multiply. I've also planted bushes with red flowers, called *coralillos,* to fill in open spaces. They are so pretty, even amidst the ruins. Not long ago I proposed to Noris, "Since the orange blossoms aren't doing well, and since you and I aren't going to see the garden in full bloom, why don't we plant species that will cover the walls?"

Mamá, always cautious, austere, and a good administrator, bought a farm with some cash Papá had left. She bought it after distributing part of the money among all of us. Pedrito received some money from the sale of a small farm he owned near his house. With that money he bought a little over ninety-three acres in the Güiza area, near San Francisco de Macorís. That purchase encouraged Mamá to purchase an adjacent farm that was for sale at seven pesos per tarea. Since she had saved some money, she bought it for some fourteen thousand pesos and put Patria and Pedrito's name on the title. She was trying to avoid problems with a family that Papá had with another woman. I mention this because this situation eventually caused some serious conflicts that made Mamá suffer tremendously.

My mother never stopped working. She took care of everything, including the plantations and the cacao harvest. She tended to the cattle... I used to visit her almost every day, and it concerned me to see her hours on end moving the cacao with her feet. But, as long as she was active, she had energy. "Mamá, stop, leave that alone," I would tell her, but she wouldn't listen to me. Later, when I saw her in her wheelchair, I missed seeing her moving around. It was as if life was over for her.

All of us inherited Mamá's strength. I certainly inherited it. I am eighty-three years old and full of energy. But, above all, I inherited her mental strength. Thanks to that strength, we never let the pain overwhelm us. What truly helped my mother and me recover was the responsibility of raising and educating my sisters' children.

Minerva Josefina (Minou) and Manuel Enrique (Manolo) were four and two years old, respectively, in November 1960. Milka Jacqueline del Rosario, María Teresa's daughter, was twenty months old. Raúl Fidel Ernesto, Patria's youngest child, had celebrated his first birthday in September. Noris Mercedes, Patria's middle child, was fifteen, and Nelson Enrique was eighteen.

After Patria's death, Nelson came to live with us. Jaimito had cleared a coffee plantation to give the land to Nelson so he could plant various crops and work the land. He tried to keep him busy and gave him other responsibilities. "It's not good for this boy to just sit around thinking. . . ." Nelson had always lived in a very stable household where he had everything he needed. He had tons of toys because, as the first son and first grandchild, all the family's love and attention had concentrated on him. Jaimito thought that with the vegetable garden, Nelson would once again become involved in something, and that is exactly what happened.

When she was released from jail, Minerva had hired Tatá Pantaleón as a private tutor for Minou, who was very sharp when it came to her studies. She learned to read and write by the time she was four. In January 1961 we knew nothing about Manolo, so I did something I thought Minerva would like: I took the child to study at the Immaculate Conception School, where Noris was studying. That way I would be able to get her away from the frightening and painful atmosphere that surrounded our home. For the nuns, having Minou there was like having a little piece of Minerva. "Minervita, Minervita," they would call her. They had her sit with them at mealtime, something they did not do with any other student, and they told me that the girl was a blessing for them. They pampered and took care of her. During the conflicts between Trujillo and the Church, and the harsh attacks against Monsignor Panal, the nuns would lock Minou and Noris in the cloister because they thought the regime's lackeys would come and take the girls away.

Manolo was released during Minou's school vacation, but he waited until she made her First Communion before taking her to the capital. In the house museum there is a photograph of Manolo with his daughter on her fifth birthday. Both seem happy and sad at the same time. At least he was able to participate in Minou's First Communion and have a photograph taken with her.

10

Manolo, 1963

Almost two years had passed since Manolo took Minou to live with him. That's when he called me to ask, "Dedé, take Minou with you because they could take her hostage so that I turn myself in." He was preparing for what was coming.

On September 23, 1963—two days before the coup against Juan Bosch—Manolo came to Salcedo to attend the burial of Alexis Brache, a 14th of June revolutionary killed by the police. That was the last time I spoke with him at length. I remember him standing with one foot resting on a bench as we talked. Jaimito told him, "Manolo, be careful. Take care of yourself!" He answered, "Don't worry. I'm not putting myself on someone's banquet table." That was the last time I saw him. After that, I spoke with him on the telephone one more time.

I learned that he had actually considered the possibility of seeking asylum in the Mexican Embassy. He entered the embassy, but a group of his comrades who had trained in Cuba, including Fidelio Despradel, pressured Manolo and reprimanded him: "The men of the 14th of June know perfectly well where the rugged mountains of Quisqueya[96] are." For that group of comrades, who were extremely motivated by Fidel's experience in Cuba, seeking asylum was treason. Manolo felt responsible for his actions and left the embassy. He hid in the home of Wiche García Saleta. The only time I attempted to talk with Manolo, Wiche took the telephone and said to me, "Dedé, hang up the phone. It's tapped." He was very upset with me for making that phone call.

Other comrades disagreed with the plan to go to the mountains to fight in order to restore the country's constitutional order. Among these were Benjamín Ramos, a physician; Máximo Bernard, a famous basketball player and member of the Basketball Federation; Vinicio Echavarría; and Pucho

---

96 Quisqueya—or "Mother of All Lands"—was the name given to the island by the native Taínos. In one of his political speeches, Manolo had stated that the 14th of June would keep up the fight from "the rugged mountains of Quisqueya." This creates a parallel with the Cuban Revolution led by Fidel Castro, which was launched from the Sierra Maestra mountains.

García Saleta . . . They, and others, did not agree with this course of action. Manolo was pressured between those who did believe in going to the mountains to fight and those who did not. Perhaps he was not completely convinced of this plan, but he felt he had to honor the promise he had made his comrades. Yolanda Vallejo, in whose home Benjamín was hiding, confirmed Manolo's conflict. She still keeps the minutes of the various meetings in which she participated. In them are documented the resolutions that were adopted.

Mamá and I knew that Manolo was committed to the establishment of a constitutional order, but we never imagined that he would actually take to the mountains. On November 22, the same day John F. Kennedy was killed in the United States, Manolo left for Santiago. From there the guerrilla fighters went up to the country's central mountain range. Once in the mountains, they all got sick. They had no weapons, and the ones they did have did not work. They were useless. It was a total disaster.

I don't criticize Manolo. He lived under a dictatorship, and he was ready to give up his life for the pursuit of freedom. He was not yet thirty-three years old. Much too young. He had lived his entire life under the dictatorship. During our youth we might make decisions based on ideals that later turn out to be less opportune as we thought.

Manolo was a leader of tremendous charisma who united all Dominicans. By going up to the mountains he kept his promise to his people, and I would say to his comrades. He made a conscientious decision that would eventually cost him his life. I found out for sure that he was up in the mountains the day they killed him. We thought it was a lie. On the one hand those from the extreme left kept saying, "Manolo is in a hotel, having a great time." On the other hand, the people on the right also attacked him.

Doña Paulina Justo, Manolo's aunt, came to visit and told us, "Manolo is up in the mountains." That was on a Friday, and the following day, on Saturday, December 21, they killed him. Our house was flooded with people. "They killed Manolo! They killed Manolo!" they shouted. I took Minou to my sister-in-law Lesbiolita's house so she would not witness the events. Jaimito and I once again left for Santiago.

This time around I didn't have the strength to go up to Las Manaclas, where they killed Manolo, outside the mountain town of San José de las Matas in the country's northwest region. So at first I waited in the home of Doña Betty Vda. Román. She was Manolo's cousin. After a while we went to the hospital to wait for the family members who had gone to the mountains to pick up their loved ones' bodies.

In the most terrible circumstances, a good man always comes along. This time, that was the engineer Víctor González, who worked in the Secretariat of Public Works. He was a handsome, serious, young man. He was loyal. His wife was related to Doña Fefita. That day he traveled up to Las Manaclas in a pickup truck from the Public Works Office. He loaded all the bodies onto the truck and drove down to Santiago. And there I went again, to the same morgue at the José María Cabral Hospital, where I had once picked up my sisters' bodies. The bodies of the seventeen guerrilla fighters were all there. All had been executed. It was evident that they had been lined up and shot.

It was a nightmare to relive the past, and now with this new tragedy on top of it. Lying there in the morgue were the seventeen destroyed bodies of the young guerrilla fighters. I recognized Manolo's face. Near his forehead were the gun powder burns left behind by a bullet. His entire body was riddled with bullets. There were bayonet stab wounds in several parts of his body. They killed him with terrible cruelty. I recognized Jaime Ricardo Socías, the husband of Manolo's sister Angela, by his moustache. Thankfully, the cold temperature up in the mountains had kept the bodies from decomposing quickly.

Other family members had gone to pick up the remains of the fallen men. We brought back Manolo and Jaime, and we buried them in Salcedo's cemetery that Monday afternoon. That was their resting place until we transferred Manolo's remains on November 2000 to the house museum, where he now rests alongside the girls in the garden, beneath the memorial in their honor. A month later, on December 21, we transferred Jaime's remains to his family's mausoleum in Montecristi, his hometown.

I left the morgue reeking of a horrible stench. Even though we transferred the bodies in an ambulance, the car in which I returned absorbed the smell of burnt flesh and retained it for several days. I could not get rid of that smell. Many months would pass before I could once again look at or much less eat a piece of meat.

For my mother and me, Manolo's death was a very difficult blow to assimilate. It was as if they had opened up an old, unhealed wound and started poking at it. Going back to the cemetery was like burying Minerva and the girls all over again. We felt the same despair. Once again, we were filled with anger and helplessness. Mamá had found comfort and support in Manolo. He was the son she always wanted to have. That's why his death was such a painful blow for her. She trusted completely in his judgment and in his sense of justice, always fighting to do the right thing.

But the pain was felt much deeper because of what Manolo meant to those who followed and believed in him. "Poor homeland, poor country," we thought. In the same way we were mourning the loss of a dear family member, our country was also suffering his loss. A leader who the Dominican people had taken thirty-two years to create, a courageous man who confronted Trujillo and epitomized the ideals of freedom and liberty held by a generation that, today, some still call the "Immortal Generation." Even the pampered children of Trujillo's closest allies supported Manolo.

He represented security, the fundamental pillar that was needed to guarantee the justice and freedom needed for our country to finally walk freely on the road to progress and democracy. We lost our guiding light, our adviser, and once again, we felt that the forces of evil had triumphed. The system, structure, and methods used by the tyrant were alive and well and had successfully swept away the first truly democratic and just government in our nation's history. And they had killed the leader of an entire generation that had finally found in Manolo a leader, a captain. He was a man who, when he was most needed, showed tremendous human qualities, a solid capacity for analysis, intellectual preparation, purity and commitment, valor and fearlessness, serenity and tolerance. He was a leader who was in love with his country and was sensitive to the needs of his people. Manolo led the way in a clear project for our nation's future, not thinking of himself, but of the Dominican people. He demonstrated all the qualities of a great leader.

III

A Time of Recovery and Commitment

Figure 3.1. Pedro, Leandro, and Manolo in jail during the visit of the OAS Commission in June 1961. Courtesy of the Fundación Hermanas Mirabal.

Figure 3.2. Manolo, a witness in the trial against the assassins of the Mirabal sisters, points to identify one of the murderers, 1962. Courtesy of the Fundación Hermanas Mirabal.

Figure 3.3. Manolo, 1963. "Mother and I knew that he was committed to the return of a constitutional government, but we never imagined that he would go to the mountains." Courtesy of the Fundación Manolo Tavárez Justo and photographer Milvio Pérez.

11

A Trial That Will Go Down in History

To help me recount all the events that impacted my family, I am going to refer to documents that, together with my personal experiences, clarify important details regarding my sisters' deaths and the events that followed. I've also gathered other important facts that will help me reconstruct the last hours of my sisters' lives as best as possible.

In the process of writing this memoir, I once again followed the route that my sisters and Rufino traveled, from the point where they were abducted to the possible location where they were killed. For years I avoided traveling through that place. But now I have reconnected with individuals from Puerto Plata who saw them or were in contact with them on November 25, 1960. I've researched important documents that I had never, until today, dared to read because the information they contained would leave me shattered.

There are details that I did not have the courage nor the strength to research, until now. There was a time when I was terrified, incapable of coming face-to-face with certain information. But now I want the truth. And I want to leave my testimony because it will shed light on the most horrific period in our nation's history. That is why I am writing this memoir: so we do not forget and so no one in my country will ever again be a victim of so much horror, so much pain.

The period between 1960 and 1965 was very intense for my family and for our country, and I was a close witness to many of the events that would change our history.

The exiled members of the Dominican Revolutionary Party returned on July 4, 1961, and immediately began to sponsor marches and political rallies throughout the country. I remember a famous march that took place in Santiago. Jaimito and I participated. During the rally, Dr. Salvador Jorge Blanco[97] delivered a speech in which he mentioned the names of various towns. Those in attendance cheered when their hometown was mentioned. Then he said, "Salcedo brings Minerva to mind, that goddess that was lost

---

97 He would be president of the Dominican Republic from 1982 to 1986.

in the ocean of life." Even today, when I remember those words, tears come to my eyes. I was there, right in the middle of the rally, standing in a corner, thin, dressed in black. All of a sudden, the public began to shout, "Dedé is here!" And they led me to the podium. I resisted because I have never liked the limelight, but the truth was it was a touching tribute to my sisters. That must have been in early July because I remember that Manolo had not yet been released from jail.

In the months that followed, the 14th of June Movement grew among the population and organized many activities. In September, there was a huge event in Salcedo to inaugurate and bless the movement's first office in the city. Invited guests spoke at the town square. I even delivered a speech in which I encouraged women to join the struggle. Chachita Brito had written it for me.

The caliés were all over town, and their offices were still in my mother's original home in Salcedo. After the rally ended, a young woman by the name of Margarita Toribio began to shout, "Down with the Trujillos!" People immediately began to chant along with her. The caliés, who lived near Jaimito's parents' house, initially reacted with aggression but then decided not to provoke the crowd. They withdrew to the nearby barracks looking for reinforcement.

Leandro and Vinicio Echavarría, from the 14th of June Movement's office in the capital, were sleeping at our house in Ojo de Agua, while Manolo slept at my mother's home in Conuco. We put our belongings in the only vehicle we had, our red pickup truck, a vehicle the caliés knew quite well. But then Jaimito thought that leaving in the truck could be dangerous, so he left it parked at his parents' house and went to look for Leonte, a driver friend of his, and asked him to take us home. We stopped to fill Leonte's car with gas. A man we knew asked us for a ride, and Jaimito got out of the car to let him in. The caliés were out looking for us but were disoriented. They spotted Jaimito and came toward us. At that moment, Jaimito ordered the driver to "move over!" He grabbed the steering wheel, took off, and passed the Volkswagen with the caliés inside. We hit the road, killed the headlights, and sped off as if the "devil were after us." When we reached Ojo de Agua we entered a dark alley instead of taking the normal way home. But when we stopped, the tail lights lit up, and the caliés spotted us. However, as we neared the house, they turned around because they knew that in the city, in Sacedo, they could count on backup from colleagues, but in the countryside, it was a completely different story.

We quickly got out of the car, and Jaimito began to call on the neighbors. "Everyone, come out! Grab rocks! The caliés are coming for us!" Days before, there was a rumor going around that they were going to burn our house down. Several men came out and gathered a ton of rocks. Many of these people had attended the rally. I remember that Leandro and his companions had a scare because when they arrived, the neighbors almost mistook them for the caliés. But that night the caliés didn't show up.

The situation was very tense during those days. Because I knew my husband's temper well, I was expecting a serious confrontation between him and the caliés. That's why I recommended that he spend some time in the United States, where one of his sisters lived.

That is what he did. But in December, when Brigadier General Pedro R. Rodríguez Echavarría led a countercoup[98] and there was a huge strike, Jaimito said he was returning to the country even if they killed him. He suffered from an ulcer, and during his trip home, it began to hemorrhage. He couldn't stand the pain and collapsed at the airport in Puerto Rico. Fortunately, Luis Fernández, who had been his school friend in San Francisco, saw him lying on the floor and asked, "Jaimito, is that you?" He replied, "Yes, and I'm dying." Luis took him to the hospital, where he received a blood transfusion. A couple of days later, when he was better, he returned home. The first thing he told me was, "Don't ask me why I came!" He didn't want me to scold him for returning when the situation was still so dangerous.

In Mamá's home everyone lived in terror. After Trujillo's death thousands of rumors circulated, and we feared that anything could happen. On several occasions, when someone heard the caliés roaming around the house, we thought they would set the house on fire. Tonó recalls that she and the other girls who took care of the children had set up an escape route: "Each of you will take one of the children and leave the house through the main hallway."

---

98 Reference to the Rebellion of the Pilots on November 19, 1961, the morning after Ramfis Trujillo, before fleeing the country, killed six of the men who had assassinated his father. He and the dictator's brothers, the generals José Arismendi (Petán) Trujillo Molina and Héctor B. (Negro) Trujillo Molina had plotted along with the SIM to massacre several political leaders and carry out a coup. To prevent this, six members of the Dominican Air Force bombed military installations so the Trujillos could not mobilize the Armed Forces to support the coup. See Homero Luis Lajara Solá, "Los pilotos de la patria," *Listín Diario*, Nov. 19, 2016. listindiario.com/la-republica/2016/11/19/443780/los-pilotos-de-la-patria.html.

Malú was in charge of Raulito, Hilda was in charge of Jacqueline, and she was in charge of Manolito. Minou was at school in La Vega.

I will always be grateful to Rodríguez Echavarría because he was the one who arrested my sisters' murderers. When I visited him in Guerra, a small town northeast of the capital, I told him how much I appreciated his courage in arresting Alicinio and the other criminals and bringing them to trial. "How did you do it?" I asked him. He explained:

> When I decided to go through with the countercoup, I was in the capital, and I didn't know what to do. I was sure there would be a massive killing, and that they were planning to kill all those who participated in Trujillo's death. That's when I got up the courage to go through with it. God gave me the courage, because I didn't know what to do at the moment. I made my decision and told the pilot, "Start up the airplane!" When I arrived in Santiago, I ran into Alicinio. I took his gun away and locked him up. I ordered the regiment to stand at attention and told them, "You will take orders from me alone, because there is an invasion on the way!" I sent an aircraft to Dajabón with the same message.

What Rodríguez Echavarría did not tell me was how he arrested Cándido (Candito) Torres Tejada and the others. But had he not intervened, Alicinio would have left the country with the Trujillos. Alicinio was waiting in Santiago for the coup so he could take over. Keep in mind that Alicinio was the head of the SIM in the Cibao.

Rodríguez Echavarría told me that before the countercoup, he had met with Manolo Tavárez in the home of Pompilio Brouwer. That was where Manolo handed him a list with the names of the five men who killed the Mirabal sisters and Rufino. We knew of Alicinio Peña Rivera's involvement because of his responsibilities as the head of the SIM office in the Cibao.

Two months after my visit with Rodríguez Echavarría, he passed away.

The question that I had always asked myself was how did Manolo find out who the murderers were? I only found out when Leandro published *1J4: De espigas y de fuegos*. In his book, Leandro reveals that when they were prisoners in Salcedo, they were being transferred to another location by car. In the front seat were two SIM caliés. Manolo was in the back seat and, because he was so tall, he must have been very uncomfortable. Leandro and another calié sat next to him. Leandro's handcuffs were on so tight that he could hardly stand the pain, so he asked the calié to loosen them a bit. He did so before they reached the town of Moca.

Sometime later, after so much had happened in the country, including the murders of the girls and Trujillo, and once some things had changed, one day Leandro was at the 14th of June Movement office on Hostos Street in the capital. Outside, a group of people were beating up a couple of caliés. A man ran up the office stairs, shouting, "Leandro! Leandro! Don't let them kill me!" Leandro recognized him and hid him to protect him from the crowd. That was a face he would never forget because it was the face of the man who had loosened his handcuffs during the car ride. He was the one who told Manolo the identities of the SIM members who had killed the girls. Leandro had two significant encounters with this killer, whose name he never knew.

What Happened on November 25?

It was through a conversation with Chujo Pimentel Líster that I found out in detail what happened on the afternoon of November 25. He lived for more than ninety years in Puerto Plata with the dignity that comes with knowing that one has fulfilled his duty. It is the testimony of one of the last persons who was in contact with my sisters on November 25, 1960. From his very lips I heard the most minute details related to those critical moments. From this conversation, I also learned how destiny intervened to place this honorable and brave man in my sisters' path when they needed it most. As Chujo himself recalled:

> Before [Patria, Minerva, María Teresa, and Rufino] arrived at my home, the SIM cars were already in the vicinity. My house, which I later lost in a fire, was situated on José del Carmen Ariza Street. When I heard the sounds of the Volkswagens: tum, tum, tum . . . , I said, "The girls are coming." They—Minerva and María Teresa— usually arrived at ten thirty in the morning. They would make themselves at home and, after lunch, they would go to the fortress to visit their husbands. That day, on November 25, they were really happy. They looked well. They even told us that when they crossed the Yásica Bridge, where there is a military post, they gave a ride to one of the guards. I told them, "But how could you do something so risky?" And Minerva said, "Naaah . . . Those guys are nothing. The bad ones are the ones giving them orders." It seems that on the way they identified themselves to the guard, who immediately said, "Drop me off here." They also told me that several days before they

had been in Montecristi, where they sold some furniture, including a stove and a refrigerator. They were carrying with them the money from the sale of the items, which totaled a couple of hundred pesos.

This time Patria was with them. It was the first time that Patria had gone along. The driver, Rufino de la Cruz, also accompanied them. In Santiago, they had stopped to purchase some sewing materials. They were getting ready to move to Puerto Plata so they could be closer to their husbands. I already had a house for them. But it seems that the permission they had received to visit their husbands was a mere farce.

That day they arrived at around eleven in the morning. They changed into more comfortable clothes. After eating they rested for a little while, then took a bath and dressed up really nice. They commented that they had to dress up nice to lift their husbands' spirits. At around two they left for the fortress. On the way back to my house, they stopped the car on the street. Minerva and María Teresa got out of the jeep to say hello to Miriam Morales, an old friend from prison. When they arrived back at my house, they seemed happy, and they said that the boys were really glad because they had told them, "Things are going to get better because we are going to see you twice a week. We are going to move close by."

They returned from the fortress at around four in the afternoon. I suggested they stay overnight and leave the following day to avoid being on the road at night. But they said, "No, if our mother doesn't see us at home, she's going to think that there's been a disaster. No, don't worry, we'll be back next week." The SIM caliés kept driving around my house, just waiting for them to leave. They were beginning to think that they were not leaving that night. They were so close to the house that we heard one of them say, "They're putting the bags into the car."

As I said, they were happy and planning their upcoming move to the house I had rented for them. And you cannot imagine the trouble I went through to get that house! No one wanted to rent to us or do anything that was related to the girls. I went to two or three places before I finally rented a house under my name. The person rented the house to me not knowing that it was for the girls. Rufino de la Cruz, the driver, was also relaxed, normal, as if there were nothing going on. I think that he was a man who was willing to serve the Mirabal sisters, no matter the circumstances.

At the house we had a huge dog that when he sniffed the presence of the caliés, he would climb on the roof and start barking like crazy. The next day, the animal was found dead. They'd poisoned him.

And then, we already know what took place that November 25 in the outskirts of Puerto Plata. They were ambushed in Mará Picá and taken to a nearby sugar cane field. And then, the disaster.

The next day I passed by the grocery store I went to every day. It was owned by my friend Raymundo Parra. My friend's wife said to me, "Compadre, you know that the girls are not coming back anymore, right?" "What do you mean they're not coming back?" I replied. "That's right," she said, and she told me that the night before, a commissioner from the town of Tamboril stopped by and said that when he passed by La Cumbre by way of the old road, he saw they were removing the bodies from the ravine where the murderers had dumped them. I never thought they would go so far as to kill them.

I attended the girls' funeral with Dr. Linda Pelegrín, but we could not enter the cemetery because it had been cordoned off by military personnel and all those thugs. They wouldn't let us through. It wasn't until later that they allowed us to leave a flower at the cemetery gate. They didn't even let us enter the cemetery. It was terrible.

Later there was a rumor going around that after killing the Mirabals and Rufino, they had also murdered Manolo and Leandro. The rumor began because they found a large bag with human remains in the cemetery. Luckily, the rumors were false.

I traveled to Montecristi, and I spent the day before Christmas Eve with Don Manuel and Doña Fefita. They were devastated. But Don Manuel was a brave and strong man. He told me how much he appreciated my visit because he knew how dangerous it was for me.

Many months later, two or three days after being released from jail, Manolo visited me to thank me, to show his appreciation, and to meet the young man that I had sent every day to deliver their meals to the prison.

I met Doña Fefita and the girls by accident. I had worked with Don Manuel Tavárez, Manolo's father. We were very close friends. I was very close to the family, almost like a relative. I visited Don Manuel and Doña Fefita quite frequently. As a matter of fact, I met Minerva during one of those visits. She was in the backyard, which was huge. She was bathing Minou, who at the time was only a few months old.

Minerva truly impressed me. That girl was capable of doing anything she set out to do.

In Puerto Plata I was visiting the home of Raymundo Parra, an excellent gentleman. We were there, in his backyard. I usually visited in the afternoons. His wife was in the grocery store, and she called out to him. He took a while to return, so I went looking for him. That's when I saw Doña Fefita, Minerva, and María Teresa. They had traveled with René Bournigal in his vehicle. René had gone to visit one of his brothers, and the three women were in the grocery store. I said, "Wow! What a pleasant surprise! What are you doing here?" They explained that they had come to confirm that the boys were alive, or if they had killed them on the way. I said to them, "Oh no! Let's go right to my house." And we went to my house. That's when they explained to me that they were buying food to leave at the jail for their husbands. They asked me to recommend someone who could deliver their meals on a daily basis. I said, "I'll take care of that." Minerva told the other women, "You see how things are working out? Don Chujo will take care of the meals." I sent the two prisoners their meals twice a day in canteens. One canteen had Manolo's name written on it, and the other said "Leandro."

Things were crazy back then. I remember there was a girl, who was also from Salcedo, who managed the pharmacy owned by Don Luis Pelegrín. It was across the street from my house. Her husband was the administrator at the Electric Company. The girl had been a school friend of the Mirabal sisters, and she stopped by to visit. They greeted and hugged one another. That was enough for the woman's husband to be fired from the Electric Company and for his world to come crumbling down around him. They were putting the final touches on a small boat they were building, but they were never allowed to launch it. The retaliation against them was terrible.

My father visited me and asked, "Are you aware of the problems you've created?" And I said, "Yes." "Are you aware of the situation?" Once again, I said yes. He, José Pimentel Loinaz, was a well-known anti-Trujillo activist. He spent Trujillo's thirty years in power knocking him down, saying, "He won't last another day. . . ." This time he told me, "Then keep doing what you're doing." During those days no one visited my house. Even my friends stayed away. One evening, the SIM agents were pulling on the doors. They were trying to knock down the doors, but they couldn't open them. Don

Luis Pelegrín, who lived across the street, turned on his lights and came out to see what was going on. The SIM agents left. It was an old building, with four front doors, no porch. We used to sit on the doorjamb. The SIM Volkswagens would pass by and almost stop, like they were threatening us, mocking us. Then they would leave. They placed microphones on the exterior wall of the house, next to the neighboring house. They carefully monitored all our movements. They would call us on the phone and ask, "Which tree in the square do you want us to hang you from for protecting enemies of the State?" They did this constantly. The tension was unbearable.

Some people said to me, "Chujo, let well enough alone. Think of your family's safety, and your children." I would answer, "I'm already involved in this, and I can't turn back now. I have to continue no matter what." Doing the contrary would have been cowardly on my part.

I worked in the insurance business. I represented the Caribbean Motors Company here, owned by Paquito Martínez, Trujillo's brother-in-law. However, I never suffered retaliation at work. I also worked for La Curacao, a furniture store. But everyone avoided me there. No one visited me, no one came around. My business crashed. Linda Pelegrín, the daughter of Luis Pelegrín, was the only person who visited us.

During the trial of the murderers of the Mirabal sisters and Rufino, I was there, and I testified. I thought there should have been a plan or something to do away with all those thugs. Do you know what they did? They were laughing while I was testifying. I remember Cruz Valerio, who people said would beat the ears of his victims with his open hands. He either killed them or drove them mad.

They asked me if I could point out the SIM members accused of the crimes. I said yes. I pointed them out and described each one. Especially on the days when the girls visited my house, the SIM agents would position themselves across the street from my house, in El Bambú. The place had a glass wall. They spied on everyone that entered and left the house. But I also saw them.

Fernando Cueto, from Puerto Plata, who in 1960 was a young man, had already been arrested and tortured along with Manolo and the other members and sympathizers of the 14th of June Movement. He was one of the individuals who ran into the girls on November 25:

That day, I arrived at Linda Pelegrín's pharmacy at ten in the morning with Guancho Escaño. The owner of the pharmacy would allow us to hide there so the dictator's henchmen wouldn't see us. The pharmacy was across the street from the home of Don Chujo Pimentel. Guancho and I, both members of the 14th of June Movement, waited for the girls just in case they needed our help running errands. At around noon the girls arrived in the jeep, and I went to greet them. Some people would regularly go and talk to them and give them things to bring to Manolo and Leandro. I remember as if it were yesterday. I specifically remember when Guancho Escaño gave them a package of candies and a box of Hollywood-brand cigarettes so they could take them to the prisoners.

Minerva asked me to leave because they had to get ready, change their clothes, so they could head over to the fortress. I even asked her what was going on and she said, "No, nothing. María Teresa is happy because she is going to see her husband." Then she asked me to stay so I could greet those who were stopping by and thank them on their behalf for their visit because they had no time to waste. I remember that Doña Rosa Morales was the last person who arrived. I said to her, "Doña Rosa, whatever it is, you can tell me because Minerva is getting ready and they have to be at the fortress on time." Doña Rosa told me, "No, sir, I have to see her and say hello to her." Minerva came out, and they hugged and talked for a while. Then they left and got in the jeep. I left and returned at around two in the afternoon. I was also trying to get them a house to rent, but the house I had found was just too far away, and they wanted a house that was in the city, surrounded by neighbors, in order to avoid problems. Then we said goodbye, and they left for the fortress.

The next day, when we heard the news about the "accident," I ran out like a madman. I really don't know why they didn't kill me. I shouted that they had been murdered. I had only been out of jail for two months.[99]

I want to include here what both Manolo and Leandro revealed about the last time they saw the girls in the jail in Puerto Plata. In his book *1J4: De espigas y de fuegos,* Leandro tells that they arrived close to two in the afternoon, as usual:

---

99   Dede's narrative does not indicate whether this was Fernando Cueto's testimony or if it was from a personal exchange.

[. . . María Teresa and Minerva] were accompanied by Patria and Rufino de la Cruz, that wonderful young man who came with them as their driver, and who we couldn't even greet because the jailers would not let us.

[. . .] To everyone's surprise, the jailers left us alone to talk. It was a blessing: we were able to talk about the political situation in general, of the martyrdom we were living, of the difficult situation they were going through, and how our emotions were being tested to the maximum but that hopefully we would flourish when the days of freedom that we dreamed of finally arrived.

A sinister shadow was cast over that conversation when the girls, intrigued, commented on Trujillo's continuous trips to Salcedo Province . . . They had heard comments about the conversation between the dictator and his friend Rafael Gómez Quezada (the one in which Trujillo said he had two problems: the priests and the Mirabal sisters) [. . .]

When they told us this, Manolo reacted as if the situation had suddenly become clear. He became agitated, raised his voice, and emphatically ordered the girls not to visit us anymore. They were not to return under any circumstances.

Minerva understood perfectly the implicit concern behind his order and responded by asking if Trujillo would be capable of daring to lift a hand against them given his standing with the international press and regional organizations.

Manolo insisted on his recommendation, and he emphasized it with a tone that was out of the ordinary. He also asked them to stay in Puerto Plata, to return to Chujo Pimentel's home, and to find a place to stay, no matter how modest the dwelling was, but where they would feel comfortable. Manolo said something else. Undoubtedly influenced by the relaxed atmosphere of privacy that the jailers' absence afforded us, he told our wives that if they stayed, that even though we were in jail, we could enjoy the meals they themselves would prepare for us.[. . .]

The conversation lifted our emotions in a special way and led to a very warm farewell. The girls looked radiant, truly beautiful. Especially María Teresa. [. . .][100]

---

100 Guzmán, *Espigas*, 155–57.

Witnesses at the Trial

During the killers' trial, there were four witnesses who had seen when the girls and Rufino were ambushed. That led many people to say, "It's true, no crime goes unpunished." The witnesses were José Gabriel Pérez, in charge of the distribution of medicine to hospitals and clinics of the Dominican Social Security and Health Services; Silvio Bienvenido Núñez, the driver of the truck; and their assistants Tomás Ortega and Romeo Molina.

The documents prepared by Investigating Judge Ambiorix Díaz Estrella included the statements made by the occupants of the Social Security truck, the only eyewitnesses to the murder. One of them, José Gabriel Pérez, made the following statement before the investigating judge:

> At the time I had the same job I have today at Dominican Social Security, which was being in charge of distributing medicine nationwide to all the hospitals and clinics of the Dominican Social Security and Health Services Department. On November 25 of last year, I was in Puerto Plata on said mission and, because I was running late, I sent the medicine that I was supposed to deliver to the town of Imbert through the postal service and left for Santiago at ten to five in the afternoon. When I was checking in at the police checkpoint upon arriving in Puerto Plata, a jeep passed us and checked in first, right at the entrance to Long Beach. A bit further on, at Kilometer 3 1/2, where there is a small cement bridge, there was a blue and white Pontiac, parked, with several men inside, more than four. After getting out of the car, they assaulted the jeep carrying the women by parking the car in the middle of the road so the jeep would not be able to pass. One of the women got out from the back of the jeep. She was wearing a yellow blouse and a brown skirt. She ran toward the truck where I was, with the driver Silvio Bienvenido Núñez and assistants Tomás Ortega and Romeo Molina. We parked the truck on the right side of the road when we saw what was going on. The lady that was running toward us screamed, "Help! Help us! They're caliés and they're going to kill us!" One of the men came running after her and pulled her hand away from the door handle on the driver's side. My partner, that is, the driver, told the lady, "Ma'am, we can't do anything." When the guy was dragging her back, she screamed at me, "Let the Mirabals know that they are going to kill us!" Just then another man came and helped his partner push her into the Pontiac because the lady

had thrown herself onto the road screaming, "They're going to kill us! They're going to kill us!" The car pulled away and disappeared. At that moment, the man that had pulled the woman away from the truck's door came toward us and said, "Be very careful about saying anything, because if you do, you're fucked. This is a delicate situation, and I'm writing down your license plate number just in case." Terrified, I told the man, "Don't worry, we're not going to say anything because I work with Villeta," who was the head of transportation at the Social Security Department at the time. The man turned around and got in the jeep with the ladies, and another man and put the driver of the jeep in the middle. They took off. Just then, a pickup truck from the Ministry of Agriculture was coming our way. The driver, known as Chulito, asked me, "José, what's going on?" I responded, "Nothing, keep going. Keep going." The pickup continued on to Puerto Plata. When we began to drive off toward Santiago, the jeep, which one of the caliés was driving, stopped. We pulled up beside him and asked him what was going on. They told us to keep going, and before we reached Kilometer 21 on the highway between Santiago and Puerto Plata, the jeep passed, and we lost sight of them.[101]

The small bridge they mentioned is known as the Mará Picá Bridge, and the woman who got out of the jeep screaming for help, saying that they were the Mirabal sisters, was Patria. I know because of the description of the clothes she was wearing.

In an article titled "The Ambush Where the Mirabal Sisters Were Killed," published in ¡Ahora! magazine, issue no. 2, dated January 31, 1962, the men said that they had mentioned Villeta (Rafael Villeta), head of transportation at Social Security. They mentioned him because he was the brother of Cholo Villeta, a very famous calié. They also highlighted a special detail that occurred after they witnessed the attack on the girls and Rufino: "Two kilometers later we saw the jeep again. The caliés were waiting for us. They passed us. At that moment, we could see who De la Rosa's partner was [...] When we reached the town of Yásica, the jeep passed us once again, and then we didn't see them again."

In that same article, the witnesses also confessed how frightened they all were and the panic they experienced for days on end, until they were finally able to get the entire story off their chests:

---

101   Citation not provided in original text.

Early the next morning (November 26, 1960), we left for Santiago by way of the San José de las Matas Highway. We saw a car parked next to a warehouse, and one of my partners thought that the man driving the car was one of the men who had assaulted the jeep. He was probably right because when we proceeded to take the highway to Montecristi to avoid approaching that car, I noticed that we were being followed, this time by one of those terrifying Volkswagens. After following the truck for several kilometers, the car decided to pass us, probably to wait for us in Montecristi.

We took advantage of the stupid maneuver made by the driver of the Volkswagen to take the Maguaca Highway, and headed toward the town of Pepillo Salcedo. We were zigzagging through the intricate network of roads owned by the Grenada Banana Company, heading toward Restauración and Bánica [in the country's northwest border region]. On Saturday night, November 26, we slept in a place known as Higüerito. We hid the truck in some nearby woods, and the following day, in the afternoon, we reached the town of San Juan de la Maguana.

That's where we found out that the young women and the driver of the jeep had been murdered, placed inside the vehicle, and thrown off a cliff along the road that connects La Cumbre, in Puerto Plata, to Peña, in order to make it look like an accident.

[...]

That is when we really began to live in terror, in agonizing silence... weeks and months of panic, just waiting for the day when, when we least expected it, we would be arrested and disappeared by the SIM, just for having been eyewitnesses to the kidnapping of those young women.

On more than one occasion when De la Rosa and Cholo Villeta were visiting Cholo's brother Fello (Villeta), we hid in Fello's office at Social Security to avoid running into this ferocious calié, afraid that this terrible henchman might remember our faces.

But if the terror we felt was overwhelming, even greater was the terrible silence we were forced to keep. That is why we felt such tremendous relief when we were called to testify in Santiago before the investigating judges. We felt that a terrible load was lifted off our chest, and without delay we said we would testify as to what we had witnessed.

On December 26, 1961, the investigating judge accompanied the witnesses who had been in the truck to Santiago's public jail to see if they could identify those who had participated in the events that took place at Kilometer 3½ along the Puerto Plata-Santiago highway. José Gabriel Pérez stated:

> I recognize the man with the streak of white hair (Ciriaco de la Rosa Luciano) as the subject who drove the Mirabal sisters' jeep after one of the sisters was pushed inside the car. The tall brown-skin man (pointing to Emilio Estrada Malleta) was the subject that stayed with the driver of the Mirabal sisters, and who later sat on the right side of the jeep, putting the driver in the middle. Also, the white one, the blonde (pointing to Manuel Alfonso Cruz Valerio), was one of the subjects who helped push the Mirabal women into the car.

Silvio Bienvenido Núñez stated:

> I only recognize the one with the streak of white hair (pointing to Ciriaco de la Rosa). He was the one that drove the jeep and told us, "Be very careful because, if not, you're fucked. I already wrote down the truck's license plate." I can't say anything about the others because I didn't get a good look at them.

Tomás Ortega:

> I recognize the one with the streak of white hair (Ciriaco de la Rosa) as the subject that drove the Mirabals' jeep.

Romero Antonio Molina:

> I recognize the one with the patch of gray hair (Ciriaco de la Rosa) as the subject who came to the truck to drag the woman away and who threatened to fuck us up. I saw the tall brown-skin man with the skinny face (pointing to Emilio Estrada Malleta) when he got out of the car. The white guy stayed in the car with the women. He was wearing a Cibao Eagles baseball cap (pointing to Manuel Alfonso Cruz Valerio).

Relevant Details Yet to be Clarified

One important detail of that tragic day, about which there has been much speculation, was the presence of a mysterious Mercedes Benz that was parked in front of the La Cumbre military checkpoint. The driver of the truck, Silvio Bienvenido Núñez Soto, said, "There was a Mercedes Benz that looked red to me parked almost across from the military post, and there were two women inside, seated in the front seat by themselves." Another witness, Tomás Ortega, said, "There was a car parked there (in La Cumbre), but I could not properly identify it. I do remember that there were women in the front seat. I didn't see any men." This witness said, "I want to add that when we were coming down from La Cumbre, a Mercedes Benz was following us with the lights turned off. It followed us until Kilometer 6, between Puerto Plata and Santiago. After that, I didn't see it anymore."

Romero Antonio Molina, one of the four men who witnessed the event, recalled, "When we no longer saw the jeep, a Mercedes Benz followed us with its lights turned off as we were leaving La Cumbre."

I have often wondered who those women in the car were and what they were doing. There must have been other occupants in the vehicle. Who were they and where were they when the eyewitnesses saw the car parked in La Cumbre? Was Alicinio Peña Rivera in the car? What did Alicinio do immediately after receiving the call from one of his agents responsible for committing the crimes, telling him that the "visitors" were in Puerto Plata?

Alicinio Peña Rivera was the man wearing the hat, standing next to the Mercedes Benz. At least, that is what I think. The assassins never revealed his identity. He was the boss, while the others were mere assassins, subordinates. They covered for him during the trial. They never identified the man with the wide-brim hat.

In his version of the events, the former SIM head Johnny Abbes placed Segundo Imbert at the crime scene and said he played a horrific part in it. That is completely untrue. If Segundo Imbert had been taken out of La Victoria to participate in the girls' murder, as Johnny Abbes wrote, the other prisoners would have noticed. There was a close bond among the political prisoners at La Victoria. Che Espaillat and Papito Sánchez were in the same cell with Segundo Imbert, and, on more than one occasion, Che Espaillat told me personally that Segundo Imbert was never removed from the cell. As a matter of fact, the Sunday after my sisters' murder, Che Espaillat's wife, Zoila Muñoz, visited her husband and was the one who told them about the crime. They wept and were deeply saddened when they heard the news. All the prisoners were shaken to the core, and that is when they realized why Pedrito had been removed from his jail cell that Saturday morning, immediately after the murders. Patria had visited him at La Victoria just a few days before.

I also discussed this issue with Dr. Fernández Caminero, who told me exactly what Che Espaillat had said: that Segundo Imbert had never been taken out of La Victoria. I have no reason to doubt these statements. Che Espaillat was an antitrujillista from childhood. They accused him of killing a very cruel calié by the last name of Cabrera. He was given a thirty-year sentence. Papito Sánchez, Segundo Imbert, and Che Espaillat, all sentenced for common crimes, enjoyed certain liberties that the political prisoners did not. They also had more opportunities to communicate with people. In prison they were tasked with taking information to the men from the 14th of June Movement, who were monitored very closely.

The *¡Ahora!* magazine article dated January 31, 1962, which I mentioned earlier, reveals the intense rumors that spread regarding the presence of an Italian by the name of Salvador Perrone, who was said to be at my sisters' crime scene. The article says that Perrone owed Trujillo favors because he had saved the Italian from bankruptcy. He was named administrator of Trujillo's farm in La Cumbre, which is why they said he supported the dictator. However, the same article states—always according to rumors—that Perrone had openly protested at the crime scene: "We can't do this! Why don't we just shoot them? [. . .] For God's sake, leave them alone . . . We aren't men . . . If we were, each one of us would shoot ourselves for what we are doing." According to the rumors, he actually fainted at the scene. That Italian, who had been the modest owner of a coffee mill, would later commit suicide by hanging himself in the bathroom of his house in the El Llano area, just a few kilometers from where my sisters and Rufino were killed. They said that he had "repented," and that he couldn't bear the torment and guilt he felt.

In my research, I have also found that there are two theories about where the murders actually took place. The first version says that they were killed in the Monte Llano cane fields, between Kilometers 8 and 9 of the Puerto Plata-Santiago Highway. The second version says that it was at the terrace of La Mansión, on Trujillo's farm in La Cumbre. An article published in the 14th of June Movement's newspaper, dated August 30, 1962, states:

> [. . .] according to most people, it was impossible for the killers of the Salcedo heroines and their driver to have been killed in the cane fields of the Monte Llano sugar mill.
>
> [. . .] The fact of the matter is that La Mansión, in La Cumbre—situated on top of a hill surrounded by a thick pine forest—was the perfect setting for Trujillo's henchmen to carry out their crime.

The same article also reveals, "[. . . I]n Puerto Plata people say that the Italian named Perrone arrived at the mansion right when they were committing the horrendous crime, and that is why he was eliminated by the regime a few weeks later. However, others say Perrone died from heart failure."

Perhaps the most interesting information regarding Salvador Perrone appears in the interrogation of his widow, Cristina Perrone, by the investigating judge, on February 5, 1962:

Q. Is it true that your husband hung himself at your house?

A. That is not true, my husband died at the hospital.

Q. Did your husband, Salvador Perrone, discover where the Mirabal sisters had been killed?

A. No, sir. He did not know anything about this.

Q. Was he the administrator of Trujillo's farm in La Cumbre?

A. He was the administrator of that farm for one year.

Q. Until when was he the administrator of the farm?

A. He was the administrator until November 27, 1960. This is not the exact date, but it was around that date.

[. . .]

Q. Did you read the magazine *¡Ahora!*? That is, the magazine that mentions the voluntary or involuntary participation of Salvador Perrone in the death of the Mirabal sisters and their driver Rufino de la Cruz?

A. Yes, sir, I read it, and I wrote a response denying all of it. It is a slanderous lie against my husband's memory. He was incapable of committing such a horrible crime. Besides, he could not walk, as he suffered from corns, and lately his feet had become very swollen because he also had albumin.

Two very important facts come to light in these statements: a) Salvador Perrone stopped being Trujillo's farm administrator in La Cumbre two days after the murders, and b) this man died a few weeks later. Because of an illness? Suicide? Was he murdered? After all the years that have passed, and being the realist that I am, I feel deeply saddened when I read these statements since we might never know exactly what happened on November 25, 1960. We will also never know who all the witnesses were and who all participated in the murders.

Judicial Records and Statements Made by the Assassins

Those involved and responsible for the crimes tried to escape, mocking the rule of law and the justice system. The investigating judge, Dr. Ambiorix Díaz Estrella, found holes in their statements in his initial investigation.

Alicinio Peña Rivera had the gall to declare, "I learned about their deaths when I was at the Military Intelligence Service office the following day, when the people started saying they had been killed in an alleged accident."

He stated that during the entire time he had been in charge of the SIM office in Santiago, he never visited the army checkpoint of La Cumbre or La Mansión.

When the trial judge asked him if he knew the four individuals who had lost their lives, he answered:

> I only knew María Teresa and Minerva because they were involved in political activities. I met Minerva when she was arrested in Montecristi, and en route to Ciudad Trujillo,[102] they stopped by my office, and I knew María Teresa because she lived in Santiago with her husband, and we even met at a social event at the home of a local family. Also, on one occasion, I was ordered to summon them both to my office in Salcedo and tell them that I had received the order to lift all restrictions on their movements throughout the country and that, consequently, they could go wherever they wanted.

In response to the question: "Did you know that the wives of Manuel Tavárez Justo and Leandro Guzmán visited them on a weekly basis in Puerto Plata?"

> His answer: Yes, sir. I was ordered to communicate to the Military Commander in Puerto Plata that those political prisoners could only be visited by their parents, siblings, wives, and children twice a week, and that the visiting days were to be assigned and spread out over the week.

The henchmen who carried out the murders conspired to repeat the same story. These are the statements made by Emilio Estrada Malleta. The others' testimonies were almost identical regarding their non-involvement in the crime. They all insisted that they turned over the Mirabal sisters to Captain del Villar at La Cuarenta.

---

102 During the dictatorship, the capital city of Santo Domingo was renamed Ciudad Trujillo (Trujillo City).

The investigating judge asked:

Q: We have called you here again so that you may respond to the murder charges presented against you, along with Alfonso Cruz Valerio, Ramón Emilio Rojas Lora, Néstor Antonio Pérez Terrero, Ciriaco de la Rosa, and Víctor Alicinio Peña, regarding the murders of Patria, Minerva, and María Teresa Mirabal and Rufino de la Cruz. What say you to this accusation?

A: One day, I don't remember the date, Peña Rivera told me to report to Sergeant De la Rosa (Ciriaco de la Rosa, alias Chaguito) and told me that he was coming from the capital to receive certain instructions. When De la Rosa arrived, we left the following day for Puerto Plata, and on the way, he told me and Alfonso Cruz Valerio, Emilio Rojas Lora, and Pérez Terrero that the instructions were to prepare an "accident" for the Mirabal sisters, but that we had to be very careful because it was a very delicate case since it involved women.

That day we saw them in Puerto Plata, accompanied by an elderly person, and we decided to return to Santiago. We made another trip on visitation day and returned again because they were accompanied by an elderly woman. On the third opportunity we saw them alone in Puerto Plata, and Ciriaco told us to wait for them in the outskirts of the city. We stopped on the right side of the highway, some kilometers away from the city. When the jeep carrying the Mirabal sisters was coming our way, we all got out of the car, except for Pérez Terrero, and Ciriaco signaled for them to stop. The jeep stopped, and we started moving the women from the jeep to the car, and that's when the truck appeared and its passengers saw the operation underway. Ciriaco went to the jeep with the Mirabals' driver, and we continued on in the car with the three women. We took the La Cumbre-Tamboril road and took them to La Cuarenta, in the capital, where we turned them over to Captain del Villar. We later returned to Santiago, except for Pérez Terrero, who stayed in the capital visiting a sick child, and we never found out what happened to them in La Cuarenta. Here in Santiago, we went to the office, and the next day Ciriaco reported to Peña Rivera since he had not been in the office the night before.

Q: Is it true that you spoke to Peña Rivera while in Puerto Plata?

A: Yes, sir. I called the Santiago office from the Puerto Plata Police

Station. I spoke to Olivero and asked him to connect me through to Peña Rivera. He answered, "Let me see if I can find him," and almost immediately, that is, some ten minutes later, they put me through to him. I told him that the visitors were in Puerto Plata, and he told me that Ciriaco had received the instructions. We were immediately cut off.

Q: Why did you... if you had received instructions, or better yet, if the instructions you received were to prepare an alleged accident on the highway... Why did you take them to La Cuarenta?

A: We made that decision because the men in the truck had seen us on the highway. When we turned them over in the capital, we didn't say anything about being seen. Later, Ciriaco said that the reason he gave them was that there was too much traffic on the road.

Q: Did you put more gasoline in the jeep to make such a long trip?

A: No, sir. I want to clarify that we left the jeep at La Cuarenta and returned in a public transportation car.

Q: Did you put gasoline in the car?

A: No, sir. I want to add that when they went to drop off Pérez Terrero at his house in the capital, I stayed at a bar on Tiradentes Avenue and ate a sandwich. They picked me up later at the same bar. I don't know if they got gas before they picked me up.

Q: What other person, aside from Captain del Villar, did you see at La Cuarenta?

A: If there were more people there, the only one that could have seen them was Ciriaco because he was the only one that got out at La Cuarenta to talk to Del Villar and hand the women over.

Q: What did the Mirabal sisters say along the way?

A: They asked where we were taking them and if there was anything pending against them, and we answered that we knew nothing and that we were following orders to take them to the capital.

When asked what time they reached the capital with the Mirabal sisters, Manuel Alfonso Cruz Valerio responded, "At around eight that evening." "How do you explain the fact that according to statements made by the military officers stationed at La Cumbre, they received the information of the jeep's accident way before nine that evening?" asked the investigating judge. "I cannot explain that," answered the man.

On the other hand, Mateo Núñez, a farmer who lived in Rio Arriba, testified that around seven that evening he heard the loud crash of the jeep when it fell from the precipice and smashed against the ground: "I was listening to *La Voz de la Reelección* on the Holy Rosary radio program when I heard the crash of a vehicle falling into the ravine. I don't know what happened because I went to bed. But later on, the authorities came and also an ambulance with its siren wailing, and they came looking for me to help remove the corpses." This farmer could recall what time it was when he heard the noise of the falling vehicle because he was listening to the radio.

Victor Alicinio Peña Rivera, a lieutenant back then, was the head of the SIM office in the Cibao. And according to what he stated during the trial, it was he who received the verbal order from Candito Torres Tejada to prepare the Mirabal sisters' "accident." They transferred SIM agent Ciriaco de la Rosa to Santiago to take part in the operation.

This is all very clear in the judicial order sent to the Criminal Court by Investigating Judge Ambiorix Díaz Estrella and by Ad-Hoc Secretary Víctor Manuel Marte, dated February 20, 1962. It states:

> That the day after Sergeant Ciriaco de la Rosa arrived in Santiago, he was assigned a vehicle where he was to be accompanied by Alfonso Cruz Valerio, Emilio Estrada Malleta, Ramón Emilio Rojas Lora, and Néstor Antonio Pérez Terrero, all members of the SIM here in Santiago;
>
> That on the aforementioned day, probably on November 18, 1960, Ciriaco de la Rosa and his four companions traveled to Puerto Plata and returned with the information that they had not carried out the crime because the Mirabal sisters were accompanied by elderly individuals and children;
>
> That on November 22, after carrying out a similar surveillance assignment, they saw the Mirabal sisters, and they returned to the SIM office in Santiago with the same abovementioned pretext;
>
> That during a trip made by Peña Rivera to the capital of the Republic, after November 22, he personally explained the situation to Navy Major Cándido Torres Tejada who, after discussing it—probably with his immediate superior Rafael Trujillo Molina—told Peña Rivera that the order had to be carried out as long as the number of casualties did not exceed five;
>
> That once the orders were delivered by Víctor Alicinio Peña Rivera, Sergeant Ciriaco de la Rosa, accompanied by the abovementioned individuals—Alfonso Cruz Valerio, Emilio Estrada Malleta, Ramón Emilio Rojas Lora, and Néstor Antonio Pérez Terrero—traveled to

the city of Puerto Plata and upon observing the jeep occupied by the Mirabal sisters in the vicinity of the fortress, they noted the license plate number and waited for them along the highway that led to Santiago, some three and a half kilometers from Puerto Plata;

In the meantime, Emilio Estrada Malleta called Peña Rivera by telephone from National Police headquarters to the SIM headquarters in Santiago to inform him that "the women had arrived" and that during this time period a truck from the Dominican Social Security Department had also arrived in Puerto Plata with four occupants, all employed by said department;

That sisters Minerva, María Teresa, and Patria Mirabal, in a jeep driven by Rufino de la Cruz, had arrived in Puerto Plata at eleven in the morning and had stayed at the home of Mr. José Eugenio (Chujo) Pimentel Líster, where they had lunch and after changing their clothing left for the penitentiary at two in the afternoon, where they stayed until four in the afternoon, cutting their visit short by one hour due to circumstances that we have not been able to clarify in this investigation;

That the jeep carrying the Mirabal sisters left Puerto Plata at 4:50 p.m., a time that has been established because said vehicle passed the truck from the Dominican Social Security Office, precisely when the truck was checking in at the Police checkpoint. The five SIM agents stopped the jeep at Kilometer 3 1/2 and forced Minerva, María Teresa, and Patria Mirabal to get into the vehicle occupied by the murderer-abductors. They were guarded by Manuel Alfonso Cruz Valerio, the driver, Ramón Emilio Rojas Lora, and Emilio Estrada Malleta, while Rufino de la Cruz was placed between Ciriaco de la Rosa and Néstor Antonio Pérez Terrero, who began to drive the jeep occupied by the Mirabal sisters.

That while said operation was being carried out, the truck from the Dominican Social Security Department appeared at the site, and the four occupants of the truck witnessed when one of the Mirabal sisters, darting out from the rear of the jeep, ran to the truck and grabbed one of the door handles, from which she was pulled away by one of the accused, dragged and forced inside the vehicle used by the SIM;

That after the two vehicles left with the future victims, somewhere along the road that leads to Santiago, probably at the farm or mansion at La Cumbre, owned by Rafael Trujillo, the horrendous assassination of Minerva, Patria, and María Teresa Mirabal and their driver, Mr. Rufino de la Cruz, was carried out. They were strangled to death after having lost consciousness due to blunt force trauma on both sides of their necks and their skulls, as we shall explain further on;

[...]

That the allegations made by the five assassins, that they took the victims to the capital of the Republic, where they said they turned them over to Captain del Villar at La Cuarenta, in their attempt to avoid the enormous responsibility that they had undertaken, have been completely dismissed based on the following: First, that the Mirabal sisters were abducted at around 5:00 p.m. and thrown from a precipice at 7:30 p.m., that is, some two hours after being kidnapped, revealing that there was no time to make a round trip to the capital of the Republic. Second, that this was not the order they were given, but quite the contrary; it was to throw them from a cliff making it look like an accident, which they did. Third, that after the accused agreed among themselves to say that they had turned over the detained persons to Captain del Villar, the investigation regarding this aspect of the events was terminated because said individual committed suicide. Fourth, that when Ciriaco de la Rosa returned from Santiago to the SIM offices, he told Peña Rivera that everything had gone perfectly and that he was going to stay a few days in the city so that his arrival would not raise suspicion in light of the alleged accident

In the summary of the investigation sent to the Criminal Court, the following was established:

That the tyrant assassinated on May 30 of the year 1961, Rafael L. Trujillo, was the intellectual author of the murder of the Mirabal sisters and Mr. Rufino de la Cruz, thereby eliminating all prosecution against him due to his death.

That among the facts proven in this investigation, there are sufficient charges and evidence to suggest that Ciriaco de la Rosa, Alfonso Cruz Valerio, Emilio Estrada Malleta, Ramón Emilio Rojas Lora, and Néstor Antonio Pérez Terrero were the material executioners of Minerva, María Teresa, and Patria Mirabal Reyes and Mr. Rufino de la Cruz [...]

That Víctor Alicinio Peña Rivera and Candito Torres Tejada may be considered accessories to the crime [...], that both, through "the abuse of power and authority," gave the instructions to commit the crime [...].

That all members of the former Military Intelligence Service (SIM) may be prosecuted for participating in criminal activities [...]; in consequence, the authorities may proceed to prosecute Ciriaco de la Rosa Luciano, Manuel Alfonso Cruz Valerio, Emilio Estrada Malleta, Ramón Emilio Rojas Lora, Néstor Antonio Pérez Terrero, Cándido Torres Tejada, Víctor Alicinio Peña Rivera, Sindito Almonte, Silvio Antonio Gómez Santana, Viterbo (Pechito) Alvarez, David Olivero Segura, and Pedro Peña Ortiz, as individuals who participated in this criminal activity.

An article published in the newspaper *El Caribe* quotes the statements made by Ciriaco de la Rosa during the trial, revelations that shook the nation to its core:

After we arrested them, we took them to a spot near the precipice, where I ordered Rojas Lora to pick up sticks and take one of the girls. He immediately obeyed the order and took one of them, the one with the long braids (María Teresa). Alfonso Cruz Valerio picked the tallest (Minerva), and I chose the shortest and chubbiest one (Patria), and Malleta took the driver (Rufino). I ordered them to take each of the victims into the cane field that was right next to the highway, and to separate themselves so that the victims would not be able to witness the others being executed. I ordered Pérez Terrero to stand guard on the highway to see if any vehicle came by or if anyone could see what we were doing. I don't want to lie to the court nor to the people. I tried to avoid the tragedy, but I couldn't because otherwise they would have killed us all.

As one can see, during the trial that began on June 27, 1962, the defendants confessed as to how they prepared the murders and coldly revealed the horrific details of the crime. Some even accused one another during the trial. That is what happened with Ramón Rojas Lara, who went so far as to compare Ciriaco de la Rosa to Satan:

"This wretch is still alive," said Ciriaco de la Rosa, referring to Minerva Mirabal, who was still alive. Just wait until we get there to finish her off. When we reached the precipice where we dumped the Mirabals, Ciriaco got out of the car enraged. He brutally pulled out the one that was still alive. She was tall and thin and had short "boyish" hair. Cursing at her, De la Rosa dragged her over the highway and the grass.

He placed her there. He looked for the club and started beating her. He finished her off completely. De la Rosa beat her numerous times with the club. He wanted to make sure she was really dead. When he stopped beating her, he was furious. He was tired and sweating profusely. He had difficulty breathing. At that moment I thought he was the image of Satan. He was, without a doubt, one of the demons of the Military Intelligence Service. He began to laugh. He seemed satisfied and pleased with his criminal work. He then called us and told us to put the girls' bodies into the jeep. We did as ordered, turned on the jeep's headlights, started the engine, and began pushing it off the cliff.[103]

The nation followed the trial closely on television and radio. There were more than thirty hearings, and it was an unprecedented event in the history of the Dominican justice system.

Finally, on November 25, 1962, Magistrate Osvaldo B. Soto from the National Penal Chamber read the ruling issued by the Dominican justice system. It sentenced Manuel Alfonso Cruz Valerio, Emilio Estrada Malleta, and Ramón Emilio Rojas Lora to thirty years of public labor, while Ciriaco de la Rosa, Néstor Antonio Pérez Terrero, Víctor Alicinio Peña Rivera, and Cándido Torres Tejada received twenty-year sentences of public labor.

Rafael (Fefé) Valera Benítez was the district attorney with federal jurisdiction. Antonio Guzmán was the attorney who represented our family during the trial, along with other prominent attorneys, such as Héctor Sánchez Morcelo, Ramón Pina Acevedo, Francisco Carvajal Martínez, and Miguel A. Vásquez Fernández. The attorney for the defendants was public defender Héctor Barón Goico.

I did not want to follow the details of the trial. I could not stand to listen to the details, nor see the killers' faces or listen to their lies. So, I decided to get some dental work done. My brother-in-law Tulio Suazo is a dental surgeon who lives in New York. I asked him to do it. And off I went to New York in mid-1962, just when they started to televise the trial. That was the first time I ever traveled outside the country.

---

[103] Tony Raful, *Movimiento 14 de Junio, historia y documentos*, 2nd ed. (Santo Domingo: Alfa y Omega, 2007), 136–137. Author's note.

Jaimito bought a big television set, and our house in Ojo de Agua would overflow with people who wanted to watch the hearings. I couldn't stand it. However, before I left, curiosity got the best of me, and I listened to some of the interrogations. But it was too painful for me to relive the tragedy. For example, I couldn't stomach watching that cynical Cruz Valerio sit there with a smirk on his face.

I was in New York for several months. I decided that I would only return to the country once the trial ended.

In regards to the scene of the crime, I agree with the conclusions reached by the members of the 14th of June Movement in Puerto Plata. It must have been very close to where they were abducted. I believe that from the very moment they were ordered to stop, my sisters were aware of their terrible plight: they were going to kill them. Knowing them, I know they would not have remained still. They knew they were going to be killed. Were they going to keep quiet, get out of the car like gentle lambs, and wait to be killed? Most certainly not. They were going to try to roll down the windows, scream, open the doors, and jump from the vehicle.

One need only consider that the moment they were abducted, Patria lost no time. She threw herself from the back door of the jeep and ran toward the oncoming truck, yelling to the occupants about what was happening. One of the abductors dragged her back. Therefore, even before they were forced to get out of the vehicle to get into the other car, they were already putting up a fight. They resisted. I am sure of that. They were packed into the car seat—there were three of them—and they would have made noise; they must have fought with the attackers while inside the car. It was still light out, and someone could take notice.

The mansion at La Cumbre is situated some forty kilometers from Mará Picá, the point where the SIM group intercepted the jeep. They were not going to take them there alive because they would not have been able to control them. I am convinced that the abductors swiftly killed them and later took the bodies to La Mansión to carry out the final details of the "accident." That is, get them ready, place them in the jeep, drive the jeep to the precipice, abandon the vehicle, and push it off the cliff. According to statements made by Rojas Lora, Minerva was barely alive when they reached La Mansión, and Ciriaco de la Rosa himself made sure to finish her off. I think it is possible that this was the part witnessed by Salvador Perrone, the manager of La Mansión.

During the trial there was ample discussion regarding the possible places where the events could have taken place, but no solid evidence was found.

Members of the 14th of June Movement in Puerto Plata always told me that they knew where they had been killed. So many years have gone by, and it is only now that I have finally dared visit the crime scene in order to fully understand the events. I went to Puerto Plata, I contacted Lillian Russo, a good friend of the girls, and her husband Fernando Cueto, a member of the Movement who had been horribly tortured along with Manolo at La Cuarenta, and whom I have already mentioned in this memoir. His father, Fernando Suárez, along with a group of individuals, was in charge of organizing the movement of internal support for the Luperón expedition in 1949, in which he was killed.[104] We first stopped at the Mará Picá bridge and walked to the monument that was built there to honor my sisters' memory. We then continued on the highway for three or four kilometers.

Fernando Cueto explained that the Catorcistas from Puerto Plata drew from statements made by the henchmen and killers during the trial, as well as their own knowledge of the area to conclude that the crimes were perpetrated in an area of the sugar cane field where the El Cupey Road began, some three or four kilometers from Mará Picá. If you travel on this highway and turn right through the narrow stretch of road, you will be completely hidden from sight.

Fernando also told me that this version of events is based on statements allegedly made by Ciriaco de la Rosa who, according to him, was later besieged by his conscience. He almost went mad, could not live with himself, and became an Evangelical Christian. It was then, after the trial ended, that he declared that the murders had taken place in the sugar cane field, on the hill that leads to El Cupey.

As we walked on this stretch of road, just a few meters from the Puerto Plata-Santiago highway, I was overtaken by strange feelings of restlessness and peace. I thought, *This was where they saw the sky for the last time, where they thought of us, their loved ones, for the last time, where they saw the demonic face of the dictatorship, personified by its henchmen, and where they spoke their last words, which we will never know for sure.*

In this place of sheer horror, I am sure that, for a moment, they saw a beautiful image of the life they so loved, embodied in part in their children, Mamá, me, their husbands, their friends . . . and in the strength that only comes with liberty.

---

104   On June 19, 1949, the first group of Dominican guerrilla fighters arrived at the Bay of Luperón, in Puerto Plata, on the north coast. It was the first attempt made by the exile movement to overthrow the dictatorship. The group left from Guatemala.

12

The Killers' Fate

In spite of the authorities' clear attempts to bring the killers to justice, especially during the first years after the murders, the collective memory of our country will forever be impacted by the shame of knowing that the majority of those who participated in the crime died in their own beds, except for Johnny Abbes and Cruz Valerio, who were both killed by François Duvalier in Haiti under suspicious circumstances.

Trujillo committed horrific crimes during his thirty-year regime. But it was the murder of the Mirabal sisters that provoked outrage across the nation. Unlike in other cases, everyone found out about the murders soon after they were carried out. The terrible news traveled like wildfire and awakened the dormant conscience of the Dominican people. The murders forever sealed the dictator's fate. Antonio de la Maza's[105] nephew Ernesto once told me that Antonio's father—a very elegant, elderly gentleman from Moca, whose son had also been murdered—scolded his remaining children: "Don't you have the balls to kill him? Will I have to go kill him myself? Go kill him! Kill him!" And when he found out about the girls' murder, he screamed, "That's it! I am going to kill him now for sure!"

At first, justice was served when it came to the murder of my sisters and Rufino. The killers, those who carried out the murders, were given thirty-year sentences. Those who orchestrated the plot received twenty-year sentences.

After the events of 1963, the year when Manolo was killed, I went to visit Leandro, who was still in jail in the Ozama Fortress. They had arrested him during the repressive campaign launched against the 14th of June political party, which had opposed the coup carried out against Juan Bosch. When the coup occurred, he did not hesitate to act against the forces that led it. Imprisonment prevented Leandro from participating in the guerrilla movement. It was through him that I found out that Alicinio Peña Rivera was a privileged prisoner. He was not being held in La Victoria as he should

---

105 He fired the shot that finally killed Trujillo.

have been, but was there, at the Ozama Fortress. He only served four of his twenty-year sentence.

It is said that during the April Revolution in 1965, when Montes Arache[106] visited the fortress, he ran into Peña Rivera. "What are you going to do with me?" asked the prisoner. "Leave," Montes Arache told him. Sometime later Fafa Taveras also entered the fortress, accompanied by a group of men who had planned to kill the murderers of the Mirabal sisters, as well as Félix W. Bernardino, another criminal who had worked for the dictatorship and was also serving time at the fortress. They were unable to execute their plan, however. The two prisoners managed to escape through the back of the fortress and swim their way to freedom through the Ozama River. Someone had obviously facilitated their escape.

It seems that when some of the Catorcistas found out that the criminals were receiving all sorts of privileges while in jail, they began forming a plan to attack the fortress and kill them.

One of them once told Minou that they had prepared a plan to attack the fortress, but that when they told Manolo, he strongly opposed the plot. He asked them, "Have you gone mad?" He explained to them that having fought so hard to achieve true justice and democracy, they couldn't now use the same methods they were trying to do away with, nor replicate the behavior they all vehemently rejected. That anecdote paints a clear and faithful picture of the Manolo I once knew: coherent, upright, pure to the point of sacrifice.

Candito Torres, the man who traveled to Santiago to deliver the instructions to kill my sisters, left the country when the Trujillos left. He still lives in the United States.[107] When I was in New York in 1961, a friend invited me to a gathering at a home in Queens. When we arrived, we found our hosts to be extremely nervous. Later on, my friend told me that Candito Torres had been at the house earlier and that when they told him I was coming, he left in a hurry.

During the provisional government installed following the 1965 revolution, police officer Neit Nivar Seijas—who later became chief of police during the Joaquin Balaguer administration—released all those who partici-

---

106 Manuel Ramón Montes Arache was a naval officer under the Trujillo regime. After the dictator was overthrown, he became an important leader of the Constitutionalist movement in the 1965 April Revolution. After his death, he was declared a national hero by President Leonel Fernández for his contribution to the country's democratic ideals.
107 Torres lived and worked in Miami for many years.

pated in my sisters' murders. At the time, all were serving their respective jail sentences. We were extremely alarmed and began to write letters in protest. But it was a hopeless cause. The head guard at La Victoria, a military officer by the last name of Despradel, declared with tremendous cynicism that someone with a voice that sounded like the president called him on the telephone and ordered him to free the prisoners. They all left the country, and the majority moved to the United States. How did they manage to obtain visas and permanent resident status in that country if they were on the run from the Dominican authorities?

The only one who remained in the country was Rojas Lora, who was from Salcedo. They also called him Caiaphas.[108] I remember that on the day of the trial, Jaimito screamed out "Caiaphas!" when he saw him. He turned around nervously. He was the man who killed María Teresa. We learned he had been a police officer in La Cementera, the local cement company. It so happened that the husband of one of Jaimito's sisters was an important executive at the company. When he told his boss, the latter responded, "You go and report him!" But that never happened. Time passed, and I never heard anything else about him.

Some five years ago a man came to visit me. He told me that Rojas Lora had died. He had slipped and fallen in the Los Mina neighborhood in Santo Domingo where he lived and he died as a result of the fall. More recently, Dr. Alcibiades González, also from Salcedo, who wrote a book on the Mirabal sisters and Rufino, told me a different story. One day a sick man arrived at his clinic situated in the eastern section of Santo Domingo. He had been referred by a high-ranking military doctor named Dr. Clarence Charles Dunlop, Balaguer's personal physician. The referral was addressed to another Dr. González, who was not seeing patients at the time, so Dr. Alcibiades attended to him. When he heard the name Emilio Rojas Lora, he was shocked by the coincidence. The sick man lived in Villa Faro and was suffering from an advanced cancer that would kill him soon after. Sometime later, a young woman in labor arrived at the clinic. She turned out to be Rojas Lora's daughter. Dr. Alcibiades overheard the bitter complaints made by the young woman's mother: Rojas Lora had left her nothing except a lot of problems. Dr. Alcibiades, a fervent admirer of the Mirabal sisters, performed a Cesarean section on the young woman. As he attended to her, he reflected on this strange twist of fate. Rojas Lora was buried in the San

---

108 In the Bible, the Jewish high priest whose conviction of Jesus led to his execution by the Romans.

Isidro Cemetery, in the eastern section of Santo Domingo. Pérez Terrero was buried in the town of Enriquillo, in the southwest border region.

For a while, Ciriaco de la Rosa and Estrada Malleta lived together in Lawrence, Massachusetts. Both were compulsive gamblers and constantly argued at the casinos. They finally went their separate ways. Estrada moved to Miami. Dominican TV personality Freddy Beras Goico interviewed him there, right around the same time he interviewed Angelita, Trujillo's daughter, as well as Alicinio Peña Rivera. Seeing the interviews turned my stomach because they presented themselves as the victims. What message is being sent to future generations by airing these interviews?

Alicinio Peña Rivera first moved to Puerto Rico, but later settled in Miami. In 1991, during the Balaguer administration, he dared to visit the country with the intention of launching the book he had written on Porfirio Rubirosa.[109] The book-launching ceremony was to take place at the National Library. In other words, a killer of women actually wrote a eulogy for this gigolo, a man who lived off women.

The Dominican afternoon daily *El Nacional* published an interview with Peña Rivera, who stated, "After 26 years, I am returning home with a clear conscience." Minou wrote a vehement letter to the newspaper's senior editor, Radhamés Gómez Pepín. We visited various television programs to protest. The people's reaction to this insufferable insult was so overwhelming that they were forced to cancel the book launch at the library. The next day at the airport there was another incident. They managed to sneak him out of the country, thanks to the protection provided by an unidentified person. Although the National Palace announced they had reissued the order that prohibited him from leaving the country, the aircraft took off with the killer on board. The press was there to report on this latest disgrace.

The following is the letter written by Minou and published by *El Nacional* on August 24, 1991, in which she expresses the feelings of our entire family. It generated overwhelming support from everyone:

Dear Mr. Director:

Sorrow, real sorrow, profound sorrow, is always silent. Perhaps this is why our family has lived its sorrow in silence. But, after reading with outraged astonishment the full-page coverage given to the statements made by Mr. Víctor Alicinio Peña Rivera, a name that

---

109   Porfirio Rubirosa was at one time Trujillo's son-in-law. He was known for his affairs with international stars, such as Ava Gardner, Zsa Zsa Gabor, Rita Hayworth, Kim Novak, and Marilyn Monroe, just to name a few.

burns my lips as well as my hands when I write it, I can't help but express my innermost thoughts to you with the hope that they will be well received in honor of the respect earned by the men and women who have given everything for their country. I can't deny that I was aghast with your coverage of the statements made by a convicted and confessed killer, a well-known fugitive of the Dominican justice system.

The reason for my consternation is that for years I have admired how your newspaper has defended ethics, morality, and justice, values that have been trampled from the article's headline to its very last line, all under the pretense of "journalistic objectivity."

Would it be naive on my part to expect that this man be referred to in the same terms applied to him by the Dominican justice system? In other words, as the killer of the Mirabal sisters? Or is it enough that this fact be merely implied in the ambiguous identifying phrase: "... tried as an accomplice and sentenced in 1962 to 20 years for the death (not the murder, m.t.m.[110]) of the Mirabal sisters?" Why give this a journalistic spin, as if you were discussing the return of a politician from unmerited exile? Why don't you highlight the real news: that this man was allowed to enter the country freely, and/or who will be responsible for defining his legal status as—not just any criminal—but a fugitive? Couldn't *El Nacional* have employed its journalists and archives to be truly objective and publish alongside his statements a history of the trial in which he was sentenced? The most objective part of the story, the only thing that contrasts with the rest of the text, is the taunting and cynical face of Peña Rivera, who would first need to have a conscience before having a clean one.

How would the Israeli press have treated a Nazi assassin that boasted so openly of his exploits? And it is important to mention the case of Israel because, as submerged as we are in a collective numbness regarding impunity, we forget that even today—50 years later—Jews are still searching all over the world for Nazi criminals in order to bring them before the justice system for the crimes they committed. Assassinations are not bound by statutes of limitations. They can't be. Every time I see my young daughter or my brother's daughters and think that my mother Minerva will never know them,

---

110   Minou Tavárez Mirabal.

my indignation over this crime resurfaces. This is a crime whose consequences endure.

Neither the daily pressures and deadlines under which journalists work, nor the competitive obsession with capturing television and headline ratings should push our journalists to the extreme of promoting injustices and lacerating the heartfelt emotions of their own readers.

I refuse to believe, Mr. Director, that the goal of this story, as well as the publication of falsehoods and inaccurate information found throughout the text, is to manipulate public opinion in order to dissociate this man from a crime that can never be erased from our national conscience, no matter how many stories and public appearances attempt to do just that.

I am particularly concerned by the tone of the story because it reminds me of the attempts made for some time now by Peña Rivera "to cleanse" himself of the crimes he committed. And this is clearly evident in the warm welcome he received in the equally "objective" television interview he gave with Freddy Beras Goico on the program *El Gordo de la Semana*. The day after the interview aired, one of my students at the university asked me to tell her the names of the men who "really" killed my mother and her sisters, because the man she had seen on television seemed "innocent."

Freddy's television interview and this story beg the question: what are the ethical standards that govern journalistic objectivity, and what interests do they serve at any given moment? On this specific occasion, I don't think they are serving the interests of the Dominican justice system, a system that has been trampled upon. Nor do they contribute—as they should—to educating future generations who have not lived through the horror and indignity that this man is now rubbing in our faces with such arrogance.

Those young individuals did not see the trial in which Peña Rivera was sentenced for the murder of the Mirabal sisters. I did not see the trial either because I was only six years old and because my grandmother, in her infinite sorrow, turned off the radio in our home forever. But those individuals who are now over 40 years old did see the trial, and can testify as to whether or not that historic trial could be labeled a "Roman circus," and if the evidence presented did not justify the guilty verdict given to this man, who was on the Santiago-San Francisco de Macorís Highway on the afternoon of November 25,

1960, monitoring by radio the details of the crime being perpetrated by the executioners. Guilty was the man who on that very evening met with the executioners at Kilometer 7 of the Santiago-Licey Highway, in the vacation home of a certain Dr. Bornia, where they would receive all the details of the operation and report back with full "loyalty and adhesion . . ." ". . . to the person and government of the *Caudillo*"[111] (the quotes and capital letters were made by Peña Rivera in his statement).

It is an insult for this man to state that he was treated unfairly. He, who was Johnny Abbes's and Trujillo's most important henchman in the Cibao region. He never took into account the rights of the thousands of Dominicans who were killed or tortured by the regime's repressive, criminal machinery, of which he was such an important part.

As a citizen and daughter of two attorneys who made the ultimate sacrifice by giving their lives in order to achieve a truly just system in their homeland, it is my obligation to confront head-on the way in which this man described the trial as a "Roman circus," daring to besmirch one of the few occasions in which our courts were used in the democratic service of justice. How could I not?

Not long ago a friend of my father told me that while Peña Rivera and his accomplices were in jail waiting for the trial to begin, he and some other friends proposed that they carry out their own justice with their own hands. Outraged, Manolo responded, "We must set an example by participating in a democratic trial that will punish the culprits." My father refused to use the same criminal methods employed by the tyranny that Peña Rivera now wants us to forget.

If back then only my father and a few others believed in one's right to an impartial trial, thus raising the standards for our court system, then now, on behalf of so many families who have mourned their dead with dignity and decorum, I write to you demanding respect for the truth and that we not forget those who were responsible for a death that to date has gone unpunished. I also write to you so that the Mirabal sisters' sacrifice, and that of my father, not be forgotten.

The justice system, the media, and Dominican society will have the last word.

Minou Tavárez Mirabal

---

111 *Caudillo* refers to a local chieftain, political/military strongman, or dictator in Latin America.

Not long ago Alicinio died from cancer in Puerto Rico. When I learned of his death, I happily blurted out, "That beast is dead!" Jaime David, who was with me at the time, looked at me in disapproval and said, "Mamá, Mamá . . . ." Ciriaco de la Rosa died in Lawrence, Massachusetts, in the United States. He had changed his name to Chago. The only one still alive, that we know of, is Estrada Malleta.

During all these years there have been some curious coincidences. In 1974, my son Jaime Enrique moved with his wife Josefina to Lawrence, Massachusetts. The great influx of Dominicans to the region was just beginning. As soon as they moved there, they received the news: "Ciriaco de la Rosa and Estrada Malleta live here. They own a red car, whose make and model are such and such." Jaime Enrique, who inherited much of his father's temper, became obsessed and even bought a sawed-off shotgun and kept it in the house.

One Sunday, when he went to a nearby bodega to purchase something, there was a strange looking man in the store, and he noticed that the store owner appeared agitated. He then saw a red car parked outside, and his heart skipped a beat. He told himself, "This guy is one of the killers." He rushed home to look for his weapon, but in the meantime, the owner of the bodega warned the assassin, "Get out! Leave. That was a nephew of the Mirabal sisters." Ciriaco de la Rosa ran out of the store, and, luckily, when my son returned with the shotgun, he saw him speed away and turn the corner. He followed him but did not catch him. That night he stayed up, on the lookout, carrying the shotgun on his shoulder. He almost froze because it was so cold outside. De la Rosa did not return to Lawrence while my son lived there. Even though I visited them to help with their newborn son, they never told me what had happened so as not to worry me.

When Donald Reid Cabral was president during the triumvirate (1963–1965), a plan was set up to compensate the victims of the dictatorship, including the widows of the men who had killed Trujillo. There was talk of a 400,000-peso payment, which was a considerable amount because the dollar and the peso were of equal value at the time. A proposal was made to include us among the beneficiaries, but we refused. However, we managed to negotiate so that Rufino's widow would receive some money. They finally agreed to give her a monthly allowance.

I don't remember how exactly, but they managed to send a message to my mother explaining that the government was willing to help her with the children's education. Her sharp response was very clear: "Thank you very much. But I don't sell my blood."

Aside from the famous telegram reporting the "accident," which did not mention Minerva by name but rather as an "unidentified" victim, there are other strange instances of erasure that now come to mind and that I do not want to leave out because I don't know if they occurred by chance.

When we went to pay my mother's and my sisters' inheritance taxes, I was surprised to find that Minerva's file was missing. We looked through all the files but never found it.

Something similar occurred with the Calasanz High School yearbook, published when Nelson's class graduated. In the space where the name of his father was to appear, it says, "Pedro González," and in the space assigned to his mother, they left out Patria's name. They only wrote "R.I.P."

Little by little I learned that only time eases the pain of deep wounds. After the tragedy suffered by my sisters, the fibers of resentment died within me. I do not harbor resentment, but I do cultivate my memories. My mother would say that this is my temperament. Over the years, without discrimination, I have met with Balaguer supporters, communists, members of the Partido Revolucionario Dominicano, and with persons from all philosophical beliefs and various political orientations.

Once, during Jaime David's first senate campaign,[112] a friend organized a fundraising activity at her home. During the reception a man came up to me and introduced himself: "Doña Dedé, how are you? I am Flicho Palma." Of course, I recognized him. He was once one of the regime's top caliés and had been our neighbor during the Trujillo dictatorship. The man had contributed to the fundraising event, and there he was. I had no choice but to greet him in return, but I could not bring myself to shake that man's hand.

When I found out about Alicinio's death, I could not hold back my joy. I remember that, although I did not personally know Ramon Antonio (Negro) Veras—a prominent attorney and one of the few members of the Panfleteros of Santiago who had survived the repressive years and who was a firm defender of human rights—it suddenly occurred to me to call and ask him to celebrate Alicinio's passing with me.

I have not forgotten. Even today, I still hurt terribly from the events that forever changed the life of my family and of my country. I learned from my mother that forgiveness is a sentiment that gives peace to humans. She would constantly tell us that if you harbor hatred and resentment, those feelings will be reflected in everything you do. However, she also taught me

---

112   He would serve as senator representing Salcedo from 1990 to 1996, in which year he was elected vice president of the Republic.

that although it is healthy to forgive, this does not mean that you have to be complacent or accept impunity.

How does one forgive the plundering of the country and stealing from poor and defenseless people? How does one tolerate that? Acts like these cannot go unpunished. How many people have made fortunes at the expense of the poor? No, we definitely cannot confuse pardon with impunity, nor respond to these bloody crimes and corrupt acts with indifference and apathy.

13

Political Events Continue To Impact Us

In 1965, in the midst of the April Revolution,[113] four revolutionaries were killed on Pedrito's farm. They had come to attack the military barracks in San Francisco de Macorís but were betrayed by the worker who transported the milk from the farm to town. Two other men were killed in the barracks. Edmundo Díaz Moreno, the brother of engineer Rubén Díaz Moreno, a member of the 14th of June Movement who had fallen alongside Manolo, and Sóstenes Peña Jáquez, another distinguished member of the Movement, died there.

A colonel by the last name of Perelló, accompanied by military troops, raided Pedrito's home and destroyed everything. He had to flee with his new wife and Raúl. They had nowhere to hide, and they decided to take refuge in my mother's home. In spite of the estrangement between our families and the friction that had arisen between us, he thought that her home was the safest place. From there they went to Uncle Fello's home in Jarabacoa. Those were truly tense, difficult times for my mother and me.

In the meantime, Jaimito had turned his pickup truck into a transportation vehicle for those who wanted to travel to the capital to join the movement, launched to reinstate the 1963 Constitution. He also transported plantains and other food items for the Constitutionalists. It was a lot of work, and his life was constantly in danger.

As a matter of fact, we hardly ever saw him because, just like Pedrito, he had to go into hiding so they would not kill him. Nelson and I told everyone that he had left for Puerto Rico, but because he was so daring, he would enter our home through a window. He risked being seen by some of Jaime David's young friends, who could have easily told on him. He would hide here or in Uca's home. She was a cousin who lived near the town of Santana. They finally caught him. He was in prison for eighteen days. I went

---

113 Dominican Civil War, April 24–September 3, 1965.

to denounce his arrest before an OAS representative who, by the way, told me that he had met Manolo during a prior mission in this country.

The day after he was released, Nelson arrived very early in the morning with the news that they were trying to steal his father's cattle. Jaimito went with him. They borrowed a couple of trucks and transferred the cattle from Pedrito's farm to ours until things quieted down.

Balaguer's victory in the June 1966 elections was a difficult blow to assimilate. Balaguer, winning in this country! After the role he played during the dictatorship! The memory of the girls' murder and of Manolo's sacrifice was still too fresh in my memory. Jaimito had openly campaigned against Balaguer, even though I did not want him to become involved in politics. But what was the use of my opposing his involvement if I could never convince him?

There is one particular story from those days that today makes me laugh, but that reflects the terribly unhappy times we were going through. Uncle David was my mother's cousin. He died the day after the elections. At his funeral I ran into various Catorcista women. We were screaming and sobbing. Someone commented that they didn't know I cared so much for that particular uncle. I didn't dare confess that I was actually letting out all the rage and frustration I was feeling. The fact that Balaguer, "the Paper Puppet," had actually won broke my heart. What a frustrating situation! Nothing in politics has hurt me more than that particular event.

During Balaguer's twelve-year regime, my home in Ojo de Agua was continuously raided, allegedly in search of weapons belonging to the 14th of June Movement. They insisted the weapons were there, hidden in the water tank in the backyard. How stupid could they be? Weapons in a water tank or in the cacao plantation! They searched everywhere. In total, they raided our home twenty-eight times. They came in at all hours of the day and night. One day the police raided our home, and one hour later, the Army came and raided us again. I guess they wanted to scare us, but Jaimito, with that temperament of his, got angrier and angrier. We were afraid they would kill him if the raids continued.

If it were not for the seriousness of the matter, I would say that the situation was actually funny because the abuse reached such extremes that once, while I was selling insurance in San Francisco de Macorís, I ran into Orlando Camilo, the person from the District Attorney's Office who had to be present during the raids. He said to me, "Dedé, what a coincidence! I've just come from your house. Since none of you were there, we had to proceed with the search."

When I got to the house, I discovered that they had taken a newspaper that had been dedicated to the first anniversary of the girls' murder, as if it were a subversive document. It included their biographies and other important photographs. I could not control myself, that's how upset I was. I sped over to the fortress and told them that I would not leave without the newspaper. They finally handed it over to me.

Once, and fearing the worst, I don't remember if it was during the April Revolution or during the Balaguer regime, we prepared an underground hideout in one of the rooms of the house. The entrance to the hideout was hidden under a bed. We had no guns there, but we thought it would serve as a hiding place if the situation became critical. We spread the dirt over the cacao groves so no one would notice. Suddenly, one day, Ramón Paja ran into the house to warn us that the troops were on their way to raid us one more time. I do not want to remember that moment. I felt for poor Rarrá, the man who was installing the door to the underground hideout. He started running around placing the mattresses here and there to trick the guards. We were scared to death. Fortunately, this time around the troops did not check the bedrooms.

Another day, when Jaimito was not at the house, the guards arrived at dawn to raid us once again. I got up quickly and hid Jaimito's gun under my blouse. One of the guards asked me about the guns, and I told him that there were none. Then he pointed to me and said, "What about that one that you just put in there?" I had no other choice than to take the gun out, and although I showed him the gun permit, he took it with him. They never returned it. Now I can talk about this and even laugh, but these were truly terrifying moments. When they ordered me to "hand over the gun," I was shaking. "Fear is free, Dedé, there are times when you feel fear and you can't help it, especially if you know that they can torture or kill you," Jaimito would tell me later.

During the Balaguer years there were always guards around, monitoring our home. That is why we forbade the children from playing in the backyard after six in the afternoon.

There were times when Jaimito hid one or two rifles in the house. I would get very nervous. In order to throw the guards off, when they got close to the hiding places, I would tell them, "Come and search in these small armoires," and my legs would not stop shaking. Jaimito would later calm me down. "Don't be embarrassed, Dedé, I actually dropped my cigarette when I saw that they were getting too close to the hiding place."

The most dangerous moments that Jaimito experienced took place in

Nagua. He always dreamed of having a farm that was bigger than the farm El Indio because, even though he was born in town, he loved the countryside as much as I did. We sold our cattle and asked the bank for a loan to purchase some land near Nagua, from a widow who had owned it since 1909. It was a tremendous opportunity. These types of farms were known as *sitios*.[114] It was a savannah situated between two lagoons, and the land was only used for rice plantations. We purchased the land at a great price. Jaimito leveled the terrain, plowed the land, planted, and organized the farm. That is when the problems got worse. Because I was still living in Ojo de Agua, I only heard bits and pieces about some of the incidents. But finally, I asked Jaimito to give me all the details of what had actually occurred during those days:

> I went looking for land around Los Jengibres, and I ran into this massive piece of land, about eight thousand or nine thousand acres, which belonged to several owners. I made the arrangements and purchased the land, but when folks around the farm saw the quality of rice I was growing, a rice so beautiful it was scary, the neighbors began to show interest and meddle. After I created footpaths, a ranch, a landing strip for fumigation aircraft, and a wooden bridge over the channeled runoff waters, Colonel Juan René Beauchamp Javier, who was from Nagua, began to covet the farm and make life difficult for me. He had taken land away from individuals or forced them to sell him their land at very low prices. He did this to the Llibre family, to Mariano Palmero—a Spaniard from Pimentel—and to Agustín Polanco, among others.
>
> They started a rumor that I was a dangerous man, that I was married to one of the Mirabal sisters, that I was a communist, and that the landing strip was so Fidel Castro's planes could land, among other things. Me, a communist! All I wanted to do was work and accumulate a lot of land, and communists don't like that.
>
> I didn't know that two or three years earlier, a guerrilla cell had become active in the region and writer Rafael Chaljub Mejía was an

---

114 In the Spanish colonial Caribbean, plots of rural land used for farming were called *sitios*, though this word commonly means simply "place" or "site." G. Friederici, *Amerikanistischer Wörterbuch und Hilfswörterbuch für den Amerikanisten*, Hamburg: Cram, de Gruyter, 1960. Cited in David Robinson, "The Language and Significance of Place in Latin America," *The Power of Place: Bringing Together Geographical and Sociological Imaginations*, eds. John Agnew and James Duncan (Boston: Unwin Hyman, 1989, 159).

active militant there. Since I would sometimes miss the entrance to the farm, for some God-known reason I decided to place a great big white cross at the entrance. That's when another rumor started to circulate: the cross was a sign to orient Fidel Castro's airplanes.

They had me under surveillance because they said that at night I met with spies. The truth is there were so many mosquitoes at the farm that if you remained still, they would cover you from head to toe. That's why in the afternoon I left the farm to have a couple of drinks, dance, fall in love, hang around, do things men do. . . . I am not going to say I was a saint or an old geezer. Dedé was living quietly in Ojo de Agua. Or so I thought.

At the intersection of Los Jengibres there was a tiny village where Eva Chaljub lived with her father. They were both very good friends of mine. It just so happened that an Air Force sergeant by the name of Emeterio Javier, Beauchamp Javier's cousin, lived around there. The sergeant told his sister-in-law that the colonel had promised him that if he killed me, they would give him a promotion and a house in San Isidro.[115] The woman sent Eva Chaljub, wife of folk musician Tatico Henríquez, to warn me. I left through the town of Abreu and reached Tenares, determined to reveal this information to anyone who could stop their plans.

One day, before I found out about the plot, I saw the sergeant as I was approaching a curve in the road. He was in uniform, and he stepped right into the middle of the road. I passed by him very closely. If I had known his intention was to kill me, I would have run him over right then and there.

A colonel friend of mine, Dr. Humberto Hernández, took me to the head of the Joint Chiefs, General Pérez Guillén. He brought in a couple of generals and colonels so they could hear me out, and he had me tell my story from the day I married Dedé. I told him everything, even the fact that Jaime Enrique had once been arrested in Nagua just because he was delivering some merchandise to our grocery store. General Pérez Guillén said to me, "Go back to Salcedo. I'll send for you with a trustworthy officer."

A few days later we heard in a news broadcast that the family of Sergeant Emeterio Javier had reported him missing. He left his house

---

115 Reference to the Air Force base in San Isidro.

and never returned. The family was told to celebrate nine masses, as was the local tradition, to honor his soul.

Beauchamp Javier was a friend of mine up front, but behind my back he was giving orders to have me killed. Men don't scare me. However, Beauchamp had such a cynical smirk that not even Trujillo's compared to his . . .

I met him at a home in Nagua. He was so nice, and I liked him. But I was later informed, 'My good man! Just a half hour ago he said that they were going to eliminate you!'

Life Went On and So Did Our Daily Routine

After my sisters' deaths, Mamá closed the front door of the house and never opened it again. Her life was limited to the house and the garden. Her seclusion lasted more than twenty years. Even her visits to church occurred under truly exceptional circumstances. Other rare outings were when she went to visit her grandson Raúl in Macorís, or the day she went to take possession of the farm she had finally recovered. They had confiscated it when the girls were arrested.

She spent each day with a rosary in her hand. She planted and took care of the garden. She never stopped working. Work gave meaning to her life. She took care of her grandchildren. She also worked in the areas set aside to dry the cacao beans. She managed the cattle farm.

Her grandchildren would say, "Mamá Chea is a witch" because while they played, she would appear out of nowhere with a rosary and a belt in her hands to give them a couple of lashes if they were misbehaving or if they climbed the many fruit trees that she herself had planted: loquat, cashew nut, tamarind, star apple, grapefruit, and tangerine. They also played tricks on folks that were walking on the nearby road. When the kids really got on her nerves, she would say to them, "You are getting away with this because the only one still alive is Dedé. If Patria were here, she would have you all under control!" And she was right because even though Patria was of such good character, she was also the strictest and most disciplined of us all.

Perhaps one of the most serious problems we faced, and which took years to resolve and truly upset both my mother and I, was the conflict with the State, and with Pedrito and his second wife, over the farm in San Francisco de Macorís. That process took many years to resolve because in our country the justice system is so terribly slow. It was also extremely painful not only for us, but especially for Patria and Pedrito's children, whom I consider my own.

Even though I was completely convinced, as the saying goes, that "it is better to have a bad agreement than a good lawsuit," My mother was so hurt that she insisted on seeing the lawsuit through until the very end. If we would have reached an agreement, whatever it was, she would have had a more peaceful death. She would have had more time to feel that she was the sole owner of her farm, that all her legal documents were in order, and that she could leave it to her grandchildren as was her wish. But life is not a dress rehearsal, and you cannot turn back time.

The sad part was that by the time the courts issued a sentence in her favor and I told her the news, she hardly reacted. Her arteriosclerosis was very advanced and had taken a toll on her. We never imagined that the lawsuit would take so long, ruining forever our family's relationship with Pedrito.

Even with a sentence issued in our favor, we continued to face challenges regarding the legal documents related to the farm. They were nowhere to be found. We later found out that the papers had gone missing because Alicinio Peña Rivera had begun a process to have the farm's title issued under his name.

These kinds of interests are just too dangerous for the unity of a family. When there are assets involved, everything should be as clear and transparent as possible. Many times, I have complained to my children that they do not help as much as they should when it comes to these issues because ever since that experience, I have gone to great lengths to make sure all documents involving our family's assets are legal and up to date. I do not want to leave the family with more of these kinds of problems. At the end of the day, as they say in the countryside, no one takes material things with them to Heaven, and "burial clothes do not come with extra pockets for keeping things."

IV

A Time to Preserve Memories

Left: Figure 4.1. Ana Antonia (Tonó) Rosario: "She, along with us, helped raise and take care of them; she was another mother to them." Courtesy of the Fundación Hermanas Mirabal.

Below: Figure 4.2. Dedé surrounded by images of her sisters. Courtesy of the Fundación Hermanas Mirabal.

Figure 4.3. Doña Chea with her granddaughter Patria Román González. The mother of the Mirabal sisters lived until 1981. "She suffered with tremendous dignity and was resigned to the comfort she found in her faith." Courtesy of the Fundación Hermanas Mirabal.

Figure 4.4. Jaime David, Dedé, and Juan Bosch. Courtesy of the Fundación Hermanas Mirabal.

Figure 4.5. Dedé with her nine children. In the first row, Noris, Jacqueline, Nelson, Minou, and Raúl. In the back row, Jimmy, Jaime Enrique, Jaime David, and Manolo. "[T]o raise them well, without pity, resentment or hatred. That was our great responsibility." Courtesy of the Fundación Hermanas Mirabal.

Figure 4.6. The garden and home that is now a museum. "Overall, people have been very supportive of everything we do to preserve the memory of the girls." Courtesy of the Fundación Hermanas Mirabal.

Figure 4.7. Dedé, the one who lived to tell the story. "I need to know that I can be useful, that when I wake up, I have a job to do." Courtesy of the Fundación Hermanas Mirabal.

14

Raising the Children Brought Us Back to Life

Mamá lived another twenty years after the girls' death. Together we worked to teach the boys and girls in our family the importance of perseverance. We made sure they were raised in an environment that was as normal and natural as possible. I wish she could have lived longer so she could have enjoyed seeing how her grandchildren have evolved. She was a bit concerned about Manolo's rebellious and mischievous character, and she would have been pleased to see the beautiful family her adored grandson has raised, as well as his tremendous success as a businessman!

If something gave her strength and satisfaction during the last stage of her life, it was having to raise those small children who, with their mischievous pranks, would sometimes exasperate her. "You are not going to drive me crazy! I refuse to go crazy!" she would snap.

Our greatest responsibility was to raise the children, tend to their needs, and try to explain to them the tragedy that had devastated their families. Our hope was to raise them in such a way that these events did not impact them psychologically or provoke resentment or hatred in them. In all, the goal was to raise them well, without pity.

As the years passed, as they were growing up, we began to adapt to each child's particular needs and interests. They were all different. When my sisters died, some of the children were already adolescents, but the majority were very small and required lots of nurturing and constant attention.

The responsibility of raising my sisters' children, and mine as well, was what forced us to continue. And I never tire of repeating it: this was what kept my mother and I alive after the tragedy.

Jacqueline and Raúl had their respective fathers. But Minou and Manolito did not. We were especially concerned about these two because we once heard that a military officer in Salcedo had commented, "Look, that's Manolo's son. Better to kill him now while he's still young." Blessed Mother of God! That was our biggest concern! My mother would not let the little boy out of her sight. She overprotected him, just like she had protected María Teresa. I became aware of her concern very early on, and I told her that if we continued to overprotect Manolo, we would turn him into a useless human being. So we decided to send him and Jaime David to the Evangelical Boarding School in Santiago.

At the school they were able to study and fit in with the rest of the children. The teachers were good to them and understood their situation. They were especially patient with Jaime David's hyperactivity and Manolo's difficult character. They took into account their particular needs and helped provide them a basic education.

The truth is everything that had to do with the children went well. Their activities were normal. They played and occupied themselves with activities that were typical of children their age. They climbed trees, flirted with danger, played hide-and-go-seek in the backyard, and sometimes bothered the folks who walked along the nearby road. Mamá was much stricter and demanding with them. I was a bit more lenient. Jaimito and I would take them to the farm and on trips to the beach. We tried to provide a normal life for them. No pity for them, nor letting them feel like little orphans. Never.

Raúl lived with his father until Pedrito's death in 1972. We then decided to take him to the capital to live with Nelson, who was already married. Tonó, who helped us raise and take care of the children, was a second mother to them. She can explain better than anyone, in her own words, how the children were raised:

> They were always together, not only Minerva, Patria, and Maria Teresa's children, but Dedé's as well. They were like normal siblings. They argued, fought, played. Jaime David was the most active. Minou loved books, and it was easier for the others to push her around a bit. Jaime Enrique and Jimmy were the oldest. They went from one house to the other. Jacqueline spent more time with Dedé, but she spent the weekends here. They were always together. Doña Chea wanted to have them all together. . . . After the girls died, I too, felt responsible for them. It was my duty to help Doña Chea.

Tonó pampered them all. She made sure to prepare the food that Nelson and Noris liked, Manolo's "coconut delight," Minou's favorite chicken and rice dish, and Jacqueline's milky mangoes. She lived so that each and every one of them would be happy. Even today she greets them with their favorite treats and pampers them all. But her weakness was always Manolo, her godchild, who lived in our house from the time he was a baby.

I don't know how, but we managed to come through as a united family in which Mamá was the center of everything. She demanded respect through discipline and insisted that they always showed good manners. We managed to raise them to love and care for one another as brothers and sisters, and they always behaved just the way we wanted: as members of a very close-knit family.

Today, as adults who lead their own individual lives, I look at them and tell myself, "They have good hearts, good intentions, they are honest and hardworking. They have earned the respect of those who know them. They adore one another, and get along well. What else can you possibly ask for, Dedé?"

Nelson Enrique, Noris Mercedes, and Fidel Raúl Ernesto

Of all of Patria and Pedrito's children, Nelson, who was already studying at the university when his mother was killed, has always stood out for his sound character. He is shy and a good-hearted soul. "You are the example," I would tell him. He was born into a happy home, and he inherited Patria's sense of discipline and organization. One only has to see how his closet is organized. His pants, shirts, sweaters . . . all in perfect order. That was Patria, extremely organized and attentive to the smallest detail. If there was a dance and Noris did not have the right bow to adorn her head, Patria would rather she not go.

I was very concerned about Nelson because I feared the tragedy would mark him forever. He was old enough to suffer, and he was very much aware of all the violence that had afflicted his family: how the caliés destroyed their beautiful and well-kept home, his father's imprisonment, as well as his own, his mother's murder. . . . However, in spite of my concerns, he managed to overcome the terrible, tragic circumstances he had to endure during his adolescent years. He was a hardworking and very responsible man, to such an extent that when he decided to get a divorce when his kids were all grown up, he expressed his concern to me: "Mamá Dedé, I'm no longer going to be an example for the rest." Then I told him that he should not concern or sacrifice himself, and that if the decision was for his own well-being, that he should go through with it.

His older children, Patricia and Nelson Enrique, now have families of their own, and his two youngest daughters, Eva and Sarah, are studying at a university in Florida.

When Patria was killed, Noris was not yet sixteen and was studying at the Immaculate Conception School in La Vega. I would accompany Patria to visit her and spend time with the nuns during the school's important celebrations.

With a truly noble, easy-going, and nurturing personality, Noris never complains about anything, not even during the difficult moments she's had to live through. She always greets you with an open and affectionate smile. She studied to become a secretary at the Luis Muñoz Rivera School, and during the nineties, she worked at the Ministry of the Environment. When I see her with her three children—Patria Mercedes, Francis Ernesto, and Cristóbal Enrique—and tending to the smallest details involving her grandchildren, I think of Patria and reflect on how quickly life passes by.

Raúl, Patria's youngest, became an industrial engineer. Nelson has always looked after him and provided him with all the support he needed, most especially in trying to guide him through a rebellious adolescence. But, above all, he is Patria's son. He inherited her organizational skills and understanding personality. He is a very hard worker, somewhat timid and reserved, and has a wonderful sense of humor. He is the owner of a company that sells industrial security equipment. Raúl and his excellent wife, Ana Amaya Hernández, have two children: Raúl Ernesto and Patria Marie, both university students.

They are also my children and, sometimes, when I see how they are carrying on with their lives and trying to build their own happiness, I feel that Patria is watching them through my eyes.

Minou and Manolito

As I said before, soon after Minerva's assassination, we sent Minou to the Immaculate Conception School. During those dangerous times—in between Minerva's death, in November 1960, and Manolo's release from jail, in July 1961—we thought she would be better protected and cared for by the nuns. This way her education would not be interrupted. Her mother had always paid great attention to Minou's intellectual development, which she had noticed early on.

Later on, Manolo decided to take her with him to the capital. Minou lived with him until 1963, when he went underground after the overthrow of the Juan Bosch administration. Manolo sent for me and asked me to take care of Minou. That year we registered the children, both Minou and Manolito, at the Sacred Heart School in Santiago.

Minou has always been super intelligent. She knew everything in school. Even when she was little, she read constantly and was very responsible when it came to her studies. I remember that when she was around twelve or thirteen, she would take the twenty-five cents that Mamá would give her for her school snack and—instead of spending it on soda pop and cookies—she would buy newspapers to read. As a matter of fact, she read all the books in Minerva's library. But she was a bit distracted. She lived so absorbed in her own world that someone once said she was not normal. That's when Mamá issued an order: "Everyone, shut up! She's just like her mother! But don't tell her that. If you tell her what they are saying, it will be worse because then she's going to want to imitate her."

She graduated high school when she was fifteen and also completed commercial trade school in Salcedo, where we had registered her so she could enter a secretarial program. At the time, Emma and Doña Fefita, Manolo's sister and mother, began to suggest that she go to the capital to study. Mamá resented the suggestion somewhat, but Minou left. And because she was not old enough to begin studying at the university, she registered at another trade school run by the teacher Consuelo Despradel.

Mamá began to worry because she said that Emma gave Minou books on the revolution, on the *Tupamaros*,[116] and on similar topics. I would say that, to a certain extent, Emma Tavárez became the head of the 14th of June when her brother was killed and once Leandro left for Mexico after having led the 14th of June for a short period of time. The group that had opposed Manolo's decision to continue the struggle in the mountains separated themselves from the organization. There were no leaders left. The organization quickly began to fall apart and splintered into various groups. Later on, Emma became a member of the Dominican Communist Party.

I remember once when Minou brought home a couple of books on politics and on Che Guevara. "And what is this?" my mother asked, and she threw them into the latrine. Minou tired of looking for them everywhere, but they never appeared. "Putting all those ideas into Minou's head? That's not going to happen!" said Mamá.

Minou was a young lady who dreamed of justice and who had inherited a legacy of fighting for it, and they had her reading all those political books, drawing her toward the Dominican Communist Party. She was being in-

---

116 A left-wing urban guerrilla group that operated in Uruguay during the 1960s and 1970s.

fluenced by her Aunt Emma. That concerned us. At one point we found out that Minou was going to travel to Moscow to participate in the World Youth Festival. At the time she had become very good friends with journalist Orlando Martínez, who was later assassinated during the Balaguer regime. He constantly wrote on democracy and against the Balaguer regime. Those were years of tremendous repression. The regime killed many young men, precisely when they were beginning to flourish as young leaders. We had reason to be concerned. I was against the trip and stood my ground: "Minou is not going. She is a minor. She was entrusted to me by Manolo, and she is my responsibility," I insisted to Emma.

That is when I think my mother, trying to remove Minou from danger, decided to send her to Canada to study English and complete a program for bilingual secretaries, even though she was only sixteen years old. When she returned to the country, she began studying literature at the Autonomous University of Santo Domingo, and she landed a good job at the Holanda Dominicana company. Mamá, ever the realist, said, "That's the job she needs so she can earn a few pesos. She can study literature later because no one makes a living from that." It's not that her granddaughter was a burden to her, but Mamá was convinced that people learned to be responsible by holding down a job.

Minou was interested in continuing her studies, and soon after, she told me she had received a scholarship to study in Cuba. I said yes because I thought her studies would last one or two years. In 1981, when Mamá died, she had not finished her studies, and she could not come to her burial, so I went to Cuba to spend a few days with her. I did not understand what it was that she was studying. "Mamá, philology is the study of languages and literature," she told me. Five years later she returned with her degree, but later returned to Cuba to complete a specialization in Hispanic American Literature.

When she returned to the country, she tried to get a job at the Autonomous University of Santo Domingo. But she was not accepted. They put up all sorts of barriers so she would not be able to teach there. She was finally hired by a private university called APEC to teach literature. At the university she became known for being a demanding professor, in whose classes you really had to study hard. She was very well prepared intellectually.

When I talk about all this, it may appear that I pressured the children not to get involved in politics. That is not the case, but we had suffered through so much that naturally we were afraid. I do admit that I would tell them, "I don't want you in politics. If members of our family gave up their lives, it means we already paid a high price in blood for our country's freedom." I told my husband the same thing when he joined the Dominican Revolutionary Party (PRD).

In the nineties Minou joined the Dominican Liberation Party (PLD), of which my son Jaime David was already a leader and senator. In 1996, she was named vice foreign minister and served in that role until 2000. In 2002, she was elected to the House of Representatives, representing the capital city, and in 2006 she was reelected for a second term. She has one daughter, Camila Minerva, and one son, Manuel Aurelio.

Manolo spent several years in Santiago's Evangelical School, where he got into serious trouble and was almost expelled. He later studied at the Superior Agricultural Institute (ISA), where Jaime David had been studying for two years. Both graduated in agricultural science from the Institute.

When the children began to finish their studies, Mamá decided to buy a house in the capital with a large garden and backyard. The idea was for Jaime David, Manolo, Raúl, and Jacqueline to live there. Minou was studying in Cuba. Although Jimmy had already married, he also moved in with them for a short while.

While he was studying industrial engineering at the Technological Institute of Santo Domingo (INTEC), I remember that Manolo got a short-term job at the Dominican Agrarian Institute. Finally, he was lucky enough to move on to the National Technical and Vocational Institute (INFOTEP), where he acquired excellent professional experience in his field. From there, he was sent to Brazil to observe the production of briquettes made from rice husks. This experience turned out to be extremely helpful because, upon returning to the country, he decided to establish Briquetas Nacionales, an innovative company in the area of renewable energy.

I have always said Manolo is the one who inherited my father's entrepreneurial spirit and vision. He has done very well as a businessman. Aside from being an agro-industrial entrepreneur, he also represents various Brazilian companies that manufacture industrial equipment and has successfully invested in the tourism industry in Las Terrenas, Samaná, on the country's north coast. He and his hardworking wife, Clara, have three children: Minerva, Minou, and Talía.

Because Minerva was so demanding with regards to the education she wanted for her children, I look at them and ask myself if she would be pleased, if she would approve of my educational methods. I am so pleased with Minou and Manolo. When I look at them and see how each is trying to give the best of themselves to their country and society, I can almost hear

Minerva saying, "Yes, Dedé. Even though I did not entrust them to you, I knew you would do a wonderful job as a substitute mother."

Jacqueline

I took charge of Jacqueline when her mother was sent to prison. She calls my husband Jaimito "Papá," and her father Leandro "Papi." She was such a good little girl. She was never a problem for us. Sometimes she would start to cough at night and I would rub her chest with turpentine. The smell would loosen her lungs to the point that Jaimito would say to me: "Hey Dedé, that treatment is really good. Look how she stopped coughing." Jacqueline was the daughter we never had. And if we'd had a daughter of our own, we would have given her the same name.

Each one of us had our own personality, and María Teresa was exceedingly kind-hearted. I believe Jacqueline inherited her mother's kindness and a bit of her mother's naivety. Her brothers would make fun of her because she believed everything they told her.

She attended school in Ojo de Agua until the fourth grade and continued in Salcedo until she completed her sophomore year. That is when we decided to send her to the Immaculate Conception School so she could finish the next two years.

When she finished high school, we sent her to study English at Lady Cliff College in New York, near West Point. She later studied hotel administration in Boston. With her father's help she finished her studies and decided to move to Madrid and then to Costa del Sol in Spain to do her internship. When she returned to Santo Domingo she began to work with Leandro, who at the time was working in the hospitality sector.

The story of how she met her husband, Fernando Albaine, has always been amusing to me. It reminds me of that popular saying about love being blind. She had moved to Puerto Plata to work in one of her father's hotels. There she came down with chickenpox, became very sick, and had an asthma attack, just like her mother used to. Fernando was the doctor who treated her, and from the moment he laid eyes on her, he fell in love, even though she looked terrible, was covered in scabs, and was skinny to the bone. They eventually married and now live in Puerto Plata.

I always say that Jacqueline is the daughter every mother wants to have: she has initiative and good taste, and she is very supportive of her brothers and sisters, as well as everyone else. She is a bit shy, and even though she hates speaking in public, she adores making new friends. With her husband, who is a kind and very family-oriented man, they have two beautiful children: María Teresa and Leandro Arturo.

If they hadn't killed her when she was twenty-five years old, María Teresa would have had several children. She always said she wanted a big family. I think my sister entrusted her to me because she knew Jacqueline would not be *like* my daughter, but that she would be *my* daughter, the one she had and whom she named Jacqueline because of me.

My Three Jaimes

My three biological sons have also embarked on their own separate paths. However, they all share the same work ethic and dedication regarding their responsibilities.

Jaime Enrique was not very studious and turned out to be quite a lady's man, like his father, until he married Josefina Salcedo Canaán, his current wife, who has been another daughter to me. They moved to the United States for a while, and their first son was born there. Their time in the United States turned out to be a real experience for him, as he himself has explained, and it helped him tremendously when he returned to the country.

Although he has not dedicated all his energies to politics, he does seem to have a calling for it. He was a PRD activist, but quickly became disenchanted with the party.

Sometimes life places us in difficult circumstances. One of these peculiar situations arose during the 1986 elections. I had to handle it with a mother's sensibility. Jaime Enrique was the PRD's senatorial candidate for Salcedo, and Jaime David was the chief of the PLD's provincial campaign. At night, after a day of campaigning, they would meet at my house and discuss the issues at hand. I was afraid they would argue, especially because Jaime Enrique had inherited his father's temper. Luckily, Jaime David is somewhat more tolerant. He has always been easy-going, and there were never any misunderstandings between them.

During the campaign Jaime Enrique took a couple of months off from his job at the brewery Cervecería Nacional Dominicana. When he finished the campaign, he was not allowed back in the company. So he partnered with Jimmy and opened an electrical equipment store in Santo Domingo. He later separated from the company and opened his own electrical equipment company.

Aside from Wanda, Jaime Enrique's daughter from his first marriage,

Jaime Enrique and Josefina have three sons: Jaime Enrique, Jaime Nelson, and José Enrique.

I remember some of the funny things Jaime Rafael would do when he was little. For instance, one day in class, when the teacher asked, "Who liberated Cuba?" Jimmy immediately replied, "Fidel Castro."

Jimmy, as we call him, was always a good student, very bright and capable. He studied at the Emiliano Tejera School in Salcedo. He registered at the Universidad Católica Madre y Maestra to study electrical engineering. Just when he was about to graduate, around 1973, the university went through a serious internal crisis, and he decided to finish his career at INTEC University in Santo Domingo. While in school, he also worked at Guridi Comercial. Soon after he graduated, he told us, "I wasn't born to be an employee." He asked us if we could support him for two or three months, until he could set himself up independently, and we said yes. But it wasn't necessary to give him anything because two months later he informed us, "I won't need any money, I'm already on my way." He is currently the owner of Electron S.A., an electrical installation company, and he is the national representative for various international companies.

Jimmy is the most open and friendly of my children. He also has sharp analytical abilities and a very practical approach to life. I remember that Monsignor Vinicio Disla once told me, "I thought that of all your sons, Jimmy was the one who would go into politics!" He likes to travel and enjoy a good wine and the best cars.

Jimmy met his wife Mayra Corominas when he was studying at INTEC. Mayra has been extremely supportive of all his projects. They have three children: María Teresa, a lawyer; Jaime Rafael, an electrical engineer; and Pedro David, a business administration student.

I have some very vivid memories of Jaime David, my youngest son. At age five, when he was too young to understand the danger that hovered over us, he would spot military officials and run up to them screaming, "Trujillo officials!" Jacqueline would come running after him. I must admit that the childhoods of Jaime David and Jacqueline are among the things that I have most enjoyed in life.

Something that distinguished Jaime David from a very early age is that he is a natural leader. The other children respected him and paid attention to what he said. For instance, he would say, "Why are you kicking balls around in the streets? Go and play baseball!"

As an adolescent, he became a community leader. He organized the first Hermanas Mirabal Games in 1977, in Ojo de Agua. The Minister of Sports attended the opening ceremony.

Dr. Concepción, a friend of the family, would say, "Minerva's heir is Jaime David." In the most spontaneous ways, he would honor the memories of his aunts Patria, Minerva, and María Teresa, but also the memory of Manolo.

Jaime David accomplished his dream of studying agricultural science when he graduated from the country's Agricultural Institute. Although he studied for one year at the Northeast Regional University, based in San Francisco de Macorís, he did not adapt to the academic approach used by the Autonomous University of Santo Domingo and transferred to INTEC University, where he finished medical school. Later, in Spain, he furthered his studies with a specialization in mental health. When he graduated, he moved to Trieste, Italy, to continue studying the latest approaches in psychiatry.

When he returned to the Dominican Republic he was named as a mental health specialist in Santiago. He also volunteered two days a week at the hospital in Salcedo. He managed to get support from the Italians and start a model program for mental health patients. The goal was to prepare these individuals to reenter society and recover the freedom they had lost due to the confinement that their families had imposed on them.

Since he made very good friends in Trieste, he was invited to return to the city to work in local mental health co-ops. Before leaving, he married Carmen Lisette (Lissy) Campos Jorge, a devoted pediatrician, who traveled with him. By year's end he was hired to work in Central America with a team of Italian doctors, specifically with refugees who were victims of the wars that had ravished the region. For the 1990 elections, his party chose him as its senatorial candidate, and he had to travel back to the country almost every week. He was elected senator on two occasions, representing the province of Salcedo, where he introduced and headed numerous development projects in health, the environment, and the fight against poverty. To advance these programs he leveraged the strong relationships he had built with various U.N. organizations and other international co-op agencies. In 1996 he was elected vice president of the Dominican Republic.

Jaime David and Lissy have three children. The oldest is Adriana, and my youngest grandchildren, Anton David and Carmen Adela, are twins.

Mamá Begins to Fade Away

Jaime David spent a lot of time with Mamá, especially in her last few years. He admired her greatly and was very loving toward her. He had a very close relationship with her. They were so close that even today it is common to hear him quote her in his speeches: "'We all fight for equality, but we do not all think the same,' as Mamá Chea used to say." He repeats this frequently. When she died, no one wept for her like he did.

Mamá lived for her grandchildren. When they were away at school or at the university, she impatiently waited for them: "Today is Friday. They're on their way," she would say. When Minou, Jacqueline, Manolito, Jimmy, Jaime David . . . when any of them were about to arrive—sometimes with friends or classmates—Mamá would tell Tonó, "Those kids like to eat a lot, prepare whatever they ask for." The arrival of her granddaughters and grandsons made her so happy. She tried to treat them all the same. Whatever she bought for one, she bought for the others, including my children.

Paradoxically, she hated nicknames, even though she was called "Chea"—her nickname—throughout her entire life. "Don't give the children nicknames. It takes away from their personalities," she would say. She would constantly fuss over the children just like a hen does with her chicks. For example, she always called Jimmy by his name: Rafael.

On Sundays, we all gathered at her house. It was an action-packed day that required a lot of preparation. The kids got into all sorts of trouble when they were together. Tonó told us that, once, they started throwing tangerine peels at the cars passing by. One driver got so upset that he began insulting the entire family. Mamá did not flinch. She stood on the porch and told him, "It's that they're kind of crazy because their mothers were killed when they were little."

In 1978, Mamá fell from her bed and broke her leg. From then on, she refused to walk and spent the last years of her life in a wheelchair. I tried to make her walk a few steps around the house, but she would tell me, "No, Dedé. Walk so I can fall again? I'd rather stay here." She also would not agree to any kind of rehabilitation program. She would sit in her wheelchair near the door and wait for us to bring her some of the flowering orchids from her collection. She would fill her pockets with corn so she could feed the chickens that came up close. Every time I think of Mamá, I am comforted by the fact that perhaps during those years her pain began to numb. On January 20, 1981, at dawn, she told Tonó that she did not feel well, that she felt nauseous. Tonó went to buy an Alka-Seltzer, but when she returned, Mamá was not breathing.

After the girls' death, many people would come visit her. There was a group of women from Puerto Plata who visited her every single year because, as I explained before, she never left the house. She only went out to attend the first anniversary mass in memory of her daughters. She visited the house in Ojo de Agua once when Jimmy broke his arm. I thought she was going to cry, but when she saw how pretty everything was, so well preserved, she was very pleased and began to tell stories of the happy times she had there.

However, on many occasions when I think of her, what comes to mind are the times when she would speak about the tragedy that took her three daughters and Manolo from her, and she would ask me, "Dedé, how do I survive with so much suffering?"

Now, when we get together at my house for anniversaries or on Sundays, with grandchildren and great grandchildren running all over, I hear their names, the chatter, and I see how my sisters have multiplied into various Patrias, a couple of María Teresas, and more than one Minerva.

It is at those moments when I understand my mother. I imagine her with that expression on her face, which was never quite fully a smile, and I understand her when she said that the life her daughters left her was what kept her from dying.

15

The Value of Work

There are no words to describe how difficult life was in the years following the tragedy. I lived as if I were on autopilot, just letting my daily routine guide my way. The sorrow, their absence, my sisters' memory, so fresh and so present. I would see Patria . . . I would dream constantly, constantly about the girls . . . Some nights, Minerva would appear beautifully dressed in a tea-length organdy dress, with a bouquet of violets at her waist. I saw them over and over again. I would dream that we would run into each other, that they had returned. And as time went on, I was convinced—as I once told a friend—that my happy years were over. However, I had my children, my nieces and nephews, my husband. That responsibility shook me back to reality.

My husband raised pigs and, one afternoon, while I was hosing them down, I came to my senses and realized I could no longer continue to live like that. I had to overcome my inertia, that feeling of not wanting to do anything, of being overpowered by so much sorrow.

The sudden death of a family friend in 1967 shook me up. She was the wife of engineer Alfredo Manzano, an important and cherished friend of our family because he had been Manolo's partner during the struggle. His wife's death led me to ask myself, *What about my kids? What will happen to them if I die?* I, who had worked with my mother and father in the family business, who had owned her own store, and who had always earned her keep. Was I going to continue living like this?

During a short trip to Santo Domingo, I unexpectedly ran into one of Jaimito's cousins who worked at the Panamerican Life Insurance Co. (PALIC). She was the one who proposed I get involved in the insurance business. "You are a very open person, and you could do really well. Come in one day so I can introduce you to Mr. Juan Amell and Mr. Ernesto Ceara. I will recommend you to them."

The next time we met she introduced me to Mr. Juan Amell, who at the time was PALIC's general manager and a pioneer in the country's insurance business. I made a good impression, especially because of the natural way I handled myself. They hired me on the spot so I could begin training immediately and start working in the company's Santiago branch. Two or three months later I sold my first insurance policy, worth 25,000 pesos, to Mr. Luis Peral from San Francisco de Macorís. He is the father of a family that I owe a lot to because of their solidarity. They treated me like a sister during those difficult times when almost everyone turned their backs on us.

That is how I was suddenly able to snap out of it. I realized I needed to restart my life and go back to being the woman who had always enjoyed working. I had to learn something new and take on that responsibility. American companies are very demanding, and I made a promise to myself that I would meet all the goals they had set for me. This new responsibility demanded a lot from me, but at the same time it brought me back to life.

Work fine-tunes the spirit. If I would have simply buckled under so much pain and sorrow, I would have never recovered. A woman's most productive years, and a man's too, usually runs between the ages of thirty-five and fifty. It is during this time that you are most creative, strong, and have the most needs. In the insurance business, when we worked on projects, we concentrated on the thirty-five-year-old population as a starting point. It is at this age when you have the greatest responsibilities, when your professional career takes off, and you begin to generate income. This is true for most people unless, of course, they inherit a fortune. In those cases, what usually happens is that people often throw away the money they had so easily received.

When I decided to become an insurance agent, I had no idea that I would eventually get divorced. What I did know was that work would give me independence. I could travel and contribute to whatever situation might present itself in the home. Being productive became a goal as part of my personal growth. And what better satisfaction than to be able to pay for your children's studies abroad, which is what happened when Jaime David decided to study psychiatry in Spain. That is why I wanted to work and decided to do so.

I could not exploit the tragedy that had befallen my family just to attract clients. Nor would I want anyone to buy insurance from me just because I was the only surviving Mirabal sister. There are people who want to take advantage of tragedies. But to me, that is something sacred. It must be respected. Also, this was a period in which an entire generation of individuals participated in the anti-Trujillo movement and fought for the freedom of all Dominicans. They were frustrated. It had impacted them economically and I would even say mentally. So they could not be my clients. That is why

I decided to introduce myself to individuals who did not necessarily "sympathize" with my tragedy.

I did take advantage of the commercial relationships I had developed while working with my father. I remember selling insurance to commission agents. I also targeted a market that had not yet been tapped, and I was successful. I often traveled to the towns of Cotuí, Nagua, Montecristi, to the capital, and to other towns where I knew a lot of people. Just a few months after I started selling insurance, I won my first important award: a trip to Guatemala, where I participated in a conference with representatives from all over Latin America. There were only three women participating in that event. I have always enjoyed working. I need to know that I can be useful and that there will be meaningful responsibilities waiting for me when I wake up in the morning.

I still wake up at six in the morning to tend to the garden and rake up the dry leaves. Jaime David tells me, "Mamá, please, leave the broom alone." And I reply that this is my daily routine, and it's what keeps me in shape.

However, I have lost the love I once had for cooking. It must be a natural reaction because I spent thirty-four years slaving away in the kitchen tending to my husband, just as I was taught to do. Thankfully, the household chores are no longer my priority. I liberated myself from all of that.

Being a saleswoman not only led me to receive awards and nominations, it also helped me grow as a person. I learned to break the ice and initiate friendly conversations on issues that are not necessarily comfortable, such as accidents and death.

I decided to retire after twenty years, even though I continued to receive special awards. Although I was strong and more than capable of continuing to work and travel, I decided to become an insurance broker and sell directly to the companies.

Everything I learned from that profession has prepared me for something else: to appear as relaxed as possible on television programs and at public events. Another thing that has helped me is the habit of reading, something Minerva so encouraged in me. However, lately I have been reacting in ways that truly upset me. When asked certain questions—questions that I have been asked hundreds and hundreds of times and that I have answered—I choke up and feel an uncontrollable urge to break down and cry. I swallow my tears and then try to cough, a technique that gives me time to recover.

My love for agriculture has never left me, and it does not bother me one bit when people jokingly say, "You're planning to live a long time if you're now planting avocados, a tree that takes five years to bear fruit!" I also need to see everything nice and tidy, that the hedges are neatly trimmed, and the fields planted. I always tell myself, "I am the niece of Tío Tilo and Juancito Fernández Mirabal, men whose fields were impeccable, all protected by nettings."

I inherited from my mother my love and knowledge of agriculture. I took over a cacao farm she left me, planted with hybrid cacao seedlings. With cacao prices hitting a critical low over the last few decades, I joined forces with fifty cacao growers, and we decided to establish the Association of Cacao Producers of the Cibao Region. Some of us decided to produce organic cacao, but it takes time to eliminate chemical residues from the farms. Some of our growers are currently involved in this process, and some have managed to achieve full organic certification. I was one of the first in the country to have my groves fully certified because for years, rather than use herbicides, I had the groves cleaned manually by hand and thus provided jobs for those who had always accompanied me. That worked in my favor.

I also have cattle and sheep, but Jaime David is the one in charge of this part of the farm. I cannot imagine living far from nature. That to me would be like dying.

I like to be close to everything happening in my cacao groves. I personally supervise the pruning and harvesting, and I anxiously wait for the rains to come because the cacao trees have deep roots, and they need rain during the flowering season so that, as we in the country say, the pods can mature. They flower until November. The cacao trees are then covered with small bunches of flowers that look like wasps or large grapes. These mature, and the beautiful purple, red, or yellow cacao pods are ready for harvest.

16

Love, Marriage, Divorce, and Stability

Someone recently asked Jaimito, in my presence, "What has Dedé meant to you in your life?" With his natural demeanor he answered, "Oh, Blessed Mother of God! . . . I'll tell you one thing: all my efforts to make something of myself was to be deserving of her. That I can say. From the time she was a little girl, Dedé was a grown woman, the motherly type. I liked her because she was very much like my mother. And my father was even more in love with her than I was for the same reasons. We spent many happy moments together."

I listened to the words of the man who had been my husband for so many years, and I could not help but think of the strange twists and turns that life takes. The truth is we had a happy and stable marriage for many years, and as a couple, we never faced any serious issues. Of course, the fact that I was not the jealous type helped tremendously. Everything I have described here shows the role my husband played in my life and in the life of my family. But I would like to go a bit deeper into this important part of my story.

Jaimito Fernández was an extremely hardworking man, a visionary, a man with ambition. He wanted to have a large farm where he could sow the land and see it produce. In the early seventies, Joaquín Balaguer declared that our farm in the town of Nagua was to be used for "public interest." We lost it. This destroyed Jaimito. That farm had been the fulfillment of all his aspirations: to have something of his own, where he could make the land produce all sorts of crops. Perhaps it was then that our relationship began to suffer.

The Balaguer government persecuted us relentlessly. With his history of being anti-Trujillo and pro-Constitutional, Jaimito was thrown in jail three times. Perhaps because they compare it with the Trujillo regime, people often forget that Balaguer's twelve-year dictatorship also carried out a multitude of crimes and selective, merciless repression.

Jaimito, who on his own terms had been a member of the 14th of June Movement and had supported the Constitutionalists in 1965, decided to stay away from politics for a while. After we lost the farm, perhaps as a reaction to what he believed was another abuse of political power, he began campaigning for the PRD. I tried to discourage him, but he wouldn't listen.

Not long after the PRD chose him as its presidential candidate, Antonio Guzmán[117] came to visit. He was accompanied by José Delio Guzmán.[118] We were sitting out on the porch when he asked Jaimito to join his campaign. He explained that he needed his support because he was an important personality in town, and everyone knew he was a hardworking and honest man who had excellent relations throughout the Cibao region.

With the passage of time, the political situation began to quiet down, especially after the PRD victory in 1978. President Guzmán made the courageous decision to remove a good number of military officials linked to the worst crimes committed by the Balaguer and Trujillo regimes. As soon as he was sworn in, Antonio Guzmán named Jaimito governor of Salcedo Province. He was now a man with a full daily agenda, with people after him looking for jobs, and he once again started having extra-marital affairs. That is when my marriage ended.

Fearless. That is a word that clearly defines Jaimito. If he said, "I'm heading in that direction," nothing could stop him. He was always looking for risky situations and provoking danger. There was always something going on. When he had the farms in Nagua and in the town of Río San Juan, he decided to live there. He constantly traveled to the region. I would sometimes accompany him, but the road was nearly impassable. To get there, we had to cross the Boba River. When the river swelled, it took the wooden bridges and its beams along with it. People would have to wait days until the waters receded in order to cross to the other side.

One time, we were traveling with the children in a pickup truck packed with people and luggage. It was early afternoon when we arrived at the already swollen Boba River. By midnight, the waters still hadn't receded. Some locals came to help us in exchange for money. "The beams are gone." "Here's another beam," they would shout, trying to tempt us. Jaimito came out of the car, looked around, and said, "Well, I'm going to cross the river." The bed of the pickup truck was packed with kids and I was beside him, screaming . . . but that did not stop him. In spite of my screams and my fierce objections, Jaimito ran the truck right into the swollen river. I was pleading, "Jaimito! Everyone is dead at my house, I'm the only one left!" "I am not turning around," is all he said. He managed to mount the wheels of

---

117   Silvestre Antonio Guzmán Fernández (1911–1982), president of the Republic from 1978 to 1982.
118   Elected senator from La Vega in 1978.

the truck on top of two beams. My only thought was, "What if something happens to these children?" But he managed to cross the river, without flinching. That was Jaimito; that was his temperament.

He was also very *machista*. He would tell the story that once God sent St. Peter back to Earth with a group of horses and chickens. He went door to door showing them the horses: a young donkey, an Arabian stallion, a honey-colored horse. If the person choosing was a woman, he would give her a chicken and continue on with the beautiful horses. After giving away many chickens, he arrived at a house where a man was the one choosing one of the animals. After St. Peter left with the horses, the woman said to her husband, "What a beautiful horse you have chosen, but I liked another one." The man called out to St. Peter and asked him to exchange his horse. The saint responded, "Here's your chicken, that's all you're getting." Even his mother Doña Lesbia suffered with her son's extreme *machismo*.

Today, when I look back on those years, I realize that I saved myself from a lot of grief and suffering by not being the jealous type. If my husband got home late, or if he had to stay overnight at the farm, it never occurred to me that he might be with another woman. Since he was such a fast driver—"Get out of the way! Here comes Jaimito!" they'd say—my only concern was that he had been in an accident. Perhaps I was naïve, but like I said, my way of looking at things saved me from an awful lot of suffering.

Jaimito's sisters would say that I was their mother's favorite. And it was true. Doña Lesbia loved me deeply because I had put up with so much from her son. I thought if I got divorced it would devastate her and Don Jaime, his father, and my mother as well. That is why I thought about it for such a long time.

In 1982, my mother had already died, and so had my father-in-law. I was fifty-eight years old and was sick and tired of putting up with so much thoughtlessness from Jaimito, so I decided to file for divorce on my own, without his knowledge.

The divorce was published in the newspaper *La Información* in 1982, around the time when President Antonio Guzmán committed suicide. I will not deny the suffering I went through, especially because Jaimito remarried the same day the divorce notice was published. They were such difficult times, with brand-new challenges for me. I overcame them by taking refuge in my work. I was completely destroyed, but I did not share my feelings with anyone, and to top it all off, I was dying of jealousy. But the truth is that in spite of the tremendous sorrow I experienced, I also felt liberated.

"Take it easy, Dedé, take it easy," I would tell myself. I slept in our bed and put a pillow by my side as an attempt to trick my loneliness. Sometimes Jaime David came over and stayed overnight with me. He became my biggest supporter. He would sit by my side and comfort me for hours. "Mamá, don't suffer so much. Let it go," he would say to me.

If I had not learned to work at a very young age and fend for myself, my divorce would have been much more difficult. The fact that I worked, that I contributed financially to my household, also helped me avoid difficult situations during the separation. In spite of his machismo, Jaimito never objected to my travels throughout the region. He gave me that freedom.

After the divorce I submerged myself in my work and in the education of my children. I always thought about the children, and that my family should remain united. That was my most important goal. My greatest happiness was, and is, that we are all at peace. That has been my greatest goal, as well as guaranteeing a sound family environment in our home.

I have forgotten many offenses and painful situations, and today Jaimito and I talk to one another with ease. We eat together, I invite him to family events, and he spends time with us. He is fine. I am happy. I do as I wish and go where I want to go. I am financially stable, and I can travel, visit other countries, and meet new people.

They say that time heals all wounds, and they must be right because now when I think of those days, I laugh out loud. The suffering I avoided by getting divorced!

I am not going to deny that, for reasons I am sure most will understand, I put up some resistance to my children's involvement in politics. However, I never stopped supporting them. As a matter of fact, my main political activities have been linked to Jaime David, who has made tremendous sacrifices in this endeavor and who can count on me for anything, as well as Minou. I have participated in their activities with great satisfaction and hope. Perhaps it is because, as they both say, "We are repeat offenders when it comes to hope."

The history of our family has been shaped by a solid commitment to the values of liberty, justice, and democracy. Because of this conviction, and with hope for the future, I have enthusiastically and actively supported them in spite of the reservations I just mentioned. I fully support the PLD moving in a new direction to lead our nation forward. As a responsible citizen and as a Dominican, I understand that the tasks involving our economic and institutional well-being are still pending, and that our efforts in politics should be geared toward improving the lives of Dominican men and women and strengthening the weak institutions left behind by the dictatorship and by the majority of the governments that followed it. Above all, we must work to build a state that is efficient and can provide its citizens with the universal services merited by everyone born in this land. I wake up every morning with these ideas in mind, and I will keep on contributing for as long as my health and age permit.

During Jaime David's senatorial campaigns and pre-campaign (1990 and 1994), his campaign for vice president (1996), and later on for president (1999 and 2003), he asked me to "take charge of Salcedo." I took on this responsibility. Some of Jaime David's friends told him that with twenty or thirty activists like me in each province, the PLD would never lose an election. I thought that was one of the nicest things anyone had ever said about my contributions to the political world.

But politics is a most ungrateful endeavor and ripe with deception. During the 1999 caucus to choose their presidential candidate, the PLD did not act rationally and did not listen to the polls and surveys that clearly indicated that Jaime David was the candidate the people wanted. During that time, I asked myself what had become of the party that Juan Bosch had founded, a party that had the capacity for political analysis and respect for the rules of the game. I never found an answer. The consequences of that "mistake" were detrimental for the Dominican Republic.

During the 2003 pre-campaign, while working with the most committed party members, I organized thirty-six support committees for Jaime David. We took to the countryside. My house was constantly packed with people. Sometimes I think that if Jaimito, with all of his selfishness, had lived here at that time, that would have been impossible. He was the man of the house, and men become selfish. Sometimes husbands become jealous even of their kids. Later on, all our work was channeled to promoting Dr. Leonel Fernández,[119] the PLD presidential candidate.

I am an austere individual, but I have helped each of my children financially, and even though my sisters' children are now well positioned and have received and done with their inheritance as they wish, they know they can always count on me.

They accuse me of being very stingy when it comes to going to an expensive restaurant or buying a luxury car. "Mamá, change that car already. It's more than ten years old!" they tell me. I tell them that the car is good

---

119 Leonel Antonio Fernández Reyna (b. 1953), president of the Republic from 1996 to 2000 and from 2004 to 2012.

for another ten years. "In another ten years that car will be really expensive," they point out, but I stand my ground because I have never wanted to spend more than is necessary, much less go into debt, acquiring superfluous things or assets. It is all about how I was raised: since a farmer never has money readily available, he must be cautious with his finances.

Farming is a risky business, and in our country, it is prone to many eventualities and frequent natural disasters. In those moments I have said that I am going to sell the farm because it only gives me problems. But I know I never will because I could not live without taking care of the land and seeing it produce food and flowers.

Traveling, Seeing the World, Gardening

In order to satisfy my longing to see the world, I personally organized tours so my fares would be covered. That is how I visited Mexico and several European countries.

Jaime accompanied me on two of these trips, which were awards earned for my success as a life insurance agent. But everything bothered him; he didn't like the hotel beds or the food. "There are too many churches here. I'm sick of all these churches and museums." It was an uncomfortable situation, and it became unpleasant to travel with him.

I have traveled to Europe on many occasions. One trip I remember fondly began at a convention in Portugal. I proposed, "Everyone: Since we're already in Europe, let's visit other countries." No one supported my suggestion, so I decided to go on my own. Someone suggested that I call a travel agency that organized tours, and that perhaps they had Spanish-speaking customers who wanted to go to the same places. It so happened that there were two Portuguese couples traveling to Greece. "Well, I'm going with them." We walked all over Athens, became friends, and visited the ruins and monuments. I truly enjoyed the presence of these unexpected travel companions.

When I started to plan these trips, my children would express their concern: "Mamá, who are you going with?" I would tell them that I would make friends along the way. It is very easy for me to start up a conversation with people around me. When I was a child, I dreamt of traveling to Russia, of crossing the Bosphorus Strait and visiting the bazaars in Istanbul. In this particular city I was surprised to see that there were hardly any women on the streets and in the plazas, just a mass of men coming and going, all well dressed, elegant, and attractive with their black moustaches.

I think my longing to travel, to see and find beauty in everything, must come from having grown up in a closed environment, in a country that was like a prison, where simply wanting to have a passport could be considered a crime. I wanted to see, to see everything, discover cities and new aromas that were different from the ones in my country. I wanted to appreciate the myriad shades of green out in the world that were different from the greens found in my valley and in the mountains of my Cibao. I wanted to see the different faces of people and their particular characteristics, similar or different from ours. This has been my way of recovering a little of the happiness they shattered into pieces.

My sisters and I inherited from our mother the love and affinity for plants and gardens. And that hobby has helped me tremendously in my life. I planted many of the trees and plants found at our home in Ojo de Agua and at my mother's home in Conuco, known today as the Mirabal Sisters House Museum. Each plant has its own particular story to tell.

When I began working in the insurance business, I brought Jacaranda trees from the town of Fantino. I planted them in the gardens of both our homes. Today, I wake up very early, take my broom in hand, and before I begin to sweep the fallen leaves, I enjoy looking at the ground carpeted with the trees' purple flowers.

Each year, with great excitement, I impatiently await the flowering of the moss silk tree at the museum's entrance. I recall with great joy my trip to Argentina and Uruguay, from where I managed to smuggle in the contraband stumps, wrapped in aluminum foil. Even Jaime David warned me, "But Mamá, that tree might not grow in the tropics." But people who come to visit cannot help but admire this strange and beautiful tree. I give anyone interested in the tree small seedlings so they can try to reproduce it. I also wonder who will rake all those pink flowers when I am no longer able to do so.

It was either while raking or picking up dry leaves, I really cannot remember which, that I hurt my shoulder some two or three years ago. I was told I had to go to therapy. I had to travel every day to Santiago or San Francisco de Macorís. When I realized how much time it took me to travel to my therapy sessions, and the money I was spending on fuel, I wondered how people with disabilities but with fewer resources than me could afford those therapy sessions. That is when I thought of opening a rehabilitation center in the town of Salcedo. I have devoted lots of time and hard work to this project, and I am very pleased to see the center in full operation in such a short time, thanks to the support of so many people, companies, and public institutions that responded to my requests to make this project possible.

I work all day, so when I am ready to go to sleep, I am out like a log. A psychologist friend believes that my well-being at my age is due not only to my good health but also to my friendly temperament, and to the energy and serenity of my character.

17

No More Room for Dictatorships

The only problem without any real solution is death. Everything else can be resolved one way or another: financial difficulties, bankruptcy, jail. But what to do when faced with death? That is why the dictatorship was so horrendous. Trujillo was not tolerant. He was not forgiving. He solved the slightest hint of dissidence by murdering his opponents. And after a person is dead, there is nothing left to do.

Those three decades of tyranny left the country in a dismal state of underdevelopment. We did not move forward, even though some like to state the contrary. All rights were violated. Even the course on morality and civics was eliminated from schools so there would be no discussion of civil rights. We lived in fear, and there is nothing more destructive than fear.

Many anti-Trujillo movements emerged during those years. Right from the very beginning of the dictatorship, many were forced into exile. I sometimes talk to the children who visit the Museum about these individuals. I tell them about Mr. Angel Morales, of a military officer named Marchena Justo, of another group of military officers that staged a revolt, as well as the Estévez and Perozo families, who were practically exterminated. I also tell them about Juancito Rodríguez, who gave his entire fortune to sponsor the Cayo Confites expedition[120] against Trujillo in 1947, among other examples.

I also talk to them about the role Balaguer played in supporting the dictatorship. And later, not as a puppet president, but during his own presidential administrations, he left us with so much misery, making people beg for handouts and establishing a degrading cronyism, practices that later became laws and impoverished the country. I do not recall ever seeing those vices in this country when I was a child.

Fortunately, these new generations will not allow a dictatorship to impose itself. Also, the Americans now have a different discourse and defend

---

120   Planned invasion of the Dominican Republic consisting of 1,500 revolutionaries, mainly Dominican exiles in Cuba but including Cuban militants. Their aim was to topple the Trujillo dictatorship, but they were arrested before launching the expedition.

democracy in other countries besides their own. Nevertheless, the Americans supported Trujillo unconditionally almost until the end of his regime was imminent, just as they had done with many other Latin American dictators.

Those of us who experienced the horror of the tyranny have the responsibility of educating the next generations so they can appreciate the courage and sacrifice of those who gave everything for liberty, and, above all, so we can assure that such tragedy and humiliation never happen again in our country.

The Mirabal Sisters House Museum

The idea came from Violeta Martínez, Minerva's friend from 1945 or 1946. She was the cousin of a schoolmate with the same name: Violeta Martínez de Ortega, from San Francisco de Macorís. Minerva met the other Violeta Martínez at her friend's home. Violeta was already concerned about the political situation and belonged to the Democratic Youth Movement. She enjoyed reading, and in 1946 or 1947, she distributed a small pamphlet against the regime. Although she was not yet nineteen, she was already working as a teacher. Despite the fact that Minerva was some three years older, they became very close friends. They exchanged books, talked about politics, and shared many common interests.

Violeta emigrated to the United States in 1950 and returned to the country to visit in 1965. So she was here when the revolution began. She came to spend a few days at our house, and during her visit, she proposed the following: "Let's gather and organize all of Minerva's things." We organized a display case, rounded up Minerva's books, and recovered some of her furniture and other belongings. That is how the House Museum began. When the conflict ended, Violeta left once again. My mother was still alive. We both continued to collect whatever items once belonged to the girls. Later, in 1982, after my mother had passed, I asked the renowned curator Reyna Alfau to evaluate what we had put together and help us give some kind of structure to the museum. We prepared the bedrooms and organized what we already had. I decided to exhibit María Teresa's braid, which I had carefully hidden from my mother in order to avoid causing her any more pain.

That is basically what we had until the early 1990s, when Violeta decided to return to the country for good, with many new ideas. Since then, she has lovingly dedicated much of her time to reorganizing the museum. We closed the house because Tonó, who was the only one living there, had to move back home to take care of her mother.

A new structure, architecturally similar to the original home, was built next to the house to expand the museum. The bedrooms where Minerva, Patria, María Teresa, and their children spent the last few months of their lives became part of the exhibit. We carefully recreated the ambience from that period. We were able to carry out the project and recover many of the items, thanks to the unselfish and generous contributions from individuals who had collaborated with my sisters in the movement, such as Miguel Feris Iglesias and Gianni Vicini, among others.

In general, everyone has been truly supportive of our efforts to keep the girls' memory alive. That solidarity became more than evident when, in the mid-1980s, television producer Freddy Beras Goico took the initiative to involve the public in creating a monument here, in Ojo de Agua, to honor the girls. He organized a contest, and the prizes were donated through his Sunday television program *El Gordo de la Semana*. The inaugural ceremony was transmitted live, nationwide, and hundreds attended the event.

At the House Museum we exhibit jewelry and other belongings that were important to the girls. They also reflect their individual tastes and their particular personalities.

Minerva's books on exhibit are those that she left here when she moved to Montecristi. The books in Manolo and Minerva's personal library in Montecristi were all destroyed by the caliés who arrested them.

There is also an important exhibit of photographs of family and friends. One particular photograph is very dear to me: it is the one the photographer Barón Castillo took of the four of us with our mother during a trip to the capital.

On display are Minerva and Manolo's university degrees, and the dress she was wearing when she was photographed for the last time, after being released from jail. When she was released, they did not give her back her identification card, which is why she had to take what turned out to be her last photograph, in Salcedo, in order to get a new ID card.

Minerva's typewriter and her cactus collection are also on exhibit, as are the jars and porcelain coffee cups that Patria collected. These and other objects are some of the things we were able to recover before the caliés auctioned off their furnishings and other personal items (beds, armoires, small antique rocking chairs . . .). We never did find out in whose homes these items ended up.

The Mirabal Sisters House Museum also features the embroidered tablecloths and knitted doilies the girls made in school. After her high school graduation, between 1946 and 1952, Minerva had plenty of time to embroider and enjoy other activities. We also have on display the hammered aluminum utensils we purchased through a Sears catalog back in those days, Patria's pencil drawings, and Minerva's oil paintings, which are almost all copies of Spanish paintings that Minerva reproduced during her years at the Immaculate Conception School. The barefoot boy was her favorite. She took it with her to Montecristi, and it was one of the very few items she brought back when she returned home. We also recovered Minerva's refrigerator, the one she sold to help Mamá with the household expenses when she moved back home.

A good number of the items on display belonged to María Teresa because, as I have explained in another section of this memoir, we had time to send for her belongings before the caliés completely ransacked their apartment in Santo Domingo.

In one of the bedrooms there are articles of clothing that Patria embroidered for her children, as well as the towel that María Teresa and Minerva would hang in their tiny cell window in La Victoria prison on visiting day to let us know they were still alive.

On exhibit in María Teresa's bedroom (she was the only one who lived in Mamá's house before she got married) is the braid that always distinguished her, a handful of letters that she and Leandro had exchanged, her sewing basket, and her impressive earring collection, among other objects.

Had it not been for Mamá's near obsession with saving everything, many of the objects that today are main attractions in the museum would not have been so well preserved. One such item is the bassinet she purchased before Patria's birth, and which she later used with each one of us and where our children were also born. Many of our grandchildren were also rocked in that bassinet.

In short, both the museum and my own home are completely full of our family's history as well as the history of each of my sisters.

Every day both homes receive visitors from all over the country and the world. According to the Secretariat of Culture, this is the most visited museum in the country. Mario Vargas Llosa was here when he was doing research for his book *La fiesta del Chivo* as well as many artists and renowned personalities. Salma Hayek and Mía Maestro also visited the museum shortly after shooting the film based on the novel written by Julia

Alvarez. Remarkably, their visit coincided with the day Ciriaco de la Rosa and one of Ramfis's sons died.

Teachers and students visit us on a regular basis. Sometimes I feel that our social memory is fading. I am surprised when I realize how little our children and youth know about our story. In the groups there are always two or three students who are genuinely interested, and they make sure they ask questions and write down the answers. However, the fact is many school children have never heard of the Mirabal sisters, or they have a distorted version of our story. As proof, I have had children ask me, "Did Trujillo want to live with all three of them?" I try to remain patient, and I once again tell them my sisters' story.

This is my responsibility, and it is the responsibility of this museum: to teach the new generations what the Trujillo regime was all about. I always highlight that my sisters represent another generation, the one that sacrificed itself for the freedoms we are able to enjoy today.

I always tell the young people that visit us the same thing: "This museum symbolizes the example set by an entire generation. My sisters, because of what happened to them, for the terrible tragedy that they suffered, are honored here, in their family home. But also honored here are the most humble and anonymous of those who fought against Trujillo."

The library, which is open to everyone, especially to the students, concentrates mainly on books that cover that ominous chapter of our national history. Our goal is that the library be used more and more.

I feel tremendous satisfaction with the work we do here. Every time we receive strangers or people we know, journalists, young people, or children who want to learn more about my sisters' lives and sacrifice, that feeling of satisfaction is once again renewed. I tell myself, "They haven't died; they are alive. Who says they are dead? The girls are more alive than I am." My work to raise awareness has become a natural part of my life, as well as an honor.

A Universal Day

One example of this honor is what happens each year on November 25. In 1998 the United Nations declared this date as the International Day for the Elimination of Violence Against Women. On that day I am invited to places near and far, from Canada and Italy, to Buenos Aires, Puerto Rico and other places.

This is a crucial day for raising awareness about the need to continue fighting to eliminate violence against women throughout the world. Every single day, many women die at the hands of those who supposedly love them. This happens not only in poor nations like ours, but also in developed and wealthy societies.

The fact that November 25 is now commemorated throughout the world has also led to increased interest in my sisters' story and legacy. I feel that this somewhat compensates in some small way the sacrifice they made.

Recently, we received a visit from some girls whose last name was Perozo. I was overtaken with emotion. I called them aside, took pictures with them, and told them, "Your family is alive, they are also present here. Your family gave it all, and almost all died fighting against the tyrant."

Children have an insatiable curiosity. When I tell them that I remained alive so I could tell them the truth, they are more than happy to listen to me tell them the story. I have to autograph each of their pamphlets personally; they will not accept a stamped autograph. I do as they wish and sign each and every one of their pamphlets by hand. They are the future generations.

Sometimes people will come looking for me during lunch, and I tell them to wait, that I am in the bathroom, so they do not feel bad. I finish my lunch, brush my teeth, and I immediately go to greet them with an open smile and a sense of humor. Visitors never bother me.

I always wanted to bring the girls' remains back to the museum. Violeta Martínez also insisted on this idea, but we could not. During the first twelve years of Joaquín Balaguer's government, one could hardly mention the Mirabal sisters. And those who participated in the events we have religiously held every November 25 to honor their memory were persecuted. The authorities reacted as if we were organizing a subversive protest. The mechanisms that Trujillo had created remained unchanged. They were intact. The government, with its military underpinnings, believed the girls represented a vibrant and living army, a threat to the regime.

Finally, on November 25, 2000, we brought back to their garden the remains of Patria, Minerva, and María Teresa. Days before, when we opened the caskets, I was surprised when I saw María Teresa's hair. Her abundant and beautiful black hair, so lush and thick, seemed to have grown. I gently took her hair and placed it on top of her bones. Her hair completely covered her bones. Her remains were then placed inside a fiberglass box to avoid the humidity and then placed in another mahogany box, a gift made in solidarity by Arlette Fernández, the widow of Colonel Rafael Fernández Domínguez, a hero of the 1965 revolution.

Through a presidential decree, the grounds of the museum were declared an extension of the National Pantheon.[121] I also transferred Manolo's remains, even though he had not yet been declared a national hero. He had once told me, "My death is imminent. If I die, don't separate me from Minerva." There were people like Violeta who did not agree because he had never lived here. But that was his last wish, and I was going to honor it. Minou and Manolo also agreed because he had given his life for the same cause. Four years later, in 2004, Congress officially declared Manolo Tavárez Justo a national hero.

Someone insisted that we place an eternal flame at the gravesite. I am more than satisfied with the water that flows through the site, with its swimming fish. The water symbolizes the continuation of life. It was Raúl's idea to use water instead. The native laurels, the star apple, and the Samán trees provide shade over the gravesite. The tree trunks are dotted with a variety of orchids, but the ones that most attract visitors' attention are the ones that look like butterflies. The girls live on in the sound of the running water; in the colorful, swimming fish; in the sound of the breeze rustling the leaves of the caimito and laurel trees; and most of all, in the perfume of their favorite flowers.

The monument at the gravesite was designed by architect Rodolfo Pou, who worked at UNESCO. We chose his design because he managed to incorporate the structure into the surrounding environment, and we all agreed that it was truly a beautiful and symbolic design. That is the way my sisters were: simple, happy, vital.

Near the gravesite, between the moss and the rocks, bathed by the rays of the sun or in the shade of the laurel trees, visitors will see the impressive busts of the girls and Manolo, sculpted by Mark Liveweavel, an American who has lived in the highlands of this province for many years.

The trees that, with their pink and purple flowers, adorn the entrance to the house are giant Alstroemerias that Minerva brought from the north coast town of Manzanillo. I remember that at first, my mother confused them with Spanish lime trees. A bit beyond the Alstroemerias, on a plot of land across the road, was an area that my mother called "the fruit bowl" because that is where, over time, she planted all sorts of fruit trees. There are mangoes, oranges, grapefruit, and mandarin trees as well as all sorts of exotic Chinese mandarin trees, the grandchildren's favorite when they were little.

---

121 The National Pantheon is a mausoleum in Santo Domingo where the remains of the country's most distinguished historical figures are buried.

A special area in the House Museum is dedicated to the memory of Rufino de la Cruz, the driver who died with my sisters. He was driving the jeep lent to us by our friend and neighbor, René Bournigal. It was the jeep René used when traveling to the mountains. He lent it to us so my sisters would not have to spend money on renting a car to go to Puerto Plata. He himself recommended that they hire Rufino, who valiantly and in solidarity agreed to accompany them. We have never forgotten his sacrifice and his infinite valor.

When I returned home with my sisters' bodies and with Rufino's, his family claimed his body because they wanted to bury him in the town of Tenares, where his relatives owned a burial plot, and not in ours, in Salcedo, as we had originally offered them during those terrible moments.

During one of the numerous visits that I receive daily, a young woman made a cruel comment: "By killing them, Trujillo immortalized them." She thought that I would be offended by her comment. Of course, it was difficult to hear that. But when I saw her sad, apologetic eyes, I felt sorry for her and told her that nothing could make up for the loss of a useful life, but that if young women like her remembered the lesson of valor and integrity set by Patria, Minerva, and María Teresa, then for sure their legacy would live on forever among the Dominican people.

There is nothing more treacherous than one's memory, which insists on keeping certain memories alive, though sometimes they hurt so very much. Each day that passes, it becomes more difficult for me to separate the past from the present. Perhaps it is because I have devoted my life to preserving my sisters' memory. That is my duty. I have already said that I do not mind that people visit me at all hours of the day, even if they interrupt me while I am eating. Nor does it bother me to give interviews and accept invitations. That is why I remained alive. Sometimes I worry when I think that perhaps, when I die, they will let all this fall apart. I will not be here to see it, nor will I see who will be responsible for taking care of all these things we so loved. In the meantime, my responsibility is to make sure that the memories of my sisters continue to flourish and to pass on their message to our youth and children.

I can proudly say I have served my country. I can proudly say I have raised an honest family. At my age, what better satisfaction than to have served my country and my family! In the cemetery, alongside my mother and father, there is a place waiting for me. In the meantime, today and each and every day, I work and live with dedication and enthusiasm.

CHRONOLOGY

1899

Violent death of dictator Ulises (Lilís) Heureaux. Juan Isidro Jimenes succeeded him.

1900

Enrique Mirabal Fernández, father of the Mirabal sisters, is born near Santiago. Their mother, Mercedes (Chea) Reyes Camilo, is born that same year.

1902

Horacio Vásquez heads a revolt against Jimenes.

1903

Alejandro Woss y Gil, president.

1904

Carlos Morales Languasco, president.

1905

The United States intervenes in the country's public finances and takes over the Customs Office. Ramón Cáceres, president.

1906

The United States approves a loan to pay the country's European debt.

1907

Signing of the Dominican-American Convention.

1908

Ramón Cáceres, reelected president.

1911

Ramón Cáceres, assassinated.

1912

Eladio Victoria, president for a brief period. Replaced by Monsignor Adolfo Alejandro Nouel.

1913

José Bordas Valdez, president.

1914

Ramón Báez, provisional president. Juan Isidro Jimenes, president.

1915

U.S. military occupation of Haiti; coincides with the opening of the Panama Canal.

1916

U.S. military occupation of Santo Domingo. Enrique Mirabal moves to Ojo de Agua, near the town of Salcedo.

1923

Enrique Mirabal Fernández marries Chea Reyes Camilo.

1924

The U.S. occupation ends. Horacio Vásquez is elected president. Patria Mirabal is born in Ojo de Agua.

1925

Bélgica Adela (Dedé) Mirabal is born in Ojo de Agua.

1926

Minerva Mirabal is born in Ojo de Agua.

1928

Horacio Vásquez extends his four-year presidential term by an additional two years.

1930

Trujillo overthrows Horacio Vásquez and is declared the winner of a fraudulent presidential election. The San Zenón hurricane devastates Santo Domingo. Virgilio Martínez Reyna and his wife are assassinated. Cipriano Bencosme revolts and is killed. Alberto Larancuent, assassinated.

1931

Desiderio Arias dies. Andrés Perozo, assassinated. Manuel (Manolo) Tavárez Justo is born in Montecristi.

193? (Exact year is unknown)

Jesús María (Chichí) Patiño, assassinated.

1934

Leoncio Blanco, assassinated.

1935

Sergio Bencosme assassinated in New York. María Teresa Mirabal is born in Ojo de Agua.

1936

Enrique Mirabal Fernández comes down with hemoptysis.

1937

Patria, Dedé, and Minerva Mirabal—on different dates—enter the Immaculate Conception School in La Vega. Killing of Haitians takes place in Salcedo region.

1938

Aníbal Vallejo, assassinated.

1939

Tancredo (Quero) Saviñón, assassinated in La Vega.

1940

Colonel Vásquez Rivera, assassinated. Enrique Mirabal Fernández suffers a stroke.

1941

Patria Mirabal, just seventeen years old, marries Pedro (Pedrito) González, originally from Conuco. World War II begins.

1942

Nelson, Patria's first son, is born.

1945

Noris Mercedes, daughter of Patria Mirabal and Pedro González, is born. End of World War II.

1946–1947

The Democratic Youth and the Popular Socialist Party (PSP) openly express their opposition to the Trujillo dictatorship. They organize marches in the capital city (Ciudad Trujillo/Santo Domingo), La Vega, and Santiago, and begin to print newspapers. Minerva's father removes her from the La Vega school, fearing that she will begin to participate in political activities. The regime uncovers the military plot organized by Captain Eugenio de Marchena.

1947

Trujillo puts an end to an interlude of tolerance and attacks the opposition. Many go into exile. The Cayo Confites expedition, organized to overthrow Trujillo, fails. Minerva Mirabal and Pericles Franco Ornes, one of the opposition leaders, share their political views and begin a close friendship. Leandro Guzmán, fifteen, meets María Teresa Mirabal.

1948

Dedé Mirabal marries Jaime (Jaimito) Fernández.

1949

Pericles Franco Ornes is released from jail and goes into exile. He would not return to the country until Trujillo's death. The Luperón Expedition fails. During the celebration of a ball in the town of San Cristóbal, Minerva, twenty-three, challenges Trujillo politically. Her father is arrested, as well as Minerva. Jaime Enrique, Dedé Mirabal's first son, is born.

1950

Mauricio Báez is assassinated in Havana. Porfirio (Prin) Ramírez Alcántara and his six companions, assassinated. Freddy Valdez, assassinated.

1951

Jaime Rafael (Jimmy) Fernández, Dedé's second son, is born while she is living in San Francisco de Macorís. The father of the Mirabal sisters is jailed once again and suffers a second stroke. Minerva Mirabal is placed under house arrest at a hotel in Santo Domingo.

1952

Andrés Requena is assassinated in New York. Minerva Mirabal registers at the university.

1953

The father of the Mirabal sisters dies. Minerva meets Manuel (Manolo) Tavárez Justo in the town of Jarabacoa.

1954

In August, after Trujillo returns to the country from his trip to Spain, Minerva is not allowed to register for her second year of courses at the university. In order to gain authorization to re-register at the university, she is forced to deliver remarks in an event organized to honor Trujillo. Construction of the Mirabal family home begins in Conuco. María Teresa Mirabal begins her university studies. Leandro Guzmán receives his degree as a civil engineer.

1955

Opening of Trujillo's International Peace Fair to commemorate the twenty-fifth anniversary of the Trujillo regime. The "Foro Público" (a daily column that appeared in the morning daily *El Caribe* to denounce Trujillo adversaries) attacks Minerva, who, that same year, married Manolo Tavárez. Another "Foro Público" criticizes his marriage to a "red communist." Pipí Hernández, assassinated in Havana.

1956

Jesús de Galíndez is kidnapped in New York and assassinated in the Dominican Republic. Octavio (Tavito) de la Maza, assassinated. Jaime David Fernández, Dedé's son, is born. Minou, Minerva and Manolo's daughter, is born. The Mirabal family moves to the house in Conuco. María Teresa, nineteen, is not allowed to participate in a beauty contest for political reasons.

1957

For financial reasons, Dedé and Jaimito move to a farm near the town of Nagua for two years. Minerva receives her law degree. Ramfis fails exams at Fort Leavenworth and is criticized by the U.S. press. An attempt to assassinate Dominican exile Tancredo Eloy Martínez fails in Mexico. Luis Escotto Gómez, assassinated.

1958

María Teresa Mirabal and Leandro Guzmán marry. Manuel Enrique (Manolito) Tavárez, son of Manolo and Minerva, is born. At the end of the year, Fidel Castro takes over in Cuba after the victory of the 26th of July Movement.

1959

Fulgencio Batista, former president of Cuba, takes refuge in Ciudad Trujillo. Juan Morales, manager of the country's Reserve Bank, is assassinated. Milka Jacqueline, daughter of María Teresa and Leandro Guzmán, is born. Minerva, Manolo, and Leandro participate in a clandestine meeting in the home of Guido (Yuyo) D'Alessandro, where Minerva proposes the creation of a movement similar to the 26th of July Movement in Cuba. Five months later, the expeditionaries participating in the Constanza, Maimón, and Estero Hondo invasion arrive in the country. Trujillo creates the Foreign Legion. In July, Ramón Marrero Aristy is assassinated. Plot organized by the mechanics at the San Isidro Air Force Base. Trujillo orders the departure of the U.S. military mission in the country. Raúl Fidel Ernesto, Patria's son, is born.

1960

JANUARY

On the ninth, in the home of Patria and Pedrito in Conuco, the 14th of June Movement celebrates its first meeting. The following day Minerva participates in a similar meeting in Mao, in the northwest region. A few days later, more than two hundred people are imprisoned throughout the country. Manolo is jailed on January 13, Leandro Guzmán on the nineteenth, and María Teresa and Minerva on the twenty-first. Nelson is also arrested, and Pedrito turns himself in. On the thirty-first, a Pastoral Letter criticizing the regime is read in all of the country's churches. Trujillo breaks with the Catholic Church.

FEBRUARY

On the eighth, Minerva and María Teresa are released from prison.

APRIL

The Eisenhower administration authorizes Ambassador Joseph Farland to secretly contact members of the opposition.

MAY

Minerva and María Teresa are once again arrested and given five-year sentences. They remain in jail until August, when they are released under house arrest. Trujillo publicly criticizes the Mirabal family and accuses them of being communists. José Almoina is assassinated in Mexico.

JUNE

Trujillo authorizes the return of some members of the Movimiento Popular Dominicano (MPD), who had taken refuge in Cuba. The attempt by Trujillo to assassinate the president of Venezuela, Rómulo Betancourt, fails. Balaguer is named president after Héctor Trujillo resigns.

AUGUST

Sina Cabral seeks asylum in the Argentine Embassy. The Organization of American States sanctions the country for the assassination attempt against Betancourt. The Latin American and U.S. Embassies recall their ambassadors and break diplomatic relations with the regime.

OCTOBER

The Eisenhower administration sends an emissary to meet with Trujillo and encourages him to leave office.

NOVEMBER

Day 8: Manolo and Leandro are transferred to the prison in Puerto Plata.

Day 17: The Mirabal sisters travel to Puerto Plata to visit their imprisoned husbands.

Day 20: Juancito Rodríguez, leader of the exile community, commits suicide in Venezuela.

Day 24: Patria visits her husband Pedrito in La Victoria prison (in the capital).

Day 25: The three Mirabal sisters are killed at nightfall.

Day 27: The Dominican press reports that the Mirabal sisters were killed in "an accident."

Day 28: Manolo and Leandro are transferred to La Cuarenta prison.

DECEMBER

Day 4: Pedrito is taken from La Victoria to La Cuarenta, where he is reunited with Leandro and Manolo. Their jailers show them press clippings about their wives' deaths and mock them.

Day 5: Due to the international uproar provoked by the murders, the Mirabal sisters' mother is pressured to declare that their deaths were due to an accident. International wires pick up her statements. The

OAS imposes economic sanctions against the Trujillo government, and the regime reacts by reaching out to the Soviets and Fidel Castro.

1961

JANUARY

Kennedy is sworn in as president of the United States.

FEBRUARY

The Alliance for Progress begins.

MARCH

Monsignor Francisco Panal criticizes Trujillo in his presence. A campaign of violence is launched against Bishops Thomas O'Reilly (San Juan de la Maguana Province) and Panal (La Vega).

APRIL

Murphy, Kennedy's envoy, meets with Trujillo. The Bay of Pigs Invasion fails.

MAY

Trujillo is assassinated. Ramfis returns to Europe.

JUNE

An OAS commission arrives in the country to meet with political prisoners. They insist on meeting with the sisters' widowers and with the Mirabal family.

JULY

Exiled Dominican Revolutionary Party (PRD) leaders return to the country. Leandro, Pedrito, and Manolo are released. The PRD holds various political rallies. Radio Caribe is destroyed. The National Civic Union (UCN) is founded. Four days after Manolo is released from jail, the 14th of June Movement becomes a political party, and members elect him as its president. It opens its first office on El Conde Street in Santo Domingo. The *paleros* (so named because they beat people with sticks and poles) attack those who attend the opposition marches. The Dominican Student Federation (FED) is founded.

AUGUST

The Partido Dominicano holds a demonstration in Santiago. Erasmo Bermúdez and others are killed during a UCN demonstration. Balaguer proposes the creation of a coalition government. The police break into the UCN and 14th of June offices in search of weapons. The first 14th of June demonstration is held in Santiago. Trujillo's widow, María Martínez, and her son Radhamés leave the country.

SEPTEMBER

An OAS committee arrives in the country. A revolt leaves various people dead on Santo Domingo's Duarte Bridge. Balaguer begins to put together a coalition government and meets with Manolo Tavárez Justo and Leandro Guzmán, leaders of the 14th of June Movement. The 14th of June organizes its first protest march in Santo Domingo. The Partido Dominicano organizes a rally.

OCTOBER

Balaguer criticizes Trujillo in a keynote speech delivered before the United Nations. U.S. counselor general in the Dominican Republic, George C. McGhee, and Ramfis Trujillo negotiate the Trujillo family's departure from the country and the lifting of sanctions. A violent demonstration takes place on Espaillat Street in Santo Domingo. The Inter-American Commission on Human Rights arrives in the country, as does Juan Bosch. Petán and Negro Trujillo, the dictator's brothers, leave the country. The 14th of June newspaper reveals the names of Military Intelligence Service (SIM) agents.

NOVEMBER

The OAS recommends a partial lifting of the sanctions.

Day 8: Manolo Tavárez, Leandro Guzmán, and other opposition leaders travel to Washington, invited by the Inter-American Commission on Human Rights. Ramfis decides to leave the country.

Day 15: Petán and Negro Trujillo return to the country.

Day 18: Ramfis kills the heroes who participated in the May 30 assassination of Trujillo and leaves the country. The United States sends a military fleet, which can be seen from Ciudad Trujillo/Santo Domingo's seaside boulevard. U.S. aircraft fly over the city. Rodríguez Echavarría organizes a coup against the San Isidro Air Force Base. Petán and Hector Trujillo leave the country.

Day 21: Manolo Tavárez and other opposition leaders return to the country. A massive rally receives them. Several of the Trujillo residences are ransacked, as well as other properties of the Trujillo family. López Molina is deported. The capital is once again named Santo Domingo.

Day 30: Trujillo's body is temporarily returned to the country. The case against the killers of the Mirabal sisters begins.

DECEMBER

Thirteen-day strike. The Council of State is established.

1962

Balaguer goes into exile. Rafael F. Bonnelly is named as the head of the Council of State. The trial against the killers of the Mirabal sisters begins in June. The accused are sentenced in November. That same month, Juan Bosch wins the first presidential elections in thirty-eight years.

1963

In February Bosch is sworn in. He is overthrown in September of that same year. A Triumvirate is established. On November 22, the same day President Kennedy is assassinated, Manolo Tavárez launches a guerrilla movement. A month later he and his companions are killed while attempting to turn themselves in.

1964

The Triumvirate controls the government.

1965

Civil war erupts on April 24. Alicinio Peña Rivera, the man who orchestrated the murders of the Mirabal sisters, is released from his prison cell at the Ozama Fortress in Santo Domingo. The victory of the Constitutionalists (those who wanted the return of Juan Bosch to the presidency) is interrupted by the U.S. military intervention. In September, Héctor García Godoy is named president.

1966

On January 28, press reports indicate that the assassins of the Mirabal sisters were released from jail and left the country. On June 1, Joaquín Balaguer wins the election, beating Juan Bosch. During Balaguer's twelve-year regime (1966–1978), the authorities raided the Mirabal home in Conuco twenty-eight times. They said they were looking for weapons.

1969

National Poet Pedro Mir publishes his poem "Amén de Mariposas."

1970 (approximately)

Balaguer declares that the farm in Nagua owned by Dedé Mirabal and her husband Jaimito is for public use.

1978

Antonio Guzmán, from the PRD, wins the presidential elections.

1981

Doña Chea, the mother of the Mirabal sisters, dies.

1982

Dedé divorces her husband. Salvador Jorge Blanco, the PRD candidate, wins the presidential elections.

1983

The Central Bank issues special coins with the images of the Mirabal sisters.

1986

Joaquín Balaguer wins the election.

1990

Balaguer remains in office for another four years. Jaime David Fernández Mirabal is elected senator.

1992

Peña Rivera, the man who orchestrated the murder of the Mirabal sisters, briefly returns to the country and is interviewed by local print and television media outlets.

1994

Balaguer wins a fraudulent election, and an agreement is reached allowing him to stay in office only until 1996. Dominican American writer Julia Alvarez publishes *In the Time of the Butterflies* in the United States. The novel has been translated into eleven languages.
Jaime David Fernández Mirabal is reelected to the Senate.

1996–2000

Leonel Fernández, from the PLD, wins the presidential elections. Jaime David Fernández Mirabal is elected vice president, and Minou Tavárez Mirabal is named vice foreign minister.

1998

The United Nations declares November 25 as International Day of Non-Violence Against Women.

2000

Jaime David Fernández Mirabal loses the presidential nomination during the PLD convention. Convention winner Danilo Medina loses the national election to Hipólito Mejía, the PRD candidate. On November 25, the remains of the three Mirabal sisters and Manolo Tavárez Justo are transferred to the Mirabal home in Conuco. By presidential decree, the grounds where they are buried are declared an extension of the National Pantheon, where the country's liberators and heroes are buried.

2001

The Hollywood production of *In the Time of the Butterflies*, produced by Salma Hayek, has its premiere.

2002

Minou Tavárez Mirabal is elected to the Lower House of Congress.

2004

Leonel Fernández wins the presidential elections. Manolo Tavárez Justo is declared a national hero by the Dominican Congress.

2006

Minou Tavárez is reelected to the legislature.

2007

The National Congress changes the name of Salcedo Province to Hermanas Mirabal Province. The Central Bank issues 200-peso bills in honor of the Mirabal sisters.

2009

Dedé's memoir, *Vivas en su jardín*, is published on May 4.

2010

During Santo Domingo's Annual Book Fair, *Vivas en su jardín* receives the prestigious Eduardo León Jimenes Award for the best book published during the previous year.

2013

Jaime Rafael (Jimmy) Fernández Mirabal dies in New York City. He was the second son of Dedé Mirabal and Jaime Fernández Camilo.

2014

On February 1, Dedé Mirabal dies in Santo Domingo. She was eighty-eight years old.

THE PLURAL CAUSE OF THINGS

Minou Tavárez Mirabal

Remarks delivered during the book launch ceremony of
Alive in Their Garden: A Memoir, April 27, 2009

There is a plural complicity in the origin of all things. A succession of chance events come together to create them.

That is why yesterday, while I was working on these acknowledgments to share with you today, I realized that, in all fairness and honesty, I had to begin by recognizing my oldest fear, the only one that, hopefully, my children will inherit. I am afraid, truly afraid, of being incapable of accepting the present for what it truly is, even in the most destabilizing circumstances: a gift where you can always, always choose between forgetting or moving forward, between losing or learning, between duty or payback, between burying or building, and between standing still or evolving with whatever changes our times may bring.

For every story, there is another story behind it. *Alive in Their Garden* is no exception. Writing those first words, which would later become Dedé Mirabal's memoir, had its ups and downs, its unsettling chaos, its complexities and long periods of waiting. It also had the support of cherished individuals.

My goal tonight is to talk about the story behind the story of *Alive in Their Garden*.

With that in mind, I would first like to begin by thanking my mother, Minerva Mirabal, because what she could not give to us in the form of affection, cuddles, and caresses, she gave to us in her eternally beautiful example and way of conducting herself.

To my aunts, Nina Patria and Tía Teté, for their courage and for the legacy of integrity and solidarity they left us.

Even though he has begged me to maintain his anonymity as a contributor to this wonderful book, I must mention Dr. Juan Tomás Estévez. He undertook this project as his own and collaborated with Angela Hernández in writing the key questions that would bring out Mamá's words. Everyone who knows her knows that this last part—getting her to openly express herself—was not difficult to do.

We asked Bernardo Vega[122] for a chronology of events. He not only prepared it, but he also carefully reviewed all the events mentioned in the book for their historical accuracy. He came back with a truly enriched draft of the original text.

On a gray December afternoon in the early eighties, as I walked down a street in Havana with Eduardo Galeano,[123] he made me promise that he would be one of the first to read this story when it was finally written. He received the draft by express mail and, in express form, he returned it by email. He generously wrote the beautiful paragraphs that appear on the book's back cover, along with comments by Julia Alvarez.

Pilar Cernuda[124] read the draft and insisted that the book had enough merit to participate in the Casa de América[125] Essay and Debate Contest. She personally entered the book in the contest and was the first to call from Madrid to tell us that, although the contest rules called for the issuance of a single award, the jury had decided to honor the book with a Special Mention because of its testimonial strength.

To the friends who read and enthusiastically edited and cared for these pages, and who made possible the publication of this beautiful edition that we are presenting today: thank you.

The draft was also read with loving care and was enriched by my brothers and sisters: Nelson, Noris, and Raúl Ernesto (Patria's children), Jacqueline (María Teresa's daughter), and Jaime Enrique and Jimmy. Manolo tirelessly insisted that the memories Mamá has narrated be printed in black and white, so they might live on. And Jaime David suggested that the title of the book be none other than the phrase that we always heard Mamá—and

---

122 Economist, historian, former Dominican ambassador to the U.S.
123 Uruguayan journalist and writer (1940–2015), considered to be one of Latin America's most influential writers. He is perhaps best known for his book *Las venas abiertas de América Latina / Open Veins of Latin America* (1971).
124 World-renowned Spanish journalist.
125 Casa de América is an important Spanish cultural center, based in Madrid, working to strengthen ties between Spain and Latin America.

Mamá Chea—repeat as we were growing up. These words appear on a stone that marks the entrance to the garden, burial site, and monument.

But, above all: thank you, Mamá.

Thank you for having the heroic humanity—in spite of the immortality of your wounds—to seize those past events from oblivion and, by telling this story, to assure that they not be lost to us and to the world. Thank you for living so you could tell the story.

In November 2000, the girls returned home, to their garden. From there, like a star, they emit a light that penetrates the terrain that surrounds them, planting in the hearts of all who come, of all who enter and pass through the house, a contagious seedling of light that has defiantly spread throughout the planet.

And thanks to that garden, where the leaves fall "without minding the wind," where doves fly "without knowing why they fly," where the sun sets because that is what the sun does: it rises and it sets. As we stand in that symbolic garden, the death of Minerva, Patria, and María Teresa is something in which we will never believe, although it be true.

And now?

What will we do now so that the Mirabals' garden becomes the garden of all Dominicans?

How can the past become the future in our small 48,000 square-kilometer garden?[126]

In this beloved garden—that is, on our share of this island—we are all responsible for pruning the fears and for weeding out complacency and despair, which, if not pulled up by its roots, will end up destroying everything, including the flowers and the grass.

The garden where Mamá Dedé declared them alive must be watered and carefully tended every single day. We must give everything we have, sowing the seeds of life, of equality, and tolerance, of justice and democracy, and of better social, economic, and political practices. We must look after it. We must care for this immense garden so that the healthy grass can support the next generation's firm steps, as well as our steps as we fulfill our obligation to build the Dominican Republic that the Mirabals dreamed of, the Dominican Republic that they lived and died for.

It is in the name of future generations that I say to you, Mamá, that the girls' death—an event that lives on in our daily consciousness—will continue to shed light upon us each day as an official, public, and familiar

---

126 Reference to the 48,000 square kilometers that comprise what today is the Dominican Republic.

part of our daily lives. Their infamous death fertilizes the garden of our nation and safeguards them from indifference and oblivion. It ensures that they thrive. It keeps them alive forever in the only place where they can be eternal: in our universal commitment, our memory, and our hearts.

Many thanks, many times over.

WHEN WE LOST EVERYTHING, YOU WERE THERE FOR US

Minou Tavárez Mirabal

Doña Dedé Mirabal passed away on February 1, 2014. The following is a letter written to her by Minou Tavárez Mirabal.

Mamá:

When ignominy violently snatched Papá Enrique, our grandfather, your dear father, away from us, you were there, during the disconcerting hustle and bustle of those days, in the warm and aromatic metal lunch box, on the road, and sitting before the dressing table . . . trying to put on a good face to confront the difficult times. That's the way you were, the way you were for yourself, for this nation that you loved so much, and how you always were for us, your family: unconditional and dignified, elegant and active, a hard worker and hardworking.

When suddenly, from one moment to the next, your three sisters became three broken bodies after being brutally clubbed, three lifeless bodies, three mute bodies lying there under your very nose, you, oh you, you made sure that they never became three lives that had passed on.

You were the one who screamed "Murderers!" to the four winds and to all those willing to listen. You gave the Dominican Republic—your country kidnapped by fear—your screaming disobedience as its only chance. Your raw indignation became our next step.

It was you, Mamá. It was you back then who became the bravest, the most desperate, the only "mad woman" in a country suffering from an excess of prudence. Or simply scared to death.

It was you, Mamá, with your "Murderers! Murderers! You killed them!" You were the one who cut the braid that kept an entire nation bound to its own cowardice.

It was you, riding in the back of the pickup truck carrying your sisters' broken bodies to the cemetery, the one who unraveled for good the history of servitude of a land enslaved by its own terror.

It was you, Mamá, so beautiful, young, and radiant, in your prime as a woman, who came home from the cemetery, buried your broken pieces, and tucked into bed not three, but nine children, whom you raised as your own from that abominable night until today.

And, of course, it was you, Mamá, who forever and until this very day, as you once told us, "gave everything for your family and your country."

It was you, Mamá, who, when we lacked everything as a nation, as a world, as a family, as sons and daughters, you were the one who was there filling the void with your committed and eternal presence, always telling the story—over and over again—a story you never tired of telling, so that your sisters would never become a part of the past.

It was you, Mamá, it was you who, when we lost everything, you gave us your all.

BIBLIOGRAPHY

Works Cited

Alvarez, Julia. *In the Time of the Butterflies*. Chapel Hill: Algonquin Books of Chapel Hill, 1994.

Awad Báez, Pilar and Eva Alvarez. *La verdad de la sangre*. Santo Domingo: Editora Búho, 2013.

Balaguer, Joaquín. "Dios y Trujillo. Una reinterpretación de la historia dominicana." *Clío. Revista de La Academia Dominicana de la Historia* 23, no. 101 (Oct.–Dec. 1954). Reproduced in Cielonaranja (2016), http://www.cielonaranja.com/balaguer-diostrujillo.htm.

Camilo, Pedro. "La Acción Clero Cultural, una organización de la resistencia antitrujillista." *Movimiento Revolucionario 14 de Junio*. Aug. 9, 2009. Accessed May 15, 2019. https://unojotacuatro.blogspot.com/2009/08/la-accion-clero-cultural-una.html.

Derby, Lauren. *The Dictator's Seduction: Politics and the Popular Imagination in the Era of Trujillo*. Durham: Duke University Press, 2009.

Domeyko, Cecilia, dir., writ. & prod. *Code Name: Butterflies (Nombre secreto: Mariposas)*. Nov. 11, 2020. Video. https://www.youtube.com/watch?v=8mrAZrVYwsU.

"Foro público." *El Caribe* (Santo Domingo, Dominican Republic), Jun. 25, 1955.

Franco, Pericles. *La tragedia dominicana. Análisis de la tiranía de Trujillo*. Santiago de Chile: Federación de Estudiantes de Chile, 1946.

Galeano, Eduardo. *Las venas abiertas de América Latina*. México City: Siglo Veintiuno Editores, 1971.

Guzmán, Leandro. *1J4: De espigas y de fuegos. Aportes para la memoria necesaria. Testimonios de un militante*. Santo Domingo: Editora de Colores, 1998.

Henríquez Castilllo, Luis. *Crímenes contra la seguridad interior y exterior del Estado dominicano*. Ciudad Trujillo/Santo Domingo: Editorial La Nación, 1960.

Horn, Maja. *Masculinity after Trujillo: The Politics of Gender in Dominican Literature*. Gainesville: University Press of Florida, 2014.

Imbert Barrera, Antonio. "Entrevista al General Antonio Imbert Barrera, uno de los ajusticiadores de Trujillo." Video. Uploaded by El Día RD, May 31, 2018. https://www.youtube.com/watch?v=iGGCN7kqONE.

Lajara Solá, Homero Luis. "Los pilotos de la patria." *Listín Diario*, Nov. 19, 2016. listindiario.com/la-republica/2016/11/19/443780/los-pilotos-de-la-patria.html.

Manley, Elizabeth. "Intimate Violations: Women and the *Ajusticiamiento* of Dictator Rafael Trujillo, 1944–1961." *The Americas* 69, no. 1 (2012), 61–94.

———. *The Paradox of Paternalism: Women and the Politics of Authoritarianism in the Dominican Republic*. Gainesville: University Press of Florida, 2017.

Minaya, Héctor. "Dictador llegó al colmo de cambiar el nombre de la capital por Ciudad Trujillo," *El Nacional* (Santo Domingo, Dominican Republic), May 26, 2016. https://elnacional.com.do/dictador-llego-al-colmo-de-cambiar-el-nombre-de-la-capital-por-ciudad-trujillo.

Mirabal, Dedé. *Vivas en su jardín. La verdadera historia de las hermanas Mirabal y su lucha por la libertad*. 3rd. ed. Santo Domingo: Editora Búho, 2014.

———. *Vivas en su jardín. La verdadera historia de las hermanas Mirabal y su lucha por la libertad*. Vintage Español. New York: Random House, 2009.

Nervo, Amado. "En paz." *Elevación*. Madrid: Editorial América, 1916.

Paulino Ramos, Alejandro. "18 de noviembre de 1961: el día en que Ramfis Trujillo asesinó a los Héroes del 30 de Mayo," Historia de la República Dominicana. Nov. 10, 2022. historiarepublicadominicana.com.do/18-de-noviembre-de-1961-el-dia-en-que-ramfis-trujillo-asesino-a-los-heroes-del-30-de-mayo.

Peña Rivera, Alicinio. *Trujillo. Historia oculta de un dictador*. New York: Plus Ultra, 1977.

Raful, Tony. *Movimiento 14 de Junio, historia y documentos*. 2nd ed. Santo Domingo: Alfa y Omega, 2007.

Robinson, Nancy. "Women's Political Participation in the Dominican Republic: The Case of the Mirabal Sisters." *Caribbean Quarterly* 52, nos. 2–3 (2006), 172–83.

Roorda, Eric Paul. *The Dictator Next Door: The Good Neighbor Policy and the Trujillo Regime in the Dominican Republic, 1930–1945*. Durham: Duke University Press, 1998.

Sang, Mu-Kein. *¡Yo soy Minerva! Confesiones más allá de la vida y la muerte*. Santo Domingo: Amigo del Hogar, 2003.

Silva, José Asunción. "Nocturne" in *The Penguin Book of Latin American Verse*, ed. and trans. Enrique Caracciolo Trejo. Harmondsworth, England: Penguin, 1971, 173–174.

Solnit, Rebecca. *Hope in the Dark: Untold Histories, Wild Possibilities*. New York: Nation Books, 2004.

Tavárez Justo, Emma. [Title of article not available] *¡Ahora!*, no. 578, December 9, 1974, n.p.

Tavárez Mirabal, Minou. *Mañana te escribiré otra vez. Minerva y Manolo. Cartas*. Santo Domingo: Fundación Hermanas Mirabal, 2013. Second edition, Santo Domingo: Aguilar, Grupo Santillana, 2014.

———. *The Letters of Minerva Mirabal and Manolo Tavárez: Love and Resistance in the Time of Trujillo*. Introduction and Trans. by Heather Hennes. Gainesville: University of Florida Press, 2022.

Taveras, Rafael. "Entrevista con Rafael (Fafa) Taveras, Comunicador," Video. Uploaded by El Día RD, Nov. 23, 2018. www.youtube.com/watch?v=4JgUzNtSMYg.

Tejeda, Darío. "Las políticas musicales del poder en la Era de Trujillo en República Dominicana, 1930–1961" In *Raíces comunes e historias compartidas: México, Centroamérica y el Caribe*. Ed. by Alain Basail Rodríguez, Inés Castro Apreza, María

Luisa de la Garza Chávez, Teresa Ramos Maza, and Mario Eduardo Valdez Gordillo, 329–44. CLACSO, 2018. https://doi.org/10.2307/j.ctvn5tzmv.19.

"Text of Pastoral Letter Read to Dominican Republic Catholics," *New York Times*, Feb. 3, 1960. https://www.nytimes.com/1960/02/03/archives/text-of-pastoral-letter-read-to-dominican-republic-catholics.html.

Turits, Richard Lee. *Foundations of Despotism: Peasants, the Trujillo Regime, and Modernity in Dominican History.* Stanford: Stanford University Press, 2003.

Valera Benítez, Rafael. *Complot develado.* Ciudad Trujillo/Santo Domingo: Editorial Handicap, 1960.

Additional References: Select Creative Works and Biographies about the Mirabal Sisters

Alonso Romero, Mercedes. *Su nombre es Patria.* Santo Domingo: Editora Búho, 2011. Biography.

Alvarez, Julia. *In the Time of the Butterflies.* Chapel Hill: Algonquin Books of Chapel Hill, 1994. Novel.

Barroso, Mariano, dir. *In the Time of the Butterflies.* 2001; Santa Monica, CA: MGM Entertainment. Film adaptation of Julia Alvarez's novel by the same title.

Galván, William. *Minerva Mirabal. Historia de una heroína.* Santo Domingo: Comisión Permanente de Efemérides Patrias, 2011. Biography.

Mariposas de Acero, writ. by Jásquez, Waddys, prod. by Pablo García. Palacio de Bellas Artes, Santo Domingo, Aug. 12, 2022. Live musical theater.

Mir, Pedro. *Amen de Mariposas.* Santo Domingo: Nuevo Mundo, 1969. Book containing poem by the same title.

Parra, Francis, dir. *Yo soy Minerva.* Teatro ECAS. Providence, RI, March 2018. Theatrical performance based on Mu-Kein Sang's monograph by the same title.

The Roar of the Butterflies, created by Juan Pablo Buscarini, dir. by Mariano Hueter, Leandro Ipiña, and Inés París. Star Original Productions. 2023. Television series.

Trópico de sangre, dir. by Juan Delánce r, 2010, Maya Entertainment, DVD. Feature film.

Sang, Mu-Kein. *¡Yo soy Minerva! Confesiones más allá de la vida y la muerte.* Santo Domingo: Amigo del Hogar, 2003. Monograph that inspired Francis Parra's theatrical adaptation by the same title.

Sisters of the Underground, prod. by Eva Longoria and Dania Ramírez. Aug. 31, 2022. Podcast, MP3 audio. iHeart Radio. https://www.iheart.com/podcast/1119-sisters-of-the-undergroun-101186016. Podcast in seven episodes.

Svitch, Caridad. *In the Time of the Butterflies/En el tiempo de las Mariposas.* 2011. Theatrical adaptation of Julia Alvarez's novel by the same name.

INDEX

1J4: De espigas y de fuegos (Guzmán), 65–66, 124–25, 167–68, 187, 194–95

Abbes, Johnny, 200
Abreu Penzo, Mario, 134
Acción Clero Cultural (Clergy-Cultural Action), xxiv
Acción Feminista Dominicana, xvi
Acevedo, Lidia, 38
Agrupación Política 14 de Junio, 172–73
¡Ahora! magazine, 202; dated January 31, 1962, 201; Emma Tavárez Justo notes in, 104–5, 114, 129, 137; and trial against assassins of Mirabal sisters, 197–98
ajusticiamiento (assassination), xxvi. *See also* judicial records, assassination trial; killers, fate of; tragedy, facing; trial against assassins of Mirabal sisters
Alive in their Garden (Dedé), xiii
Alix, Juan Antonio, 106
Almánzar, Ana, 37
Almonte, Caonabo, 132–33
Alvarez, Julia, 265
Amaya Hernández, Ana, 240
Amell, Juan, 250–51
Aníbal González, Francisco (Pachico), xxiv, 133
Anna Karenina (Tolstoy), 53
antitrujillistas, xxiv, 55, 127,
Antuña, Bartolo, 59
apazote, herb, 38
April Revolution, xxvii–xxviii, 9, 55, 214, 223, 225
Arache, Montes, 214
Arias, Desiderio, xv
Aristy, Amaury Germán, 168
Aristy, Elsa, 42
Ariza, Doña Lucila, 35

Association of Cacao Producers, 253
assassination. *See* judicial records, assassination trial; killers, fate of; tragedy, facing; trial against assassins of Mirabal sisters
Atidó, Bodó, 43–44
Autonomous University of Santo Domingo (UASD), 133, 247
Aybar, Gisela and Zaida, 42

Báez, Cayo, 23
Balaguer, Joaquín, xiii, xxix, xxvii, 67, 163, 171, 214, 254, 281; administration of, 214–15; regime of, 168, 224–25, 242
Balaguer, Lope, 67
Baló, Joaquín, 155
Bay of Luperón, 212
Bécquer, Gustavo Adolfo, 50
Bello, Andrés, 51
Benedicto, Thelma, 59
Beras Goico, Freddy, 216, 218, 264
Bermúdez, Poppy, 59
Bermúdez Espaillat, Erasmo, 171
Bernard, Máximo, 177
Bernardino, Félix W., 214
Betancourt, Rómulo, 145, 148, 163
Blanco, Salvador Jorge, 185
Bobea, Mario, 56
Bogaert, Charlie, 129–30
Bohemia magazine, 155
Bonnelly, Carlos Sully, 59
Bonnelly, Rafael, 174
Bordas, Diego, 27
Bosch, Juan, 174, 177
Bosch Gaviño, Juan Emilio, xxvii, 155, 171n94, 174
Bournigal, René, 155, 269
Brache, Alexis, 177
Brache, Julito, 93

296 · Index

Brito, Chachita, 95
Buckalew, Charles R., 24
Burgos, Arturo, 20, 86
Burgos, Miriam, 47
business ventures, 30–32, 95–96
Butterflies. *See* Mirabal sisters

Cabral, Manuel del, 53–54
Cabral, Sina, 139, 143
Cabral, Tobías Emilio, 61–64
cacao trees, 253
Caja Dominicana de Seguros Sociales, 157
caliés, xxxv, 24, 55, 68, 90, 132, 134–36, 138, 140, 143, 146, 152, 156–57, 167–68, 174, 186–91, 196–98, 201, 221, 239, 264
Camilo, Basilio, 135
Camilo, Chilín, 89–90
Camilo, David, 37
Camilo, Jesús María, 162
Camilo, Lesbia, 57–58
Camilo, María de los Angeles, 23–25
Camilo, Nicolás, 38–39
Camilo, Orlando, 224
Camilo, Patria, 67
Camilo, Víctor (Vitico), 159
Canadian Confederation, 30
Campos Jorge, Carmen Lisette (Lissy), 247
Caribe, El (Caribbean, The), xix–xx, 109, 120–21, 151, 162, 166–67
Carmela, Aunt, 23–25, 37, 120
Carrel, Alexis, 53
Carta Pastoral, La (Pastoral Letter, The), xxv. *See also* Catholic Church Pastoral Letter
Carvajal Martínez, Francisco, 210
Casa Museo Hermanas Mirabal, 130. *See also* Mirabal Sisters House Museum, xxviii
Castillo, Barón, 264
Castro, Fidel, xxiii
Catholic Church, 127
Catholic Church Pastoral Letter, 141–42
caudillos, xv
Cayo Confites Expedition, xxii, 55, 262
cepillos, xix
Cerro de la Cruz, hill, 28–29
Cervecería Nacional Dominicana, 245
Césaire, Aimé, 53

Chea. *See* Reyes Camilo, Mercedes (Chea; Doña Chea)
childhood: births, 33–34; early school days, 34–38; education during, 38–43; health during, 38–43; memories of Bodó and Fefa, 43–44
children, raising: Jacqueline, 244–45; Mamá fading away, 248–49; Minou and Manolito, 240–44; Nelson Enrique, Noris Mercedes, and Fidel Raúl Ernesto, 239–40; overview, 237–39; three Jaimes, 245–47
chronology: early years, 271–72; eighties, 281; fifties, 274–76; forties, 273–74; later years, 282–83; nineties, 281–82; seventies, 281; sixties, 276–80; thirties, 272–73; twenties, 272
Ciudad Trujillo, 203n102. *See also* Trujillo, Rafael
Clergy-Cultural Action, 127
Clisante, Pedro, 172
Cold War, xx, xxii
Colegio Mayor Universitario San José de Calasanz, 133
Concepción, Dr. 247
Conde, Chelito, 96
coralillos, 175
Cordero, Marcia, 42
Corominas, Mayra, 246
Crimes Committed against the National and International Security of the Dominican State, 149
Cruz, Alia, 37
Cruz, Rufino de la, xxvii, 126, 155, 158, 190, 195, 202, 204, 207–8, 269; death of, 157–63
Cruz Inoa, Daniel, xxiv, 127
Cruz Valerio, Manuel Alfonso, 205, 210
Cuban Revolution, xxiii
Cuesta, Ana Matilde, 168
Cueto, Fernando, 130–31, 131, 193–94, 212

D'Alessandro, Guido (Yuyo), 127–28, 170–71, 173
Delio Guzmán, José, 255
Derby, Lauren, xvii
Despradel, Consuelo, 61
Despradel, Fidelio, 177

Día, El (program), xxiv
Díaz, Brinio Rafael, 171
Díaz, Pedro, 136–37
Díaz, Tamara, 114
Díaz Estrella, Ambiorix, 148, 150, 196–99, 203, 206
Díaz Moreno, Edmundo, 223
dictatorships, remembering: International Day for the Elimination of Violence Against Women, 266–69; Mirabal Sisters House Museum, 263–66, 269; new generations, 262–63. *See also* Trujillo, Rafael
Disnalda María, 152
Distribuidora Olivetti, 128
Doce Años, Los, xxvii–xxviii
Dominican Communist Party, 241–42
Dominican Liberation Party (PLD), 243, 245, 257–58, 281–82
Dominican Republic, 247; characterizing politics in, xv–xvi; and era of Trujillo, xv–xxi; 14th of June Revolutionary Movement in, 127–49; jailed women in, 139–46; legal training in, 108; Mirabel Reyes family in, xiii–xv; resistance in, xxi–xxv; survival, fortitude, and memory, xxvi–xxix; tragedy in, xxv–xxvi; wounds left by 1916 American occupation, 23–25
Dominican Revolutionary Movement, 40
Dominican Revolutionary Party (PRD), 171, 185, 243, 245, 255, 278, 281–82
Ducoudray, Juan, 55
Dunlop, Clarence Charles, 215
Durán, Isabel, 33–34

Echavarría, Leandro and Vinicio, 186
Echavarría, Vinicio, 177
education, 38–43. *See also* Mirabal sisters
Emiliano Tejera School, 246
Era of Trujillo. *See* Trujillo, Rafael
Espaillat, Che, 200
Espaillat, José (Che), 21–22, 170
Estrada Malleta, Emilio, 203, 210, 216, 220
Estrada Medina, Manuel de Jesús, 107
Estrella, Fifa, 164
Estrella Liz, Víctor Rafael, 171

Estrella Sadhalá, Salvador, 164
Estrella Ureña, Rafael, xvi
Expedition of Constanza, Maimón, and Estero Hondo, xxiii

Familia, La, magazine, 105–6
family: business ventures, 30–32; childhood, education, and friends, 33–44; childhood, education, and friends, 33–44; love, marriage, divorce, and stability, 254–61; marriage of parents, 26–30; raising children, 237–49; remembering dictatorships, 262–69; settling in Ojo de Agua, 21–22; value of work, 250–53; working with Papá, 30–32; and wounds left by 1916 American occupation, 23–25. *See also* Reyes Camilo, Mercedes (Chea); Mirabal Fernández, Enrique; Mirabal Reyes, Aída Patria Mercedes; Mirabal Reyes, Antonia María Teresa; Mirabal Reyes, Bélgica Adela (Dedé); Mirabal Reyes, María Argentina Minerva; Mirabal sisters; tragedy, facing
Father of the New Nation. *See* Trujillo, Rafael
Faxas Canto, Rafael (Pipe), xxiv
Fefa, aunt, 37–38, 43–44, 106
Fefa, cook, 43–44
Fefé. *See* Valera Benítez, Rafael
Fefita, aunt. *See* González de Garrido, Josefa
Fefita, Doña. *See* Justo de Tavárez, Josefa
Fellito, death of, 94
Fello, uncle 21–22
Feris Iglesias, Miguel, 264
Fernández, Abel, 47
Fernández, Adela, 21
Fernández, Celeste, 154
Fernández, Jaime (father-in-law), 27, 69
Fernández, Jaimito, 68–72; as being *machista*, 256; divorcing from, 256–57; "fearless" as word defining, 255–56; as member of 14th of June Movement, 254–55; political situation of, 255
Fernández, Leonel, 258
Fernández, Lesbiolita, 57–58
Fernández, Luis, 187

Fernández Caminero, José, 154, 200
Fernández Domínguez, Rafael, 267
Fernández Mirabal, Jaime David, 107, 157, 220–21, 223; campaigns of, 258–59; raising, 245–47; and value of work, 252
Fernández Mirabal, Jaime Enrique, 72–73, 151, 220, children 246; raising, 245–47
Fernández Mirabal, Jaime Rafael (Jimmy), 72–73; raising, 245–47; children 246
Ferreras, Chino, 113
Fiallo, Fabio, 50
Flores, Juan Antonio, 160
folktales, telling, 35–36
Foro Público, xix, 109, 275
14th of June Revolutionary Movement, xxii–xxiv; and fierce repression, 171–72; first formal meeting, 130; founding of, 129–39; and jailed women, 139–46; newspaper, 201–2; original copies of detailed minutes, 130–31; overview of period of, 127–29; receiving official name, 129–30; second arrests, 146–49; stashing weapons, 131–32; structuring, 132
Franco Ornes, Pericles, xxii, 57, 60–61, 89

games, 34–38
García, Carlos, 113
García, Gladys, 41
García, Láutico, 174
García, Leyda, 41
García Monclús, Pedro, 171
García Saleta, Pucho, 177
García Trujillo, Virgilito, 144
gardening, 259–61
Garrido, Flor, 37
Garrido, Victor, 145–46
gavilleros, 23
Geraldino, Horacio, 109
Gómez Pepín, Radhamés, 216
González, Alcibiades, 215
González, Ezequiel, 46, 165
González, Leví, 48
González, Murat, 146
González, Pedro (Pedrito), 24, 42, 46, 119, 169
González, Renán, 88

González, Renato, 133
González, Víctor, 179
González de Garrido, Josefa (Aunt Fefita), 23–24, 26, 37, 68
González Mirabal, Fidel Raúl Ernesto (Raúl), 81, 132, 175, 223, 228, 235, 237–38, 239–40, 243, 276, 286
González Mirabal, Nelson Enrique, 175–76, 239–40
González Mirabal, Noris Mercedes, 239–40
González Reyes, Antonio Ezequiel, xxiv
Gordo de la Semana, El, 264
grace, fall from: events impacting family, 94–101; party in San Cristóbal, 85–88; repression against family, 88–93
Guillen Gómez, Wenceslao (Wen), xxiv
Guridi Comercial, 246
Guzmán, Antonio, 210, 255–56
Guzmán Abreu, Marino, 171
Guzmán Mirabal, Jacqueline, 4, 117, 141, 147, 151, 158, 175, 188, 237–39, 244–48
Guzmán Rodríguez, Leandro, xxvi, xxx, 78–80, arrest of, 146–49; and children, 241, 244–45; chronology of, 274–79; describes María Teresa, 65–66; and founding of 14th of June Movement, 128–39; in prison in 1963, 213; marrying María Teresa, 120–25; release of, 166–73; tragedy, 150–76; and trial of assassins, 185–212

Ḥāfeẓ, Khwāja Shams-ud-Dīn Muḥammad, 62
Haitian Massacre, xviii, 43–44
Hayek, Salma, 265
health, childhood and, 38–43
Henríquez, Rafael David, 95
Hermanas Mirabal Games, 247
Hostos, Eugenio María de, 39
Hotel Jaragua, 125–26
Hugo, Victor, 53
Hurricane San Zenón, xvii, 25

Imbert, Ramón (Moncho), 170
Imbert, Segundo, 200
Imbert Barrera, Antonio, xxvi
Immaculada Nursery, 56

Immaculate Conception School, xiv, xxii, 29, 39–40, 42, 106, 240, 265
Immortal Generation, 180
In the Time of the Butterflies (Alvarez), 116
Información, La, 256
INFOTEP. *See* National Technical and Vocational Institute
INTEC. *See* Technological Institute of Santo Domingo
Internal Revenue Service, 27–28
International Day for the Elimination of Violence Against Women, 5, 266–69
ISA. *See* Superior Agricultural Institute

Jiménez, Doña Emilia, 113
Jiménez, Juan Isidro, xv
Jiménez, Onésimo, 157
Jiménez Guzmán, Fausto, 171
José María Cabral Hospital, 179
José, uncle (José Reyes Camilo), 54–55
Juan Pablo Duarte Bridge, 171
judicial records, assassination trial: defendant confession, 209–10; February 20, 1962, judicial order, 206–8; finding holes in initial investigation, 203–6; summary of investigation, 208–9. *See also* killers, fate of, tragedy, facing; trial against assassins of Mirabal sisters
Justo, Doña Paulina, 178
Justo, Marchena, 262
Justo de Tavárez, Josefa (Doña Fefita), 138, 148, 151, 173, 179, 191–92, 241
Juventud Democrática (Democratic Youth), xxii

killers, fate of: after events of 1963, 213–14; collective memory, 213; compensation, 220; death of Alicinio Peña Rivera, 220; death of Rojas Lora, 215–16; fate of Candito Torres, 214; interviews, 216–19; missing files, 221–22; releasing from prison, 214–15; support for family, 216–19. *See also* political events, impact of; tragedy, facing; trial against assassins of Mirabal sisters
Krant, María, 41

Lalía, aunt, death of, 23, 46, 120, 155, 165–66
Lama, Miguel, 169
Larry. *See* Cabral, Tobías Emilio
Lima house, 25
Listín Diario, 45, 109
Lithgow Ceara, Enrique, 102–3
Llenas, Rafael, 59
Lora, Jacinto, 89
Luis Muñoz Rivera School, 240
Luperón Expedition of 1949, xxii

machismo, term, 110
Maestro, Mía, 265
Mamá. *See* Reyes Camilo, Mercedes (Chea)
Mamá Chichí. *See* Camilo, María de los Angeles
Man, the Unknown (Carrel), 53
Manley, Elizabeth, xvi, xx
Manolito. *See* Tavárez Mirabal, Manuel Enrique
Manolo. *See* Tavárez Justo, Manuel Aurelio
Manzano, Alfredo, 250
Mará Picá, 191, 197, 211–12
Marcial, Hortensia, 96
Marrero, Colombina, 42
Marte, Víctor Manuel, 206–8
Martínez, Alejo, 172
Martínez, Orlando, 242
Martínez, Violeta, 42, 89, 263–66, 267
Martínez Cabrera, Manuel, 171
Mary Queen of Scots (Zweig), 53
Mayer, Isabel, 86, 107
Maza, Antonio de la, 41, xxvi
Maza, Pirolo de la, 169
Mejía Ricart, Magda, 121
memories, preserving. *See* family
Mercedes Benz, 199–200
Michel, María, 22
Michel, Mercedes, 67
Military Intelligence Service (SIM), 55, 135, 137, 140, 144, 146, 149–51, 166, 187–93, 198, 200, 203, 206–9, 21, 279
Minervino Matías, Américo Dante, 135, 150
Minou. *See* Tavárez Mirabal, Minerva Josefina
Mir, Pedro, 116
Mirabal, Antonio, 160

Mirabal, Gustavo, 94
Mirabal, Simeón (Mon), 67
Mirabal Fernández, Enrique, xiii, 21, 46, 90, 92, 103, 125, 162, 175, 244, 271; and Aída Patria Mercedes, 48–49; and Antonia María Teresa, 64–66; and Bélgica Adela, 67–73; and births, 33–34; death of, 96–101; describing, 29; and education, 39–40, 42; events impacting, 95; and fall from grace, 86–90, 92–93; health of, 26; and María Argentina Minerva, 49–64; work schedule of, 28; working with, 30–32
Mirabal Núñez, Simeón, 21
Mirabal Reyes, Aída Patria Mercedes, xiv, 14–18, 29, 42, 78, 81, 87; and arrests of her family, 146–49; birth of, 33–34; childhood, games, and school, 34–38; dealing with repression against family, 93; death of, 157–63; and death of Enrique Mirabal, 96–101; fortunate encounters of, 102–26; and founding of 14th of June Movement, 129–39; health and education, 38–43; relationship with Antonia María Teresa, 64–66; relationship with María Argentina Minerva, 49–64; at San Cristóbal party, 85–88; as supportive one, 45–49
Mirabal Reyes, Antonia María Teresa, 138; being intelligent and kind, 64–66; birth of, 33–34; death of, 157–63; diary of, 96–101; facing tragedy, 150–63; and founding of 14th of June Movement, 129–39; going to university, 120–25; health and education of, 38–43; marrying Leandro, 120–25; and other jailed women, 139–46; second arrest, 146–49
Mirabal Reyes, Bélgica Adela (Dedé): birth of, 33–34; birth of sons of, 72–73; business ventures of, 95–96; childhood, education, and friends, 33–44; personality of, 67–69; and era of Trujillo, xv–xxi; events impacting family of, 94–101; facing tragedy, 150–63; fall from grace, 85–88; falling in love with Jaimito, 68–72; family of, 21–32; and fate of killers, 213–22; and 14th of June Revolutionary Movement, 127–49; health and education of, 38–43; impact for political events on, 223–29; and jailed women, 139–46; life in El Indio, 116–20; love, marriage, divorce, and stability, 254–69; and Mirabel Reyes family, xiii–xv; and most difficult act of heroism, 3–6; at party in San Cristóbal, 85–88; on raising children, 237–49; and resistance movements, xxi–xxv; survival, fortitude, and memory, xxvi–xxix; staying alive, 7–11; temperament, ideas, and life choices, 45–73; and tragedy, xxv–xxvi; traveling, seeing the world, gardening, 259–61; and trial against assassins of Mirabal sisters, 185–212; value of work, 250–53
Mirabal Reyes, family, xiii–xv. See various entries
Mirabal Reyes, María Argentina Minerva: arrest of, 57–58, 92, 137–38; arriving at Immaculate Conception School, 55–56; birth of, 33–34; communion of ideals, 107–16; death of, 157–63; facing tragedy, 150–63; and founding of 14th of June Revolutionary Movement, 129–39; friendships of, 61–64; going off to university, 95–96; happiest years for, 58–59; health and education of, 38–43; illness of, 113–14; interest in painting, 57; interest in politics, 54–55; interrogating, 144; as jealous individual, 115–16; laying stone path at home, 57; learning about, 49; learning to drive, 58; in love with Manolo, 102–7; missing file of, 221–22; and other jailed women, 139–46; other qualities of, 56; at party in San Cristóbal, 85–88; reading and reciting poetry, 50–54; relationship with Pericles Franco Ornes, 60–61; relationship with siblings, 49–50; repression against family, 88–93; second arrest of, 146–49; as spirited young woman, 49–64; stashing weapons, 130–31; writings of, 110–13
Mirabal Reyes, Víctor Enrique, 33
Mirabal sisters: and 14th of June Revolutionary Movement, 127–49; childhood, education, and friends, 33–44; chronology of, 271–83; events impacting family, 94–101; facing tragedy, 150–63; fall from grace, 85–88; family of, 21–32; fate of killers of,

213–22; fortunate encounters of, 102–26; and Mirabal Sisters House Museum, 263–66, 269; political events impacting, 223–29; temperament, ideas, and life choices, 45–73; trial against assassins of, 185–212
Mirabal Sisters House Museum, 7, 260, 263–66, 269
Miss University, competition, 120–25
MLD. *See* Movimiento de Liberación Dominicana
Molina, Romeo, 196–99. *See also* trial against assassins of Mirabal sisters
Molina, Romero Antonio, 200
Monroe Doctrine, xv
Montecristi, Dominican Republic, 113
Montes de Oca, Porfirio, 27, 69
Morales, Angel, 262
Morales, Juan Carlos, 130–31
Morales, Santo, 143
Morales Languasco, Carlos Felipe, xv
Movimiento de Liberación Dominicana (MLD), xxiii
Movimiento Revolucionario 14 de Junio. See 14th of June Revolutionary Movement
Moya, Manuel de, 87
Muñoz, Zoila, 200

Nacional, El, 216–19
National Pantheon (Santo Domingo), 268
National Technical and Vocational Institute (INFOTEP), 243
negro, term, 43–44
Neruda, Pablo, 50
Nervo, Amado, 50
Nivar Seijas, Neit, 214–15
Northeast Regional University, 247
November 25. *See* International Day for the Elimination of Violence Against Women
Núñez, Mateo, 205–6
Núñez Soto, Silvio Bienvenido, 196–200. *See also* trial against assassins of Mirabal sisters

Ojo de Agua, xiv; and Haitian Massacre, 43–44; learning to read and write in, 38–39; life going on in, 228–29; Mirabal Sisters House Museum in, 263–66; origins of, 26–27; settling in, 21–22; raiding home in, 224–25; against Trujillo regime, 55; watching assassin trial from, 210–12; wedding in, 108–9. *See also* Mirabal sisters
O'Reilly, Tomás, 143
Organization of American States, xxvii, 145, 148, 169
Ornes, Francisco, 89
Ortega, Tomás, 196–99. *See also* trial against assassins of Mirabal sisters, 200
Osorio, Juan, 23
Ozama Fortress, 92–93, 213–14, 280

PALIC. *See* Panamerican Life Insurance Co.
Palma Sola Massacre, 85
Panal, Francisco, 143
Panamerican Life Insurance Co. (PALIC), 250–53
panfleteros, xxiv
Pantaleón, Luis, 135
Pantaleón, Tatá, 176
Papá. *See* Mirabal Fernández, Enrique
parents, marriage of, 26–30
Parra Beato, Alfredo, 109
Parsley Massacre, xviii
Partido Democrático Revolutionario Dominicano (PDRD), xxii
Partido Dominicano (Dominican Party), xx–xxii
Paulita, Doña, 88
PDRD. *See* Partido Democrático Revolutionario Dominicano
Peña Jáquez, Sóstenes, 223
Peña Rivera, Víctor Alicinio, 9, 132, 144, 174, 200, 203, 210, 213–14, 216–20
Peral, Luis, 251
Peralta, Antigua, 89
Perdomo, Eugenio, 168
Perdomo Pérez, Virgilio, 168
Pérez, Gilda, 60–61
Pérez, José Gabriel, 196–99, 196–99. *See also* trial against assassins of Mirabal sisters
Pérez, Victoriana, 42
Pérez Terrero, Néstor Antonio, 210
Perrone, Salvador, 202
Pimentel, Rafael (Chujo), 151
Pimentel Líster, Chujo, 189–93

Pina Acevedo, Ramón, 210
PLD. *See* Dominican Liberation Party
Plot Discovered (Benítez), 149
poetry, reading and reciting, 50–54
political events, impact of: Balaguer election victory, 224; Jaimito, 223–24; life moving on, 228–29; Nagua incident, 225–28; raiding home of Pedrito, 223; raiding Ojo de Agua home, 224–25. *See also* struggle, times of; tragedy, facing; Trujillo, Rafael
Portorreal, Candito, 138
Portorreal, Otilio, 138, 141
Pou, Rodolfo, 268
Prasmoski, Peter, 48
PRD. *See* Dominican Revolutionary Party
Puerto Plata, 27, 32, 38, 42, 57, 65, 244, 249, 269, 277; and assassin trial, 185, 189–94; finding holes in investigation, 203–7, 211–12; jailed women from, 139; representing at 14th of June Movement, 130; tragedy near, 151–56, 162, 165, 171; trial witnesses, 196–202
Puerto Plata-Santiago Highway, 199, 201, 212

Quebrada Prieta, La, 26
Quisqueya, 177

Ramfis. *See* Trujillo Martínez, Rafael Leónidas
Ramírez, Porfirio (Prin), 155
Ramírez Alcántara, Miguel Angel, 155
Ramón, Pedro, 133
Ramos, Benjamín, 177
Ramos, Gustavo, 56
Rebellion of the Pilots, 187
recovery and commitment, time of: fate of killers, 213–22; impact of political events, 223–29; trial against assassins of Mirabal sisters, 185–212
Reid Cabral, Donald, 220
repression, start of, 88–93
Reyes, Miguel Angel, 23
Reyes Camilo, Mercedes (Chea), 212, 237–39; and Aída Patria Mercedes, 48; and Antonia María Teresa, 64; and Bélgica Adela, 67–73; birthing Mirabal sisters, 33–34; and business ventures, 30–32; in childhood of Mirabal sisters, 34–43; children health and education, 38–43; death of, 96–101; and death of Mirabal sisters, 152, 154, 156–60 162; and death of Enrique Mirabal, 96–101; and end of fifties, 125–26; fading of, 248–49; and fate of killers, 220; and founding of 14th of June movement, 133–39; and jailed women, 139–40, 146–48; life going on for, 228–29; and Manolo, 178–79; and María Argentina Minerva, 50–51, 54–55, 57–58; María Teresa going to university, 120, 123; marriage of, 26–30; and Minerva and Manolo in love, 102–9, 115–16; and Minou and Manolito, 240–43; in mourning, 165, 168, 172, 175; period of very hard work, 119–20; raising children, 237–49; start of repression against family, 88–93
Ricart, Josefina, 127–28, 128
Rodríguez, Emma, 42, 128–29
Rodríguez, Juan, Jr., 169
Rodríguez, Juancito, 152, 262
Rodríguez, Rafael, 59
Rodríguez, Víctor, 27, 69
Rodríquez, José Horacio, 152
Rodríguez Echavarría, Pedro R., 174, 187–8
Rodríguez Mesa, Fausto, 143–44
Rodríguez Núñez, Tomás, 92
Rodríguez Reyes, Miguel, 85–88, 96
Rojas, Juan, 27, 69
Rojas, Olga and Deysi, 41
Rojas Lora, Ramón Emilio, 210, 215–16
Román, Betty, widow of, 178
Román Fernández, José René, 144–45
Romano González, Cristóbal Enrique, 240
Romano González, Francis Ernesto, 240
Roosevelt, Theodore, xv
Rosa, Ciriaco de la, 9, 210, 216, 220
Rosario, Ana Antonia, 29, 136, 162, 233
Rosario, Milka Jacqueline del, 175
Rubio, Cesarina, 42
Rubirosa, Porfirio, 216
Russo, Domingo, 168
Russo, Lillian, 212

Sacred Heart School, 157, 240
Salcedo Casino, 57–58
Salcedo Club, 67
Sánchez, Papito, 200

Sánchez Morcelo, Héctor, 210
San Cristóbal: party in, 85–88; repression following party in, 89–93
San Francisco de Macorís, 24–25, 131; moving to, 58
Sang Ben, Mu-Kein Adriana, 51
San José Declaration, 145
Santa Teresita School, 173
Santo Domingo, modernization of, xvii
Santos, Juan Bautista, 135
school, 34–38
second arrests, 146–49
Servicio de Inteligencia Militar (SIM). See Military Intelligence Service
Servio, Félix, 55
Silva, José Asunción, 50
Silvana, o una página de la intervención (Osorio), 23
Silverio, Germán, 130–31
SIM. *See* Military Intelligence Service
sitios, 226
Socías, Jaime Ricardo, 134
Solnit, Rebecca, 5
Soto, Osvaldo B., 210
state control, establishment of, xix
St. Isidore's Day, 69–70
struggles, time of: death of Fellito, 94; death of Papá, 96–101; events impacting family, 94–101; facing tragedy, 150–63; fall from grace, 85–93; fortunate encounters, 102–26; 14th of June Revolutionary Movement, 127–49; people in mourning, 164–76
Suazo, María Cristina, 67
Superior Agricultural Institute (ISA), 243
Suro, Rubén, 59, 89

Tavárez Justo, Emma, 104–5, 113-14, 129
Tavárez Justo, Manuel Aurelio (Manolo), xxii, 4, 138, 175–76, 188, 268; communion of ideals with Minerva, 107–16; death of, 178–80; in love with Minerva, 102–7; and Minou and Manolito, 240–44; in 1963, 177–80; release of, 166–73. *See also* political events, impact of; tragedy, facing; trial against assassins of Mirabal sisters
Tavárez Mayer, Carmen, 173
Tavárez Mirabal, Minerva Josefina (Minou), 4, 175–76, 240–44; "Plural Cause of Things, The," 285–88; "When We Lost Everything, You Were There for Us," 289–90
Taveras, Fafa, 132
Technological Institute of Santo Domingo (INTEC), 243, 246–47
Tejada Florentino, Manuel, 138
Terrero, Pérez, 216
Tilo, uncle, 33-36
Tolstoy, Leo, 53
Tonó. *See* Rosario, Ana Antonia
Toribio, Margarita, 186
Toribio, María Teresa, 67
Torres, Candito, 214
Torres Tejada, Cándido, 210
tragedy, facing: continuation of tragedies, 164–66; death of sisters, 157–63; and end of Trujillo era, 173–76; heading to Puerto Plata, 154–56; house arrest, 150–51; jail transfer to Puerto Plata, 151–54; "The Mirabal Sisters' Husbands Are Alive," 166–73; seeking asylum, 150; Trujillo going on tour, 151. *See also* recovery and commitment, time of
Tragedy of King Christophe, The (Césaire), 53
traveling, 259–61
trial of assassins of Mirabal sisters: discussions of, 211–12; fate of killers, 213–22; final ruling of, 210–11; judicial records and statements, 203–12; November 25 events, 189–93; overview of, 185–89; relevant details to be clarified, 199–202; witnesses, 196–99
Trinitaria, La, movement, 132
Trujillato, era. *See* Trujillo, Rafael
Trujillo, Petán, 86
Trujillo, Romeo (Pipí), 134
Trujillo Martínez, Rafael Leónidas (Ramfis), 170–71
Trujillo Molina, Rafael Leónidas, xiii; and 14th of June Revolutionary Movement, 127–49; arrests ordered by, 132–33; assassination of, 170–72; Catholic Church Pastoral Letter against, 141–42; coming to Salcedo, 164–65; compensating victims killed by, 220; and death of Mirabal sisters, 157–63; end of era of, 173–76; and end of fifties, 125–26; era of, xv–xxi; and fate of killers, 213–22;

on tour, 151; growth of opposition to, 116; and jailed women, 139–46; most repressive years of, 127–29; organizing assassination attempt, 148; owing favors to, 201; at party in San Cristóbal, 85–88; and people in mourning, 164–76; repression against family, 88–93

Tupamaros, 241

UASD. *See* Autonomous University of Santo Domingo
UGRI. *See* Unión de Grupos Revolucionarios Independientes
Unión de Grupos Revolucionarios Independientes (UGRI), xxiv
United States, 4, 9, 22, 37, 39, 44, 59, 61, 108, 125, 178, 187; 1916 occupation wounds, 23–25; Candito Torres living in, 214; chronology of involvement in DR, 271, 277–79, 281; in early sixties, 145; emigrating to, 61–62, 124; Minerva interest in politics, 54–55; Mirabal sisters' killers living in, 215, 220; occupying Dominican Republic, xv–xvi; second invasion from, 55; and three Jaimes, 245; Violeta emigrating to, 263
Universidad Católica Madre y Maestra, 246
University of Santo Domingo, 242; going to, 95–96

U.S. Marines, 21

Valera Benítez, Rafael, 149
Vargas, Aniana, 42
Vargas Llosa, Mario, 265
Vásquez Fernández, Miguel A., 210
Vásquez Lajara, Horacio, xvi
Vega, Bernardo, 4, 8
Vicini, Gianni, 264
Victoria National Penitentiary, La, xxv
viuda (*Vda.*), 102–3
Volkswagen Beetles, xix

"Way of the Cross of the Mirabal Sisters, The" (tribute), 164
women: jailing, 139–46; participation of, xx–xxi
work, value of, 250–53
World Youth Festival, 242

Yo soy Minerva (Sang Ben), 51

Zorrilla, Tulio, 89
Zweig, Stefan, 53

Dedé Mirabal Reyes (1925–2014) was the surviving sister of Patria, Minerva, and María Teresa Mirabal, known as the Butterflies, whose brutal murder by the Trujillo regime in the Dominican Republic sparked widespread outcry. In this memoir, she shares her story of family, love, loss, survival, and hope.

Ana (Nani) E. Martínez is a journalist, translator, and interpreter living in the Dominican Republic.

Heather Hennes is professor of Spanish at Saint Joseph's University, which has provided financial support for this project.

www.ingramcontent.com/pod-product-compliance
Lightning Source LLC
Chambersburg PA
CBHW021153230426
43667CB00006B/382